D1567588

Designing and Deploying 802.11 Wireless Networks

A Practical Guide to Implementing 802.11n and 802.11ac Wireless Networks For Enterprise-Based Applications

Second Edition

Jim Geier

Cisco Press

800 East 96th Street

Indianapolis, IN 46240

Designing and Deploying 802.11 Wireless Networks

Second Edition

Jim Geier

Published by:
Cisco Press
800 East 96th Street
Indianapolis, IN 46240 USA

ISBN-13: 978-1-58714-430-1

ISBN-10: 1-58714-430-1

Printed in the United States of America

2   16

Library of Congress Control Number: 2015936629

Warning and Disclaimer

This book is designed to provide information about wireless networking, which includes Cisco products. Every effort has been made to make this book as complete and as accurate as possible, but no warranty or fitness is implied.

The information is provided on an "as is" basis. The authors, Cisco Press, and Cisco Systems, Inc. shall have neither liability nor responsibility to any person or entity with respect to any loss or damages arising from the information contained in this book or from the use of the discs or programs that may accompany it.

The opinions expressed in this book belong to the author and are not necessarily those of Cisco Systems, Inc.

Trademark Acknowledgments

All terms mentioned in this book that are known to be trademarks or service marks have been appropriately capitalized. Cisco Press or Cisco Systems, Inc. cannot attest to the accuracy of this information. Use of a term in this book should not be regarded as affecting the validity of any trademark or service mark.

Corporate and Government Sales

The publisher offers excellent discounts on this book when ordered in quantity for bulk purchases or special sales, which may include electronic versions and/or custom covers and content particular to your business, training goals, marketing focus, and branding interests. For more information, please contact: **U.S. Corporate and Government Sales** 1-800-382-3419 corpsales@pearsontechgroup.com

For sales outside the United States, please contact:
International Sales international@pearsoned.com

Feedback Information

At Cisco Press, our goal is to create in-depth technical books of the highest quality and value. Each book is crafted with care and precision, undergoing rigorous development that involves the unique expertise of members from the professional technical community.

Readers' feedback is a natural continuation of this process. If you have any comments regarding how we could improve the quality of this book, or otherwise alter it to better suit your needs, you can contact us through e-mail at feedback@ciscopress.com. Please make sure to include the book title and ISBN in your message.

We greatly appreciate your assistance.

Publisher: Paul Boger	**Business Operation Manager, Cisco Press:** Jan Cornelssen
Associate Publisher: Dave Dusthimer	**Executive Editor:** Mary Beth Ray
Technical Editors: Jonathan Christman and George Stefanick	**Managing Editor:** Sandra Schroeder
Copy Editor: Kitty Wilson	**Senior Development Editor:** Eleanor C. Bru
Indexer: Brad Herriman	**Project Editor:** Seth Kerney
Proofreader: Debbie Williams	**Editorial Assistant:** Vanessa Evans
Book Designer: Mark Shirar	**Composition:** Trina Wurst

Americas Headquarters	**Asia Pacific Headquarters**	**Europe Headquarters**
Cisco Systems, Inc.	Cisco Systems (USA) Pte. Ltd.	Cisco Systems International BV
San Jose, CA	Singapore	Amsterdam, The Netherlands

Cisco has more than 200 offices worldwide. Addresses, phone numbers, and fax numbers are listed on the Cisco Website at **www.cisco.com/go/offices.**

CCDE, CCENT, Cisco Eos, Cisco HealthPresence, the Cisco logo, Cisco Lumin, Cisco Nexus, Cisco StadiumVision, Cisco TelePresence, Cisco WebEx, DCE, and Welcome to the Human Network are trademarks; Changing the Way We Work, Live, Play, and Learn and Cisco Store are service marks; and Access Registrar, Aironet, AsyncOS, Bringing the Meeting To You, Catalyst, CCDA, CCDP, CCIE, CCIP, CCNA, CCNP, CCSP, CCVP, Cisco, the Cisco Certified Internetwork Expert logo, Cisco IOS, Cisco Press, Cisco Systems, Cisco Systems Capital, the Cisco Systems logo, Cisco Unity, Collaboration Without Limitation, EtherFast, EtherSwitch, Event Center, Fast Step, Follow Me Browsing, FormShare, GigaDrive, HomeLink, Internet Quotient, IOS, iPhone, iQuick Study, IronPort, the IronPort logo, LightStream, Linksys, MediaTone, MeetingPlace, MeetingPlace Chime Sound, MGX, Networkers, Networking Academy, Network Registrar, PCNow, PIX, PowerPanels, ProConnect, ScriptShare, SenderBase, SMARTnet, Spectrum Expert, StackWise, The Fastest Way to Increase Your Internet Quotient, TransPath, WebEx, and the WebEx logo are registered trademarks of Cisco Systems, Inc. and/or its affiliates in the United States and certain other countries.

All other trademarks mentioned in this document or website are the property of their respective owners. The use of the word partner does not imply a partnership relationship between Cisco and any other company. (0812R)

About the Author

Jim Geier has 30 years' experience planning, designing, analyzing, and implementing communications systems, wireless networks, and mobile devices. Jim is founder and principal consultant of Wireless-Nets, Ltd., providing wireless analysis and design services to product manufacturers. He is also president and CEO and co-founder of Health Grade Networks, providing wireless network solutions to hospitals, airports, and manufacturing facilities. Jim is the author of more than a dozen books on mobile and wireless topics, including *Designing and Deploying 802.11n Wireless Networks* (Cisco Press), *Implementing 802.1X Security Solutions* (Wiley), *Wireless Networking Handbook* (New Riders), and *Network Re-engineering* (McGraw-Hill). He has been an active participant in IEEE standards organizations, such as the IEEE 802.11 Working Group and the Wi-Fi Alliance. He has served as chairman of the IEEE Computer Society, Dayton Section, and various conferences. He has served as a testifying expert for patent litigation cases focusing on technologies dealing with wireless networking and cellular systems.

You can e-mail Jim Geier at jimgeier@wireless-nets.com.

About the Technical Reviewers

Jonathan E. Christman is vice-president of technology and co-founder at Health Grade Networks. He has more than 25 years of networking experience with more than 20 years dedicated to healthcare IT. He holds numerous certifications, including Cisco CCNP-Wireless, CCNA Routing and Switching, and CCDA, as well as other vendor-specific and vendor-neutral certifications. For the past 10 years, Jon has been working exclusively with wireless technologies, RFID/RTLS systems, and VoIP and VoWiFi systems in healthcare. Jon lives in the Firelands area of north-central Ohio with his beautiful wife and has two grown daughters.

George M. Stefanick, Jr. is a wireless architect employed by the Houston Methodist Hospital, where he manages 7 wireless distributions, 3,500 access points, and 30,000 wireless clients. George has been in wireless communications since 1997 and holds various vendor-specific and vendor-neutral certifications. George focuses on high-density indoor deployments in the healthcare vertical, leveraging his hands-on experience in site survey, RFID, and voice designs. George has consulted internationally and on many *Fortune 500* accounts. George was a Cisco Support Community VIP in 2012, 2013, and 2014, and an Aruba MVP in 2014 and 2015.

Dedication

I dedicate this book to my wife, Debbie.

Acknowledgments

I want to thank the Pearson production team for their time and effort with creating this book.

I also want to thank Jon Christman and George Stefanick for providing technical feedback on the many topics that this book covers.

Contents at a Glance

Contents

Icons Used in This Book

Access
Point

Mesh Access
Point

Lightweight
Access Point

WLAN
Controller

Wireless LAN
Router

Wireless
Bridge

Router

Multilayer
Switch

Ethernet
Switch

Hub

Repeater

Call
Manager

Voice
Gateway

IP Telephony
Router

PC

Laptop

Printer

Server

Web
Server

Database

Cell Phone

PDA

Wireless
Inventory/Manufacturing
Device

Phone

Camera/PC
Video

WiMax Base
Station

Network Cloud

Introduction

The 802.11ac amendment to the IEEE 802.11 wireless LAN (WLAN) standard was ratified in 2013, enabling 802.11 systems to provide significantly higher performance in the 5-GHz band. Network equipment manufacturers now offer 802.11ac-compliant equipment in addition to 802.11n (2.4 GHz) as their primary WLAN solutions. WLANs based on earlier versions of the standard (802.11a, 802.11b, and 802.11g) are considered "legacy," and there is significant risk that these existing non-802.11n/ac systems will become obsolete. As a result, organizations deploying new WLANs should definitely implement 802.11ac and 802.11n-compliant equipment. In addition, organizations with existing non-802.11n/ac WLANs should begin planning the migration to 802.11ac and 802.11n-compliant networks.

This book focuses on planning, designing, installing, testing, and supporting 802.11ac and 802.11n wireless networks for a variety of applications. The methods, recommendations, and tips in this book are based on the author's many years of practical experience deploying WLANs. Organizations with no existing wireless network and those migrating from legacy wireless networks to 802.11ac- and 802.11n-compliant networks will find this book to be a valuable guide.

Goals and Methods

The overall goal of this book is to guide you through the steps of deploying an 802.l1n WLAN. To accomplish this, the book includes the following elements:

- **Step-by-step approach:** The book breaks each phase of WLAN deployment into clearly defined steps that provide the basis for understanding and planning the details of the phase.

- **Case studies:** The book includes several case studies that provide explanations of concepts and methods as they are practiced in actual deployments.

- **Hands-on exercises:** The book includes exercises that make use of free and inexpensive tools that help you gain practical experience with concepts described in the chapter.

- **Notes:** Concise notes are distributed throughout the book and provide insightful information related to deploying WLANs.

Who Should Read This Book?

This book is intended for a variety of people, from someone with basic knowledge of networking to those who have years of experience working with WLANs but have little or no experience implementing 802.11 networks.

How This Book Is Organized

Although this book can be read cover to cover, it is designed to be flexible and allow you to easily move between chapters and sections of chapters to learn just the information that you need.

This book covers the following topics:

- **Part I, "Fundamental Concepts":** This part of the book includes chapters that cover important underlying concepts that must be understood before deploying an 802.11 wireless network. Readers already familiar with WLANs may be able to skip one or more of the chapters in this part of the book.

  - **Chapter 1, "Introduction to Wireless LANs":** This chapter defines the markets and applications of WLANs and the wireless technologies that support them.

  - **Chapter 2, "Radio Wave Fundamentals":** This chapter explains radio wave fundamentals so that you have a basis for understanding the complexities of deploying WLANs.

  - **Chapter 3, "Wireless LAN Types and Components":** This chapter describes ad hoc, mesh, and infrastructure WLAN types and various components, such as access points, controllers, client radios, and amplifiers.

  - **Chapter 4, "Wireless LAN Implications":** This chapter explains the impacts of radio signal interference, security vulnerabilities, multipath propagation, roaming, and battery limitations on WLANs.

- **Part II, "The 802.11 Standard":** This part of the book provides in-depth coverage of the most current medium access and physical layers of the IEEE 802.11 standard (including 802.11ac and 802.11n functionality). The focus here is on the elements of the standard that you should know to be successful at deploying and supporting 802.11 wireless networks.

  - **Chapter 5, "Introduction to IEEE 802.11 and Related Standards":** This chapter provides background on the 802.11 standards and an overview of the 802.11 standard and related standards, such as IEEE 802.2.

  - **Chapter 6, "IEEE 802.11 Medium Access Control (MAC) Layer":** This chapter explains details of the 802.11 standard that you need to know to help you best configure and troubleshoot 802.11 WLANs.

  - **Chapter 7, "IEEE 802.11 Physical (PHY) Layers":** This chapter describes the modulation functions that are part of the 802.11 physical layers.

- **Part III, "Wireless Network Design":** This part of the book includes chapters that cover steps necessary to design an 802.11 wireless network for various scenarios.

- **Chapter 8, "Planning a Wireless LAN Deployment":** This chapter provides an overview of the steps you need to complete when deploying a WLAN and details on defining the project scope, developing a work breakdown structure, identifying staffing, creating a schedule, developing a budget, evaluating risks, and analyzing feasibility.

- **Chapter 9, "Defining Requirements for a Wireless LAN":** This chapter explains how to gather, analyze, and document requirements for an 802.11 WLAN.

- **Chapter 10, "System Architecture Considerations":** This chapter explains what to consider when designing the access network and distribution system for an 802.11 WLAN.

- **Chapter 11, "Range, Performance, and Roaming Considerations":** This chapter explains the various trade-offs for enhancing the range, performance, and roaming capabilities of an 802.11 wireless LAN.

- **Chapter 12, "Radio Frequency Considerations":** This chapter covers important radio frequency (RF) design considerations for 802.11 WLANs, such as frequency band selection, transmission channel settings, difficult-to-cover areas, and radio signal interference reduction techniques.

- **Chapter 13, "Security Considerations":** This chapter explains important methods and techniques for securing a WLAN, including encryption, authentication, rogue access point detection, RF shielding, and security policies.

- **Part IV, "Wireless Network Installation and Testing":** This part of the book explains the steps necessary to install and test an 802.11 wireless network.

  - **Chapter 14, "Test Tools":** This chapter describes the tools that you need to effectively design and support an 802.11 WLAN.

  - **Chapter 15, "Performing a Wireless Site Survey":** This chapter explains the steps and techniques, such as inspecting the existing network, analyzing radio signal interference, and performing signal propagation testing, that are needed to determine the optimum installation locations for access points.

  - **Chapter 16, "Installing and Configuring a Wireless LAN":** This chapter explains how to plan the installation, stage the components, install the access points, and document the installation of a WLAN.

  - **Chapter 17, "Testing a Wireless LAN":** This chapter describes the steps and techniques necessary to test a wireless LAN, including signal coverage testing, performance testing, in-motion testing, security testing, acceptance testing, simulation testing, prototype testing, and pilot testing.

- **Part V, "Operational Support Considerations":** This part of the book explains what to consider when supporting an 802.11 wireless network. Readers will learn how to establish specialized support for wireless networks and perform help desk operations, network monitoring, and troubleshooting.

- Chapter 18, "Managing a Wireless LAN": This chapter describes important operations and maintenance functions that you should consider when supporting a WLAN, including help desk, network monitoring, maintenance, engineering, configuration management, security management, trouble ticket coordination, operational support tools, and operational support transfer preparation.

- Chapter 19, "Troubleshooting a Wireless LAN": This chapter explains how to identify problems, such as connectivity and performance issues, and determine the underlying causes.

- Chapter 20, "Preparing Operational Support Staff": This chapter describes what you should consider when evaluating the experience and education of staff for supporting a wireless LAN.

- Glossary: The glossary defines terms that this book uses.

Hands-on Exercises

As mentioned in the "Goals and Methods" section, this book includes exercises that make use of free and inexpensive tools that help you gain practical experience with the concepts described. You can find these exercises on the following pages:

Chapter 4:

Hands-on Exercise: Passively Monitor a Wireless LAN—78

Hands-on Exercise: Understand Basic Performance Impacts of Radio Signal Interference—94

Chapter 6:

Hands-on Exercise: Observing 802.11 Dynamic Rate Shifting—130

Hands-on Exercise: Observing 802.11 Active Scanning—139

Hands-on Exercise: Observing the 802.11 Connection Process—143

Hands-on Exercise: Observing 802.11 Beacons—158

Hands-on Exercise: Observing 802.11 Frames Resulting from Typical User Traffic—164

Chapter 7:

Hands-on Exercise: Understanding Performance Impacts of Increasing 802.11n Spatial Streams—182

Hands-on Exercise: Understanding Performance Impacts of 802.11n Channel Bonding—183

Chapter 11:

Hands-on Exercise: Analyzing Impacts on Range Using Different Data Rate Settings—293

Chapter 1

Introduction to Wireless LANs

This chapter will introduce you to:

- Wireless LAN Markets and Applications
- Benefits of Wireless Networks
- Wireless LAN Technologies
- Wireless LANs: A Historical Perspective

Applications of wireless local-area networks (WLANs) have become commonplace in many markets throughout the world. Newer WLANs based on the 802.11n and 802.11ac standards now offer the performance needed to effectively support a high density of users and a broad range of high-end applications, such as voice, video, and image processing. This chapter defines the markets and applications of WLANs and the wireless technologies that support them.

Wireless LAN Markets and Applications

In general, WLANs are applicable to all markets with a need for user mobility or when the installation of physical media is not feasible. WLANs are especially useful when employees must process information on the spot via electronic-based forms and interactive menus. Wireless networking makes it possible to place portable computing devices in the hands of mobile users, such as doctors, nurses, warehouse clerks, inspectors, claims adjusters, real estate agents, and salespeople.

The implementation of portable devices with wireless connectivity facilitates access to a common database and applications that meet the needs of users, eliminate unnecessary paperwork, decrease errors, reduce processing costs, and improve overall efficiency. It also introduces user mobility by allowing the user to move from one WLAN to another seamlessly. The alternative to this, which many companies still employ today, is using paperwork to update records, process inventories, and file claims. This method processes information much more slowly, produces redundant data, and is subject to input errors caused by illegible handwriting. The approach to mobile computing over a WLAN using a centralized database enhances productivity and is clearly a superior approach.

The sections that follow provide a general description of the WLAN market and applications within that market. This will help stimulate ideas with regard to how WLANs will benefit your company or organization.

Retail

Retail organizations need to order, price, sell, and manage inventories of merchandise. A wireless network in a retail environment enables clerks and storeroom personnel to perform their functions directly from the sales floor. Salespeople are equipped with a pen-based computer or a small computing device with bar code reading and printing capabilities, while connected to the store's database via the WLAN. They can then complete transactions such as pricing, labeling bins, placing special orders, and taking inventory from anywhere within the store.

When printing price labels that will be affixed to items or shelves, retailers often use a handheld bar code scanner and printer to produce bar coded or human-readable labels. A database or file contains the price information located either on the handheld device, often called a batch device, or on a server somewhere in the store. In batch mode, the price clerk scans the bar code (typically the product code) located on the item or shelf edge, the application software uses the product code to look up the new price, and then the printer produces a new label that the clerk affixes to the item.

In some cases, the batch-based scanner/printer has enough memory to store all the price information needed to perform the pricing functions throughout a shift or an entire day. This situation makes sense if the user needs to update pricing information in the database through the day, typically during the evening. The clerks load the data onto the device at the beginning of their shifts and then walk throughout the store, pricing items. However, if the memory in the device is not large enough to store all the data or if updates to the server need to be done in real time, a wireless network is necessary. If the handheld unit is equipped with a wireless network connection, the handheld can be configured for a WLAN, and data can be stored on a centralized server and accessed each time an item's bar code is scanned. In addition, a wireless network–based solution has merit if downloading information to a batch device is too time consuming.

Warehousing

Warehouse staff must manage the receiving, shelving, inventorying, picking, and shipping of goods. These responsibilities require the staff to be mobile. Warehouse operations traditionally have been paper intensive and time consuming. An organization can eliminate paper, reduce errors, and decrease the time necessary to move items in and out by giving each warehouse employee a mobile handheld computing device with an Intermec bar code scanner, for example, connected via a wireless network to a warehouse inventory system.

Upon receiving an item for storage within the warehouse, a clerk can scan the item's bar coded item number and enter other information from a small keypad into the database via the handheld device. The system can respond with a location by printing a put-away label. A forklift operator can then move the item to a storage place and account for the procedure by scanning the item's bar code. The inventory control system keeps track of all transactions, making it very easy to produce accurate inventory reports. In addition, the online interaction with a database will identify mistakes immediately, enabling the operator to correct a mistake before it becomes a problem.

As shipping orders enter the warehouse, the inventory system produces a list of the items and their locations. A clerk can view this list from the database via a handheld device and locate the items needed to assemble a shipment. As the clerk removes the items from the storage bins, the database can be updated via the handheld device. All these functions depend heavily on wireless networks to maintain real-time access to data stored in a central database.

Warehouses involve a host of functions where the use of wireless IP phones can provide significant benefits. Clerks end up being scattered throughout the warehouse facility, which can be quite expansive, and communications with other clerks and managers is essential to perform various functions. In most cases, it is not practical for the clerks and managers to meet face to face to communicate. In fact, it is often not possible for them to even find each other because of the numerous rows of bins and products. For example, an order may come in for the shipment of a particular item to a customer. Rather than wait for a clerk to return to the main office, it is much faster and productive for the shipping department to call a clerk directly and have the clerk pick the item.

Wireless Bar Code System for Warehouses

A manufacturer in North America is a leading provider of bar code printers and supplies. As part of the company's goal to streamline processes within its manufacturing plant and warehouse, a process improvement team applied the use of mobile handheld bar code scanning and printing devices with the support of a WLAN within its central distribution center (CDC).

Before the system was implemented, the CDC was experiencing inefficiencies because clerks needed to walk back and forth between stacks of finished goods and a desktop terminal used to determine a warehouse storage location for the items. The clerks would collect information from the finished goods by writing it down on a piece of paper, and then they would walk to the terminal to query the company's warehouse management system for a recommended storage location. The clerk would write this location information on a large label, walk back to the product, and affix the label to the product's container. Later, a forklift operator would come by and place the container in the correct location on the warehouse floor. The process of walking back and forth between the products and the terminal made inefficient use of the clerk's time, which slowed the movement of products through the plant.

The solution to this problem consists of a bar code scanner equipped with a radio card and a WLAN. 802.11 access points throughout the warehouse connect to an Ethernet network that interfaces to a server running a warehouse management system. The clerk can now scan the finished product's bar code, which is used to query the warehouse management system for a valid put-away location. The system then prints a label on a printer connected to the bar code scanner indicating the applicable location information.

Through the use of this scan, print, and apply function, the solution eliminates the need for the clerk to walk back and forth to the terminal, increasing productivity by 50 percent. In addition, the solution provides significant gains in accuracy through the elimination of human error.

Many warehouses already have existing WLANs; however, because these wireless networks primarily support relatively low-performance bar code solutions for implementing inventory management functions, such an existing WLAN will likely not have enough capacity to support a large number of wireless IP phones. In most cases, the much higher capacity of 802.11n and 802.11ac networks is necessary to support voice applications in warehouses.

Healthcare

Healthcare centers, such as hospitals and doctor's offices, must maintain accurate records to ensure effective patient care. A simple mistake can cost someone's life. As a result, doctors and nurses must carefully record test results, physical data, pharmaceutical orders, and surgical procedures. This paperwork often overwhelms healthcare staff, taking 50 percent to 70 percent of their time.

Doctors and nurses are also extremely mobile, going from room to room as they care for patients. The use of electronic patient records, with the capability to input, view, and update patient data from anywhere in the hospital, increases the accuracy and speed of healthcare. This improvement is made possible by providing each nurse and doctor with a wireless pen-based computer, coupled with a wireless network connected to databases that store critical medical information about the patients.

A doctor caring for someone at the hospital, for example, can place an order for a blood test by keying the request into a handheld computer. The laboratory will receive the order electronically and dispatch a lab technician to draw blood from the patient. The laboratory will run the tests requested by the doctor and enter the results into the patient's electronic medical record. The doctor can then check the results via the handheld appliance from anywhere in the hospital.

Wireless LANs also help patients in hospitals. Patient monitoring devices, such as those from Draeger and Mindray, monitor the vital signs of patients and wirelessly send the information to monitors located in the patient rooms and nursing stations. This allows patients to get out of bed and move around their room without the nuisance of cables attaching them to monitoring equipment.

Another application for wireless networks in hospitals is the tracking of pharmaceuticals. The use of mobile handheld bar code printing and scanning devices dramatically increases the efficiency and accuracy of all drug transactions, such as receiving, picking, dispensing, inventory taking, and tracking of drug expiration dates. Most importantly, though, it ensures that hospital staff is able to administer the right drug to the right person at the right time. This would not be possible without the use of wireless networks to support a centralized database and mobile data collection devices.

Hospitals were some of the first users of wireless IP phones, mainly because of the significant needs for effective communications among high-valued medical staff. The ability for doctors and nurses to respond quickly with verbal instructions is crucial in saving the lives of patients. Patients receive a higher level of care, which leads to faster recovery. Wireless IP phones allow hospital staff to not waste time looking for a phone to use.

An issue with deploying voice over wireless solutions in hospitals, however, is the difficulty in providing adequate WLAN coverage. Hospitals include x-ray rooms surrounded by lead, irregular metal objects, and unpredictable traffic flows of people. This leads to significant attenuation and multipath propagation. In addition, radio frequency (RF) interference from other wireless systems operating in the 2.4-GHz band, such as frequency-hopping spread spectrum devices, can cause degradation in performance. As a result, a wireless site survey is absolutely necessary to ensure that the network fully meets all requirements.

Hospitality

Hospitality establishments check customers in and out and keep track of needs such as room service orders and laundry requests. Restaurants need to keep track of the names and numbers of people waiting for entry, table status, and drink and food orders. Restaurant staff must perform these activities quickly and accurately to avoid making patrons unhappy. Wireless networking satisfies these needs very well.

Wireless computers are very useful in situations where there is a large crowd, such as a sports bar restaurant. For example, someone can greet a restaurant patron at the door and enter his name, the size of the party, and smoking preferences into a common database via a wireless device. The greeter can then query the database and determine the availability of an appropriate table. Those who oversee the tables use a wireless device to update the database to show whether the table is occupied, being cleaned, or available. After obtaining a table, the waiter transmits the order to the kitchen via the wireless device, eliminating the need for paper order tickets. Keep in mind, however, that the wireless network approach in finer restaurants may not be appealing to patrons. In that case, the patrons may expect waiters to memorize their orders.

Voice over WLAN

Voice over WLAN (VoWLAN) systems are an extension to wired VoIP systems and an alternative to traditional analog and digital voice communications. VoWLANs offer significant benefits of providing mobility and wirelessly converging voice with data applications. With VoWLANs, hospitals, enterprises, retail stores, warehouses, and homeowners can reduce telephony costs and enable mobile applications.

Examples of the systems that VoWLANs can replace include the following:

- Wired telephones

- Cellular telephones

- Two-way radios

With VoWLANs, individuals and teams can use VoWLAN phones to communicate by voice over the WLAN to others inside and outside a facility. The experience is similar to using a traditional wired telephone; however, the user is free to roam about the building where Wi-Fi has been deployed. Furthermore, a VoWLAN phone can operate from many of the growing number of Wi-Fi hotspots, allowing a person to make use of the same mobile phone while within or away from the office or home. Some cellular phones incorporate VoWLAN capability, which allows users to make calls over traditional cellular networks when no WLAN is available and then switch to a WLAN seamlessly when the user roams onto the Wi-Fi-enabled network.

Figure 1-1 illustrates the basic usage models of a VoWLAN system. The optimum approach depends on user requirements and existing telephone hardware.

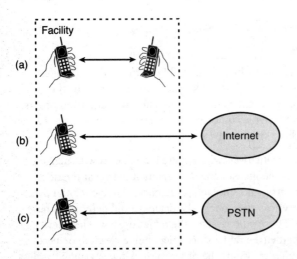

Figure 1-1   *VoWLAN Usage Models: (a) Local-Only, (b) Telephone via Internet, (c) Telephone via PSTN*

Video Surveillance

Several companies sell small video cameras that relay moving images to monitors and recording devices over WLANs. The installation of these cameras is much easier than with traditional ones because there is no need to run wires between the cameras and the company's network. The video signals flow over a WLAN and into a video server or PC. As a result, a company can set up a Wi-Fi video surveillance system much faster and in scenarios where it is not feasible to install traditional wired cameras.

Wireless video surveillance is beneficial for many industries. For example, the San Mateo County Courthouse installed Wi-Fi video cameras. With this system, security officials could keep a continual eye on crowds and their behavior. In addition, public facilities, such as hotels and shopping malls, use Wi-Fi cameras to watch over shopping areas, inside elevators, and near exit doors. Enterprises are also taking advantage of Wi-Fi cameras to monitor lobby entrances and parking lots.

Home and Small Office

With a WLAN, employees can bring laptops home from work and continue working just as they do from their offices. For many professions, this makes it possible for people to work from home more effectively, whether it is to spend a few more hours researching on the Internet or to enable telecommuting on a daily basis.

Of course with a wireless laptop, a person can truly work from any place in the house. There is nothing tying you down to a desk in a particular room. You are free to use the Internet or access files on other computers while relaxing in a comfy chair in front of a TV, lounging on the patio breathing fresh air, or sitting at a desk in a quiet bedroom.

WLANs at home are good for PCs, too. Unlike in companies, most homes are not wired with Ethernet cabling. That makes wireless the best way to connect stationary PCs to the network. You will have much more flexibility in locating a PC to any part of the house without being near the broadband modem.

Many homes now have more than one computer. After purchasing a new PC, homeowners will generally hold on to the older PC. It might not be the best for running some of the newer games, but it still offers a good station for browsing the web and interacting with e-mail. Of course, some people will also bring a laptop home from work or purchase one instead of upgrading to a newer PC.

With multiple computers, it is extremely beneficial for home users to connect to the same broadband connection. Because of the ease of installation, a WLAN is the best solution for sharing access to the Internet and other PCs in the home. Just be sure to install a WLAN router (not an access point) to ensure that you have Network Address Translation (NAT) and Dynamic Host Configuration Protocol (DHCP) services, which are necessary for all the computers to share a single official IP address supplied by your Internet service provider.

Without a WLAN, most home users must cable their printer directly to a PC or the Ethernet connector on a broadband modem. This limits the number of places that the printer can reside. Generally, it must sit within a few feet of the PC or modem.

A Wi-Fi print server, however, enables the printer to be accessible over the WLAN. This makes printer placement extremely flexible. For example, you might find it most useful to have the printer in the family room, where you do most of your laptop computing. Or it might make more sense to have the printer just inside the door that leads to your patio. You can also easily move a Wi-Fi-connected printer to new locations whenever you want to.

General Enterprise Systems

In the past, the implementation of a WLAN was relatively expensive compared to the implementation of higher-performing Ethernet networks. This required a WLAN application to provide a tremendous gain in efficiency to make it cost effective. As a result, many existing applications of WLANs are in markets such as healthcare, warehousing, and retail, where mobility provided efficiency gains capable of significantly lowering operational costs. With WLAN prices continuing to drop and performance increasing with 802.11n and 802.11ac, though, many enterprise information system managers are beginning to seriously consider the use of WLANs rather than traditional Ethernet. The benefits are provision of mobile and portable access to general network functions such as e-mail, Internet browsing, access to databases, and so on and elimination of the time and expense of installing and supporting physical cable. Thus, WLANs are now effectively satisfying applications in horizontal markets.

An oil exploration company operating in Colombia, South America, experienced high expenses when relocating its drilling rigs. The oil-drilling setup required two control rooms in portable sheds separated 5,000 feet from the drilling platform to provide 500 Kbps computer communication between the sheds and the drilling rig. The existing communications system consisted of Ethernet networks at each of the three sites. Each shed had four PCs running on the network, and the drilling site had one PC for direct drilling-control purposes.

Every time the oil company needed to move to a different drilling site, which occurred four or five times each year, it had to spend between $50,000 and $75,000 to reinstall optical fiber through the difficult terrain between the sheds and the drilling platform. With rewiring expenses reaching as high as $375,000 per year, the onsite system engineer designed a wireless point-to-point system to accommodate the portability requirements to significantly reduce the cost of relocating the drilling operation. The solution includes a spread-spectrum radio-based wireless system that uses directional antennas to establish point-to-point communication between the sheds and the drilling platform.

The cost of purchasing the wireless network components was approximately $10,000. Wherever the oil company now moves its drilling operation, it will save the costs of laying a new cabling infrastructure between the sites.

Location-Aware Wireless Applications

More and more companies are beginning to apply location-based services over wireless networks to enable rather interesting enhancements to applications. In general, a location-based system (LBS) keeps track of the position of users on the network as they roam throughout the facility. A centralized system collects and integrates this positioning information to drive additional functions that identify the position of users in relation to the facility and pertinent areas, such as information booths, emergency centers, stores, products, and so on.

Within healthcare facilities, doctors, nurses, and, sometimes, patients are very mobile. As a result, many hospitals have WLANs to support patient monitoring, electronic patient records, and narcotics tracking. In this situation, an LBS can also track doctors throughout the hospital, which enables a nurse to know whether a particular doctor is nearby and able to take care of a specific emergency.

In addition, an LBS enables hospital staff to track the whereabouts of patients, and if they go astray or anything adverse happens to them, an alarm system will alert the closest doctors and nurses. For example, some homes for the elderly implement LBSs over WLANs to trigger an alarm when patients try to leave the facility.

Hospitals also need to track expensive equipment that is often required to save lives. An LBS enables hospital administration to know the exact location of this equipment for accountability and usability purposes. If a nurse needs a specific portable x-ray machine in the emergency room, stat, the LBS can display where to find it. If it leaves the facility, chokepoints can be installed in major corridors or exits, showing when a piece of equipment or a user leaves a given area of the hospital or passes through an exit where a chokepoint is installed.

Department stores and shopping malls can reap huge benefits from LBSs. A customer can use his or her smart phone to download an interactive store map and find the exact location of any item within the store. By entering a few search criteria, the smart phone can provide a description of where the item has been moved on the WLAN. The same concept also applies to shopping malls. A WLAN can cover the entire parking lot and the inside of a large shopping mall, and customers using a smart phone are able to more easily find stores. Once a customer is in the mall, a real-time map constantly shows the shopper where each store is in relation to his/her position. The LBS can also send promotions from specific stores as shoppers pass by them.

An LBS also provides convenience to people in large public areas. In a convention center, for example, a wireless user can take advantage of moving maps that identify meeting rooms, positions of vendors on a tradeshow floor, and emergency exits in relation to the position of the user.

As a patron using a smart phone passes a specific display case at a museum, an LBS can download voice and possibly video information describing the contents of the display. The user can move about the museum and receive location-based information, which enhances the learning and enjoyment of the visitor.

Similar to a convention center, in an airport, wireless users can also easily find their way around by using an LBS solution. For example, the LBS can display routes to various locations, such as restaurants, coffee shops, and emergency exits. Tenants within the airport can also display location-aware advertisements, which offer the airport a revenue stream for advertising in addition to network access.

An LBS can make the job of security guards immensely easier. The security control room can constantly track the position of every guard and alert others when there is an incident occurring in an area. All of this traverses the WLAN. Of course, this means that the WLAN requires enhanced security mechanisms to ensure that this information is not available to thieves.

Because of the vast amounts of data, such as maps and tracking updates, that an LBS generates, the higher performance and reliability of 802.l1n and 802.11ac are imperative. This is especially true when supporting LBS in addition to other wireless applications, such as voice.

Case Study 1-1: Acme Healthcare Is Ready to Go Wireless

Acme Healthcare is a fictitious 250-bed acute care hospital that surfaces throughout this book to emphasize the primary considerations when deploying an 802.11 wireless network.

Acme Healthcare serves the healthcare needs of a medium-sized community in the United States. The hospital has very few wireless networks, which are mainly operated independently by several of the clinics. The existing networks are a mix of 802.11g and 802.11n networks, and they primarily serve connections between laptops and the hospital's healthcare information system.

The hospital CIO, Arthur, has attended a couple of healthcare conferences and learned that many of the other hospitals are in the process of deploying WLANs to support mobile applications, such as voice communications, electronic medical records, x-ray image distribution, video surveillance, asset tracking, patient monitoring, and foreign language translator systems. Arthur envisions similar applications and substantial resulting benefits for his hospital. With the masses of baby boomers getting older, Acme Hospital's profit has been increasing steadily over the past few years, and Arthur is now ready to move forward with a hospital-wide wireless system.

Note   Upgrade your existing network to all 802.11n and 802.11ac to support higher-speed mobile applications and avoid implications of the legacy WLANs (802.11a, 802.11b, 802.11g) that have become obsolete.

Benefits of Wireless Networks

The emergence and continual growth of WLANs are being driven by the need to lower the costs associated with network infrastructures and to support mobile networking applications that offer gains in process efficiency, accuracy, and lower business costs. The following sections explain the mobility and cost-saving benefits of WLANs so that you can better justify the expense of deploying a WLAN.

Mobility

Mobility enables users to move physically while using an appliance, such as a wireless laptop, smart phone, or data collector. Many employers require their employees to be mobile in an effort to increase efficiency. Inventory clerks, healthcare workers, police officers, and emergency care specialists, for example, are ideal candidates who can benefit from wireless mobility.

Of course, wired networks require a physical tether between a user's workstation and a network's resources, which makes access to these resources impossible while roaming about their work environment. Wireless mobility increases the users' freedom of movement and results in significant return on investment because of gains in efficiency.

Mobile applications requiring wireless networking include those that depend on real-time access to data, which is usually stored in centralized databases. If your applications require mobile users to be aware immediately of changes made to data, or if information put into the system must immediately be available to others, you have a definite need for wireless networking. For accurate and efficient price markdowns, for example, many retail stores use wireless networks to interconnect handheld bar code scanners and printers to databases containing current price information. This enables the printing of the correct prices on the items, making both the customer and the business owner more satisfied.

Installation in Difficult-to-Wire Areas

The implementation of wireless networks offers many tangible cost savings when performing installations in difficult-to-wire areas. If rivers, freeways, or other obstacles separate buildings you want to connect, a wireless solution may be much more economical than installing physical cable or leasing communications circuits, such as T1 service. Some organizations spend thousands or even millions of dollars on installing physical links with nearby facilities. 802.11n bridges, coupled with directional antennas, can easily provide wireless connectivity over thousands of feet, depending on obstacles along the path.

The asbestos found in older facilities is another problem that many organizations encounter. The inhalation of asbestos particles is extremely hazardous to your health; therefore, you must take great care when installing network cabling within these areas. When taking necessary precautions, the resulting cost of cable installations in these facilities can be prohibitive.

Some organizations, for example, remove the asbestos, making it safe to install cabling. This process is very expensive because you must protect the building's occupants from breathing the asbestos particles agitated during removal. The cost of removing asbestos covering just a few flights of stairs can be tens of thousands of dollars. Obviously, the advantage of wireless networking in asbestos-contaminated buildings is that you can avoid the asbestos removal process, resulting in tremendous cost savings.

In some cases, it might be impossible to install cabling. Some municipalities, for example, might restrict you from permanently modifying older facilities with historical value. This could limit the drilling of holes in walls during the installation of network cabling and outlets. In such a situation, a wireless network might be the only solution. Right-of-way restrictions within cities and counties might also block the digging of trenches in the ground to lay optical fiber for networked sites. Again, in this situation, a wireless network might be the best alternative.

Increased Reliability

A problem inherent in wired networks is downtime because of cable faults. Moisture erodes metallic conductors via water intrusion during storms and accidental spillage or leakage of liquids. With wired networks, a user might accidentally break his/her network connector when trying to disconnect his/her PC from the network to move it to a different location. Imperfect cable splices can cause signal reflections that result in unexplainable errors. The accidental cutting of cables can bring down a network immediately. Wires and connectors can easily break through misuse and normal use. These problems interfere with users' ability to use network resources, causing havoc for network managers. An advantage of wireless networking, therefore, results from the use of less cable. This reduces the downtime of the network and the costs associated with replacing cables.

Reduced Installation Time

The installation of cabling is often a time-consuming activity. For LANs, installers must pull twisted-pair wires or optical fiber above the ceiling and drop cables through walls to network outlets that they must affix to the wall. These tasks can take days or weeks, depending on the size of the installation. The installation of optical fiber between buildings within the same geographic area consists of digging trenches to lay the fiber or pulling the fiber through an existing conduit. You might need weeks or possibly months to receive right-of-way approvals and dig through ground and asphalt.

The deployment of wireless networks greatly reduces the need for cable installation, making the network available for use much sooner. Thus, many countries that lack network infrastructure have turned to wireless networking as a method of providing connectivity among computers without the expense and time associated with installing physical media. This is also necessary within the United States to set up temporary offices and rewire renovated facilities.

Long-Term Cost Savings

Companies reorganize, resulting in the movement of people, new floor plans, office partitions, and other renovations. These changes often require rewiring the network, incurring both labor and material costs. In some cases, the rewiring costs of organizational changes are quite substantial, especially with large enterprise networks. A reorganization rate of 15 percent each year can result in yearly reconfiguration expenses as high as $750,000 for networks that have 6,000 interconnected devices. The advantage of wireless networking is again based on the lack of cable: You can move the network connection by just relocating an employee's PC or IP phone.

Productivity Gain Is the Answer

For compelling reasons to install WLANs, you need to show continual productivity benefits. For example, consider using 802.11-equipped laptops. This enables users to read and respond to e-mail and browse the Internet during office meetings, assuming that the user can be responsive when needed at the meeting while plunking away at a laptop. Even though this seems trivial, the productivity gains can be significant.

Assume that a person attends three hours of meetings each day. If the user spends approximately 15 minutes per hour responding to e-mail and other Internet-related tasks during each meeting, the user will have 45 more minutes each day to work on other tasks. This seems pretty reasonable, considering the average person and office setting.

A 45-minute productivity gain equates to company cost savings that depend on the person's cost per hour. At $50 per hour, the savings will be $37.50 per person-day. A smaller company with 20 users will save $750 per day, $15,000 per month, $180,000 per year, and so on. After including WLAN installation costs, you may see a positive ROI in just a few months. Even if you factor in the cost of new laptops for everyone, you should still see a positive ROI in less than a year.

As a result, the use of WLANs can prove financially beneficial in common office environments, even if it only enables people to make better use of their time during meetings. Once a WLAN is in place, however, you will surely think of additional productivity-enhancing applications.

Determining Benefits of a VoWLAN System

The calculation of savings resulting from a VoWLAN solution includes the combination of quantitative and qualitative benefits. Let's take a look at each of these types of benefits and see how they can help justify VoWLAN costs.

Quantitative Benefits

The quantitative benefits comprise the actual dollar savings resulting from the deployment of a VoWLAN solution. This is generally cash that a company avoids paying for particular services, but it can also include sales of hardware that the VoWLAN system is replacing. The following are the types of quantitative benefits that you can realize with a VoWLAN solution:

- Reduced long-distance telephone charges: The routing of inter-company VoIP telephone calls is nearly free; therefore, a VoWLAN system can eliminate the long-distance charges (toll bypass) associated with each VoWLAN user.

- Fewer wired telephone lines: A company can eliminate the need for a wired telephone line for each VoWLAN user, which saves any associated fees. Because VoWLAN users are wireless, there is no need to rewire telephone lines when changes are made to the workforce.

- Increased productivity: This one is somewhat difficult to define in some cases, but it allows employees to complete work faster and better server customers. This results in higher revenues for the company, which is certainly a benefit.

Qualitative Benefits

Qualitative benefits enhance the operation of the company, but they do not result in definable dollar savings. These types of benefits often lean management toward funding the project when quantitative benefits are marginal or not well defined. The following are the types of qualitative benefits that you should consider when performing an ROI study for a VoWLAN solution:

- **Improved safety:** This is certainly important to any company. In some cases, the regular use of VoWLAN phones can provide vital and immediate communications in emergency situations.

- **Better image to customers:** With the use of VoWLAN phones, customers will see company employees getting things done faster and more efficiently, which makes the customer more inclined to do business with the company.

- **Increased employee morale:** Employees equipped with VoWLAN handsets have less frustration because they don't have to deal with telephone tag or search for phones when they need them.

Note　For details on implications of WLANs, such as radio frequency interference and security issues, refer to Chapter 4, "Wireless LAN Implications."

Wireless LAN Technologies

Wireless LAN technologies offer wireless connectivity in building, campus, and city-wide environments. Figure 1-2 illustrates the basic concept of a WLAN. The 802.11 standard has been evolving for more than a decade, resulting in today's 802.11n and 802.11ac and several legacy standards (see Figure 1-3).

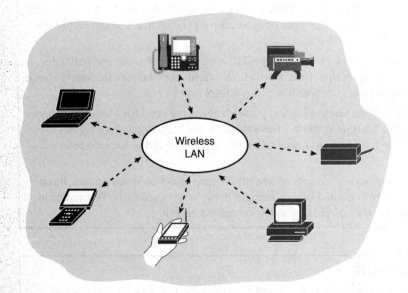

Figure 1-2　*Wireless LANs Support Wireless Communications Among a Variety of Client Devices*

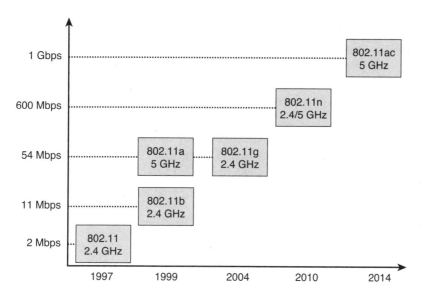

Figure 1-3 *IEEE 802.11 Standardization Has Led to Higher Performance*

In most cases, a standards organization defines the specific protocols and radio technology, and an industry group certifies the products based on the standard. For example, the IEEE 802.11 Working Group defines the 802.11 standard for WLANs, and the Wi-Fi Alliance provides interoperability testing for 802.11 products.

Note 802.11a, 802.11b, and 802.11g are considered legacy WLAN technologies because they have become obsolete.

Several different types of WLANs exist in companies and organizations. As a result, it is important that you understand the different WLAN types and their capabilities. In most cases, especially if there is an existing wireless network, it will be cost-effective to deploy an 802.11n or 802.11ac WLAN and make use of the existing legacy networks by configuring the access points to allow connections for older clients (e.g., 802.11g). Over time, as the needs arise and the funding is available, you should focus on migrating all users and applications to only 802.11n and 802.11ac.

The following sections provide a brief overview of the WLAN standards. The emphasis of this book is on IEEE 802.11–compliant WLANs because 802.11 is expected to continue being the preferred standard for supporting WLAN application. Other technologies, such as 802.16 (WiMAX), 802.15.3 (Bluetooth), and 802.15.4 (ZigBee), may better suit your needs in some situations, however. For example, WiMAX may be best for providing networking over large areas, such as cities. Bluetooth is the predominant technology for personal area networks, and ZigBee is ideal for very-low-power applications.

Initial 802.11

The initial IEEE 802.11 WLAN standard, ratified in 1997, specifies the use of both direct-sequence spread spectrum (DSSS) and frequency-hopping spread spectrum (FHSS) for delivering 1-Mbps and 2-Mbps data rates in the 2.4-GHz band. DSSS and FHSS are different forms of transmitting data over a WLAN.

The lower data rate provided by the initial 802.11 standard was more than enough bandwidth at the time to support bar code applications, which were the first commercial uses of WLAN technology. In general, however, the products based on this initial standard did not proliferate because of their high costs. In addition, some of the wireless data collector vendors were reluctant to move from proprietary wireless technologies to 802.11-based devices, primarily because they wanted to continue selling their own wireless base stations and only allow their data collectors to operate on them.

802.11a

In 1999, the 802.11 group ratified the 802.11a standard, which offers data rates up to 54 Mbps in the 5-GHz band, using orthogonal frequency-division multiplexing (OFDM). Even though the 802.11a standard was available in 1999, 802.11a access points and radio cards did not become commercially available until several years later. The primary reasons for the delay to market were the difficulties in developing 5-GHz, 802.11 hardware and the weak market potential for WLAN components that did not interoperate with the existing 2.4-GHz WLANs. 802.11a products had been available for several years, but their use was somewhat limited to specialized applications, especially where high performance was necessary (and interoperability with 2.4-GHz systems was not necessary).

A significant advantage of 802.11a is that it offers very high capacity compared to other legacy WLANs. The reason is that the 802.11a, 5-GHz spectrum defines a greater number of RF channels that do not overlap in frequency. Another advantage of 802.11a is that it operates in the 5-GHz band, which is mostly free from sources of RF interference. Microwave ovens, Bluetooth devices, most cordless phones, and the majority of neighboring WLANs operate in the 2.4-GHz band of frequencies. The lower noise floor in the 5-GHz band affords lower retransmission rates and higher resulting throughput compared to 802.11b and 802.11g systems.

802.11b

To provide higher data rates when operating in the 2.4-GHz band, the 802.11 group also ratified the 802.11b physical layer in 1999, enhancing the initial DSSS physical layer to include additional 5.5-Mbps and 11-Mbps data rates. The 802.11b access points were backward compatible with original 802.11 DSSS client devices. Soon after ratification of the 802.11b standard, 802.11b access points and radio cards began shipping with those improvements. It was a fairly easy modification to existing 802.11 DSSS devices to become 802.11b compliant. In fact, most users could upgrade their existing access points and radio cards with simple firmware upgrades. For several years, 802.11b devices proliferated throughout the industry and became the most commonly installed WLAN hardware.

Unfortunately, a great deal of RF interference resides in the 2.4-GHz band, which impacts 802.11b, 802.11g, and 2.4-GHz 802.11n users. A microwave oven can cause significant degradation in throughput because radio waves from a microwave oven can block 802.11b (and 802.11g) radio cards from accessing the medium or create bit errors in the 802.11 frames in transit. The potential for RF interference in the 2.4-GHz band is one reason a company would strongly consider using 5-GHz solutions.

A limiting factor of 802.11b is that it supports only up to three non-overlapping radio cells in the same area. The 2.4-GHz frequency spectrum is roughly 90-MHz wide, and an 802.11b radio card or access point uses approximately 30 MHz when transmitting. To avoid inter-access point interference (also referred to as co-channel interference), 802.11b access points must be set to specific channels. For example, access points in the United States can be set to channels 1, 6, and 11 to avoid overlap and mutual interference. This is especially important if there are many active wireless users. As a result of this frequency plan and limited data rates, 802.11b has limited capacity (and data rates).

802.11g

802.11g, ratified in 2004, further enhances 802.11b to include data rates up to 54-Mbps in the 2.4-GHz band, using OFDM. 802.11g is backward compatible with 802.11b, which is referred to as 802.11b/g mixed-mode operation. For example, an 802.11b radio card can associate with an 802.11g access point. Because of its support for data rates up to 54-Mbps, 802.11g offers higher performance than 802.11b systems. Capacity is still somewhat limited, however, because 802.11g operates in the 2.4-GHz band, which still limits the number of non-overlapping channels to 1, 6, and 11, as with 802.11b. As a result, 802.11g systems have less capacity than 802.11a WLANs. 802.11g, for example, can have up to three non-overlapping channels with 54 Mbps per channel.

A single 802.11b station associating with an 802.11g access point invokes the use of protection mechanisms, such as request-to-send/clear-to-send (RTS/CTS). The reason this is necessary is that 802.11b and 802.11g use different modulation, which means that they cannot interoperate and coordinate transmissions according to the 802.11 protocol. The access point informs all stations that an 802.11b station is present by setting an applicable bit in the body of each beacon frame. As a result, all stations begin using protection mechanisms.

The RTS/CTS protection mechanism requires each station to implement the entire RTS/CTS process for each data frame needing transmission. The problem with this requirement is that throughput suffers because of the RTS and CTS frames. As a result, some 802.11 stations are designed to implement a CTS-to-self mechanism as a protection. In this case, a station needing to send data first transmits a CTS frame to itself, using a modulation type understandable by all stations and indicating to other stations how long the sending station will need to access the medium in order to send a data frame. This may decrease the number of frame transmissions, but it still introduces a considerable amount of overhead. Thus, a mixed environment of 802.11b and 802.11g users significantly degrades the throughput of the WLAN, often by as much as 30 percent, which reduces the number of simultaneous voice calls that the network can support.

This is why most vendors allow administrators to configure access points to allow only 802.11g station associations, referred to as 802.11g-only mode. Of course the problem with this is that all users must have 802.11g radio cards. 802.11b-equipped devices will not be able to associate with the access point. But at least the throughput will remain relatively high.

Some vendors also allow you to disable protection mechanisms in mixed mode, which supports both 802.11b and 802.11g connections. This is a good approach if there are a limited number of active users because the probability of 802.11b and 802.11g devices transmitting at the same time is minimal.

Many 802.11g implementations use 802.11b-only mode to avoid interoperability issues and maximize range. Sometimes 802.11b client radios have trouble connecting to 802.11g access points, and administrators often fix the problem by switching the 802.11g access points to b-only mode. 802.11b also has slightly better range because of lower minimum data rates. 802.11b can operate with data rates as low as 1 Mbps, whereas 802.11g can operate only as low as 6 Mbps. The lower minimum data rate operation of 802.11b allows longer-range operation compared to 802.11g.

In addition, most 802.11g access points set to b-only mode will send beacons as 1 Mbps instead of 2 Mbps (which is what 802.11g generally uses). This extends the reach of 802.11b access points beyond 802.11g access points. In addition, the use of b-only mode eliminates the need for the access point to use protection mechanisms since users are all 802.11b and not a mix of 802.11b and 802.11g.

Current Standards: 802.11n and 802.11ac

The 802.11n standard, ratified in 2009, specifies data rates well above 100 Mbps and at much better throughput than legacy systems. In 2008, the Wi-Fi Alliance started certifying WLAN products based on Draft 2.0 of the 802.11n standard, which offers a solid technology that requires only software upgrades to be compatible with the ratified version of the 802.11 standard. Draft 2.0 802.11n differs from earlier pre-802.11n, which was based on several earlier and differing 802.11n drafts. A problem is that most of the pre-802.11n products do not interoperate between vendors. As a result, it is likely not possible to upgrade pre-802.11n products to the Draft 2.0 or ratified versions of the standard.

802.11n supports operation in both the 2.4-GHz and 5-GHz bands, which provides flexibility for satisfying a multitude of wireless requirements. In addition, 802.11n is backward compatible with 802.11g and 802.11a legacy WLANs, and protection mechanisms are necessary to coordinate access to the network, similar to 802.11b/g mixed-mode operation. Of course, protection mechanisms impose a great detail of overhead, which hampers throughput. The backward compatibility makes it possible to continue use of existing legacy WLAN devices; however, to achieve the full performance potential of 802.11n, you should implement 802.11n-only client devices.

802.11n does a better job than legacy systems (802.11a, 802.11b, and 802.11g) at providing higher performance, availability, and predictability of the network because of multiple-input multiple-output (MIMO) operation, channel bonding, and more efficient protocols, such as packet aggregation. With 802.11n, usage of the wireless network is comparable to wired Ethernet connections. In addition, support costs are relatively low because there isn't as much need to continually fine-tune the network as there is in legacy networks. The MIMO technology of 802.11n overcomes interference issues, which improves reliability and reduces the time needed to troubleshoot related problems.

802.11ac was ratified in 2014 and is an enhancement to the 802.11n standard in the 5-GHz band. 802.11ac increases data rates in the Gbps range to play effectively with Gigabit Ethernet. 802.11ac provides higher data rates through wider RF channels, more spatial streams, and higher-order modulation. Typical dual-band access points today implement 802.11n in the 2.4-GHz band and 802.11ac in the 5-GHz band. This combination of technologies offers substantial performance for meeting the needs of a wide variety of wireless applications and utilization levels today and in the foreseeable future.

Comparison of 802.11 Standards

Table 1-1 provides a comparison of the different characteristics of the 802.11a, 802.11b, 802.11g, 802.11n, and 802.11ac standards.

Table 1-1 *802.11 Standards Comparison*

	RF Spectrum	Max Speed	Compatibility	RF Interference Impacts	Date Ratified
802.11a	5 GHz	54 Mbps	Does not work with 802.11b or 802.11g	Slight	1999
802.11b	2.4 GHz	11 Mbps	Works with 802.11g	Moderate	1999
802.11g	2.4 GHz	54 Mbps	Works with 802.11b	Moderate	2004
802.11n	2.4 GHz and 5 GHz	600 Mbps	Works with 802.11a/b/g	Slight	2009
802.11ac	5 GHz	Gbps range	Works with 802.11a or 5 GHz 802.11n	Slight	2014

Wi-Fi Certification

The Wi-Fi Alliance (which was originally known as the Wireless Ethernet Compatibility Alliance [WECA]) is an international nonprofit organization focusing on the manufacturing, marketing, and interoperability of 802.11 WLAN products. The Wi-Fi Alliance pushes the term (actually brand) "Wi-Fi" to cover all forms of 802.11-based wireless networking (whether 802.11a, b, g, n, or ac); it is also the group behind Wi-Fi Protected Access (WPA), the stepping-stone between the much-criticized WEP and the 802.11i security standard.

> **Note**   For a current list of certified Wi-Fi equipment, refer to the Wi-Fi Alliance website, at www.wi-fi.org.

The Wi-Fi Alliance has the following goals:

- Promote Wi-Fi certification worldwide by encouraging manufacturers to follow standardized 802.11 processes in the development of WLAN products

- Market Wi-Fi-certified products to consumers in the home, small office, and enterprise markets

Wi-Fi certification is a process that assures interoperability between 802.11 WLAN equipment, including access points and radio cards complying with a variety of form factors. After completing a testing program, WLAN vendors receive Wi-Fi certification for their products. All Wi-Fi-certified products include a label, as shown in Figure 1-4.

Figure 1-4   *A Product Bearing This Label Verifies Compliance with Wi-Fi Standards*

The Wi-Fi Alliance follows an established testing program to certify that products are interoperable with other Wi-Fi-certified products. Certification consists of independent testing labs located in North America, Europe, and Asia. After a product successfully passes every test, the manufacturer is granted the right to use the Wi-Fi Certified logo on that particular product and its corresponding support material, such as packaging and manuals.

For a manufacturer, the main reason to obtain Wi-Fi certification is that it helps sell products. Wi-Fi certification is meant to give consumers confidence that they are purchasing WLAN products that have met multivendor interoperability requirements. A Wi-Fi Certified logo on the product means that it has met interoperability testing requirements and will definitely work with other vendors' Wi-Fi-certified products. If a product says Wi-Fi Certified, consumers should feel confident that it will work.

There is certainly merit in having products guaranteed to interoperate with those from other vendors. IT managers generally deploy access points from a single vendor, but they often do not have control over the use of different vendors for radio cards found in user devices. This can pose compatibility issues unless all devices undergo interoperability testing, such as the Wi-Fi certification process. Thus, Wi-Fi certification enables WLAN sales because IT managers are more likely to buy certified devices than ones that do not have Wi-Fi certification.

The 802.11 standard enables significant interoperability; however, there are no conformance mandates to ensure that a particular vendor follows all the rules precisely. IT managers realize this and therefore see the value in the conformance that Wi-Fi demands.

In fact, the general public is starting to recognize Wi-Fi as a brand and buzzword that is more significant than 802.11 alone.

With this said, a company wanting to sell mainstream WLAN products needs Wi-Fi certification to be competitive. The importance of Wi-Fi certification will only grow as more and more mixed-vendor WLANs proliferate in public markets.

> **Note**   Refer to Chapters 5, "Introduction to IEEE 802.11 and Related Standards," 6, "IEEE 802.11 Medium Access Control (MAC) Layer," and 7 "IEEE 802.11 Physical (PHY) Layers," for more details on the IEEE 802.11 standard.

Case Study 1-2: Acme Healthcare Chooses 802.11n and 802.11ac

Acme Healthcare, the fictitious hospital introduced earlier in this chapter, decided that 802.11n and 802.11ac will best meet the hospital's wireless networking needs. Arthur, the hospital CIO, consulted with several of his IT staff, and the consensus was that the higher throughput and reliability of 802.11n and 802.11ac as compared to the legacy 802.11 systems is absolutely necessary to support demanding applications that the hospital plans to deploy. It will be imperative that the wireless network be able to effectively support a relatively large number of time-sensitive applications, such as voice communications and patient monitoring, as well as currently unknown applications that the hospital may implement in the future. In addition, the surge of hospital workers having multiple wireless computing devices, such as smart phones and laptops, has increased potential utilization to levels that the legacy technologies will not support.

Note that this case study surfaces throughout this book to emphasize the primary considerations in deploying an 802.11n and 802.11ac wireless network.

Wireless LANs: A Historical Perspective

You may be interested in knowing how WLAN technologies got started and how they have developed over the years. The evolution of WLANs has been taking place for decades, leading to continual gains in performance, security, and reliability. This section starts with the historical roots and then explores what has led to the 802.11n and 802.11ac standards.

The Early Days

Network technologies and radio communications were brought together for the first time in 1971 at the University of Hawaii as a research project called ALOHANET. The ALOHANET system enabled computer sites at seven campuses spread out over four islands to communicate with the central computer on Oahu without using the existing unreliable and expensive phone lines. ALOHANET offered bidirectional communications in a star topology between the central computer and each of the remote stations. The remote stations had to communicate with each other via the centralized computer.

In the 1980s, amateur radio hobbyists, hams, kept radio networking alive in the United States and Canada by designing and building terminal node controllers (TNCs) to interface their computers through ham radio equipment. A TNC acts much like a telephone modem, converting the computer's digital signal into a signal that a ham radio can modulate and send over the airwaves by using a packet-switching technique. In fact, the American Radio Relay League (ARRL) and the Canadian Radio Relay League (CRRL) have been sponsoring the Computer Networking Conference since the early 1980s to provide a forum for the development of wireless WANs. Thus, hams have been using wireless networking for years, much earlier than the commercial market.

In 1985, the FCC made possible the commercial development of radio-based LAN components by authorizing the public use of the Industrial, Scientific, and Medical (ISM) bands. These frequencies reside between 902 MHz and 5.85 GHz, just above the cellular phone operating frequencies. The ISM band is attractive to wireless network vendors because it provides a part of the spectrum on which to base their products, and end users do not have to obtain FCC licenses to operate the products. The ISM band allocation has had a dramatic effect on the wireless industry, prompting the development of WLAN components. Without a standard, however, vendors began developing proprietary radios and access points.

Initial 802.11 Standardization

In the late 1980s, the Institute of Electrical and Electronics Engineers (IEEE) 802 Working Group, responsible for the development of LAN standards such as Ethernet and Token Ring, began development of standards for WLANs. Under the chairmanship of Vic Hayes from NCR, the IEEE 802.11 Working Group developed the Wireless LAN Medium Access Control and Physical Layer specifications. Before the ratification of the standard, companies began shipping proprietary WLAN radio cards and access points operating in the 902-MHz ISM band. In the early 1990s, the first WLAN products, NCR WaveLAN and Motorola Altair, appeared on the market. At that time, there were no applicable standards, and prices were relatively high, at around $1,500 per wireless adapter. As a result, only companies having applications with significant benefits from wireless connectivity, such as inventory management and price marking, could afford to deploy WLAN solutions.

The IEEE Standards Board approved the standard on June 26, 1997, and the IEEE published the standard on November 18, 1997. The finalization of this standard prompted vendors to release 1-Mbps and 2-Mbps 802.11-compliant radio cards and access points throughout 1998. Proliferation of WLANs at that point was slow, mainly because performance of the initial 802.11 devices was slow (and pricing was still high) compared to wired Ethernet networks. In addition, there was significant criticism of the security of 802.11 networks because of issues with the Wired Equivalent Privacy (WEP) encryption protocol.

In December 1999, the IEEE released supplements to the 802.11 standard to increase performance of WLANs. 802.11a provided up to 54 Mbps in the 5-GHz band, and 802.11b offered up to 11 Mbps in the 2.4-GHz band. Vendors began shipping 802.11b devices throughout 2000 at prices of less than $200 per radio card. This caused 802.11b sales to skyrocket. The 54-Mbps 802.11a WLANs did not become available for a couple years after 802.11b products. As a result, the proliferation of 802.11a was very low because of the significant installed base of 802.11b (and lack of interoperability between 802.11b and 802.11a).

Later, in 2004, IEEE released 802.11g, which further extended data rates in the 2.4-GHz band to 54-Mbps, using OFDM. The higher-data-rate 802.11 standards 802.11a, 802.11b, and 802.11g offer adequate capacity for supporting most applications. 802.11a, however, provided the highest capacity, mainly because the RF channels in the 5-GHz band do not overlap with each other, as they do in the 2.4-GHz band.

Another improvement to the 802.11 standard was security; 802.11i includes much stronger encryption and authentication mechanisms than the initial standard. The use of TKIP/RC4 and CCMP/AES, along with 802.11i protocols, makes WLANs very secure. The ratification of the 802.11e standard, which offers quality of service important for VoWLAN applications, was an important step toward making 802.11 WLANs more reliable.

In the past few years, the prices for WLAN adapters have decreased to well under $100 each. This dramatic drop in prices has fueled the proliferation of WLANs for a variety of applications in all markets. The Wi-Fi Alliance has also been actively promoting WLANs through the Wi-Fi brand and mandating interoperability testing.

802.11n and 802.11ac Standardization

A major improvement to WLAN technology was the development of the 802.11n standard. The first official 802.11n development began with a presentation in January 2002 to the Wireless Next Generation Standing Committee (WNG SC) of the IEEE 802.11 Working Group. In September 2002, the High Throughput Study Group (HTSG) had its first meeting and completed the Project Authorization Request (PAR) to begin the High Throughput Task Group (TGn), which would then continue with the development of the standard. The PAR emphasized the development of an amendment to the 802.11 standard to modify the Physical (PHY) Layer and Medium Access Control (MAC) Layer specifications to satisfy high performance needs of residential, enterprise, and hotspot environments. At its first meeting in September 2003, TGn created functional requirements.

The following is a list of the key requirements that the 802.11n PAR identifies:

- At least 100-Mbps throughput in a single 20-MHz channel
- Spectral density of at least 3 bps/Hz
- Support for operation in the 5-GHz band
- Backward compatibility with 802.11a
- Integration of 802.11e within workstations

It is interesting to note that there was no initial requirement for 2.4-GHz operation, but if it were to become part of the standard (which it eventually did), it would have to be backward compatible with 802.11g.

TGn issued a call for proposals on March 17, 2004. There were several proposals, but eventually the TGn Sync and WWiSE proposals emerged. TGn Sync, founded by Intel, Cisco, Agere, and Sony, emphasized providing wireless connectivity for PCs, enterprises, and consumer electronics. WWiSE, founded by Broadcom, Conexant, and Texas Instruments, focused on a simple upgrade to 802.11a. Both proposal groups defined 40-MHz channels and MAC enhancements such as frame aggregation.

Unsuccessful attempts were made from 2005 to 2006 to confirm one particular proposal. This resulted in merging the TGn Sync and WWiSE proposals. Meanwhile, some of the first "802.11n" products were made available to the public starting in 2007, but they are more appropriately referred to as pre-N products because they are based on differing versions of draft 802.11 standards. The pre-N products do not provide guaranteed interoperability. These single-vendor systems were primarily sold to the home and small business market, where it is not as important to have interoperability.

The merged 802.11n proposal passed confirmation vote (unanimously) within TGn in January 2006, and the merged proposal was converted to a draft 802.11 standard amendment (Draft 1.0). In March 2006, Draft 1.0 of the standard (referred to as a Letter Ballot) was distributed to the entire 802.11 Working Group, but it did not receive the required 75 percent necessary for adoption. The reviewers of the draft proposal generated 6,000 comments.

Resolution of the comments began in May 2006, and TGn submitted the updated draft standard (Draft 2.0) for the Letter Ballot in February 2007. This time, the 802.11 Working Group adopted Draft 2.0 with a favorable vote of 83 percent. This process, however, generated 3,000 comments that the TGn would have to resolve. Because the 802.11 Working Group adopted Draft 2.0, the Wi-Fi Alliance started certifying 802.11n products based on Draft 2.0 of the 802.11n standard. This was done so that the vendors could start selling 802.11n products while the 802.11 Working Group was finalizing the standard. Draft 3.0 of the 802.11n standard was ready in September 2007. Instead of being a Letter Ballot, Draft 3.0 was sent to the IEEE 802.11 Working Group as a Recirculation Ballot, which required that comments only address changes that had taken place since the previous draft.

On September 11, 2009, the 802.11n amendment to the 802.11 standard was ratified.

Because of falling prices and substantial performance of 802.11n, WLANs took on a much larger role in horizontal enterprise applications. In addition, many organizations, such as hospitals and airports, began replacing existing legacy (mostly 802.11g) wireless networks with 802.11n infrastructures. During 2012, the IEEE 802.11ac Task Group produced Drafts 2.0 and 3.0 of the 802.11ac standard, with final ratification in January 2014. Soon after the drafts of the standard were released, vendors started selling 802.11ac products based on the draft standard.

Summary

Wireless LANs provide significant benefits to enterprises, hospitals, warehouses, and any other establishment where mobility is important. A host of organizations, such as hospitals, enterprises, and warehouses, have many tangible benefits based on the use of wireless IP phones and other bandwidth-intensive mobile applications. 802.11n- and 802.11ac-based WLAN solutions have the performance and reliability necessary for supporting these types of applications, especially when it's not clear what applications may need to be supported down the road.

Chapter 2

Radio Wave Fundamentals

This chapter will introduce you to:

- Radio Wave Attributes

- RF System Components

- RF Signal Propagation

- RF Mathematics

As the basis for understanding the installation, operation, and troubleshooting of wireless LANs (WLANs), it is important that you have a good knowledge of how radio waves propagate through an environment. Every Wi-Fi deployment requires that the systems engineer understand the fundamentals of how radio waves move and react within the environment. For example, in a WLAN, radio waves carry information over the air from one point to another. Along the way, the waves encounter various obstacles or obstructions that can impact range and performance, depending on the characteristics of the radio wave. In addition, regulatory rules govern the use and limitations of radio waves. This chapter explains the fundamentals of radio waves so that you have a good basis for understanding the complexities of deploying WLANs.

Radio Wave Attributes

A radio wave is a type of electromagnetic signal designed to carry information through the air over relatively long distances. Sometimes radio waves are referred to as radio frequency (RF) signals. These signals oscillate at a very high frequency, which allows the waves to travel through the air similar to waves on an ocean.

Radio waves have been in use for many years. They provide the means for carrying music to FM radios and video to televisions. In addition, radio waves are the primary means for carrying data over a wireless network. As shown in Figure 2-1, a radio wave has amplitude, frequency, and phase elements. These attributes may be varied in time to represent information.

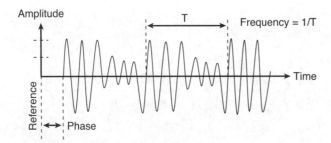

Figure 2-1   *The Amplitude, Frequency, and Phase Elements of a Radio Wave*

Amplitude

The amplitude of a radio wave indicates its strength. The measure for amplitude is generally power, which is analogous to the amount of effort a person needs to exert to ride a bicycle over a specific distance. Similarly, power in terms of electromagnetic signals represents the amount of energy necessary to push the signal over a particular distance. As the power increases, so does the range.

Radio waves have amplitudes with units of watts, which represent the amount of power in the signal. Watts have linear characteristics that follow mathematical relationships we are all very familiar with. For example, the result of doubling 10 milliwatts (mW) is 20 mW. We certainly do not need to do any serious number crunching to get that result.

As an alternative, it is possible to use dBm units (decibels referenced to 1 mW) to represent the amplitude of radio waves. The dBm is the amount of power in watts referenced to 1 mW. Zero (0) dBm equals 1 mW. By the way, the little m in dBm is a good reminder of the 1 mW reference. The dBm values are positive above 1 mW and negative below 1 mW. Beyond that, math with dBm values gets a bit harder. Refer to the section "RF Mathematics," later in this chapter, to learn how to convert between watts and dBm units and understand why it is preferable to use dBm units.

Note   You can adjust the transmit power of most client cards and access points. For example, some access points allow you to set the transmit power in increments from −1 dBm (0.78 mW) up to 23 dBm (200 mW).

Frequency

The frequency of a radio wave is the number of times per second that the signal repeats itself. The unit for frequency is Hertz (Hz), which is actually the number of cycles occurring each second. In fact, an old convention for the unit for frequency is cycles per second (cps).

802.11 WLANs use radio waves having frequencies of 2.4 GHz and 5 GHz, which means that the signal includes 2,400,000,000 cycles per second and 5,000,000,000 cycles per second, respectively. Signals operating at these frequencies are too high for humans to hear and too low for humans to see. Thus, radio waves are not noticed by humans.

The frequency impacts the propagation of radio waves. Theoretically, higher-frequency signals propagate over a shorter range than lower-frequency signals. In practice, however, the range of different frequency signals might be the same, or higher-frequency signals might propagate farther than lower-frequency signals. For example, a 5-GHz signal transmitted at a higher transmit power might go farther than a 2.4-GHz signal transmitted at a lower power, especially if electrical noise in the area impacts the 5-GHz part of the radio spectrum less than the 2.4-GHz portion of the spectrum (which is generally the case).

Phase

The phase of a radio wave corresponds to how far the signal is offset from a reference point (such as a particular time or another signal). By convention, each cycle of the signal spans 360 degrees. For example, a signal might have a phase shift of 90 degrees, which means that the offset amount is one-quarter (90/360 = 1/4) of the signal.

RF System Components

Figure 2-2 illustrates a basic RF system that enables the propagation of radio waves. The transceiver and antenna can be integrated inside the client device or can be an external component. The transmission medium is primarily air, but there might be obstacles, such as walls and furniture.

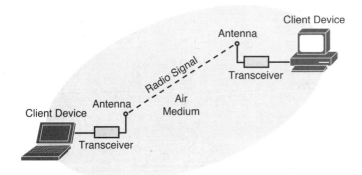

Figure 2-2   *An RF System Consists of RF Transceivers, Antennas, and a Transmission Medium*

RF Transceiver

A key component of a WLAN is the RF transceiver, which consists of a transmitter and a receiver. The transmitter transmits the radio wave on one end of the system (the "source"), and the receiver receives the radio wave on the other side (the "destination") of the system. The transceiver is generally composed of hardware that is part of the wireless client radio device (sometimes referred to as a client card).

Figure 2-3 shows the basic components of a transmitter. A process known as *modulation* converts electrical digital signals that represent information (data bits, 1s and 0s) inside a computer into radio waves at the desired frequency, which propagate through the air medium. Refer to the section "RF Modulation" for details on how modulation works. The amplifier increases the amplitude of the radio wave signal to a desired transmit power prior to being fed to the antenna and propagating through the transmission medium (consisting primarily of air in addition to obstacles, such as walls, ceilings, chairs, and so on).

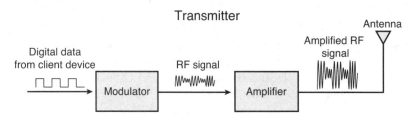

Figure 2-3   *A Transmitter Consists of a Modulator, an Amplifier, and an Antenna*

At the destination, a receiver (see Figure 2-4) detects the relatively weak RF signal and demodulates it into data types applicable to the destination computer. The radio wave at the receiver must have amplitude that is above the receiver sensitivity of the receiver; otherwise, the receiver will not be able to "interpret" the signal, or decode it. The minimum receiver sensitivity depends on the data rate. For example, say that the receiver sensitivity of an access point is –69 dBm for 300 Mbps (802.11n) and –90 dBm for 1 Mbps (802.11b). The amplitude of the radio wave at the receiver of this access point must be above –69 dBm for 300 Mbps or above –90 dBm for 1 Mbps before the receiver will be able to decode the signal.

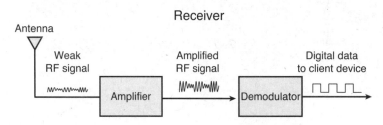

Figure 2-4   *A Receiver Consists of an Antenna, an Amplifier, and a Demodulator*

RF Modulation

RF modulation transforms digital data, such as binary 1s and 0s representing an e-mail message, from the network into an RF signal suitable for transmission through the air.

This involves converting the digital signal representing the data into an analog signal. As part of this process, modulation superimposes the digital data signal onto a carrier signal, which is a radio wave having a specific frequency. In effect, the data rides on top of the carrier. To represent the data, the modulation signal varies the carrier signal in a manner that represents the data.

Modulation is necessary because it is not practical to transmit data in its native form. For example, say that Kimberlyn wants to transmit her voice wirelessly from Dayton to Cincinnati, which is about 65 miles. One approach is for Kimberlyn to use a really high-powered audio amplifier system to boost her voice enough to be heard over a 65-mile range. The problem with this, of course, is that the intense volume would probably deafen everyone in Dayton and all the communities between Dayton and Cincinnati. Instead, a better approach is to modulate Kimberlyn's voice with a radio wave or light carrier signal that's out of range of human hearing and suitable for propagation through the air. The data signal can vary the amplitude, frequency, or phase of the carrier signal, and amplification of the carrier will not bother humans because it is well beyond the hearing range.

The latter is precisely what modulation does. A modulator mixes the source data signal with a carrier signal. In addition, the transmitter couples the resulting modulated and amplified signals to an antenna, which is designed to interface the signal to the air. The modulated signal then departs the antenna and propagates through the air. The receiving station antenna couples the modulated signal into a demodulator, which derives the data signal from the signal carrier.

Amplitude-Shift Keying

One of the simplest forms of modulation is amplitude modulation (sometimes referred to as amplitude-shift keying), which varies the amplitude of a signal to represent data. Figure 2-5 illustrates this concept. Frequency-shift keying (FSK) is common for light-based systems whereby the presence of a 1 data bit turns the light on and the presence of a 0 bit turns the light off. Actual light signal codes are more complex, but the main idea is to turn the light on and off to send the data. This is similar to giving flashlights to two people in a dark room and having them communicate with each other by flicking the flashlights on and off to send coded information.

Amplitude modulation alone does not work very well with RF systems because there are signals (noise) present inside buildings and outdoors that alter the amplitude of the radio wave, which causes the receiver to demodulate the signal incorrectly. These noise signals can cause the signal amplitude to be artificially high for a period of time; for example, the receiver would demodulate the signal into something that does not represent what was intended (for example, 10000001101101 would become 10111101101101). To combat impacts from noise, modulation for RF systems is more complex than using only amplitude modulation.

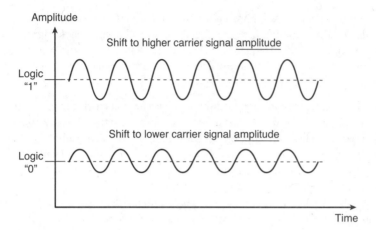

Figure 2-5 *Amplitude-Shift Keying Varies the Amplitude of the Signal to Represent Digital Data*

Frequency-Shift Keying

FSK makes slight changes to the frequency of the carrier signal to represent data in a manner that's suitable for propagation through the air at low to moderate data rates. For example, as shown in Figure 2-6, modulation can represent a 1 or 0 data bit with either a positive or negative shift in frequency of the carrier. If the shift in frequency is negative—that is, a shift of the carrier to a lower frequency—the result is a logic 0. The receiver can detect this shift in frequency and demodulate the results as a 0 data bit. As a result, FSK avoids the impacts of common noise that exhibits shifts in amplitude.

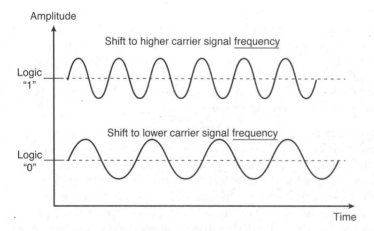

Figure 2-6 *Frequency-Shift Keying Makes Use of Changes in Frequency to Represent Digital Data*

Phase-Shift Keying

Some systems use phase-shift keying (PSK), which is similar to FSK, for modulation purposes for low to moderate data rates. With PSK, data causes changes in the signal's phase, while the frequency remains constant. The phase shift, as Figure 2-7 depicts, can correspond to a specific positive or negative amount relative to a reference. A receiver can detect these phase shifts and realize the corresponding data bits. As with FSK, PSK is mostly immune to common noise that is based on shifts in amplitude.

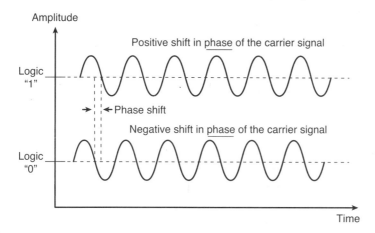

Figure 2-7   *Phase-Shift Keying Makes Use of Changes in Phase to Represent Digital Data*

Quadrature Amplitude Modulation

Quadrature amplitude modulation (QAM) causes both the amplitude and phase of the carrier to change to represent patterns of data, often referred to as symbols. The advantage of QAM is the capability of representing large groups of bits as a single amplitude and phase combination. In fact, some QAM-based systems, for example, make use of 64 different phase and amplitude combinations, resulting in the representation of 6 data bits per symbol. Higher-order combinations of phase and amplitude in QAM make it possible for standards such as 802.11n and 802.11ac to support higher data rates.

Note   See Chapter 7, "IEEE 802.11 Physical (PHY) Layers," for details on the modulation and transmission frequencies that 802.11a, 802.11b, 802.11g, 802.11n, and 802.11ac use.

Spread Spectrum

After modulating the digital signal into an analog carrier signal using FSK, PSK, or QAM, some WLAN transceivers spread the modulated carrier over a wider spectrum to comply with regulatory rules. This process, called *spread spectrum*, significantly reduces the possibility of outward and inward interference. As a result, regulatory bodies generally do not require users of spread spectrum systems to obtain licenses. Spread spectrum, developed originally by the military, spreads a signal's power over a wide band of frequencies (see Figure 2-8).

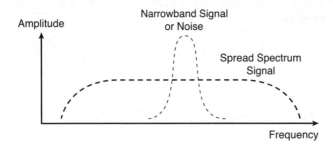

Figure 2-8   *Spread Spectrum Occupies a Wide Portion of the RF Spectrum*

Spread spectrum radio components use either direct sequence or frequency hopping for spreading the signal. Direct sequence modulates a radio carrier by a digital code with a bit rate much higher than the information signal bandwidth. Figure 2-9 is a hypothetical example of direct sequence that represents the transmission of three data bits (101) serially in time. The actual transmission is based on a different code word that represents each type of data bit (1 and 0). As shown in the figure, when sending a data bit 1, the radio sends the code word 00010011100 to represent the data bit. Similarly, when sending a data bit 0, the radio sends the code word 11101100011. The increase in the number of bits sent that represents the data effectively spreads the signal across a wider portion of the frequency spectrum.

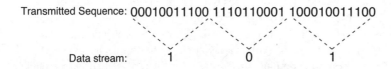

Figure 2-9   *Direct Sequence Is a Type of Spread Spectrum*

Frequency hopping uses a different technique to spread the signal by quickly hopping the radio carrier from one frequency to another within a specific range. Figure 2-10 illustrates this concept. The boxes labeled A, B, C, D, and E in the figure represent bursts of data that are sent at different times and frequencies. This also effectively spreads the signal across a wider part of the spectrum.

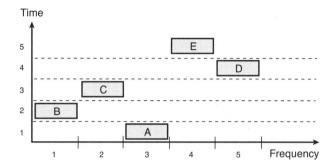

Figure 2-10 *Frequency Hopping Is a Type of Spread Spectrum*

The Advent of Frequency-Hopping Spread Spectrum

Hedy Lamarr, who was a well-known film actress during the 1940s, conceived the idea of frequency-hopping spread spectrum during the early part of World War II to keep the Germans from jamming the radios that guided U.S. torpedoes against German warships. (Lamarr was desperate to find a way she could help win the war against Germany. She was strongly opposed to the Nazis; in fact, she left her first husband for selling munitions to Hitler.)

Lamarr's idea was to transmit communications signals by randomly hopping from frequency to frequency to prevent the enemy from knowing what radio signal frequency to send for jamming purposes. It is amazing that she had no technical education but still thought of this very important communications concept.

Lamarr and film score composer George Antheil, who had extensive experience in synchronizing the sounds of music scores with motion pictures, set out to perfect the idea. One problem was how the torpedo's receiver was to know the frequency to listen to at specific times, because the idea was to send a random sequence of frequencies. Antheil was able to devise methods to keep a frequency-hopping receiver synchronized with the transmitter. His idea was to send signals to the torpedo using a long pattern of different frequencies that would appear to be random. The receiver, knowing the secret hopping pattern, would be able to tune to the correct frequency at the right time. This pseudo-random hopping sequence is what the frequency-hopping systems use today and what led to the development of other spread spectrum technologies.

Lamarr and Antheil sent details of their invention to the National Inventors Council. Charles Kettering, the director of the council, encouraged them to patent the idea. They filed the patent in 1941. Lamarr and Antheil then teamed with electrical engineers from MIT to provide the technical design. On August 11, 1942, Lamarr and Antheil received U.S. Patent Number 2,292,387 for their idea.

Because of the newness of the technology and clumsy mechanical nature of the initial design, spread spectrum was never used during World War II. The initial prototype used many moving parts to control the frequency of transmission and reception.

In the 1950s, Sylvania began experimenting with frequency hopping, using newly developed digital components in place of the initial mechanical system. By then, Lamarr and Antheil's patent had expired. Sylvania, under contract with the U.S. Navy, used spread spectrum for the first time on ships sent to blockade Cuba in 1962. In the mid-1980s, the U.S. military declassified spread spectrum technology, and commercial companies began to exploit it for consumer electronics.

Lamarr and Antheil conceived an excellent modulation technique; however, they never received any compensation for their idea. Their main interest, expressed in a high degree of patriotism, was to help win the war against the Nazis. In March 1997, Lamarr and Antheil were honored with the Electronic Frontier Foundation's Pioneer Award at its San Francisco convention, the Computers, Freedom, and Privacy Conference.

Orthogonal Frequency-Division Multiplexing

Instead of using spread spectrum, higher-speed WLANs make use of orthogonal frequency-division multiplexing (OFDM). OFDM divides a signal modulated with FSK, PSK, or QAM across multiple subcarriers occupying a specific channel (see Figure 2-11). OFDM is extremely efficient, which enables it to provide the higher data rates and minimize multipath propagation problems. OFDM has also been around for a while, supporting the global standard for asymmetric digital subscriber line (ADSL), a high-speed wired telephony standard.

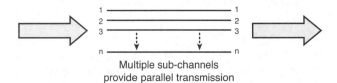

Multiple sub-channels
provide parallel transmission

Figure 2-11   *OFDM Sends Multitudes of Data Simultaneously in Parallel*

Note   Some WLANs, such as 802.11ac, further increase data rate capability through spatial separation, which involves using the same modulation simultaneously within different portions of the frequency band.

RF Signal Propagation

A radio wave propagates fairly freely through the air and with some resistance through obstacles, such as walls and furniture. When deploying WLANs, you must be aware of several impairments, such as attenuation, noise, and multipath propagation, which impede the capability of a radio wave to successfully carry data to the destination.

Attenuation

As a radio signal propagates through the transmission medium, it experiences a decrease in amplitude (signal loss) referred to as *attenuation*. For example, a radio wave might have a signal amplitude of 20 dBm as it leaves the antenna at the source transceiver. After completing its journey of propagating through the transmission medium, the amplitude of the radio wave might be only –75 dBm.

Free Space Loss

A large part of the decrease in amplitude with attenuation results from what is known as free space loss (FSL), as depicted in Figure 2-12. The atmosphere causes the modulated signal to attenuate exponentially as the signal propagates farther away from the antenna. Therefore, the signal must have enough power to reach the desired distance at an acceptable signal level that the receiver needs for decoding purposes. The amplitude of a radio wave is proportional to the inverse of the square of the distance from the source. For example, if you double the distance between the transmitter and receiver, the amplitude of the radio wave at that location will be one-quarter of its initial value. Likewise, the amplitude of a radio wave is proportional to the inverse of the square of the radio wave's frequency.

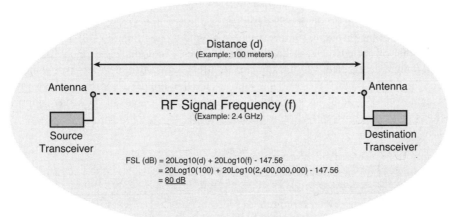

Figure 2-12 *Propagation of RF Signals Through the Air Medium Causes Significant Attenuation (FSL) to RF Signals*

You can calculate the attenuation (in dB) of a radio signal in free space (line of sight with no obstructions) by using the following formula:

$$\text{FSL (dB)} = 20\text{Log}10(d) + 20\text{Log}10(f) - 147.56$$

where d is the distance from the transmitter in meters, and the f is the frequency in Hertz.

For example, referring to Figure 2-12, you can calculate the FSL for an 802.11n (2.4 GHz signal) propagating over 100 meters as follows:

FSL (dB) = 20Log10(100) + 20Log10(2,400,000,000) − 147.56 = approximately 80 dB

If using 5-GHz frequencies for an 802.11n or 802.11ac implementation, the FSL at 100 meters would be as follows:

FSL (dB) = 20Log10(100) + 20Log10(5,000,000,000) − 147.56 = approximately 86 dB

Thus, the attenuation of radio waves based on FSL of a typical 802.11ac system is 80 to 86 dB over 100 meters. A 2.4-GHz signal with an amplitude at the source transceiver of 20 dBm, for instance, would only be −60 dBm (20 dBm − 80 dB) at 100 meters away from the source. Keep in mind that the preceding free space loss calculation is for completely open space, and other factors—such as the shape of the room and obstacles—might make the attenuation more or less. Also, note that the attenuation increases as the frequency increases; however, the actual effective range of the signal might be greater for the 5-GHz system because of less noise and interference in the 5-GHz band.

Physical Obstacles

As radio waves travel through physical obstacles, such as walls and ceilings, they decrease much more when compared to traveling through open air. The amount of attenuation varies significantly depending on the material, but a typical radio wave used in WLANs at signal amplitude of −60 dBm, for example, will decrease to approximately −63 dBm after going through an interior wall of a building (see Figure 2-13). In addition to walls, other obstacles, such as filing cabinets, shelves, fire doors, elevator shafts, and air conditioning ducts, offer varying amounts of attenuation. Also, be aware that some areas of the facility might have relatively high attenuation (50 dB or more), such as x-ray rooms in hospitals. In addition, some buildings have extensive steel and concrete support structures that can significantly attenuate radio waves.

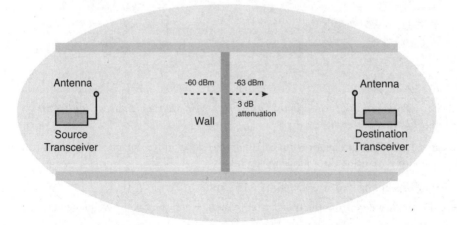

Figure 2-13   *Obstacles Contribute to the Attenuation of RF Signals*

If you are installing a wireless network outdoors, keep in mind that rain, fog, and snow increase the amount of water in the air and can cause significant attenuation to the propagation of modulated wireless signals. Smog clutters the air, adding attenuation to the communications channel, too. In addition, leaves on trees block transmissions in the spring and summer.

Note See Chapter 15, "Performing a Wireless Site Survey," for details on how to ensure that a WLAN compensates for various transmission impairments.

Multipath Propagation

Multipath propagation occurs when portions of a radio wave take different paths when propagating from source to destination (see Figure 2-14). A portion of the signal might go directly to the destination, and another part might bounce from a desk to the ceiling and then to the destination. As a result, some of the signal will encounter delay and travel longer paths to the receiver.

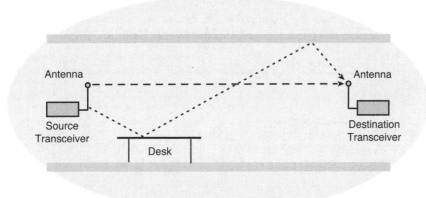

Figure 2-14 *Obstacles Get in the Way and Cause the Signal to Bounce in Different Directions*

Note For more information about the impacts of multipath propagation, see Chapter 4, "Wireless LAN Implications."

Noise and Signal-to-Noise Ratio

The capability of a receiver to make sense of the radio waves it receives depends on the presence of other nearby radio waves, referred to as interfering signals, or noise. This noise can distort the communications, making it difficult for the receiver to correctly understand the data being sent. As an analogy, imagine two people, Evan and Shanna, trying to carry on a conversation while they are 20 feet apart. Shanna, acting as the transmitter, is speaking just loud enough for Evan, the receiver, to hear every word. If their baby, Kimberlyn, is crying loudly nearby, Evan might miss a few of Shanna's words. In this case, the interference of the baby has made it not possible to effectively support communications. Evan and Shanna need to move closer together, or Shanna needs to speak louder, or they need to find some way to make the baby stop crying. This is no different from the transmitters and receivers in wireless systems using radio waves for communications. It is possible to improve communications by either moving the transceivers closer together, increasing the transmit power, or reducing the surrounding noise.

In general, an average noise of –95 dBm (often referred to as *noise floor*) exists because of the electromagnetic impacts of the atmosphere. In addition to the noise floor, other electromagnet devices, such as microwave ovens, cordless phones, and other wireless networks, may operate sporadically and increase the average noise level to –90 dBm and even –80 dBm in some areas. As a result, it is very important to measure the noise and factor it in when designing a WLAN.

An important signal measurement is the signal-to-noise (SNR) ratio, which provides a figure of merit for a particular radio wave. The SNR (in dB) at a particular point (and point in time) in a network is simply the signal power (in dBm) of the radio wave minus the noise power (in dBm) at that point. Figure 2-15 illustrates the SNR.

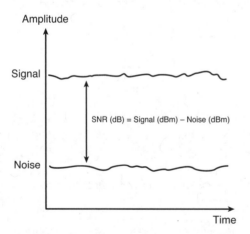

Figure 2-15   *SNR Is the Difference Between the Signal and Noise Power of a Signal at a Given Point in Time*

For example, a signal power of –65 dBm and noise power of –90 dBm yields an SNR of 25 dB. (The difference between values in dBm results in units of dB.) In other words, the signal in this example is 25 dB higher than the average noise, which generally provides excellent performance for 802.11 wireless networks. Even though the signal level is above the sensitivity of the receiver, the SNR must be positive to enable the receiver to distinguish the signal from the noise. For 802.11 wireless networks, it is important to ensure that the SNR at the receiver is at least 15 to 20 dB (maybe higher for some applications) to provide a safety margin to ensure that noise fluctuations do not cause too many retransmissions. Because of the varying operation of interfering sources, such as cordless phones, the noise levels (and corresponding SNR) can vary dramatically over time.

Note   For more details on radio frequency interference, see Chapter 4.

RF Mathematics

When working with WLANs, it is eventually necessary to perform RF mathematics, which involves converting units and dealing with gains and losses.

Converting Units

A problem is that technical literature for WLANs refers to both linear (watts) and logarithmic (dBm) units. The output power of an access point, for example, is generally given in mW. Most analyzers, though, display output power in dBm. Often, you must perform conversions so that all values are in the same units to determine path loss, calculate EIRP, and so on.

The following are relationships between mW and dBm:

dBm = (10Log10(mW))

and:

mW = 10(dBm/10)

As mentioned previously, dBm values do not fit into the linear world. For example, doubling the equivalent power in watts of 20 dBm is not 40 dBm. You can see this for yourself by using a calculator and finding the value in watts for 20 dBm. The answer is 100 mW. Now perform the calculation for 40 dBm, and you get 10,000 mW. That's much more than doubling the power!

If you have a calculator with a logarithm (LOG) key, just punch in the numbers to get the results. For example, plug 100 mW into the equation for dBm, and you should find that the answer is 20 dBm. Try another one by converting 26 dBm to mW. You should get 400 mW. Instead of using a calculator, you can use a spreadsheet program, such as Microsoft Excel, to solve these types of problems.

To make life easier, you can memorize some simple relationships so that you can do RF mathematics easily without a calculator. A simple relationship is that if you multiply a value in mW by 10, the equivalent value in dBm increases by 10. (That is, dividing mW by 10 decreases dBm by 10.) The following are some typical equivalent values worth memorizing based on this rule:

0 dBm = 1 mW

10 dBm = 10 mW

20 dBm = 100 mW

30 dBm = 1000 mW (1 watt)

Also, if you multiply the value in mW by 2, the equivalent value in dBm increases by 3 dB (divide the value in mW by 2 and subtract 3 dB). For example, 10 dBm is equivalent to 10 mW. If you multiply 10 mW by 2, the resulting value in dBm is 13 dBm (10 dBm + 3 dB), which is equivalent to 20 mW. Similarly, if you divide 10 mW by 2, the resulting value in dBm is 7 dBm (10 dBm − 3 dB), which is equivalent to 5 mW. Thus, an antenna having 3 dB of gain doubles the transmit power of 100 mW (20 dBm), resulting in 200 mW (23 dBm). You could do this on a calculator, but it is much easier to calculate by remembering these simple rules.

Note   In communications systems, a dB (decibel) refers to the difference between one absolute value and another. For example, the difference between 12 dBm and 15 dBm is 3 dB.

As a practical example, say that you want to know the overall effective power in dBm of an access point that is set to 100 mW transmit power with an antenna having 6 dB gain. You might find yourself going through this exercise to know if the system is within regulatory limitations. You could use a calculator and convert 100 mW to dBm using the formula from above. Or, if you remember that 20 dBm equals 100 mW, all you have to do is add 6 dBm to 20 dBm, and you will end up with the correct answer of 26 dBm. The antenna gain of 6 dB adds 3 dBm to the value twice (that is, it doubles the power twice).

With a little practice, you will be quick with this type of mathematics. You might want to have a calculator nearby at first to check your work, but you will soon be running through these types of problems in your head.

Note   There are many online calculators for converting between dBm and milliwatts, such as the one at http://www.cpcstech.com/dbm-to-watt-conversion-information.htm.

Summary

Wireless LANs use radio waves to carry information between client devices and access points. A transceiver is a hardware component that transmits and receives radio waves. Modulation is a process that a transmitter implements to prepare the radio waves for propagation through the air medium. While en route between the source and destination, the radio waves encounter impairments, such as attenuation, noise, and multipath propagation, which can substantially reduce the amplitude and quality of the radio waves. SNR is a measurement that provides a figure of merit that characterizes the ability of a receiver for demodulating the radio wave successfully into information that the WLAN is conveying. To successfully decode a radio wave, the signal amplitude must be higher than the sensitivity of the reviver, and the SNR at the receiver must be high enough for the receiver to distinguish the signal from the noise.

Chapter 3

Wireless LAN Types and Components

This chapter will introduce you to:

- Types of Wireless LANs
- Wireless LAN Components
- Network Infrastructure Components

The 802.11 standard specifies details on how wireless LANs (WLANs) operate, with emphasis on stations (often referred to as client radios, or cards) and access points, which form ad hoc and infrastructure types of WLANs. This chapter defines each of these primary configuration types and components, as well as others.

Types of Wireless LANs

It is possible to configure WLANs into different architectures, depending on the requirements of the system. The physical architectures include the following:

- Ad hoc
- Infrastructure
- Mesh

Ad Hoc Wireless LANs

Ad hoc WLANs (sometimes referred to as "peer-to-peer" WLANs), as shown in Figure 3-1, only require 802.11 client radios in the client devices that connect to the network. Because there is no access point or WLAN controller and the stations are within range of each other, data transmitted by a particular source station travels directly to the applicable destination station. The rationale behind the ad hoc form of networking is to enable users to spontaneously set up WLANs. Access points are not necessary, which makes peer-to-peer networks easy to set up and take down. This can be beneficial, for example, if you want to establish a WLAN among several laptops in a conference room for a meeting in a building that has no WLAN that the laptops can connect to. These networks require no administration and very little preconfiguration. All that's needed to set up an ad hoc WLAN is to set the 802.11 radio in Microsoft Windows-based client devices to ad hoc mode.

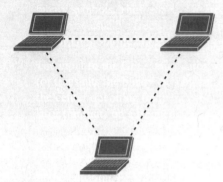

Figure 3-1   *An Ad Hoc Wireless LAN Provides Connectivity to Multiple Client Devices Within Radio Range of Each Other*

Note   The 802.11 standard refers to an ad hoc WLAN as an independent basic service set (IBSS).

The ad hoc form of communications is especially useful in public-safety and search-and-rescue applications. Medical teams require fast, effective communications when they rush to a disaster to treat victims. They cannot afford the time to run cabling and install networking hardware. The medical team can use 802.11-equipped laptops and enable broadband wireless data communications as soon as they arrive on the scene.

The absence of an access point in an ad hoc network means that an ad hoc WLAN must take on more of the MAC-layer responsibilities. The first active ad hoc station (802.11-equipped client device set to ad hoc mode) establishes an IBSS and starts sending beacon frames, which are needed to announce the presence of the ad hoc network and maintain synchronization among the stations. Other ad hoc stations can join the network after receiving a beacon and accepting the IBSS parameters (for example, beacon interval) found in the beacon frame.

Each station that joins the ad hoc network must send a beacon periodically if it does not hear a beacon from another station within a short random delay period after the beacon is supposed to be sent. The random delay minimizes the transmission of beacons from multiple stations by effectively reducing the number of stations that will send a beacon. If a station does not hear a beacon within the random delay period, the station assumes that no other stations are active, and a beacon needs to be sent. After receiving a beacon, each station updates its local internal clock with the timestamp found in the beacon frame, assuming that the timestamp value is greater than the local clock. This ensures that all stations can perform operations, such as beacon transmissions and power management functions, at the same time.

Infrastructure Wireless LANs

Most companies, public hotspots, and homeowners implement infrastructure WLANs. An infrastructure WLAN, as shown in Figure 3-2, offers a means to extend a wired network. In this configuration, one or more access points interface wireless mobile devices to the distribution system. Each access point forms a radio cell, also called a basic service set (BSS), which enables wireless users located within the cell to connect to the access point. This allows users to communicate with other wireless users, as well as with servers and network applications connecting to the distribution system. A company, for example, can use this configuration to enable employees to access corporate applications and the Internet from anywhere within the facility.

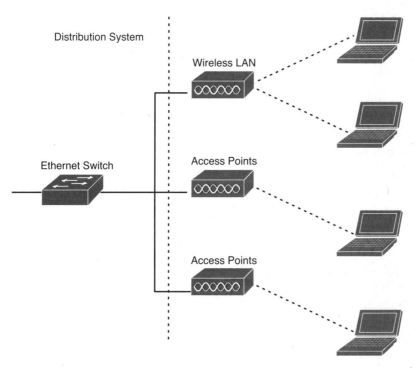

Figure 3-2   *An Infrastructure Wireless LAN Interfaces Client Devices to a Wired Distribution System and Extends Coverage Through Use of Access Points*

Each access point in the infrastructure WLAN broadcasts beacon frames, which identify the presence of the WLAN and synchronizes various events, such as 802.11 power management. Each access point creates a radio cell, with a coverage area that depends on the construction of the facility, chosen PHY layer, transmit power, and antenna type. This range is typically 100 feet in most enterprise facilities, depending on the data rate and environmental factors, such as building construction.

The desired level of performance, however, can impact the effective range of the access points. Lower data rates offer longer range than do higher data rates.

Note   The 802.11 standard refers to an infrastructure WLAN as an extended service set (ESS).

If a company installs access points with overlapping radio cells, as shown in Figure 3-3, then users can roam throughout the facility without any noticeable loss of connectivity. The radio card within the user's mobile device will automatically re-associate with access points having stronger signals. For example, a user might begin downloading a file when associated with access point A. As the user walks out of range of access point A and within range of access point B, the client radio automatically re-associates the user to access point B and continues the downloading of the file through access point B. The user generally does not experience any noticeable delays, but voice over WLAN phones might drop connections if the roaming delay exceeds 150 milliseconds.

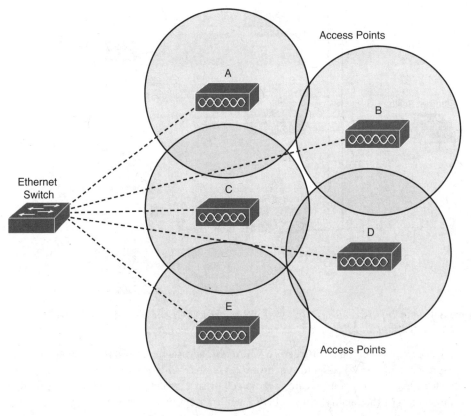

Figure 3-3   *Multicell Wireless LAN with Overlapping Cells Supports Roaming*

In infrastructure WLANs, data transmissions do not occur directly between the wireless clients. Data traffic going from one wireless user to another user must travel through an access point (see Figure 3-4). The access point receives the data traffic going from client A to client B, for example, and retransmits the data to client B. As a result, significant data traffic between wireless users decreases throughput because of the access point needing to relay the data to the destination user. If the source wireless user is sending data to a node on the distribution system, then the access point does not need to retransmit the data to other wireless users. The access point (if it is an autonomous type) delivers the data directly to the distribution system for routing to the applicable node. In the case of a controller-based WLAN, the access point hands over the data to an applicable controller, and the controller delivers the data to the distribution system.

In addition to overlapping cells, the 802.11 standard also supports collocated and disjointed radio cells, as shown in Figure 3-5.

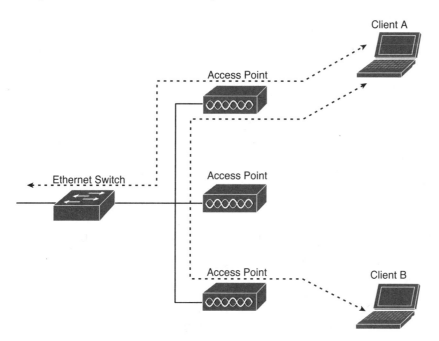

Figure 3-4   *Typical Flow of Data Through an Infrastructure Wireless LAN*

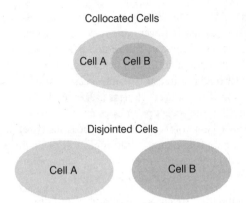

Figure 3-5   *Collocated and Disjointed Wireless LANs*

The collocated radio cell configuration is useful if a company needs greater capacity than a single access point can deliver. In this scenario, two or more access points are set up so that their radio cells overlap significantly. This works well if the access points are set to non-conflicting radio channels. A portion of the users in the area, for example, associate with access point A, and the other users associate with access point B. This boosts the capacity of that particular area.

A company can install disjointed access points when complete coverage throughout the facility is not necessary. For example, the company might install an access point in each conference room and not the rest of the building. If the radio cells are disjointed, then users will temporarily lose connection to the network and then re-associate when they come within range of another access point. An 802.11 network, though, supports this form of network, similarly to roaming with the overlapping radio cells. The re-association delay is a function of the time it takes the user to move into range of the next access point. The wireless application in use, however, might or might not be able to tolerate this longer roaming delay.

Wireless Mesh Networks

Wireless mesh networks make use of mesh nodes, which are similar to access points, except that mesh nodes connect to each other wirelessly rather than via Ethernet, as do most infrastructure wireless networks (see Figure 3-6). Thus, mesh networks avoid the need for Ethernet connections. You can install them just about anywhere, as long as electrical power is available (or you can use solar power for most outdoor installations).

A mesh network is beneficial in areas where it is not feasible to install a traditional WLAN consisting of access points. For example, a mesh network approach makes sense in residential and city-wide Wi-Fi networks. The deployment of cabled access points over larger, open areas is a daunting task because of the massive amount of data cabling that must be installed and the countless permissions. Other places where installations of cabled access points are difficult include convention centers, college campuses, stadiums, marinas, parks, and construction sites.

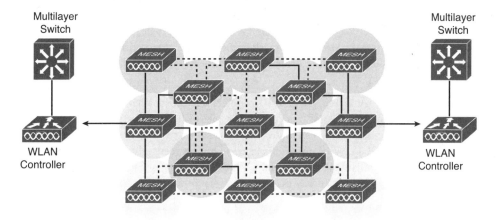

Mesh Access Points

Figure 3-6 *A Mesh Network Includes Mesh Access Points That Connect with Each Other Wirelessly*

Client devices connect to a mesh node similar to the method used for connection to an access point in an infrastructure network. Each mesh node implements a routing protocol that routes packets between client devices and wired connections to the Internet and servers. A mesh network offers multiple paths from source to destination, and intelligent routing algorithms allow each node to make a decision on which path to forward packets through the network to improve performance. If the link between a pair of nodes along one of the paths is congested, for example, then the algorithms establish another path that avoids the congested link. Also, if a node goes down, an alternate route is chosen based on the routing algorithms.

Note To extend the capability of 802.11 serving large-scale outdoor wireless networks, the 802.11 Working Group published an amendment to the 802.11 standard (802.11s) in 2011 to address special functions related to mesh networking. For example, 802.11s includes the Hybrid Wireless Mesh Protocol (HWMP), which provides a common multi-hopping routing protocol across mesh nodes.

Latency can vary significantly on mesh networks, depending on the number of users and hops that are necessary for moving packets through the backhaul network. Roaming and routing delays can affect performance, especially for VoIP applications. Even if the data rate between the user and the local backhaul node is kept high, which many of the mesh network vendors claim, the delays across the network might be substantial.

Often the lack of electrical power for mesh nodes in some areas leads to installation delays and unforeseen costs. In outdoor installations, some light poles do not supply adequate electrical power, or occasionally mounting assets, such as rooftops, do not have any readily available power. In these cases, the use of solar panels can be an option for generating power for mesh nodes and backhaul equipment. In this case, the network equipment actually runs off a battery, and the solar panel generates electricity to recharge the battery and power the mesh node if the battery is charged. Without a battery, there would be no power available at night or when something, such as clouds, obstructs the sunlight.

The use of solar energy is free, which can save electricity costs when running a mesh network. A problem, however, is that the cost of solar panels and batteries can be several hundred dollars for each mesh node. This makes the use of solar power generally feasible only where the cost of installing electrical lines is relatively expensive or where electricity is very unreliable. For example, Chittagong in Bangladesh decided to power some mesh nodes with solar energy because electrical power there is not stable enough.

If using solar panels for generating electricity for mesh nodes is appealing, then be certain to investigate average sunlight on a daily basis and ensure that the solar panels and batteries specified will supply an adequate amount of power for the equipment. This can be a bit tricky because predicting the amount of sunlight might not be accurate enough to satisfy network availability requirements.

Wi-Fi Mesh Hot Zones

Many large municipalities have installed or are planning to install Wi-Fi networks for creating city-wide wireless coverage. These deployments have had ups and downs in terms of signal coverage and performance, and they are very costly. As an alternative to covering large expansive areas, some municipalities and private entities, such as home and apartment owners, are building smaller-scale Wi-Fi networks (hot zones) that offer wireless Internet connectivity to smaller groups of people. This appears to be a more feasible approach.

For example, a municipality might install a Wi-Fi network to cover a 1- or 2-mile stretch of the town's main street, where it is likely that businesses and the public can strongly benefit from free Internet connectivity or mobile access to the Internet. Furthermore, an apartment owner might provide coverage to tenants, or a homeowner or an entrepreneur might offer Internet connectivity to a specific neighborhood. In many cases, the benefits of enabling web browsing, e-mail, and possibly voice telephony are enough to warrant the installation of a Wi-Fi hot zone.

Wireless LAN Components

Several different types of components comprise a WLAN.

Client Devices

As with a wired LAN system, a WLAN needs a way for users to gain access to applications and services. Whether the network is wireless or wired, a client device is an interface between the user and the network. Figure 3-7 illustrates examples of the client devices that can interface with a WLAN. In addition to client devices that people use, a wireless network can interface to machines, such as robots, and control systems. In this case, the client device is an end system, not a user device.

Figure 3-7   *Wireless LANs Support a Multitude of Client Devices*

The selection of the right client devices significantly impacts the usability of an application and the corresponding return on investment of the network. Think about application requirements and choose devices with the optimum weight, keypad, screen, battery longevity, and ruggedness. Client devices in warehouses, for example, will probably undergo more physical abuse than those in use in a typical office setting. Thus, in this scenario, choose rugged user devices that will withstand an industrial environment. Before rolling out hundreds of client devices to users, carry out testing at pilot sites with a representative group of users. That way, you will be sure that the chosen devices will best fit requirements. Also, involve upper management in the trials to receive adequate levels of buy-in, which of course is sometimes necessary to continue funding for a wireless project.

Implementing Client Device Wipe Functions

More and more companies are beginning to deploy device wipe functions (which erase a device's memory) to ensure that wireless client devices are secure in case they are lost or stolen. For example, an employee who's lost his/her device can inform a system administrator that the device is gone, and the administrator can issue a command to the device to wipe the memory and applications from the device. In case the device is out of range of the wireless network, functions of the device itself can be preconfigured to automatically perform the wiping if someone mistakenly enters the wrong username and password too many times. Just be sure to do a good job of replicating the device data on a server!

Client Radio

A client radio implements the 802.11 MAC-layer functions and a specific PHY layer, such as 802.11a, 802.11b, 802.11g, 802.11n, or 802.11ac. Figure 3-8 illustrates the primary internal components of an 802.11 client radio. Firmware on the radio implements

802.11 MAC-layer functionality, and a transceiver provides the actual transmitting and receiving tasks corresponding to the specific 802.11 PHY layer implemented. The bus interface binds the client radio to the client device (for example, laptop computer) via a bus interface standard. The software driver interfaces the client radio to the client device operating system, such as Microsoft Windows or Linux.

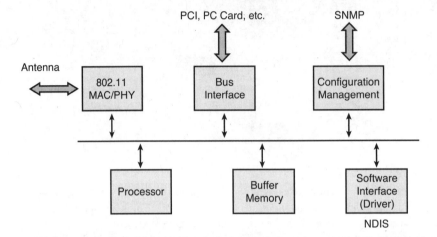

Figure 3-8   *An 802.11 Client Radio Includes Components Necessary to Interface Client Devices to an 802.11 Network*

Note   The 802.11 standard refers to client radio functionality as an 802.11 station (sometimes abbreviated as STA).

Multimode radios make it possible for client devices to associate with networks implementing different PHY layers. For example, an 802.11n client radio is backward compatible with 802.11g. With this dual-mode capability, for example, a user is equipped with WLAN interfaces that maximize interoperability and capability to migrate from 802.11g to 802.11n networks.

Computers process information in digital form, with low direct current (DC) voltages representing data 1s and 0s. These signals are optimum for transmission within the computer, not for transporting data through wired or wireless media. A client radio device couples the digital signal from the end-user appliance to the wireless medium, which is air, to enable an efficient transfer of data between sender and receiver. This process includes the modulation and amplification of the digital signal to a form acceptable for propagation to the receiving location.

The interface between the client device and the radio device includes a software driver that couples the client's operating system software to the card. This driver must be compatible with the operating system that the client device implements. Most client radios have drivers for Microsoft Windows, for instance. Drivers for Linux might be available, but they are sometimes difficult to find.

The client radio generally takes the shape of a wireless network interface card (NIC) that facilitates the modulator and communications protocols. The radio card conforms to one of several form factors that defines a physical and electrical bus interface that enables the radio card to communicate with a computing device. The following are types of standard form factors for interfacing client radios to client devices:

■ Industry Standard Architecture (ISA)

■ Peripheral Component Interconnect (PCI)

■ Mini-PCI

■ PC card

■ ExpressCard

■ CompactFlash (CF)

■ Universal Serial Bus (USB)

Figure 3-9 includes photos of some of the various form factors.

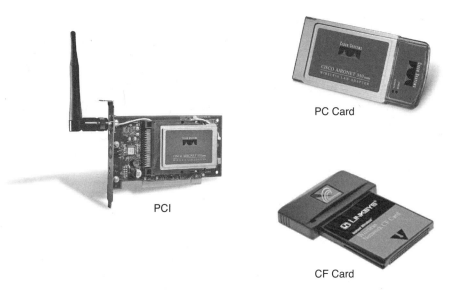

PC Card

PCI

CF Card

Figure 3-9 *Client Radio Cards Have Various Form Factors and Electrical Interfaces*

The sections that follow cover the form factors in greater detail.

Industry Standard Architecture

The Industry Standard Architecture (ISA) bus is a common bus interface in the desktop PC world. ISA has been around since the early 1980s for use in the IBM PC/XT and PC/ AT. Because of this, the proliferation of ISA has been significant in desktops. Despite its lack of speed (2 Mbps), nearly all PCs manufactured up until a short time ago had at least one ISA bus. The ISA bus has failed, however, to advance at the pace of the rest of the computer world, and higher-speed alternatives are now available. It is not advisable to deploy ISA radio cards because of the likelihood that they will become obsolete.

Peripheral Component Interconnect

The Peripheral Component Interconnect (PCI) bus, which is the most popular bus interface for PCs today, has a throughput rate of 264 Mbps. Intel originally developed and released PCI in 1993, and it satisfies the needs of most recent generations of PCs for multimedia, graphics, and networking cards. PCI cards were the first to popularize Plug and Play (PnP) technology. PCI circuitry can recognize compatible PCI cards and then work with the computer's operating system to set the resource allocations for each card. This helps save time and prevents installation headaches.

An example of a PCI radio card is the Linksys Wireless-N PCI Adapter.

Note To ensure good connectivity with an access point, think about purchasing PCI cards that have external antenna connectors to allow the placement of an antenna on top of or next to the desk to avoid having the desk block the radio waves.

Mini-PCI

A Mini-PCI card is a small version of a standard desktop PCI card. It has all the same features and functionality of a normal PCI card but is about one-quarter the size. Mini-PCI cards are integrated in laptops as an option to buyers, with antennas that are often integrated out of view within the monitor's case or even up next to the LCD screen. A strong advantage of this form of radio card is that it frees up the PC card slot for other devices. In addition, manufacturers can provide Mini-PCI-based wireless connectivity at lower costs.

The Mini-PCI card is not without disadvantages, however. If you want to replace a Mini-PCI card yourself, you may have to disassemble most of the laptop—and doing so could void the manufacturer's warranty. Mini-PCI cards might also lead to lower performance because they require the computer to do some, if not all, of the processing. Despite these drawbacks, the Mini-PCI card has revolutionized the wireless laptop world.

PC Card

Developed in the early 1990s by the Personal Computer Memory Card International Association (PCMCIA), a PC card is a 16-bit credit card–sized peripheral device that can provide extended memory, modems, connectivity to external devices, and, of course, WLAN capabilities to laptops. Some PC card NICs are referred to as CardBus, which is a 32-bit implementation of a PC card. CardBus is faster and more likely to be the basis for 802.11n radio cards.

Antennas are generally integrated into a wireless PC card, with a stub that extends outside the PC card slot and provides omnidirectional RF propagation patterns. In most cases, these integrated antennas provide good performance. Some PC cards, however, come with optional removable antennas in case you have a need to use alternative, possibly higher-gain, antennas.

Some access points incorporate PC card radio NICs and are easily replaceable, accommodating newer technologies (for example, 802.11ac) as they become available. In most cases, end users can swap the radio NICs and do relatively simple firmware upgrades. This extends the life of the access point hardware, which of course saves money in the long run.

ExpressCard

ExpressCard provides high performance in a smaller form factor—about half the size of a PC card. PCMCIA developed the ExpressCard standard with assistance from the USB Implementers Forum (USB-IF) and the Peripheral Component Interconnect-Special Interest Group (PCI-SIG). Many feel that ExpressCard is the next generation of client card technology and will eventually replace PC card and CardBus. Because of its small design, ExpressCard radios are ideal for "closed box" wireless devices, such as data collectors.

CompactFlash

SanDisk Corporation first introduced CompactFlash (CF) in 1994, and WLAN radio cards based on CF form factors became available roughly a decade later. A CF card is very small, weighing half an ounce and less than half the thickness and one-quarter the volume of a PC card radio card. A CF card also draws very little power, which enables batteries to last longer than for devices using PC cards. Some PDAs come with direct CF interfaces, which results in a very lightweight and compact wireless PDA.

Universal Serial Bus

The majority of external 802.11 radio devices, such 802.11 modems and print servers, connect to client devices via Universal Serial Bus (USB), which provides electrical power and data interface to connected peripherals, such as 802.11 radios. The USB-IF has developed a series of USB specifications. USB 1.0, introduced in 1994, has a speed of 12 Mbps. In 2000, the USB-IF released USB 2.0, with a higher data rate of 480 Mbps. USB 3.0 (referred to as SuperSpeed USB), released in late 2008, has a speed that's 10 times faster than USB 2.0.

Note   In practice, you should limit the length of a USB cable to 16 feet.

Access Points

Similar to a client radio, an access point implements the common MAC functions and specific physical layers and provides a connection to a common distribution system (generally Ethernet). The access point is the primary component of an infrastructure WLAN. Figure 3-10 illustrates the primary internal components of an 802.11 access point.

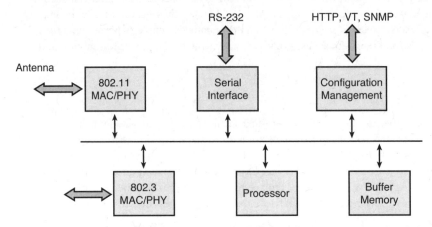

Figure 3-10 *An 802.11 Access Point Includes Components Necessary to Form an Infrastructure Wireless LAN*

Client radios associate with a single access point and can roam to different access points as the need arises, such as when roaming through a facility. In many cases, access points have multiple radios. For example, an access point might have a 2.4-GHz radio and a 5-GHz radio. This makes it possible to maintain some clients operating on 2.4-GHz channels and some clients operating on 5-GHz channels. For example, a lower-performance data application could operate at 2.4 GHz, and higher-performance applications, such as Wi-Fi phones, could operate at 5 GHz. That way, the phones won't be bogged down by data applications.

Autonomous Access Points

Most WLANs implemented in the past made use of autonomous access points (see Figure 3-11), and many of those networks still exist today. An example of an autonomous access point is any Cisco access point that implements Cisco IOS software. An autonomous access point is relatively intelligent and implements enough functions to be able to interconnect with other access points via conventional Ethernet switches. The configuration of the access points is either done through specialized management software or by logging in to each access point individually.

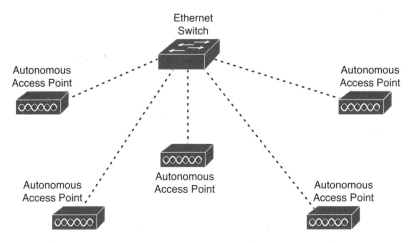

Figure 3-11 *Autonomous Access Points Offer Distributed Management and Control*

Controller-Based Access Points

As an alternative to traditional intelligent access points, some companies offer "lightweight" access points that implement the basic 802.11 functions (see Figure 3-12). An example of a lightweight access point is any Cisco access point that implements Cisco Lightweight Access Point Protocol (LWAPP) or the IETF standard Control and Provisioning of Wireless Access Points (CAPWAP). These lightweight access points connect to a WLAN controller, which provides centralized enhancements for management, security, and performance.

Note   You can find an up-to-date list of 802.11-certified access points and client radio devices at the Wi-Fi Alliance website: www.wi-fi.org.

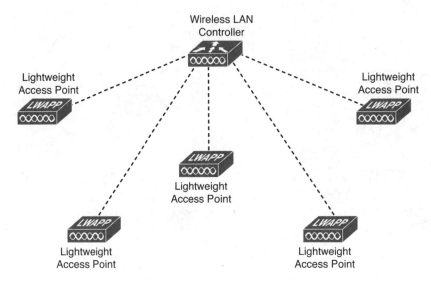

Figure 3-12 *Controller-Based Access Points Provide Centralized Management and Control*

Wi-Fi Routers

By definition, a router transfers packets between networks. The router chooses the next best link to send packets on to reach the destination. Routers use IP packet headers and routing tables, and they use internal protocols to determine the best path for each packet. Most routers connect a LAN (like the one in your home or office) to a WAN (like the cable system running your cable modem) by interfacing a broadband modem to the network within the enterprise, small office, or home.

A WLAN router, such as the Linksys WRT300N, adds the function of an access point to a multiport Ethernet router. This combines multiple Ethernet networks with wireless connections, too. A typical WLAN router includes four Ethernet ports, an 802.11 access point, and sometimes a parallel or USB port so it can be a print server. This gives wireless users the same ability as wired users to send and receive packets over multiple networks.

There might be some confusion over the difference between WLAN routers and access points. The main thing to remember is that access points allow wireless clients access to a single network, while WLAN routers allow clients to browse several different networks. A router always takes the IP address into account to make decisions on how to forward (route) the packet; on the other hand, access points ignore the IP address and forward all packets.

In addition, WLAN routers implement the Network Address Translation (NAT) protocol, which enables multiple network devices to share a single IP address, generally provided by the Internet service provider (ISP). Wireless LAN routers also have the capability to provide port-based control, firewall management, and Dynamic Host Configuration Protocol (DHCP) services for client devices. These functions make the WLAN router much more versatile than an access point.

Consider using a WLAN router for the following reasons:

■ **Sharing IP addresses:** Wireless LAN routers offer strong benefits in home and small office settings. For example, you can subscribe to a cable modem service that provides a single IP address through DHCP to the router, and the router then provides IP addresses via DHCP to clients on your local network. Figure 3-13 illustrates this concept. In such a setup, NAT maps a particular client on the local network to the ISP-assigned IP address whenever that client needs to access the Internet. As a result, you should use a WLAN router if you plan to have more than one networked device on a local network sharing a single ISP-assigned address. Instead of having one box for the router and another box for the access point, you can use a WLAN router that provides both in the same box.

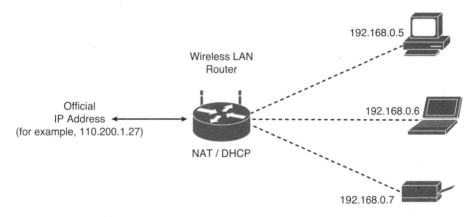

Figure 3-13 *Wireless LAN Routers Are Beneficial for Sharing a Single Official IP Address and Distributing Unique IP Addresses to Each Client Radio*

Note For larger WLANs, such as for a hospital, it is generally best to make use of a dedicated DHCP server. In that case, the installation of access points rather than WLAN routers will be the most cost-effective and easiest to manage.

■ **Connecting multiple networks:** Wireless LAN routers are ideal for wireless networks in public areas, especially if multiple networks are accessible. For instance, a university might have a separate network in each of its buildings. Students sitting outside might want to gain access to one or more of these networks and also surf the Internet. A WLAN router enables them to access everything through the wireless connection.

■ **Improving network performance:** Because routers send packets only to specific, directed addresses, they do not forward the often numerous broadcast packets that are sent out by other devices. This results in an increase in throughput because of lower utilization on the network and less work needed by the router. This enables WLANs to operate much more effectively. The router, however, will offer more delay than an access point, but the impacts are generally unnoticeable.

■ **Increasing security:** A strong advantage of WLAN routers is that they provide an added layer of security, on both the wired and wireless sides. The wired side is usually protected by a firewall and has extensive access control filters. These filters can be set based on MAC address, IP address, URL, domain name, and even a set schedule that allows access only at certain times. If an unauthorized user tries to access the network, an e-mail alert is immediately sent to the network administrator. For supporting sensitive information, many WLAN routers support multiple and concurrent IPsec sessions, so users can more securely access networks through a range of virtual private network (VPN) clients.

Mesh Nodes

A mesh node is the primary component of a mesh network. Each mesh node includes an access point, which implements 802.11 and inter-node wireless connectivity to enable communications between mesh nodes. Client devices equipped with an 802.11 radio device connect to the access point functionality of the mesh node. A single radio can implement both the access point and the inter-node wireless connectivity. In multi-radio implementations, the access point can operate independently on a dedicated RF channel, while the internode communications takes place on a different RF channel. In this case, communications between the client devices and the mesh node can occur simultaneously with the internode communications. As a result, multi-radio mesh nodes provide better performance than single-radio solutions.

Antennas

An antenna couples RF energy between the radio transceiver and the air medium. The transmitter within a radio device sends an RF signal to the antenna, which acts as a radiator and propagates the signal through the air. The antenna also operates in reverse, capturing RF signals from the air and making them available to the receiver.

Some radio devices have integrated antennas that you cannot change. For example, laptops that have integrated wireless capability generally integrate the antenna within the cover or body of the laptop, which is not visible or changeable by the user. Some client devices, such as bar code scanners, use permanently mounted antennas. With these types of products, you have no choice but to use the antenna the vendor supplies. Other WLAN devices, however, have antennas that are interchangeable. In fact, it is a good idea to purchase access points with removable antennas. These allow more flexibility by enabling the selection of an antenna having characteristics best suited for the specific application.

The following are common antenna characteristics:

■ **Antenna bandwidth and power:** For 802.11 WLANs, you need to use an antenna tuned for either 2.4 GHz or 5 GHz, depending on the spectrum on which the system is designed to operate. An antenna will work efficiently only if the frequency range of the antenna matches that of the radio. Antennas can handle a specific amount of power put out by the transmitter. In the case of 802.11, the antenna will generally be rated greater than 1 watt to handle the maximum peak transmit power of the radio device. For most applications, the antenna power specification will not be of too much concern to you because of the relatively low power that WLANs transmit.

■ **Radiation pattern:** Antenna manufacturers provide illustrations indicating the radiation pattern of the antenna. The radiation pattern defines how radio waves propagate in relation to the antenna. This radiation pattern applies to both transmit and receive functions of the antenna. The antenna allows the transceiver to have a particular range in different directions for both sending radio waves and receiving them. The actual propagation of radio waves conforms to the radiation pattern. If you increase the transmit power of the transceiver, the range of the radio waves will increase with the same shape as the radiation pattern.

■ **Antenna gain:** The gain of an antenna represents how well it increases effective signal power, with decibels (dB) as the unit of measure. Most antenna manufacturers specify antenna gains with dBi unit, which is the true gain of the antenna relative to an isotropic antenna. An isotropic antenna has a radiation pattern that resembles a beach ball with an antenna at its center. An antenna with isotropic radiation pattern is theoretical and not physically used in practice.

■ **Antenna diversity:** Antenna diversity, which makes use of multiple antennas for a single radio, can aid in combating multipath propagation. An access point may implement a spatial diversity antenna system, which consists of two antennas that interchangeably receive and transmit radio signals. An access point will receive a signal on both antennas, but many times, because of multipath propagation and interference, the same signal will not reach both antennas at the same time and strength. The access point will then perform internal calculations to optimize the received signal. The main benefits of spatial diversity antenna systems are improved coverage and signal reception.

The most common antenna types for WLANs have omnidirectional radiation patterns (see Figure 3-14). Omnidirectional antennas propagate RF signals in all directions equally on a horizontal plane but limit the range on the vertical plane. This radiation pattern resembles a very large doughnut with the antenna at the center of the hole. Omnidirectional antennas, having gains ranging up to 6 dBi, apply to most applications inside buildings. Omnis provide the widest coverage and make it possible to form somewhat circular overlapping cells from multiple access points located throughout the building. Most access points ship with standard omnis having relatively low gain. Consider using higher-gain ones to increase range, which enables wider spacing of access points. This can reduce the number of access points and reduce costs. To take advantage of the range benefits, though, the client devices must have equivalent gain antennas and transmit power of the access points.

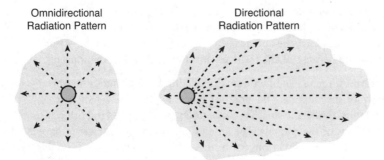

Figure 3-14   *Omnidirectional and Directional Radiation Patterns of Antennas*

> **Note**   It is important to note that the actual propagation of radio waves in relation to an antenna might be somewhat different than the radiation pattern (which is based on an open area). Obstructions such as walls and office furniture attenuate the signals, which might cause them to travel differently than the radiation pattern.

A directional antenna (often called a yagi) transmits and receives RF signals more in one direction than others (refer to Figure 3-14). This radiation pattern is similar to the light that a flashlight or spotlight produces. Directional antennas have higher gain, such as 9 or 12 dBi, and have a narrower beam width, which limits coverage on the sides of the antennas.

Directional antennas work best for covering large, narrow areas or supporting point-to-point links between buildings. In some cases, a directional antenna will reduce the number of access points needed within a facility. For example, a long loading dock of a distribution center might require three access points having omnis, but the use of a high-gain directional antenna would likely require only a single access point.

RF Amplifiers

Similar to the gain associated with an antenna, an external RF amplifier increases the effective power of the RF signal. An amplifier is installed between the antenna and the access point, as shown in Figure 3-15, and it must be designed to amplify the frequency range in which the WLAN operates (for example, 2.4 or 5 GHz). RF amplifiers for WLANs specify a range of power inputs and deliver a constant power output. For example, a 4-watt RF amplifier will deliver 4 watts to the antenna when the input to the amplifier is between 1 and 100 mW. An amplifier also has a receive gain specification (for example, 12 dB), which defines how well the amplifier can increase the power of the signals that it receives. If the antenna is mounted outdoors, it is important to use a lightning protector and properly ground the system. To avoid excessive cable attenuation, use low-loss coaxial cable and keep cable runs as short as possible.

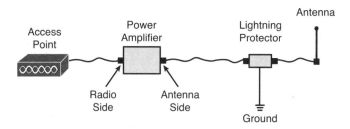

Figure 3-15 *Power Amplifiers Boost RF Signals to Increase Range*

> **Note**   When purchasing RF amplifiers, you must comply with special licensing requirements.

Consider using an RF amplifier to extend the range of an access point, especially for outdoor areas. For example, you might have an area needing signal coverage where it is not practical to install an access point or a mesh node. In this case, the amplifier might be able to increase transmit and receive gains enough to cover the area.

Repeaters

A repeater regenerates radio signals to extend the range of a WLAN. As shown in Figure 3-16, a repeater does not physically connect by wire to any part of the network. Instead, a repeater receives radio signals (802.11 frames) from an access point, a wireless client device, or another repeater on a particular RF channel and retransmits the frames without changing the frame contents on the same RF channel. This makes it possible for a repeater located between an access point and a distant user to act as a relay point for frames traveling back and forth between the user and the access point. As a result, wireless repeaters are an effective solution to overcome signal impairments such as RF attenuation. The wireless repeater fills in the coverage holes.

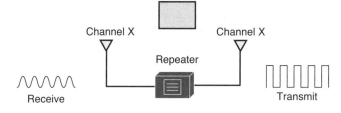

Figure 3-16 *A Repeater Reshapes RF Signals and Extends the Range of a Wireless LAN*

A downside of using a wireless repeater, however, is that it will reduce throughput capacity of the WLAN by roughly 50 percent in the area covered by the repeater. A repeater must receive and retransmit each frame on the same RF channel, which effectively doubles the number of frames that are sent over the WLAN. This problem compounds when using multiple repeaters because each repeater duplicates the number of frames sent. Thus, be sure to plan the use of repeaters sparingly and keep the total count within a particular area below three.

Bridges

A bridge provides a method for connecting dissimilar networks. A remote bridge connects networks that are not next to each other, such as networks in different buildings. With remote bridges, directional antennas are most often used to form a point-to-point or point-to-multipoint network. Workgroup bridges are advantageous for connecting one or more client devices (which do not have wireless client radios) to a WLAN. These types of connections offer a substitute for a client radio device, making it useful when the device, such as a printer, PC, or video game console, has an Ethernet port and no 802.11 radio card. In some cases, you might have no way of adding a radio device to a particular client device, which makes using a bridge the only way to go wireless. Figure 3-17 illustrates various bridge configurations.

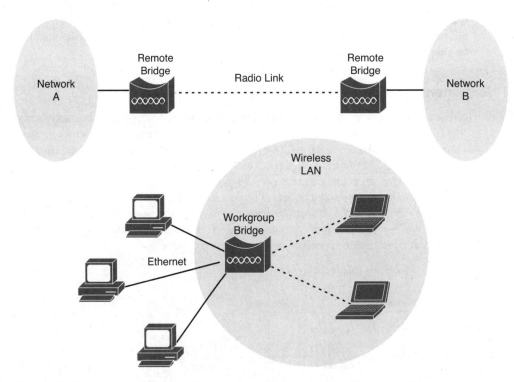

Figure 3-17   *Bridges Offer Multiple Methods for Connecting Client Devices and Networks*

A bridge receives packets on one port and retransmits them on another port. A bridge will not start retransmission until it receives a complete packet. Some bridges retransmit every packet on the opposite port, whether or not the packet is heading to a station located on the opposite network. A learning bridge, which is more common, examines the destination address of every packet to determine whether it should forward the packet based on a decision table that the bridge builds over time. This increases efficiency because the bridge will not retransmit a packet if it knows that the destination address is on the same side of the bridge as the sending address. Learning bridges also age address table entries by deleting addresses that have not been heard from for a specified amount of time.

Network Infrastructure Components

A complete wireless system consists of more than what the 802.11 standard specifies. Other components are necessary to fully depict an architecture that satisfies application requirements. You need to specify these components when designing a system. Some of these components, such as a distribution system, might already be present in the facility where you are installing a WLAN. Companies generally have existing distribution systems, such as Ethernet LANs and WAN connectivity.

The following types of components compose a network infrastructure:

- Network distribution system

- Power over Ethernet

- Application connectivity software

The sections that follow cover the infrastructure components in greater detail.

Network Distribution Systems

Designers of the 802.11 standard purposely avoided defining a particular distribution system (refer to Figure 3-2) for connecting access points; rather, they left system architects the freedom to implement 802.11-compliant networks as effectively as possible, given the situation. As a result, you need to decide what technologies and products will constitute a distribution system if multiple access points are necessary to extend the range of a complete wireless system.

In most cases, you can specify an Ethernet network infrastructure to act as the distribution system. All enterprise 802.11 access points are capable of connecting to Ethernet networks. Even mesh nodes generally have Ethernet ports for enabling a mesh node to communicate with a central tower for backhaul purposes.

Switches

An 802.3-based distribution system (also referred to as the wired backbone) consists of switches or hubs that tie together users (PCs and access points) equipped with 802.3 client cards. The switch or hub is somewhat analogous to an 802.11 access point. The main difference, obviously, is that the hub or switch provides the connections over a physical medium, and an access point uses radio waves.

A hub offers a single collision domain among multiple wired users. When one user's Ethernet NIC sends data, all other stations connected to the LAN hold off sending data until the medium is idle. A traditional access point most closely resembles a hub. A switch is more sophisticated than a hub and connects one user to another without blocking access of other users. The switch improves throughput because of the smaller resulting collision domains. Users do not have to wait until others are finished before sending data. This is why you should use switches rather than hubs for interconnecting wireless access points and controllers, especially for 802.11ac networks. Hubs are considered "old" technology and are used only in very small networks; they are nearly nonexistent in enterprise networks.

Figure 3-18 compares the flow of packets through a hub and through a switch.

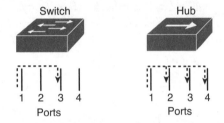

Figure 3-18   *Hubs and Switches Treat Frames Differently*

In a WLAN, the switch or hub connects access points. This creates a wired backbone and enables WLAN roaming protocols to work. Most access points accommodate connection to a switch or hub via an RJ-45 connector and twisted-pair wiring. The Ethernet cable can be up to roughly 300 feet long. As a result, you need to plan the installation of hubs or switches to avoid exceeding this distance. If distances exceed 300 feet, you can interconnect switches via optical fiber and place switches close to access points in various parts of the facility.

Consider the following when deploying a distribution system for a WLAN:

- **Use a hub only for very small deployments:** If the WLAN consists of only a few access points, then you can probably get by with a hub. There is no need to pay extra money for a switch for smaller deployments in this situation if you have an older hub lying around. In addition, digital subscriber line (DSL) and cable modem interfaces generally come equipped with a built-in, four-port Ethernet hub.

- **Use switches for enterprise-wide deployments:** A larger WLAN with many access points will benefit from the use of Ethernet switches. For very large networks, consider implementing a master switch that interconnects a series of smaller switches. Connect the switches together using optical fiber to improve security and increase the range of the distribution system.

- **Select the appropriate data rate:** In most cases, 10-Mbps Ethernet was sufficient to support interconnections among 802.11b access points, but you need 100 Mbps/1 Gbps (preferred) data rates for 802.11n and possibly higher data rates for 802.11ac.

- **Create a separate IP domain for the WLAN or SSID:** Some network devices continuously send broadcast packets that propagate freely throughout Ethernet networks. Access points also forward these broadcast packets to all users on the WLAN. In many enterprise scenarios, the broadcast packets will flood the WLAN and severely limit performance for wireless users. So separate the WLAN (or possibly each SSID) from the rest of the corporate network through a router or separate virtual LAN (VLAN). Keep in mind that a controller-based network may block broadcast packets by default, making it unnecessary to use separate domains for blocking broadcasts.

Optical Fiber

If you need a very high degree of noise immunity or information security, consider using optical fiber rather than UTP. Optical fiber is a medium that uses changes in light intensity to carry information from one point to another. An optical-fiber distribution system consists of a light source, optical fiber, and a light detector. A light source changes digital electrical signals into light (that is, on for a logic 1 and off for a logic 0), the optical fiber transports the light to the destination, and a light detector transforms the light into an electrical signal.

The main advantages of optical fiber are very high bandwidth (megabits per second and gigabits per second), information security, immunity to electromagnetic interference, lightweight construction, and long-distance operation without signal regeneration. As a result, optical fiber is superior for bandwidth-demanding applications and protocols, operation in classified areas and between buildings, and installation in airplanes and ships. Most municipalities have optical fiber installed along most streets, and it is possible (especially for city governments) and advantageous to use this optical fiber for connecting WLANs in different buildings.

> **Tip**   Use optical fiber to connect hubs and switches and provide connections between buildings. This will be more expensive than using twisted-pair wiring, but benefits such as higher data rates and less possibility of interference on inter-building links generally outweigh the higher cost.

Power over Ethernet

Power over Ethernet (PoE) avoids the need for an electrical outlet (or electrical extension cord) for powering access points and other system components. Figure 3-19 depicts several PoE configuration options. A PoE solution only requires technicians to deploy a single Ethernet cable to the access point for supplying both power and data. The most common PoE in use today is based on the IEEE 802.3af standard (ratified in 2003), which specifies up to 15.4 watts of power. This is generally enough to support the operation of a wireless access point, but additional power equipment may be necessary to support access points operating both 2.4-GHz and 5-GHz radios simultaneously. The newer 802.3at version of PoE (ratified in 2009) provides up to 25 watts of power and can easily support dual radios, but 802.3at is less commonly available in existing switches installed in organizations. With PoE, power sourcing protocols automatically detect the presence of an appropriate "powered device" (for example, an access point) and inject current into the cable. An access point using PoE can operate solely from the power it receives through the data cable.

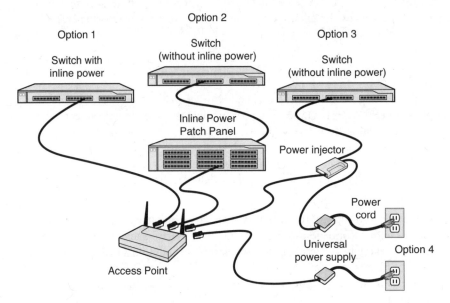

Figure 3-19   *Several Options Exist for Supporting Electrical Power to Access Points over Cabling*

PoE solutions have the following benefits as a result of not needing AC power cords:

- **Cost savings:** PoE significantly reduces the need for electricians to install conduit, electrical wiring, and outlets throughout a facility. In larger installations, these items can be relatively expensive. Consider an installation of 50 or more access points. This requires lots of conduits, outlet boxes, and electrical wiring, as well as the time of a qualified electrician. The low costs of deploying PoE compared to traditional electrical circuits lead to worthwhile returns on investment.

- **Flexible access point locations:** With PoE, a WLAN designer has greater freedom to locate access points. You do not need to depend on only locations within short distances from AC outlets. The independence from electrical outlets also makes it easier to relocate access points in the future, if needed, to fine-tune RF coverage or increase capacity. Thus, PoE enables companies to more easily maximize the performance of a WLAN.

- **Higher reliability:** Systems with fewer wires tend to be more reliable. With WLANs not using PoE, cleaning people may unplug an access point to use its AC outlet to power vacuum and buffing equipment. Electricians rewiring electrical circuits could inadvertently cut power to an access point. PoE eliminates the possibility of such situations disrupting the operation of the network.

■ **Enhanced operational support:** Many PoE devices implement Simple Network Management Protocol (SNMP), which enables support staff to remotely manage the electrical power supplied to the access points. For example, support staff can disable a PoE-enabled access point by shutting off its power after detecting a security breach. The temporary disabling of the access point can protect against an intruder continuing to access corporate systems. Other SNMP-based features enable the monitoring of the condition and consumption of power, which enhances the ability to ensure smooth and efficient network operations.

■ **Simpler international development:** For manufacturers, PoE offers the benefit of the vendor not needing to provide different power cords for various countries. This not only helps keep the cost of access points down, it means installers need to worry about one less piece of equipment. Standards for PoE are still under development within the Institute of Electrical and Electronics Engineers (IEEE).

Many vendors incorporate inline PoE into their enterprise-class access point solutions; you seldom find PoE in inexpensive home networking products. This is the most basic type of PoE system, connecting only one access point at a time to a power source. This is done through a PoE injector, which fits between the source signal (modem, switch, and so on) and the access point via Category 5 or higher cable. The injector connects to a power outlet through a regular electrical cord. For optimum benefits, you can plan the placement of the injector near a power outlet, such as within the communications room near the switch.

The injector receives current from the power outlet and sends it through the Cat5 cable to the access point. Think of this configuration as a T, with the injector at the intersection, the source signal and access point at either side of the top line, and the power outlet at the bottom point.

Inline PoE devices are best for small office applications. Because there are very few access points (or even just one) in these applications, the costs for the injectors are less than the cost of purchasing a more elaborate PoE hub. In some cases, smaller installations will not even benefit from PoE because you can generally locate the access point close enough to an electrical outlet to use a traditional (old-fashioned) power cord.

Another way to implement PoE is to install a "power hub" between the source signal and the access points. This implementation follows the same concept as the inline PoE system, except that the hub feasibly supports multiple access points rather than just one. Multiple Ethernet cables run from the switch into the power hub, which connects directly to a power outlet. Multiple power-infused Ethernet cables run from the other side of the hub to various access points.

Using PoE hubs is a good approach when dealing with a large-scale installation that has existing switches, such as adding a WLAN to an existing wired Ethernet network. PoE hubs give an installer the ability to run power to multiple access points while using only one power outlet, saving time and preventing the huge headache caused by dealing with too many wires (and electricians). PoE hubs can each usually support up to 12 access points.

The most convenient way to implement PoE is to integrate it into a switch. This eliminates the need to buy extra equipment, making it most cost-effective to deploy a WLAN. The switch itself connects to a power outlet, and each port includes PoE capability integrated within the switch. The access points connect directly to the PoE-based switch ports to receive both electrical power and data over the Cat5 cable.

Integrated PoE is an optimum solution for providing electrical power to access points. It is definitely the approach to use when installing a new, large-scale network. Unfortunately, most large companies already have an existing wired Ethernet network, and replacing the existing switches is impractical and expensive. If a company is just starting up or replacing its existing wired backbone, however, integrated PoE is the ideal approach.

Application Connectivity Software

The traditional components of a wireless network (for example, radio cards and access points) provide a path for data to flow between the end-user device and a wired network that has connectivity to the host or server. To communicate effectively, wireless systems must also include connectivity between the end user and the application software and system databases. The following sections describe the primary methods for providing wireless application connectivity.

Terminal Emulation

Terminal emulation software makes an end-user device appear as a terminal to application software running on a host-based operating system, such as UNIX and AS/400. For example, Virtual Terminal (VT) emulation software interfaces with an application running on a UNIX host. Likewise, 5250 emulation software interfaces with an application running on an IBM AS/400. Terminal emulation software on wireless appliances generally communicates with the host using Telnet over TCP/IP protocols. After a connection is made with the host, the application software residing on the host can send display information (such as login prompts, menus, and data) to the appliance, and keyboard strokes will be sent to the application. Thus, the software on the host provides all application functionality.

A Case for Terminal Emulation

A police station in Florida was losing track of evidence that it acquired through the investigation of crimes. This had become a big problem because when the court needed the evidence, police officials could not find the evidence in a timely manner. This often delayed trial proceedings. As a result, the police chief decided to implement an asset-tracking system to manage the items and their specific locations. This system, based on the use of bar codes and handheld scanning equipment, needed a wireless network to support mobility when performing asset-management functions (such as picking and inventory) in the relatively large room that contained the evidence.

Because no IS staff members were available to do the project, the police chief outsourced the complete system implementation to a reliable system integrator. After careful analysis of functionality requirements and the existing system, the integrator developed a design that specified the use of off-the-shelf asset-management software, two 802.11-compliant handheld scanners, an 802.11 access point, and connectivity software. The asset-management software was hosted on the existing UNIX server that supported the police station's jail management software. The access point interfaced the wireless handheld scanners to an existing Ethernet network, providing a network connection to the UNIX server.

When dealing with the connectivity software, the integrator narrowed the choices to either terminal emulation or middleware. Direct database connectivity was not an option because there was no way to interface directly with the database. All interaction with the database was done through the application software only.

The integrator decided to use terminal emulation (VT220) for several reasons. First, there would have been no significant gain in performance by using middleware with only two wireless appliances sending data over the wireless network. The relatively small amount of data sent between appliances and the UNIX application offered very little impact to the 2-Mbps wireless network. In addition, the price for two terminal-emulation licenses for the appliances was much lower than the cost of purchasing middleware software. Also, the police station had no plans to move to a client/server system. Overall, terminal emulation was the lowest-cost form of connectivity software, based on the police station's requirements.

Some companies implement terminal controllers that provide an efficient interface between an end-user device and the host. The terminal controller provides effective management of the wireless end-user devices while maintaining constant connections with the host. The problem with these controllers is that they generally do not support forms of connectivity other than terminal emulation. For example, they do not support interfaces to databases via open database connectivity (ODBC), as many of the newer end systems require.

Note If a wireless appliance running terminal-emulation software does not connect to the host, be sure that the host is running TCP/IP. It is common to not implement TCP/IP software for host computers (especially mainframes) if the original implementation did not interface with a network. In these cases, you will have to install the TCP/IP software to establish communications between the appliance and the host.

Browser-Based Approaches

The explosive use of smart phones, tablets, and the Internet is prompting the rapid development of browser-based application connectivity technologies and standards for interfacing with information and applications at websites on the Internet and company intranets. A major problem with accessing the web wirelessly today, however, is that most web pages are written to display information on large desktop screens over relatively high-bandwidth physical connectivity. These pages do not work well over lower-data-rate wireless connections and small handheld device screens. In addition to solving these performance issues, the wireless Internet revolution is fueling the need for interoperability in the way mobile devices access web-based information.

Direct Database Interfaces

Some companies develop customized versions of application software that run on an end-user device and interface directly with a database on a server via ODBC or proprietary protocols. With this configuration, the software on the end-user device generally provides all application functionality. The application software with direct database connectivity generally uses TCP/IP software as a basis for communicating with the server. Some programmers refer to this form of development as *socket programming*.

Note   The advantage of writing the appliance software to interface with ODBC is that it provides an open interface to the many databases that are ODBC compliant. This enables you to write one application that can interface with databases from different vendors.

Wireless Middleware

Wireless network middleware is an intermediate software component generally located on the wired network between the wireless end-user devices and the application or data residing on the wired network (see Figure 3-20). Middleware client software runs on the end-user device and communicates using efficient (often proprietary) wireless protocols with middleware software (controller) residing on a platform such as UNIX or Microsoft Windows 2000. The middleware controller software communicates with host applications and databases over a wired connection.

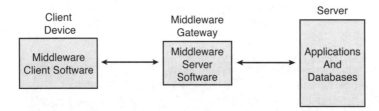

Figure 3-20   *Wireless Middleware Resides Between a Client Device and an Application Server*

With the continuing need to support bandwidth-intensive applications, companies will implement wireless middleware as part of their wireless network solutions, with the goal of increasing performance. To accomplish this, middleware attempts to counter wireless network impairments, such as limited bandwidth and disruptions in network connections. Middleware enables highly efficient and reliable communications over a WLAN, while maintaining appropriate connections to application software and databases on the server/host via the more reliable wired LAN.

Traditionally, middleware suppliers could only enable a limited set of end-user devices and only interface with a specific end system. Presently, suppliers are striving to make middleware as open as possible by incorporating many different end-user devices, hosts, and servers. End-user companies generally select middleware software based on the ability to interface with their specific end systems, which tend to be IBM AS/400s, Microsoft 2000 Server machines, or UNIX hosts. In addition, end users generally want wireless middleware software capable of supporting a variety of end-user devices provided by different vendors. This minimizes limitations when adding additional end-user devices in the future.

The following vendors provide wireless middleware solutions:

- **Connect:** www.connectrf.com

- **Iona:** www.iona.com

- **NetMotion:** www.netmotionwireless.com

- **Wavelink:** www.wavelink.com

A Case for Wireless Middleware

A boat-building company in Maine decided to implement a quality-assurance system to improve the efficiency of the inspections is performs periodically. Several times throughout the process of manufacturing each boat, inspectors need to walk throughout the plant and record flaws as the boats are being assembled. The new system includes a handheld PC with an 802.11-compliant radio card that communicates to the corporate information system. For each boat, the inspector enters the boat's serial number, and then the system prompts the inspector through a series of questions that pertain to the quality of specific items of that particular boat. As the inspector answers the questions, the wireless network transports the data back to the corporate information system for viewing by construction managers.

The company's corporate information system consists of an IBM mainframe that supports most of the company's application software, servers that host databases, 3,270 terminals that interface with the mainframe applications, PCs that run client application software and interface with the databases, and an Ethernet network that ties everything together. The information that the new quality-assurance system uses is located on both the mainframe and the database servers. As a result, the corporate IS group had to pay close attention to the type of connectivity software to use to satisfy the requirements of both operating environments.

The IS group evaluated several alternatives for connectivity software: the use of terminal emulation, direct database connectivity, and middleware. Terminal emulation for the handheld PCs would interface easily with the mainframe system, but it would not provide an interface to the database servers. Likewise, direct database connectivity would interface with the database servers but not the mainframes. For this project, middleware was clearly the best alternative. The need to seamlessly interface with both the mainframe and the database server systems was imperative.

Summary

As you can see from this chapter, the implementation of a WLAN involves more than just installing radio cards and access points. The implementation might also include the use of WLAN routers, bridges, repeaters, and amplifiers. The limited connectivity you might have with a WLAN will negatively impact performance of other aspects of the system that might not be optimized for wireless applications. As a result, you need to consider the wired backbone that will interconnect the access points, software that interfaces with the servers, and IP address assignments. Attention to these elements in addition to the core WLAN components will maximize the performance and success of your WLAN implementation.

Chapter 4

Wireless LAN Implications

This chapter will introduce you to:

- Security Vulnerabilities
- Radio Signal Interference
- Impacts of Multipath Propagation
- Roaming Issues
- Battery Limitations
- Interoperability Problems
- Installation Issues

As Chapter 1, "Introduction to Wireless LANs," describes, wireless LANs (WLANs) offer tremendous benefits. When designing and supporting a WLAN, however, you must be aware of potential implications, such as security vulnerabilities, radio signal interference, multipath propagation, and other issues. This chapter explains the impacts of these problems and introduces some ways to resolve them. Later chapters explain more details on how to combat the implications.

Security Vulnerabilities

Network security refers to the protection of information and resources from loss, corruption, and improper use. With WLANs, security vulnerabilities fall within the following areas (see Figure 4-1):

- Passive monitoring
- Unauthorized access
- Denial-of-service attacks

The sections that follow explain these security problems in greater detail.

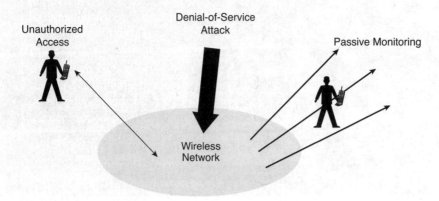

Figure 4-1 *Wireless LAN Security Vulnerabilities Include Passive Monitoring, Unauthorized Access, and Denial-of-Service Attacks*

Passive Monitoring

Wireless LANs intentionally propagate data throughout buildings, campuses, and even cities. As a result, the radio signals often go beyond the limits of the area an organization physically controls. For instance, radio waves easily penetrate building walls and can be received from the facility's parking lot and possibly a few blocks away, as illustrated in Figure 4-2. It is possible for an unauthorized person to passively retrieve a company's sensitive information by using a laptop equipped with a radio card from this distance without being noticed by network security personnel. A hacker, for example, might be sitting in an automobile outside a business, capturing all 802.11 transmissions using a freely available packet sniffer, such as WireShark. After capturing the data, the hacker will be able to retrieve contents of e-mails and user passwords to company servers. Of course, the hacker can use this information to compromise the security of the company. This problem also exists with wired Ethernet networks, but to a lesser degree. Current flow through the metallic wires emits electromagnetic waves that someone could receive by using sensitive listening equipment. The person must be much closer to the cable, though, to receive the signals. Thus, in terms of passive monitoring, WLANs are not as secure as wired networks.

The method for resolving the issues of passive monitoring is to implement encryption between all client devices and the access points. Encryption alters the information bits in each frame, based on an encryption key, so that the hacker cannot make sense of the data he captures via passive monitoring. An example of an 802.11 encryption process is Wired Equivalent Privacy (WEP), which was part of the original 802.11 standard ratified in 1997. WEP is fairly easy to crack, however, so it is not recommended for encrypting sensitive information. Other encryption methods, such as Wi-Fi Protected Access (WPA), offer much stronger security.

Note   See Chapter 13, "Security Considerations," for more details on WEP and WPA.

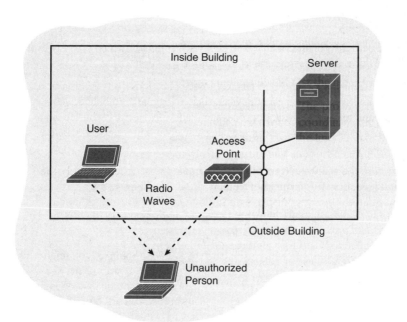

Figure 4-2   *Without Effective Encryption, an Unauthorized Person Can Listen in on Wireless LAN Data Transmissions*

Retail Store Loses Credit Card Numbers over Wireless LAN

A garden supplies store implemented a WLAN to support communications between portable point-of-sale (PoS) terminals and servers. This allowed the store to temporarily move the PoS terminals outdoors during seasonal periods to sell garden equipment. The store did an effective job of advertising this capability, which brought more shoppers (and sales) to the store.

After the system was operational for a few months, customers of the store began contacting the store management to say that their credit card numbers had been used fraudulently soon after shopping at the store. The store found that the affected credit cards had been processed over the wireless PoS terminals, not the terminals that connect to the servers via Ethernet only. The store immediately shut down the wireless PoS terminals. After consulting with an information security consultant, the store learned that encryption was needed to keep hackers from passively monitoring the 802.11 transmissions and stealing the credit card numbers. The store had not implemented any form of encryption.

The consultant recommended that the store implement Advanced Encryption Standard (AES) encryption, which is part of WPA2 and the 802.11i standard. This keeps hackers from understanding the data in the 802.11 transmissions. The store implemented this solution and is now back to using the wireless PoS terminals without any security problems.

Hands-on Exercise: Passively Monitor a Wireless LAN

This exercise gives you some experience seeing potentially sensitive information that a WLAN transmits through the air.

Perform the following steps:

Step 1. Obtain a wireless protocol analyzer, such as WireShark (which is freely available) or other analyzers described in Chapter 14, "Test Tools."

Step 2. Identify wireless applications to test. Choose applications that you or your organization use from wireless client devices, such as logging in to online accounts, sending and receiving e-mail, or processing credit cards, so that you can get a good idea of what a hacker can see while passively monitoring your wireless network.

Step 3. Configure the analyzer to record 802.11 frame transmissions on only the radio frequency (RF) channel of your WLAN. This helps reduce extraneous frames that the analyzer displays by filtering out frames from other channels. With fewer frames, you will be able to more easily pinpoint the 802.11 data frames applicable to your applications.

Step 4. For initial tests, turn off encryption (such as WPA); of course, you might only want to do this on a test network, separate from the operational network. Now the WLAN will not encrypt 802.11 data frame contents, which includes the information associated with the application that you are testing. This will give you an idea of what the WLAN exposes to potential hackers if you are not implementing encryption.

Step 5. While using each application you chose to test, record a packet trace with the protocol analyzer. View the recorded packet trace and look at the frame body of the 802.11 data frames pertaining to the application you are testing. To narrow down the search, try applying a filter on the packet trace corresponding to only 802.11 data frames associated with the wireless client device you are using the application from. What sensitive information, such as the user's username and password when logging into an online bank account, are you able to find? If you are testing an e-mail application, can you interpret the contents of e-mails being sent or received via the wireless client device?

Step 6. Turn on encryption and repeat step 5. View the recorded packet trace and note the impact of enabling encryption. This allows you to see the impact of encryption and the difficulties a hacker will have when trying to acquire sensitive information from a WLAN implementing encryption. With encryption on, what sensitive information in the packet trace pertaining to your applications can you find?

With encryption turned off, you will probably not be able to find the username and password when logging into bank accounts because the session is likely encrypted between the client device and the bank's website via Secure Sockets Layer (SSL), assuming that the online bank account implements secure web pages (HTTPS). You will likely find that many non-financial online accounts, such as hobby sites and e-mail systems, however, do not use SSL when logging into accounts. As a result, you will probably spot the usernames and passwords for those types of accounts. This is a significant issue if users have the same username and password for all accounts (which is common). The hacker just needs to monitor the user logging into a completely non-secure account, view the username and password in the packet trace, and use that username and password to log into the user's bank account. That's why it is a good idea to use different usernames and passwords for different online accounts. With encryption turned off, you will probably be able to find the contents of e-mail (unless encrypted by the e-mail server). Of course by turning on encryption, the WLAN will scramble (and thus hide) application-oriented information because it encrypts the frame body of all 802.11 data frames.

Unauthorized Access

If someone can connect to a WLAN, she can potentially access anything on the network, including client devices, servers, and applications, as illustrated in Figure 4-3. Some organizations do a good job of locking down servers and applications, but others do not. A hacker who can connect to a WLAN will look for backdoors and other security glitches to compromise the security of the network. For example, a hacker connected to an access point can use a TCP port scanner to implement a scan for open (unsecured) ports on servers. If one is found, the hacker has access to the port's utilities, which might allow her to directly access sensitive information or reconfigure the network in a manner that makes it less secure (and thus easier to access more sensitive information).

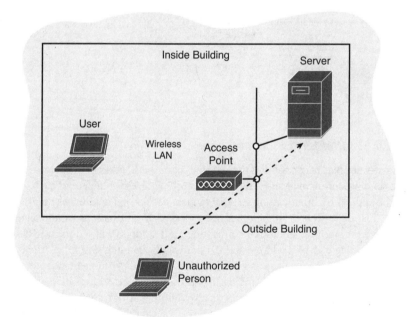

Figure 4-3 *Unauthorized Access Enables Someone to Gain Access to an Organization's Servers and Applications*

One way that a hacker can gain unauthorized access to a WLAN is to stage a man-in-the-middle attack, as illustrated in Figure 4-4. There are a variety of methods to set up a man-in-the-middle attack. One is to exploit the TCP/IP Address Resolution Protocol (ARP) functions. ARP is a crucial function that a source station (such as an 802.11 radio) uses to discover the physical address of a destination station. This physical address is the MAC address, which is embedded in the client radio by the manufacturer and unique from any other client device or network component. The MAC address is analogous to the street address of your home. Just as someone must know this address to send you a letter, a sending 802.11 radio must know the MAC address of the destination. The 802.11 radio understands and responds to only the physical MAC address.

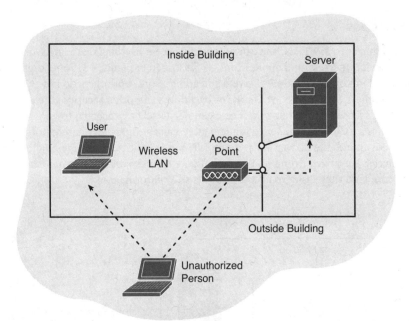

Figure 4-4   *A Hacker Can Hijack a Session Away from a Legitimate User*

The application software that needs to send the data will have the IP address of the destination, but the sending station must use ARP to discover the corresponding physical address. It gets the address by broadcasting an ARP request packet that announces the IP address of the destination station to all the other network devices. All stations within range hear this request, and the station that has the corresponding IP address will return an ARP response packet containing its MAC address and IP address. The sending station will then include this MAC address as the destination address in the 802.11 data frame being sent. The sending station also stores the corresponding IP address and MAC address mapping in a table for a period of time or until the station receives another ARP response from the station having that IP address. This is where ARP introduces a security risk.

A hacker can fool a station by sending (from an unauthorized laptop) a fictitious ARP response that includes the IP address of a legitimate network device, such as a wireless access point, and the MAC address of the client radio in the unauthorized laptop. This causes all legitimate stations on the network to automatically update their ARP tables with the false mapping to the unauthorized laptop. This causes these stations to send future 802.11 data frames to the rogue device rather than the legitimate access point. This is a classic man-in-the-middle attack, which enables a hacker to manipulate user sessions. As a result, the hacker can obtain passwords, capture sensitive data, and even interface with corporate servers as if she were the legitimate user.

A critical security concern of IT managers is the presence of rogue wireless access points on the corporate network. A rogue access point is one that the company does not authorize for operation. The trouble is that a rogue access point often does not conform to WLAN security policies, which enables an open, insecure interface to the corporate network from outside the physically controlled facility. Figure 4-5 illustrates a scenario where a rogue access point is providing open access to the network from outside the physically controlled area of a facility.

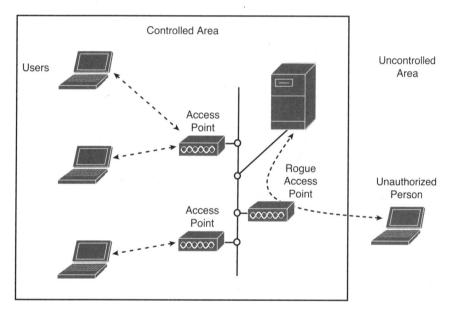

Figure 4-5   *A Rogue Access Point Can Offer an Unsecured Opening to the Network*

Employees have relatively free access to a company's facility, which makes it possible for them to inadvertently install a rogue access point. An employee, for example, might purchase an access point at an office supply store and install it without coordinating with the IT organization to support wireless printing or access to the network from a conference room. Or developers working on wireless applications might connect an access point to the corporate network for testing purposes. In most cases, employees deploying these types of access points do not understand the security issues they're creating. These scenarios often lead to access points not conforming to adequate security practices. As a result, the corporate network is left wide open for a casual snooper or hacker to attack.

A hacker can install a rogue access point to provide an open, non-secure interface to the corporate network. To do this, the hacker must directly connect the access point to an active network port within the facility. This requires the hacker to pass through physical security, and it is easier to do than most companies assume. Nevertheless, the hacker will need to physically traverse the facility and install the access point without being noticed. It is unlikely that someone would do this unless the company has resources that are critical enough for a hacker to go to the trouble and risk of planting the rogue.

A way to counter unauthorized access is to employ an authentication system that verifies the identity of users, client devices, and access points before allowing them to operate on the WLAN. The user provides a form of credentials, such as username and password or digital certificate, and an authentication server determines whether the person (or client device) can access the network. If not, the network does not allow the client device to connect to the access point. As a result, the access point on the WLAN acts as a security gate to the network. In addition, for added protection, a company can keep all traffic on the WLAN on a virtual LAN (VLAN) that is separate from VLANs supporting sensitive applications and servers. This way, the company can limit the implications resulting from unauthorized access to only the applications and servers supporting the wireless network. A company can even go as far as keeping all WLAN traffic outside the company firewall and requiring all wireless users to implement virtual private network (VPN) client software similar to when connecting to the corporate network from public networks.

Unauthorized Access Leads to Compromise of Financial Data

A large private company in California implemented a WLAN to support enterprise mobility. The system was seemingly working great and providing significant benefits to its users. Over a year after the system went operational, the IT department noticed, through a routine network security audit, that several of its printers in the financial department had been configured to send all printed data to a file at a suspicious IP address. Unfortunately, the IT department had not locked down the administrative access ports on these printers. Even though all the details of what happened here are not known, it is likely that a hacker gained unauthorized access to the WLAN (which did not implement any form of authentication) and ran a port scan to find the open printer administration port. With the open port's IP address (resulting from the scan), the hacker could easily log in to the administrative port and set the printer to send all print jobs to a file located on the hacker's laptop. The printer would then continue to print on paper and also send the print data to the hacker's laptop. Of course this would send to the hacker everything that the printer would print, such as internal goals and objectives, company sales information, employee salaries, and so on. After discovering this issue, the company promptly implemented an authentication system to disallow all unauthorized people from accessing the WLAN.

Note   See Chapter 13 for more details on solutions for guarding against unauthorized access.

Denial-of-Service Attacks

A denial-of-service (DoS) attack is an assault that can cripple or disable a WLAN. Wireless networks are extremely vulnerable to DoS attacks (even when using modern security mechanisms), which can cause a WLAN to slow to crawling speeds or even quit working. This causes a company that's dependent on a WLAN to experience delays, which can be costly for some applications, such as wireless security cameras, inventory systems, and PoS terminals.

One form of DoS attack is the "brute-force" method. This type of attack can come in one of two forms:

- A huge flood of packets that uses up all the network's resources and forces it to shut down

- A very strong radio signal that totally dominates the airwaves and renders access points and radio cards useless

One of the ways a hacker can perform a packet-based brute-force DoS attack is to use other computers on the network to send large numbers of useless packets to the server. This adds significant overhead on the network and takes away usable bandwidth from legitimate users. The use of a very strong radio signal to disrupt the access points and radio cards is a rather risky attack for a hacker to attempt. Because a very powerful transmitter at a relatively close range must be used to execute this type of attack, the owners of the WLAN can find the hacker through the use of homing tools.

Another form of DoS attack fiddles with the 802.11 protocols in a way that disables the network. This can be done via specialized software running on a laptop without connecting to any of the network's access points. For example, the software can continuously send 802.11 disassociation frames to all client radios, which causes them to disconnect from the access points with which they are associated. This cuts off the client devices from the network, which of course disables them from communicating on the network, accessing applications, and so on. This method and others are well known by network culprits and published readily on the Internet.

DoS attacks are not common, and they are generally implemented over the air, thus disturbing only a small portion of a WLAN. For example, a malicious hacker with a wireless laptop might be outside a building containing a WLAN and begin broadcasting disassociation frames, but only the client radios within range of the malicious person will receive the disassociation frames and disconnect from their respective access points. Other client radios operating farther inside the building, far enough away to not receive disassociation frames, will continue operating.

Sometimes a DoS occurrence on a wireless network might not be intentional. Because the 2.4-GHz version of 802.11n resides in such a crowded spectrum, 2.4-GHz cordless phones, microwave ovens, Bluetooth devices, and other devices that use the 2.4-GHz spectrum might cause a significant reduction in WLAN performance. As a result, a company should fully investigate the use of these devices and possibly put limits on their usage before a WLAN is deemed operational.

There is not much that you can do to entirely prevent a DoS attack. A company can minimize the possibility of DoS attacks against a WLAN by making the facility as resistive as possible to incoming radio signals. This includes using directive antennas near the periphery of the building and aiming the directive side of the antenna indoors to reduce the listening capability of the antenna to signals originating outdoors. In addition, the use of RF shielding paint and window film can add significant attenuation to the exterior walls of the buildings to nearly eliminate jamming signals from outdoors. The problem with these solutions, however, is that they can be expensive and also cut off the usage of other wireless devices, such as cell phones. Also, they are not effective if a hacker somehow gets inside the building to stage the DoS attack. Of course that's where good physical security practices come into play.

Note   See Chapter 12, "Radio Frequency Considerations," for more information about implementing methods for guarding against DoS attacks.

Because of the potential harm, you must consider potential DoS attacks before launching mission-critical applications on a WLAN. If a DoS attack is even a remote possibility, think about how you will get by if the network is not available for an indefinite period of time. The benefits of the WLAN in the long term, however, will likely outweigh the disruption of an occasional DoS attack, assuming that the organization does not depend entirely on the wireless network. Something that should be put in place for any mission-critical WLAN application is a backup plan. A company should not be so dependent on its wireless network that if it goes down, everything grinds to a halt.

As with wired networks, a company should also have a "Plan B" in case the WLAN becomes unavailable because of a DoS attack. For example, a large retail store might use a wireless network to support wireless PoS terminals. In case the wireless network becomes inoperative (possibly due to a DoS attack), the retail store should have a backup plan, such as batching sale transactions for later processing when the network becomes available or when it is possible to connect the terminal to the retail system via a cable.

Be Aware of DoS Attacks on Video Surveillance Systems

When deploying a Wi-Fi video surveillance system, you must be aware that it is possible to deny the service of a WLAN. A culprit, for example, could transmit a jamming signal that holds off the video cameras from transmitting. 802.11 makes use of carrier sense multiple access (CSMA), which Wi-Fi uses to control access to the air medium. With CSMA, client radios in user devices take turns transmitting over a common RF channel. If another client radio is transmitting or an interfering (or jamming) signal is present, then all client radios within range of the jamming signal will hold off from transmitting. This situation will disrupt the video camera signals. As a result, be very careful to not depend heavily on Wi-Fi video cameras, especially if there are serious risks involved in the cameras not working!

Radio Signal Interference

Radio signal interference involves the presence of unwanted, interfering radio signals that disrupt normal WLAN operations. Because of the 802.11 Medium Access Control (MAC) protocols, an interfering radio signal of sufficient amplitude and frequency can appear as a bogus 802.11 station transmitting a packet. This causes legitimate 802.11 stations to wait for indefinite periods of time before attempting to access the medium until the interfering signal goes away.

To make matters worse, radio signal interference does not abide by the 802.11 protocols, so the interfering signal might start abruptly while a legitimate 802.11 station is in the process of transmitting a packet, as illustrated in Figure 4-6. If this occurs, the destination station will receive the packet with errors and not reply to the source station with an acknowledgement. In return, the source station will attempt to retransmit the packet, adding overhead on the network.

Radio signal interference causes wireless clients and access points to hold off transmitting, which causes delay and reduced throughput. As a result, interference lasting for longer periods of time (referred to as duty cycle) will cause more damage to the signal, and interference present for shorter periods of time may have less impact on the signal. The resulting decrease in performance caused by interference can make browsing websites and downloading files sluggish and severely limit the number of active voice users. In cases where interfering signals are strong enough, the wireless clients might not be able to access the WLAN at all for an indefinite period of time. This is rare but possible. As a result, companies need to be aware of potential sources of radio signal interference, such as microwave ovens and cordless phones, operating within the WLAN environment.

Of course this all leads to network latency and unhappy users. In some cases, 802.11 protocols will attempt to continue operation in the presence of radio signal interference by automatically switching to a lower data rate, which also slows the use of wireless applications. The worst case, which is fairly uncommon, is that the 802.11 stations will hold off until the interfering signal goes away completely, which could be minutes, hours, or days.

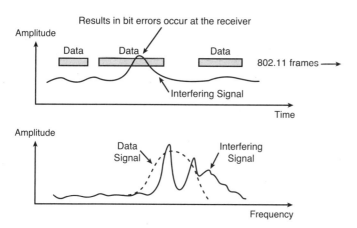

Figure 4-6   *Radio Signal Interference Can Damage 802.11 Frames En Route Between Client Radios and Access Points*

Radio Signal Interference Halts a Wireless LAN

A large marketing firm in Washington, D.C., is situated along the Potomac River. The consulting firm's main conference room is along the side of the building facing the river. After deploying a WLAN within the building, the company found that the majority of wireless client devices in the conference room (and other offices on the side of the building facing the river) were experiencing significant delays when using applications on the network. For example, a user walking from the opposite side of the building toward the conference room could successfully browse the Internet, but web pages would freeze after the user entered the conference room. The company contacted the contractor that had installed the network to see what it could do to fix the problem. After analyzing the situation, the contractor found that a military base on the other side of the river was periodically transmitting radio signals. The interfering signals were strong enough for the 802.11 client radios to misinterpret them as data traffic, forcing the stations to wait indefinitely. When originally installing the network, the contractor had verified that the signal strength was sufficient throughout the building, but the contractor had not investigated the presence of radio signal interference. The presence of radio signal interference was causing the signal-to-noise ratio (SNR) to be very low and even negative. Fortunately, the contractor was able to reposition access points to increase the SNR high enough along the Potomac side of the building that client devices were able to operate.

The problem with radio signal interference is that it will likely change over time. For example, a neighbor might purchase a 2.4-GHz cordless phone and start using it frequently, or the use of WLANs in your area might increase. This means that the resulting impacts of radio signal interference could grow over time, or they could come and go. As a result, rather than wait to investigate radio signal interference as an underlying problem for poor performance, investigate the potential for radio signal interference in a proactive manner. You can then attempt to reduce the sources of interference and design a WLAN to accommodate certain types of interference.

Note   In some facilities, it is imperative to comply with electromagnetic compatibility (EMC) standards, especially in hospitals where WLANs interfere with medical devices implanted in humans and other RF equipment.

The sections that follow explore the various sources of radio signal interference.

Microwave Oven Interference

Microwave ovens emit damaging interfering signals at up to 25 feet or so from an operating oven. Some microwave ovens emit radio signals that occupy only a third of the 2.4-GHz band, whereas others occupy the entire band. This means that it might be possible to tune an access point near a microwave oven to a noninterfering channel. Keep in mind that the microwave oven's interfering signal is present only while the oven is operating, which might not be often. For example, a microwave oven in a break room might be in use only a few times during lunch and sit idle during the rest of the day. Thus, microwave ovens present within the facility might not significantly impact the use of the WLAN.

Figure 4-7 shows the output of a Bantam spectrum analyzer depicting the presence of microwave oven interference at ranges of 10 and 25 feet. These measurements were taken while the microwave oven was cooking a bag of popcorn, which takes about 2 minutes. As you can see, the interfering signals occupy the majority of the 2.4-GHz band. What is seen in the image is actually a quasi-peak value, which is the peak signal value with a discharge that takes a few seconds. In this case, it is not possible to completely avoid the interference by changing the access point channels. Each microwave oven has a different interference signature. In fact, we have tested other microwave ovens that have had more interference in the upper third of the 2.4-GHz band, which makes it possible to avoid the interference by tuning the access points near the microwave oven to the lower RF channels.

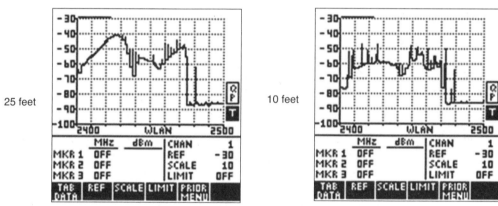

Figure 4-7 *Radio Frequency Interference Originating from a Microwave Oven*

Dueling with Microwave Ovens

My consulting firm, Wireless-Nets, Ltd., routinely tests microwave ovens in facilities where companies are planning to install a WLAN to understand how much impact the microwave ovens will have on WLAN operation. One particular microwave oven, made by GoldStar, resides in a break room of a small company. The label on the back of the microwave indicates that it consumes 1200 watts of power and operates at 2450 MHz, which is close to the 2.4-GHz 802.11 channel 9.

We set up an 802.11n access point for test purposes about 20 feet from the microwave oven. We set the access point to the 2.4-GHz channel 9 (a probable worst-case situation), and took some signal measurements in the break room to use as a baseline (without the microwave oven operating). The signal level resulting from the access point beacons within the break room was –63 dBm, which is sufficient for solid performance. We ran throughput tests, which indicated 667 packets per second (pps) while sending 1,532-byte frames.

While holding the wireless client device (a laptop) within 1 foot of the microwave, we recorded some signal measurements while the microwave was set to high and heating up a large bowl of water. The throughput fell to 90 pps. As a result, using a wireless client device very close to the operating microwave made the throughput plunge by over 85 percent. This is a substantial reduction in performance, but it is the worst-case situation. The access point was set to the same frequency of the microwave oven, and it is unlikely that someone would use a wireless client so close to the oven.

A more realistic distance from the microwave is from one of the break tables, which is about 8 feet away from the microwave oven. At this range, we reran the throughput tests and got 178 pps throughput. This still equates to around a 75 percent decrease, which is still substantial. To see what it was like to experience a 75 percent decrease in throughput, we tried surfing to a website having a few graphics. With the microwave running, the pictures would come in painfully slowly. We also surfed around a bit to other pages, and sometimes the pages would freeze. After turning off the microwave oven, we cleared the browser cache and found no problems surfing the same web pages.

We also repeated the tests down the hall, about 20 feet away, with the microwave oven running, and we still experienced fairly sluggish responses. In fact, throughput from there was still only 260 pps. Obviously, the microwave oven was making the WLAN very slow at surprisingly great distances. Something to consider is that these tests were run with only one active wireless client. The results would have been much worse if there had been more active users on the network.

We were curious to know what channels the microwave oven would affect the most, so we reran the throughput tests again while the access point was set to different channels. With the access point set to channels 1, 2, 3, 4, 5, 6, 7, 8, 9, 10, and 11, the throughput was 660 pps, 658 pps, 655 pps, 651 pps, 643 pps, 574 pps, 434 pps, 258 pps, 178 pps, 191 pps, and 210 pps, respectively. Based on these numbers, the microwave was most critically impacting channels 8, 9, 10, and 11, which is the upper third of the 2.4-GHz spectrum. This particular microwave oven had very little if no impact on the lower channels.

Cordless Phone Interference

Cordless phones cause interference with WLANs. Today, a person can purchase cordless phones that operate in a variety of unlicensed frequency bands: 900 MHz, 2.4 GHz, and 5 GHz. A cordless phone will cause interference only with WLANs operating in the same frequency bands as the phone. For example, a 2.4-GHz cordless phone can interfere with WLANs operating in the 2.4-GHz band but not the 5-GHz band.

Many of these phones use direct-sequence spread spectrum (DSSS) and automatically choose the least congested channel. As a result, they can tune around WLAN access points. If there are several phones actively in use at the same time, however, the phones might monopolize the entire spectrum and cause interference with the WLAN access points. Figure 4-8 shows the output of a Bantam spectrum analyzer depicting the presence of interference approximately 2 feet from a DSSS cordless phone. Some cordless phones use frequency-hopping spread spectrum (FHSS), which distributes radio signals over the entire band. As a result, they nearly always cause significant interference with WLANs operating in the same frequency band as the phone.

The use of 2.4-GHz cordless phones is very common. In this case, consider implementing 802.11ac or the 5-GHz version of 802.11n to avoid interference. As a last resort, the use of cordless phones should be prohibited in cases where it is critical to maximize the capacity of a WLAN, such as when maximizing the number of active voice users.

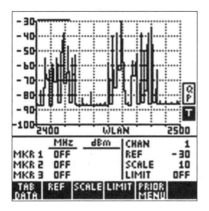

Figure 4-8 *Radio Frequency Interference Originating from a Cordless Phone*

Dueling with Cordless Phones

My consulting firm, Wireless-Nets, Ltd., has had an opportunity to do some Wi-Fi interference testing with several Plantronics 2.4-GHz cordless phones. We found that the cordless phones, when switched on (with or without a dial tone), always transmit a 10-MHz-wide signal in the 2.4-GHz ISM band, which is roughly 90 MHz wide. We could clearly see from a spectrum analyzer that turning on a second phone would produce another 10-MHz-wide signal in an unoccupied part of the band. Apparently, the phones search for the least congested area and tune their transmitters to that frequency. With a fairly clean spectrum, with no Wi-Fi or Bluetooth devices operating, we could turn on six of the phones, which filled approximately two thirds of the spectrum. Based on the way that the phones were operating, the use of cordless phones (at least the Plantronics model we tested) will reduce the capacity for supporting Wi-Fi signals. Because a Wi-Fi access point operating in the 2.4-GHz band uses one third of the spectrum, the operation of six phones would leave enough room for a single access point. If there is a need for operating nine phones in the same general area as an access point, then interference between the access point and the phones (the three using a frequency that overlaps with the access point) will occur. The result is distorted voice heard over the phone when talking to someone and a much higher frame retransmission rate at the access point. Keep in mind that varying cordless phone models operate differently, so it is worthwhile to test them if they will be used in conjunction with a WLAN.

Cordless Phone Dodges Access Points

My consulting firm, Wireless-Nets, Ltd., tested a VTech 2.4-GHz cordless phone in an office environment. The product box states that the phone is "Wi-Fi friendly." This is the first time that we have seen cordless phone makers mention this. After some quick testing, we found that this VTech phone automatically tunes to different channels to avoid interfering with a WLAN access point set to a specific channel. This is a great feature. We have experienced cordless phones without this interference avoidance mechanism that severely degrade the performance of a WLAN. Some companies are now offering 6.0-GHz cordless phones, however, to completely dodge radio frequency interference issues with WLANs.

Bluetooth Interference

Similar to 802.11 WLANs, Bluetooth devices operate within the 2.4-GHz band. The difference is that Bluetooth uses FHSS (at 1,600 hops per second) to hop over the entire 2.4-GHz band. 802.11, on the other hand, occupies only approximately one third of the 2.4-GHz band. As a result, Bluetooth hops all over 802.11 transmissions. Figure 4-9 shows the output of a Bantam spectrum analyzer depicting the presence of interference approximately 2 feet from a Bluetooth headset. Adaptive frequency hopping, introduced by the Bluetooth Special Interest Group (SIG) and part of most Bluetooth devices, helps reduce the impact of Bluetooth interference, but it is still wise to be aware of the impacts and implement other anti-interference methods.

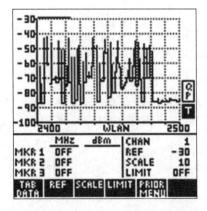

Figure 4-9   *Radio Frequency Interference Originating from a Bluetooth Headset*

Because of the potential for collisions, 802.11 (and Bluetooth) networks can suffer lower performance. The full impact of radio signal interference depends on the use and proximity of Bluetooth devices. Interference can occur only when both Bluetooth and 802.11 devices transmit at the same time. Users might have Bluetooth devices in their PDAs or laptops, but no interference will exist if their applications are not using the Bluetooth radio to send data. Some Bluetooth applications, such as printing from a laptop or synchronizing a tablet to a desktop, use the radio for only a very short period of time. In this case, the Bluetooth devices will generally not be active long enough to noticeably degrade the performance of an 802.11 network. For example, a user might synchronize his tablet to his desktop when arriving at work in the morning. Other than that, his Bluetooth device might be inactive the rest of the day.

The biggest impacts occur when a company implements a larger-scale Bluetooth network, such as one that enables mobility for doctors and nurses using wireless devices throughout a hospital. If the Bluetooth network is widespread and under moderate to high levels of utilization, the Bluetooth system will probably offer a substantial number of collisions with an 802.11 network residing in the same area. In this case, Bluetooth and 802.11 would have difficulties coexisting, and performance would likely suffer.

In addition to use, the proximity of the Bluetooth devices to 802.11 client radios and access points has a tremendous effect on the degree of interference (see Figure 4-10). The transmit power of Bluetooth devices is generally much lower than that of 802.11 WLANs. Thus, an 802.11 station must be relatively close (within 10 feet or so) of a transmitting Bluetooth device before significant interference can occur. A typical application fitting this scenario is a laptop user having Bluetooth supporting connections to a tablet and printer and 802.11 for accessing the Internet and corporate servers. The potential for interference in this situation is enormous, especially when the user is operating within the fringe area of the 802.11 network (that is, at the range that just supports the required data rate). The low-power Bluetooth signal will likely drown out the weaker 802.11 signal because of the distance of the access point.

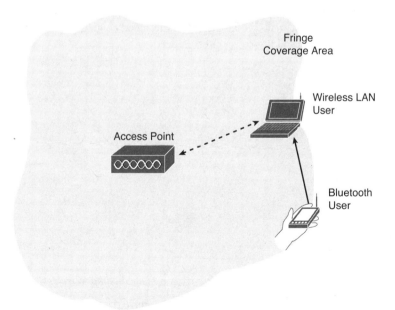

Figure 4-10 *Bluetooth Devices Offer the Greatest Impact on Wireless LANs in Fringe Coverage Areas*

> **Note**   See Chapter 12 for more information about solutions for counteracting radio signal interference.

Neighboring Wireless LAN Interference

With the growing proliferation of WLANs, it is likely that neighboring wireless networks will exist in the area where an organization installs the WLAN. In most cases, the neighboring networks will implement a version of 802.11 that is compatible with your network. The advantage of this is that both your network and the neighboring one coordinate access to the common medium.

Interference between different WLANs occurs when the access points within range of each other are set to the same RF channel. As a result, a radio cell from one network overlaps a radio cell of the other network. In this case, with no data traffic occurring within each of the overlapping cells, there is insignificant interference. The only interference results from the periodic transmission of 802.11 access point beacons and other management frames.

Figure 4-11 shows the output of a Bantam spectrum analyzer depicting the presence of interference approximately 50 feet from a neighboring WLAN. In this case, the neighboring WLAN access point is set to one of the lower RF channels in the 2.4-GHz band. To counteract this potential for interference with its WLAN, the organization should avoid the lower RF channels near the side of the building next to the neighboring access point. It is likely possible to use the lower RF channels farther inside the building because the additional distance and walls would attenuate the signal coming from the neighboring WLAN to levels that will not cause interference.

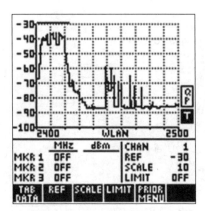

Figure 4-11   *Radio Frequency Interference Originating from a Neighboring Wireless LAN*

When client devices in both cells begin to actively send and receive data over the WLAN, the client devices will share access of the medium, based on the 802.11 MAC protocols. (See Chapter 6, "IEEE 802.11 Medium Access Control (MAC) Layer," for details on how these protocols work.) They will share the capacity of the RF spectrum, which reduces the potential performance that the networks can deliver. Because the interactivity between the client devices does not result in a significant increase in retransmissions, similar to interference from other sources such as microwave ovens (because the client devices are sharing the medium politely), the performance degradation might not be noticeable as compared to a client device operating from one of the cells while the neighboring cell has no activity. Thus, interference from neighboring networks is a problem only as utilization increases.

Throughput Degradation Due to Beacons

My consulting firm, Wireless-Nets, Ltd., performed throughput tests between a wireless client device and an 802.11n access point, with and without the presence of a neighboring access point set to the same channel. We measured degradation of only a few percent in throughput when the interfering access point was active as compared to when it was not (without any client device traffic). This indicates that there was not much impact from the beacons of a neighboring access point set to the same channel. For larger networks, you'll likely experience more degradation at a specific location, depending on the number of access points that are within range of each other at that location. For networks having many access points within range of each other (generally caused by improper design), the degradation may be higher, such as 50 percent. In the past, it was common for organizations to install FHSS WLANs (both proprietary and 802.11 based), especially in hospitals and warehouses. Not many of the WLAN vendors sell FHSS equipment anymore, but these systems are still operating in some facilities. All the FHSS systems operate in either the 900-MHz or 2.4-GHz bands, not the 5-GHz band.

Because FHSS WLANs transmit signals over the entire 2.4-GHz band, FHSS causes significant interference with 802.11b, 802.11g, and 802.11n operating in the 2.4-GHz band. Figure 4-9, which shows a spectrum analyzer display of interference originating from a Bluetooth headset, depicts similar interference from an FHSS system. No matter what channel you set in the access point, the FHSS signal always interferes. A 2.4-GHz 802.11 signal, however, only interferes with roughly one third of the FHSS signal, which does not cause nearly as much damage to the 802.11 signal. As a result, FHSS interferes more with 2.4-GHz 802.11b/g/n than the other way around. As mentioned before, Bluetooth and some 2.4-GHz cordless phones also use FHSS, which can cause similar interference with 2.4-GHz 802.11b/g/n WLANs.

802.11 FHSS Systems Are Still Out There

My consulting firm, Wireless-Nets, Ltd., has seen recent existing cases of 802.11 FHSS systems interfering with 2.4-GHz 802.11b/g/n networks. We have tested it in lab scenarios and assisted several clients with interference mitigation efforts. For example, when we recently performed a wireless site survey and WLAN design for a hospital, we found that the existence of a FHSS WLAN throughout the emergency department of the hospital was causing approximately a 40 percent decrease in throughput on the 2.4-GHz 802.11n network we were testing in the same location.

Hands-on Exercise: Understand Basic Performance Impacts of Radio Signal Interference

This exercise helps you understand the impact that radio signal interference, such as interference from microwave ovens and cordless phones, has on the performance of a WLAN from a user perspective.

Perform the following steps:

Step 1. Identify sources of radio signal interference to test. For example, you might choose to test a microwave oven, cordless phone, Bluetooth headset, or any other devices that operate in the 2.4-GHz or 5-GHz bands.

Step 2. Configure a 2.4-GHz 802.11n wireless client device to test performance against a point located on the wired network. For example, you can run a throughput test from the client device against an online performance tester, such as the one at http://performance.toast.net. The main idea is to measure performance for comparison purposes as you test different sources of interference.

Step 3. Run a performance test with a client device configured with a 2.4-GHz radio (and associated with a 2.4-GHz 802.11n access point) within close proximity to the source of interference. This will give you an idea of the maximum impacts on performance because the interfering signals will be strongest. Perform the test with the interference active and inactive. For example, place the client device 1 or 2 feet away from a microwave oven and run the performance test while the microwave oven is on (maybe while heating a cup of water). Note the performance. With the microwave oven off, rerun the performance test and note the corresponding performance. Compare the two performance levels. How much did the interference degrade the performance?

Step 4. Repeat the performance tests with the applicable access point set to different RF channels. How does a different access point channel setting impact the performance when the interference is active and inactive? What changes do you see in baseline performance (when the interference is not present) among the different channels?

Step 5. Repeat the performance tests with the client device configured with a 5-GHz client radio and associated with a 5-GHz 802.11n access point. How does moving to the 5-GHz band impact the performance when the interference is active and inactive? What changes do you see in baseline performance when moving from the 2.4-GHz band to the 5-GHz band?

Step 6. Repeat the performance tests with the client device located farther away from the interference source. This will provide insight on more practical impacts on performance, based on areas where users would likely use the WLAN.

You might or might not notice any degradation in performance, depending on the part of the spectrum that the interference is present in relation to your access point channel. Probably the largest drop in performance will occur when testing a microwave oven within close range of a 2.4-GHz client device with the associated access point set to a channel that falls within the frequency range of the microwave oven. You will probably notice an increase in baseline performance when moving from the 2.4-GHz band to the 5-GHz band.

Note Before installing a WLAN, perform a thorough wireless site survey to fully understand the presence of radio signal interference. See Chapter 15, "Performing a Wireless Site Survey," for more on how to counteract radio signal interference.

Impacts of Multipath Propagation

Delays caused by multipath propagation result in the information symbols represented in the radio wave smearing (see Figure 4-12). This is often referred to as intersymbol interference (ISI). Because the shape of the signal conveys the information being transmitted, the receiver will make mistakes when demodulating the signal's information. If the delays are great enough, bit errors in the packet will occur, especially when data rates are high. The receiver will not be able to distinguish the symbols and interpret the corresponding bits correctly. When multipath strikes in this way, the receiving station must have an error-checking process to ensure that the data it receives is okay. WLANs employ a protocol that causes the source transceiver to retransmit the data if the destination transceiver detects errors in the data at the destination.

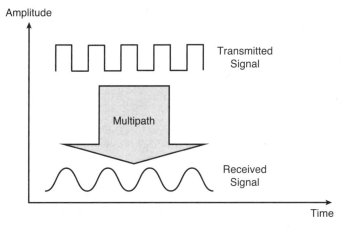

Figure 4-12 *Multipath Propagation Decreases the Quality of the Signal at the Receiver*

Because of retransmissions, users encounter lower performance when multipath is significant. For example, 802.11 signals in homes and offices might encounter 50 nanoseconds of multipath delay, while for users in a manufacturing plant it could be as high as 300 nanoseconds. Metal machinery and racks in a plant provide a lot of reflective surfaces that cause radio waves to bounce around and take erratic paths. As a result, be wary of multipath problems in warehouses, processing plants, and other areas full of irregular metal obstacles.

Wireless LAN manufacturers compensate for the effects of multipath propagation by using special processing techniques. For example, equalization and antenna diversity are methods for reducing the number of problems arising from multipath propagation. See Chapter 12 for more details on using diversity to combat multipath propagation.

Roaming Issues

An extremely beneficial aspect of Wi-Fi networks is mobility. For example, a person can walk through a facility while carrying on a conversation over a Wi-Fi phone or when downloading a large file from a server. The 802.11 radio inside the user device automatically roams from one access point to another, as needed, to provide seamless connectivity.

In general, wireless technologies provide access point roaming protocols. For example, with 802.11 networks, the client radio makes a decision to hand off to the next access point when retransmissions and received signal levels indicate a need to hand off. A decision to hand off too soon generally leads to skipping back and forth between access points. As a result, client radio manufacturers generally choose to dampen the handoff process and wait until it is absolutely necessary to hand off to the next access point.

Every model radio device behaves differently when roaming because of proprietary mechanisms, and some cards do better than others. Keep in mind that roaming might take much longer than expected with WLAN applications, especially wireless voice applications, which are not tolerant to roaming delays exceeding 150 milliseconds. The use of wireless middleware can also help accommodate patterns of broken communications between the client and the server caused by roaming delays.

Is Wi-Fi Roaming Really Seamless?

My consulting firm, Wireless-Nets, Ltd., has completed roaming testing to determine the impacts of handoffs between access points. We configured one 802.11n access point (AP-1) set to channel 1 in the 2.4-GHz band and the other access point (AP-2) set to channel 6 in the 2.4-GHz band. Other settings were default values, such as beacon interval of 100 milliseconds, RTS/CTS disabled, and so on. The access points were installed in a typical office facility in a manner that provided a minimum of 25 dB SNR throughout each access point's radio cell, with about 20 percent overlap between cells. The roaming client in this test was a laptop equipped with an internal 802.11n radio.

While standing with the wireless client within a few feet of AP-1, we used AirMagnet Laptop Analyzer (installed on the same laptop and interfacing with a separate 802.11 radio) to ensure that the laptop was associated with AP-1. We then initiated an FTP transfer of a large file from the server to the laptop and started measuring the 802.11 packet trace, using AirMagnet Analyzer. With the file downloading throughout the entire test, we walked toward AP-2 until we were within a few feet of it. With the packet trace, we were able to view the exchange of 802.11 frames, calculate the roaming delay, and see if there was any significant disruption to the FTP stream.

Once the client radio decided to re-associate, it issued several 802.11 disassociation frames to AP-1 to initiate the re-association process. The radio then broadcasted an 802.11 probe request to get responses from access points within range of the wireless client. This is done to ensure that the client radio has up-to-date information (beacon signal strength) of candidate access points prior to deciding which one to re-associate with. AP-2 responded with an 802.11 probe response. Because the only response was from AP-2, the client radio decided to associate with AP-2. As expected, the association process with AP-2 consisted of the exchange of 802.11 authentication and association frames (based on 802.11 open system authentication). See Chapter 6 for details on how these protocols work.

The re-association process took 68 milliseconds, which is the time between the client radio issuing the first dissociation frame to AP-1 and the client receiving the final association frame (response) from AP-2. This is quite good, and we have found similar values with other vendor access points. The entire roaming process, however, will interrupt wireless applications for a much longer period of time. For example, based on our tests, the FTP process halts an average of 5 seconds prior to the radio card initiating the re-association process (that is, issuing the first disassociation frame to AP-1). We measured 802.11 packet traces indicating that the client radio card re-retransmits data frames many times to AP-1 (because of weak signal levels) before giving up and initiating the re-association with AP-2. This substantial number of retransmissions disrupts the file download process, which makes the practical roaming delay in our tests an average of 5 seconds. Some cards roam better than others, so it is worthwhile to perform your own testing to fully understand the roaming of the client radios you plan to use on your network.

Note   See Chapter 11, "Range, Performance, and Roaming Considerations," for more on how to implement effective WLAN roaming.

Battery Limitations

When performing an inventory in a warehouse or caring for patients in a hospital, it is probably too cumbersome—if not impossible—to plug your mobile computer into an electrical outlet. Therefore, you will need to depend on the computer's battery. The extra load of the radio card in this situation can significantly decrease the amount of time available to operate the computer before needing to recharge the battery. The operating time, therefore, might decrease to less than an hour if the client device accesses the network often or performs other functions, such as printing.

To counter this problem, most vendors implement power management techniques in the client devices and radios. Without power management, radio-based wireless components normally remain in a receptive state, waiting for any information. For example, some vendors incorporate two modes to help conserve power:

- **Doze mode:** The doze mode, which is the default state of the product, keeps the radio off most of the time and wakes it up periodically to determine whether any messages await in a special mailbox. This mode alone generally uses approximately 50 percent less battery power.

- **Sleep mode:** The sleep mode causes the radio to remain in a transmit-only standby mode. In other words, the radio wakes up and sends information if necessary, but it is not capable of receiving any information.

Note   See Chapter 6 for details on how 802.11 power management protocols work.

When deploying wireless client devices, such as bar code scanners, for performing regular functions, such as inventory control, plan on installing battery recharge stations. When the client devices are not in use, the client devices can be left in the charging station. That way, they'll be ready to go when they are needed.

Interoperability Problems

Client cards and access points compliant with the 802.11n standard are backward compatible with the common 802.11 versions, such as 802.11a, 802.11b, and 802.11g. In addition, 802.11ac is backward compatible with 802.11n (5 GHz) and 802.11a. You will likely not have interoperability issues with the basic 802.11 functions, such as association and data transfer, especially if all the devices on your network have undergone successful Wi-Fi interoperability testing. An 802.11g client radio, for example, can associate with an 802.11n access point and enable a user to browse the Internet.

Even with standards, however, you still face interoperability issues. For example, proprietary enhancements generally do not work across multiple vendor devices. Vendor-specific enhancements to 802.11-compliant products often make interoperability questionable. For example, a vendor might include a special performance enhancement in its access points, but it will work only if you use the same vendor's client radios. To ensure interoperability with WLANs, it is best to implement client radios and access points (if possible) from the same vendor. You can implement multivendor WLANs successfully, but that reduces the WLAN features to the lowest common denominator, which is what the 802.11 standard specifies.

Note   To maximize interoperability, deploy WLAN components that have Wi-Fi certification.

Installation Issues

With wired networks, planning the installation of cabling is fairly straightforward. You can survey the site and look for routes where installers can run the cable. You can measure the distances and quickly determine whether cable runs are possible. If some users are too far away from the network, you can design a remote networking solution or extend the length of the cable by using repeaters. When the design is complete, installers can run the cables, and the cable plant almost always supports the transmission of data as planned.

A WLAN installation is not as predictable. It is difficult if not impossible to design a WLAN by merely inspecting the facility. Predicting the way in which the contour of the building will affect the propagation of radio waves is difficult. As Chapter 2, "Radio Wave Fundamentals," explains, omnidirectional antennas propagate radio waves in all directions if nothing gets in the way. Walls, ceilings, and other obstacles attenuate the signals more in some directions than others and even cause radio waves to change their paths of transmission. Even the opening of a bathroom door can change the propagation pattern. These events cause the actual radiation pattern to distort, taking on a jagged appearance, as shown in Figure 4-13.

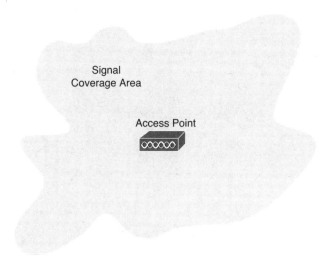

Figure 4-13 *The Radiation Pattern of an Omnidirectional Antenna Within an Office Building Is Irregular and Unpredictable*

To avoid installation problems, an organization should perform a thorough wireless site survey to assess the coverage of the network. Neglecting to do so might leave some users in a coverage hole without reliable connections to the network. Propagation tests give you the information necessary to plan optimum installation locations for access points, allowing coverage over required areas.

Note   For more on how to perform a wireless site survey, see Chapter 15.

Summary

As this chapter explains, you must consider certain implications when designing, installing, and supporting a WLAN. It is imperative that you consider security vulnerabilities, such as passive monitoring, unauthorized access, and denial-of-service (DoS) attacks. Encryption and authentication, respectively, are ways to counteract passive monitoring and unauthorized access. The threat of a DoS attack is a bit more difficult to resolve, and it makes sense to have a "Plan B" in case the WLAN becomes inoperable, especially for mission-critical applications. Irregular propagation of radio signals through a facility and radio signal interference, coming from microwave ovens, cordless phones, and other devices, are unforeseen things that can reduce the performance of the WLAN. As a result, it is important to perform a wireless site survey before installing a WLAN. As part of deploying a WLAN, you also need to consider and possibly test for other implications, such as multipath propagation, roaming delays, battery limitations, and interoperability problems.

Chapter 5

Introduction to IEEE 802.11 and Related Standards

This chapter will introduce you to:

- The Importance of Standards
- The IEEE 802 LAN Standards Family
- IEEE 802.11 Features

Before getting into the details of the 802.11 standard, you need to first understand the overall architecture of the 802.11 standard. This chapter explains basic functions of 802.11 and how it interacts with non-802.11-related protocols.

The Importance of Standards

Wireless LAN manufacturers and users in the early 1990s initially expected markets to dive head-first into implementing wireless networks. Markets did not respond as many had hoped they would, and flat sales growth of wireless networking components prevailed through most of the 1990s. Relatively low data rates, high prices, and especially the lack of standards kept many users from purchasing wireless forms of media. For those having applications suitable for lower data rates and enough cost savings to warrant purchasing relatively expensive solutions, the only choice before 1998 or so was to install proprietary hardware to satisfy WLAN requirements. In response to lacking standards, the Institute of Electrical and Electronics Engineers (IEEE) developed the first internationally recognized WLAN standard: IEEE 802.11.

Types of Standards

There are two main types of standards:

- **Official:** An official standard is published and known to the public, but it is controlled by an official standards organization, such as the IEEE. Government or industry consortiums normally sponsor official standards groups. Official standards organizations generally ensure coordination at both the international and domestic levels.

- **Public:** A public standard is similar to an official standard, except it is controlled by a private organization, such as the Wi-Fi Alliance or the Internet Engineering Task Force (IETF). Public standards, sometimes called de facto standards, are common practices and written specifications that have not been produced or accepted by an official standards organization. These standards, such as TCP/IP and Wi-Fi Protected Access (WPA), result from widespread proliferation. In some cases, public standards that proliferate, such as the original Ethernet, eventually pass through standards organizations and become official standards.

Companies should strive to adopt standards and recommended products within their organizations for all aspects of information systems. What type of standards should you use? For most cases, focus on the use of an official standard if one is available and proliferating. This will help ensure widespread acceptance and longevity of your wireless network implementation. If no official standard is suitable, a public standard would be a good choice. In fact, a public standard can often respond faster to changes in market needs because it usually has less organizational overhead for making changes. Be sure to avoid non-standard or proprietary system components unless no suitable standards are available.

Note   Some manufacturers of 802.11-compliant hardware implement numerous non-standard enhancements, such as automatic transmit power control. The corresponding products still provide connectivity as defined by the 802.11 standard, but these enhanced features are often realized only if using access points and client radios sold by the same manufacturer.

802.11 Versus Proprietary Standards

A large retail store based in Sacramento, California, needed to implement a wireless network to provide mobility within its 10 warehouses in northern California. The application called for clerks within a warehouse to use new handheld wireless data collectors to perform inventory management functions.

The company, which already had one vendor's data collection devices (we will call these Brand X), decided to use that vendor's Brand Y proprietary wireless data collectors and its proprietary wireless network. (The vendor did not offer an 802.11-compliant solution.) This decision eliminated the need to work with additional vendors for the new handheld devices and the wireless network.

A year passed after the installation, and enhancement requirements began to pour in for additional mobile appliances that were not available from the Brand X vendor. This forced the company to consider the purchase of new Brand Z appliances from a different vendor. The problem, though, was that the Brand Z appliances, which were 802.11 compliant, did not interoperate with the installed proprietary Brand Y wireless network. In addition, the Brand Y wireless network had no upgrade path to 802.11. Because of the cost associated with replacing its network with one that was 802.11 compliant, the company could not implement the new enhancement cost-effectively.

The company could have eliminated the problem of not being able to implement the new enhancement if it had implemented the initial system with 802.11-compliant network components, because most vendors offer products that are compatible with 802.11 but not with all the proprietary networks. This would have given the company the ability to consider multiple vendors for a wider selection of appliances.

Institute of Electrical and Electronics Engineers

The Institute of Electrical and Electronics Engineers (IEEE) is a nonprofit professional organization founded by a handful of engineers in 1884 for the purpose of consolidating ideas dealing with electrotechnology. The IEEE plays a significant role in publishing technical works, sponsoring conferences and seminars, accreditation, and standards development. With regard to LANs, the IEEE has produced some very popular and widely used standards. For example, the majority of LANs in the world use network interface devices based on the IEEE 802.3 (Ethernet) standards.

Before someone can develop an IEEE standard, he or she must submit a Project Authorization Request (PAR) to the IEEE Standards Board. If the board approves the PAR, IEEE establishes a working group to develop the standard. Members of the working groups serve voluntarily and without compensation, and they are not necessarily members of the institute. The working group begins by writing a draft standard and then submits the draft to a balloting group of selected IEEE members for review and approval. The ballot group consists of the standard's developers, potential users, and other people who have a general interest.

Before publication, the IEEE Standards Board performs a review of the Final Draft Standard and then considers approval of the standard. The resulting standard represents a consensus of broad expertise from within IEEE and other related organizations. All IEEE standards are reviewed at least once every five years for revision or reaffirmation.

Note   In May 1991, a group led by Victor Hayes submitted a PAR to IEEE to initiate the 802.11 Working Group. Hayes became chair of the working group and led the standards effort to its completion in June 1997.

Benefits of the 802.11 Standard

The many benefits of using standards such as those published by IEEE include the following:

- Appliance interoperability
- Fast product development
- Stable future migration
- Price reductions
- Avoiding silos

The following sections explain these benefits of standards compliance, especially as related to IEEE 802.11.

Appliance Interoperability

Compliance with the IEEE 802.11 standard makes possible interoperability between multiple vendor appliances and the chosen wireless network type. This means you can purchase an 802.11-compliant bar code scanner from one manufacturer and another one from a different manufacturer, and they will both interoperate within an 802.11 wireless network. Standards compliance increases price competition and enables companies to develop WLAN components with lower research and development costs. This enables a greater number of smaller companies to develop wireless components.

As shown in Figure 5-1, the interoperability of multiple brands of 802.11 devices prevents dependence on a single vendor for appliances. Without a standard, for example, a company having a non-standard proprietary network would be dependent on purchasing only appliances that operate on that particular network. With an 802.11-compliant wireless network, you can use any equivalent 802.11-compliant appliance. Because most vendors have migrated their products to 802.11, you have a much greater selection of appliances for 802.11-compliant networks.

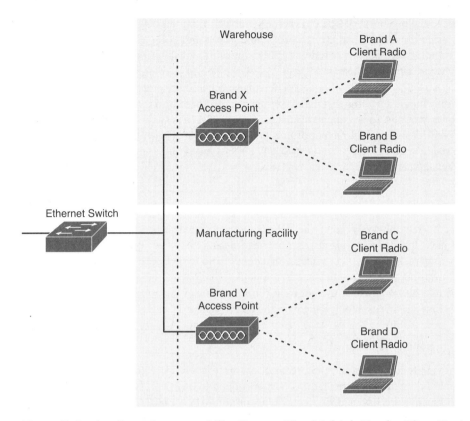

Figure 5-1 *Appliance Interoperability Ensures That Multiple Vendor Client Devices Will Communicate Over the Same Wireless LAN*

Fast Product Development

The 802.11 standard is a well-tested blueprint that product developers can use to implement wireless devices. The use of standards decreases the learning curve required to understand specific technologies because the standard-forming group has already invested time in smoothing out wrinkles in the implementation of the applicable technology. This leads to the development of products in much less time. Because standards generally mean longevity of a technology, integrated circuit manufacturers usually invest in the development of chips that support the standard technology. This has definitely been the case with 802.11.

Stable Future Migration

Compliance with standards helps protect investments that users put into their information systems; when choosing standards-compliant systems, users can avoid ending up with legacy systems that must be completely replaced in the future as proprietary products become obsolete. The evolution of WLANs has been occurring in a fashion similar to the evolution of 802.3 (Ethernet). Initially, Ethernet began as a 10-Mbps standard, using coaxial cable media. The IEEE 802.3 working group enhanced the standard over the years by adding twisted-pair cable, optical fiber cable, and 100-Mbps and 1000-Mbps data rates. Just as IEEE 802.3 did, the 802.11 Working Group recognizes the investments organizations make in network infrastructure and the importance of providing migration paths that maximize the installed base of hardware. It has already demonstrated this, for example, by ensuring that 802.11n is backward compatible with the past widespread deployment of 802.11b/g devices. 802.11 will likely continue offering a stable migration path from existing WLANs as even higher-performance wireless networking technologies become available.

Price Reductions

High costs have always plagued the WLAN industry; however, prices for WLAN components have dropped significantly as more vendors and users have complied with 802.11. One of the reasons for lower prices is that vendors no longer need to develop and support lower-quantity proprietary subcomponents, which helps them cut design, manufacturing, and support costs. Ethernet went through a similar lowering of prices as more and more companies began complying with the 802.3 standard.

Avoiding Silos

Over the past couple decades, IS organizations have had a difficult time maintaining control of network implementations. The introduction of PCs, LANs, and visual-based development tools has made it much easier for non-MIS organizations, such as manufacturing departments, to deploy their own applications. One part of a company, for example, might purchase a wireless network from one vendor, while another part of the company might buy a different wireless network. As a result, non-interoperable systems, called *silos*, appear within the company, making it very difficult for MIS personnel to plan and support compatible systems. Some people refer to these silos as *stovepipes*.

Acquisitions bring dissimilar systems together, too. One company with a proprietary system might purchase another company that has a different proprietary system, resulting in non-interoperability. For example, as Figure 5-1 illustrates, a company's warehouse might have 802.11-compliant Brand X access points with a mix of 802.11-compliant Brand A and Brand B client radios, and the company's manufacturing facility might have 802.11-compliant Brand Y access points with a mix of 802.11-compliant Brand C and Brand D client radios. All the wireless devices can interoperate because of compliance with the 802.11 standard, which minimizes the occurrence of silos.

Problems with Mixed Standards

A company located in Barcelona, Spain, specializes in the resale of women's clothes. This company, whose IS group has little control over the implementation of distributed networks in major parts of the company, has projects under way to implement wireless networks for an inventory application and a price-marking application.

Non-IS project managers located in different parts of the company lead these projects. They have little desire to coordinate their projects with IS because of past difficulties. As a result, the project managers end up implementing incompatible proprietary wireless networks to satisfy their networking requirements.

The project managers install two systems: one that covers the sales floor space of the 300 stores (for price marking) and one that encompasses 10 warehouses (for doing inventory functions). Even though the systems are not compatible, all is fine for the users operating the autonomous systems.

The problems with this system architecture, though, are the difficulty in providing operational support and inflexibility. The company must maintain purchasing and warranty contracts with two different wireless network vendors, service personnel need to acquire and maintain understanding of the operation of two networks, and the company cannot share appliances and wireless network components between the warehouses and the stores. As a result, the silos in this case make the networks more expensive to support and limit their flexibility in meeting future needs. The implementation of standard 802.11-compliant networks would have avoided these problems.

The IEEE 802 LAN Standards Family

The IEEE 802 Local and Metropolitan Area Network Standards Committee is a major working group chartered by IEEE to create, maintain, and encourage the use of IEEE and equivalent International Electrotechnical Commission/International Organization for Standardization (IEC/ISO) standards. The IEEE formed the committee in February 1980, and it meets as a plenary body at least three times per year. The IEEE 802 committee produces the series of standards known as IEEE 802.x, and the Joint Technical Committee (JTC) 1 series of equivalent standards is known as ISO 8802-nnn.

IEEE 802 includes a family of standards, as depicted in Figure 5-2, which fits within the lower layers of the Open Systems Interconnection (OSI) reference model. The MAC and physical layers of the 802 standard were organized into a separate set of standards from the logical link control (LLC) layer because of the interdependence between medium access control, medium, and topology. 802.3 and 802.11 are examples of 802 data link and physical layers. There are other 802.x standards, too, such as 802.15 and 802.16, that Figure 5-2 does not depict.

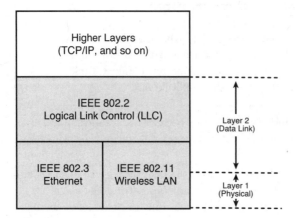

Figure 5-2   *The IEEE 802 Family of Standards Falls Within the Scope of Layers 1 and 2 of the OSI Reference Model*

Note   To review the OSI reference model, refer to www.itu.int/rec/T-REC-X.200-199407-I/en.

Note   Visit the IEEE 802 LAN/MAN Standards Committee website at www.ieee802.org for more information on 802 LAN standards.

In a logical sense, WLANs provide functionality that corresponds to layer 1 (physical layer) and layer 2 (data link layer) of the OSI reference model. Figure 5-3 illustrates the logical architecture of 802.11. 802.11 WLANs define a portion of the data link layer—the MAC sublayer—that interacts with the IEEE 802.2 logical link control (LLC) layer. There are several different 802.11 physical layers, such as 802.11, 802.11b, 802.11g, 802.11n, and 802.11ac. Some of the 802.11 physical layers, such as the original 802.11 direct-sequence and frequency-hopping spread spectrum, are not shown in Figure 5-3.

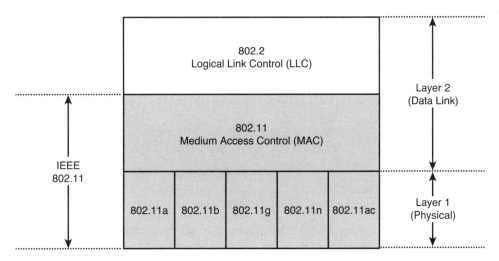

Figure 5-3 *A Wireless LAN Provides Functions Related to the Data Link and Physical Layers of a Network's Architecture*

802.11 MAC Sublayer

The 802.11 MAC sublayer resides within the data link layer and enables multiple client devices (also referred to as stations) to share the common air transmission medium via a carrier sense protocol. This protocol coordinates access to the common medium so that the stations can share the same frequency and space in the radio spectrum. In addition, MAC functions provide reliable delivery of data over the somewhat error-prone wireless medium.

As an analogy, consider a room of people engaged in a single conversation in which each person can hear if someone speaks. This represents a fully connected bus topology, where everyone communicates using the same frequency (audio voice) and space (the room). To avoid having two people speak at the same time, a person wanting to say something must (or should) wait until another person has finished talking. This simple protocol ensures that only one person speaks at a time, offering a shared use of the communications medium. 802.11 WLANs operate in a similar fashion, except the communications are by way of radio wave signals. A station wanting to transmit data first senses the medium, and if idle, might go ahead and transmit the data, depending on additional rules that 802.11 defines, as explained in Chapter 6, "IEEE 802.11 Medium Access Control (MAC) Layer." If the medium is busy (which indicates that another station is transmitting), the station holds off transmission. This protocol is referred to as carrier sense multiple access (CSMA).

802.11 WLANs handle error control by having each station check incoming data for altered bits. If the destination station does not detect errors, it sends an acknowledgement back to the source station. If the station detects errors, the data link protocol ensures that the source station re-sends the packet. To continue the analogy, consider two people talking to each other outside. If one person is speaking and a disruption occurs, such as a plane flying overhead, the dialog might become distorted. As a result, the listener asks the speaker to repeat a phrase or two.

Because of propagation delays, it is possible that two wireless stations might sense that the medium is not busy and both begin transmitting. This is similar to two people starting to talk at the same time. They sense that no one is talking, and they both start speaking at the same time. In that case, each person will generally stop talking, wait for a short period of time, and then start talking again, with hopes of avoiding another collision. 802.11 WLANs follow a similar process for mediating transmission collisions.

Note   To learn more about the 802.11 MAC layer, see Chapter 6.

802.11 Physical Layer

Generally speaking, a physical (PHY) layer of a network provides for the transmission of bits through a communications channel. This includes all specifications needed for defining the physical composition of the signals that are sent through the wireless network. For example, the 802.11 PHY layer defines modulation types, frequencies, and signal synchronization procedures. The 802.11 standard includes a different PHY layer specification for each of the WLAN types (that is, 802.11a, 802.11b, 802.11g, 802.11n, and 802.11ac). All these PHY layers share common MAC sublayer functions.

Note   For details on the 802.11 PHY layers, see Chapter 7, "IEEE 802.11 Physical (PHY) Layers."

IEEE 802.2

The LLC is the highest layer of the IEEE 802 OSI reference model and provides functions similar to the traditional data link control protocol: High-Level Data Link Control (HDLC). ISO/IEC 8802-2 (ANSI/IEEE Standard 802.2), dated May 7, 1998, specifies the LLC. The purpose of the LLC is to exchange data between end users across a LAN using an 802-based MAC controlled link. The LLC provides addressing and data link control, and it is independent of the topology, transmission medium, and medium access control technique chosen.

Higher layers, such as TCP/IP, pass user data down to the LLC, expecting error-free transmission across the network. The LLC in turn appends a control header, creating an LLC protocol data unit (PDU). The LLC uses the control information in the operation of the LLC protocol. Before transmission, the LLC PDU is handed down through the MAC service access point (SAP) to the MAC layer, which appends control information at the beginning and end of the packet, forming a MAC frame. The control information in the frame is needed for the operation of the MAC protocol.

The LLC provides the following three services for a network layer protocol:

- Unacknowledged connectionless service

- Connection-oriented service

- Acknowledged connectionless service

These services apply to the communication between peer LLC layers (that is, one located on the source station and one located on the destination station). Typically, vendors provide these services as options that a designer can select when writing drivers for the equipment.

All three LLC protocols employ the same PDU format that consists of four fields, as illustrated in Figure 5-4.

8 Bits	8 Bits	8 bits	Variable
Destination SAP	Service SAP	Control	Data

Figure 5-4   *The LLC PDU Consists of Data Fields That Provide the LLC Functionality*

The destination service access point (DSAP) and source service access point (SSAP) fields each contain addresses that specify the destination and source stations of the peer LLCs. One bit of the DSAP indicates whether the PDU is intended for an individual station or a group of stations. One bit of the SSAP indicates whether it is a command or response PDU.

The format of the LLC control field is identical to that of HDLC, using extended sequence numbers. The control field has bits that indicate whether the frame is one of the following types:

- **Information:** Carries user data
- **Supervisory:** Flow control and error control
- **Unnumbered:** Various protocol control PDUs

The data field contains the information from higher-layer protocols that the LLC is transporting to the destination.

Unacknowledged Connectionless Service

The unacknowledged connectionless service is a datagram-style service that does not involve any error-control or flow-control mechanisms. This service does not involve the establishment of a data link layer connection (such as between peer LLCs). This service supports individual, multicast, and broadcast addressing. This service simply sends and receives LLC PDUs, with no acknowledgement of delivery. Because the delivery of data is not guaranteed, a higher layer, such as TCP, must deal with reliability issues.

The unacknowledged connectionless service offers advantages in the following situations:

- If higher layers of the protocol stack provide the necessary reliability and flow-control mechanisms, it would be inefficient to duplicate them in the LLC. In this case, the unacknowledged connectionless service would be appropriate. TCP and the ISO transport protocol, for example, already provide the mechanisms necessary for reliable delivery.

■ It is not always necessary to provide feedback pertaining to successful delivery of information. The overhead of connection establishment and maintenance can be inefficient for applications involving the periodic sampling of data sources, such as monitoring sensors. The unacknowledged connectionless service would best satisfy these requirements.

Using Unacknowledged Connectionless Service to Minimize Overhead

The executive office building of a high-rent advertising agency in southern California has 20 sensors to monitor temperatures throughout its building for input to the heating and air-conditioning system. These sensors send short information packets every minute to an application on a centralized server that updates a temperature table in a database. The heating and air-conditioning system uses this information to control the temperature in different parts of the building.

For this application, the server does not need to acknowledge the receipt of every sensor transmission because the information updates are not critical. The system can maintain a comfortable temperature throughout the building even if the system misses a temperature update from time to time.

In addition, it is not feasible to require the sensors to establish connections with the server to send the short information packets. As a result, designers of the system chose to use the LLC unacknowledged connectionless service to minimize overhead on the network, making the limited wireless network bandwidth available to other applications.

Connection-Oriented Service

The connection-oriented service establishes a logical connection that provides flow control and error control between two stations that need to exchange data. This service involves the establishment of a connection between peer LLCs by performing connection establishment, data transfer, and connection termination functions. The service can connect only two stations; therefore, it does not support multicast or broadcast modes. The connection-oriented service offers advantages mainly if higher layers of the protocol stack do not provide the necessary reliability and flow-control mechanisms, which is generally the case with terminal controllers.

Flow control is a protocol feature that ensures that a transmitting station does not overwhelm a receiving station with data. With flow control, each station allocates a finite amount of memory and buffer resources to storing sent and received PDUs.

Networks, especially wireless networks, suffer from induced noise in the links between network stations that can cause transmission errors. If the noise is high enough in amplitude, it causes errors in digital transmission in the form of altered bits. This will lead to inaccuracy of the transmitted data, and the receiving network device may misinterpret the meaning of the information.

The noise that causes most problems with networks is impulse noise, which is characterized by long quiet intervals followed by high-amplitude bursts. This noise results from lightning and switching transients (such as microwave ovens). Impulse noise is responsible for most errors in digital communication systems and generally provokes errors that occur in bursts.

To guard against transmission errors, the connection-oriented and acknowledged-connectionless LLCs use error control mechanisms that detect and correct errors that occur in the transmission of PDUs. The LLC Automatic Repeat Request (ARQ) mechanism recognizes the possibility of two types of errors:

- **Lost PDU:** A PDU fails to arrive at the other end or is damaged beyond recognition.

- **Damaged PDU:** A PDU arrives, but some bits are altered.

When a frame arrives at a receiving station, the station checks whether there are any errors present by using a cyclic redundancy check (CRC) error detection algorithm. In general, the receiving station will send back a positive or negative acknowledgement, depending on the outcome of the error detection process. In case the acknowledgement is lost en route to the sending station, the sending station will retransmit the frame after a certain period of time. This process is often referred to as ARQ.

Overall, ARQ is best for the correction of burst errors because this type of impairment occurs in a small percentage of frames, thus not invoking many retransmissions. Because of the feedback inherent in ARQ protocols, the transmission links must accommodate half-duplex or full-duplex transmissions. If only simplex links are available because of feasibility, it is impossible to use the ARQ technique because the receiver would not be able to notify the transmitter of bad data frames.

Note   When single-bit errors predominate or when only a simplex link is available, a forward error correction (FEC) algorithm and associated processing can provide error correction. FEC algorithms provide enough redundancy in data transmissions to enable the receiving station to correct errors without needing the sending station to retransmit the data.

The two approaches for retransmitting unsatisfactory blocks of data using ARQ are continuous ARQ and stop-and-wait ARQ, as described in more detail in the sections that follow.

Continuous ARQ

With continuous ARQ, often called a sliding window protocol, the sending station transmits frames continuously until the receiving station detects an error. The sending station is usually capable of transmitting a specific number of frames and maintains a table indicating which frames have been sent.

The system implementer can set the number of frames sent before stopping via configuration parameters of the network device. If a receiver detects a bad frame, it will send a negative acknowledgement back to the sending station, requesting that the bad frame be sent again. When the transmitting station gets the signal to retransmit the frame, several subsequent frames may have already been sent (because of propagation delays between the sender and receiver); therefore, the transmitter must go back and retransmit the bad data frame.

There are a couple ways the transmitting station can send frames again using continuous ARQ:

- **Go-back-*n* technique:** The source retrieves the bad frame from the transmit buffer and sends it and all frames following it. A problem is that when *n* (the number of frames the transmitter sent after the bad frame plus 1) becomes large, the method becomes inefficient because the retransmission of just one frame means that a large number of possibly good frames will also be re-sent, thus decreasing throughput.

  The go-back-*n* technique is useful in applications where receiver buffer space is limited because all that is needed is a receiver window size of one (assuming that frames are to be delivered in order). When the receive node rejects a bad frame (that is, sends a negative acknowledgement), it does not need to buffer any subsequent frames for possible reordering while it is waiting for the retransmission because all subsequent frames will also be sent.

- **Selective repeat:** The selective repeat method selectively retransmits only the bad frame and then resumes normal transmission at the point just before getting the notification of a bad frame. It is obviously better than continuous go-back-*n* in terms of throughput because only a bad frame needs retransmission. With this technique, however, the receiver must be capable of storing several frames if the frames are to be processed in order. The receiver needs to buffer data that has been received after a bad frame was requested for retransmission since only the damaged frame will be sent again.

Stop-and-Wait ARQ

With the stop-and-wait ARQ method, the sending station transmits a frame and then stops and waits for some type of acknowledgement from the receiver on whether a particular frame was acceptable. If the receiving station sends a negative acknowledgement, the frame will be sent again. The transmitter will send the next frame only after it receives a positive acknowledgement from the receiver.

An advantage of stop-and-wait ARQ is that it does not require much buffer space at the sending station or receiving station. The sending station needs to store only the current transmitted frame. However, stop-and-wait ARQ becomes inefficient as the propagation delay between source and destination becomes large. For example, data sent on satellite links normally experiences a round-trip delay of several hundred milliseconds; therefore, long block lengths are necessary to maintain a reasonably effective data rate. The trouble is that with longer frames, the probability of an error occurring in a particular block is greater. Thus, retransmission occurs often, and the resulting throughput is lower.

Using ARQ to Reduce Errors

A mobile home manufacturer in Florida uses robots on an assembly line to perform welding. Designers of the robot control system had to decide whether to use ARQ or FEC for controlling transmission errors between the server and the robots. The company experiences a great deal of impulse noise from arc welders and other heavy machinery.

In the midst of this somewhat hostile environment, the robots require error-free information updates to ensure that they function correctly. Designers of the system quickly ruled out the use of FEC because of the likely presence of burst errors due to impulse noise. ARQ, with its capability to detect and correct frames having lots of bit errors, was obviously the best choice.

Acknowledged Connectionless Service

As with the unacknowledged connectionless service, the acknowledged connectionless service does not involve the establishment of a logical connection with the distant station. But the receiving stations with the acknowledged version do confirm successful delivery of datagrams. Flow and error control is handled through use of the stop-and-wait ARQ method.

The acknowledged connectionless service is useful in several applications. The connection-oriented service must maintain a table for each active connection for tracking the status of the connection. If the application calls for guaranteed delivery, but a large number of destinations need to receive the data, then the connection-oriented service may be impractical because of the large number of tables required. Examples that fit this scenario include process control and automated factory environments that require a central site to communicate with a large number of processors and programmable controllers. In addition, the handling of important and time-critical alarm or emergency control signals in a factory would also fit this case. In all these examples, the sending station needs an acknowledgement to ensure successful delivery of the data; however, the urgency of transmission cannot wait for a connection to be established.

Note   A company that has a requirement to send information to multiple devices needing positive acknowledgement of the data transfer can use the acknowledged connectionless LLC service. For example, a marina might find it beneficial to control the power to different parts of the boat dock via a wireless network. Of course, the expense of a wireless network might not be justifiable for this application alone.

Other applications, such as supporting data transfers back and forth between cash registers and gas pumps and the use of data collection equipment for inventorying rental equipment, can share the wireless network to make a more positive business case. For shutting off the power on the boat dock, the application would need to send a message to the multiple power controllers and then expect an acknowledgement to ensure that the controller receives the notification and that the power is shut off. For this case, the connectionless (rather than connection-oriented) transfer makes sense because it would not be feasible to make connections to the controllers to support such a short message.

IEEE 802.11 Features

The initial 802.11 PAR states that "the scope of the proposed [WLAN] standard is to develop a specification for wireless connectivity for fixed, portable, and moving stations within a local area." The PAR further says that "the purpose of the standard is to provide wireless connectivity to automatic machinery and equipment or stations that require rapid deployment, which may be portable, handheld, or which may be mounted on moving vehicles within a local area."

The resulting standard, which is officially called "IEEE Standard for Wireless LAN Medium Access (MAC) and Physical Layer (PHY) Specifications," defines over-the-air protocols necessary to support networking in a local area. As with other IEEE 802–based standards (such as 802.3, Ethernet), the primary service of the 802.11 standard is to deliver MAC service data units (MSDUs) between peer LLCs. Typically, a radio device and access point provide functions of the 802.11 standard.

Note   To download the IEEE 802.11 standard, go to http://standards.ieee.org/getieee802/802.11.html.

The 802.11 standard provides MAC and PHY (physical layer) functionality for wireless connectivity of fixed, portable, and moving stations moving at pedestrian and vehicular speeds within a local area. Specific features of the 802.11 standard include the following:

- Support for asynchronous and time-bounded delivery services

- Continuity of service within extended areas via a distribution system, such as Ethernet

- Accommodation of multiple high-speed transmission

- Prioritized delivery of information based on differing quality of service requirements

- Multicast (including broadcast) services

- Network management services

- Authentication and encryption services

- Backward compatibility with legacy 802.11 WLANs (for example, 802.11b and 802.11g)

Target environments for use of the standard include the following:

- Inside buildings, such as offices, banks, shops, malls, hospitals, manufacturing plants, and residences

- Outdoor areas, such as parking lots, campuses, building complexes, and outdoor plants

The 802.11 standard takes into account the following significant differences between wired LANs and WLANs:

■ **Security mechanisms:** Because wireless LANs transmit signals over much larger areas than LANs using wired media, WLANs, in terms of privacy, require protecting a much larger area. Thus, 802.11 implements a variety of encryption and authentication methods.

■ **Bandwidth efficiency methods:** Radio frequency spectrum offers limited bandwidth for sending signals as compared to the metallic and optical fiber cabling that Ethernet uses. As a result, the 802.11 MAC and PHY layers must implement specialized functions for making transmissions as efficient as possible.

■ **Power management:** Because 802.11 radios are installed in smaller handheld devices that have limited battery power, 802.11 includes options for activating a power save mode that conserves battery power.

The 802.11 standard defines services that provide the functions that the LLC layer requires for sending MSDUs between two entities on the network. These services, which the MAC layer implements, fall into two categories:

■ **Station services:** These include authentication, deauthentication, privacy, and MSDU delivery.

■ **Distribution system services:** These include association, disassociation, distribution, integration, and re-association.

The following sections define the station and distribution system services.

Station Services

The 802.11 standard defines services for providing functions among stations. A station might be within any wireless element on the network, such as a handheld PC or handheld scanner. Each of these client devices might have more than one station. In addition, all access points implement station services. To provide necessary functionality, these stations need to send and receive MSDUs and implement adequate levels of security.

Authentication

Because WLANs have limited physical security to prevent unauthorized access, 802.11 defines authentication services to control LAN access to a level equal to a wired link. Every 802.11 station, whether part of an independent basic service set (BSS) or an extended service set (ESS) network, must use the authentication service prior to establishing a connection (referred to as an *association*, in 802.11 terms) with another station with which it will communicate. Stations performing authentication send a unicast management authentication frame to the corresponding station.

Deauthentication

When a station wants to disassociate from another station, it invokes the deauthentication service. Deauthentication is a notification and cannot be refused. A station performs deauthentication by sending a deauthentication management frame to the station it wants to terminate authentication.

Privacy

With a wireless network, all stations and other devices can hear data traffic taking place within range on the network, seriously affecting the security level of a wireless link. IEEE 802.11 counters this problem by offering a privacy service option (that is, encryption) that raises the security level of the 802.11 network to that of a wired network.

> **Note**   See Chapter 6 for more information about how 802.11 provides various services.

Distribution System Services

Distribution system services, as defined by 802.11, provide functionality across a distribution system. Access points provide distribution system services. The following sections describe the services that distribution systems need in order to provide proper transfer of MSDUs.

Association

Each station must initially invoke the association service with an access point before it can send information through a distribution system. The association maps a station to the distribution system via an access point. Each station can associate with only a single access point, but each access point can associate with multiple stations. Association is also a first step to providing the capability for a station to be mobile between BSSs.

Disassociation

A station or an access point may invoke the disassociation service to terminate an existing association. This service is a notification; therefore, neither party may refuse termination. Stations should disassociate when leaving the network. An access point, for example, might disassociate all its stations if being removed for maintenance.

Distribution

A station uses the distribution service every time it sends MAC frames across a distribution system. The 802.11 standard does not specify how the distribution system delivers the data. The distribution service provides the distribution system with only enough information to determine the proper destination BSS.

Integration

The integration service enables the delivery of MAC frames through a portal between a distribution system and a non-802.11 LAN. The integration function performs all required media or address space translations. The details of an integration function depend on the distribution system implementation and are beyond the scope of the 802.11 standard.

Re-association

The re-association service enables a station to change its current state of association. Re-association provides additional functionality to support BSS-transition mobility for associated stations. The re-association service enables a station to change its association from one access point to another. This keeps the distribution system informed of the current mapping between access point and station as the station moves from one BSS to another within an ESS. Re-association also enables changing association attributes of an established association while the station remains associated with the same access point. The mobile station always initiates the re-association service.

Station States and Corresponding Frame Types

The state existing between a source and destination station (see Figure 5-5) governs which IEEE 802.11 frame types the two stations can exchange.

The following types of functions can occur within each class of frame:

- Class 1 frames:

Control frames:

- Request-to-send (RTS)

- Clear-to-send (CTS)

- Acknowledgement (ACK)

- Contention-free (CF)

Management frames:

- Probe request/response

- Beacon

- Authentication

- Deauthentication

- Announcement traffic indication message (ATIM)

Data frames

- Class 2 frames:

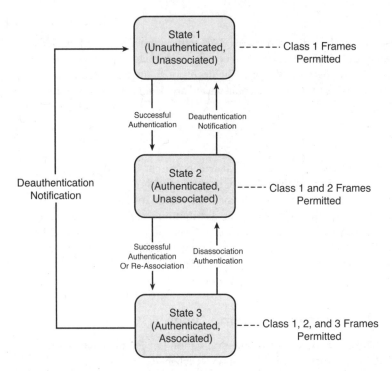

Figure 5-5 *The Operation of an 802.11 Station Depends on Its Particular State*

Management frames:

- Association request/response

- Re-association request/response

- Disassociation

- Class 3 frames:

Data frames

Management frames:

- Deauthentication

Control frames:

- Power Save Poll

To keep track of station state, each station maintains two state variables:

- **Authentication state:** Can have a value of unauthenticated and authenticated.

- **Association state:** Can have a value of unassociated and associated.

Note   Keep up-to-date on the IEEE 802.11 Working Group activities by periodically visiting its website at www.ieee802.org/11/.

Summary

As mentioned in this chapter, the 802.11 WLAN standard certainly has benefits that an organization should consider when selecting components that provide LAN mobility. IEEE 802 is a solid family of standards that will provide much greater multiple-level interoperability than proprietary systems. The 802.11 standard has the backing of IEEE, which has an excellent track record of developing long-lasting standards, such as IEEE 802.3 (Ethernet) and earlier versions of 802.11.

Chapter 6

IEEE 802.11 Medium Access Control (MAC) Layer

This chapter will introduce you to:

- Primary 802.11 MAC Layer Functions
- Connectivity
- Timing and Synchronization
- 802.11 MAC Frame Structures
- MAC Frame Types
- Interoperability

To design and implement an effective wireless LAN (WLAN), it is important to have a good understanding of the operation of the 802.11 MAC layer. The description of the MAC layer in the 802.11 standard is rather lengthy and focuses on details that developers must know when designing and implementing 802.11 radios; however, it is not necessary that those deploying wireless LANs understand all the fine points. This chapter explains the parts of the 802.11 standard that you need to know to configure and troubleshoot 802.11n and 802.11ac WLANs.

Primary 802.11 MAC Layer Functions

The 802.11 standard specifies a common Medium Access Control (MAC) layer, which provides a variety of functions that support the operation of 802.11-based WLANs. In general, the MAC layer manages and maintains communications between 802.11 stations (client radios and access points) by coordinating access to a shared radio channel and using protocols that enhance communications over a wireless medium. Often viewed as the "brains" of the network, the 802.11 MAC layer interfaces with a specific 802.11 physical (PHY) layer, such as 802.11a, 802.11b, 802.11g, 802.11n, or 802.11ac, to perform the tasks of carrier sensing, transmission, and receiving of 802.11 frames. (See Chapter 7, "IEEE 802.11 Physical (PHY) Layers," for details.)

The MAC layer provides the following main functions:

- **Data delivery:** The delivery of data between stations is the primary function of the MAC layer. This includes medium access, exchange of data frames, error recovery, frame aggregation, fragmentation, quality of service (QoS), encryption, and multicasting.

- **Connectivity:** Before an 802.11 station can send and receive data, it must connect to the network. This includes scanning for an available network and authenticating and associating with the network.

- **Timing and synchronization:** Because of the sharing of the wireless medium, 802.11 stations must adhere to strict timing and synchronization rules.

- **Power management:** 802.11 power saving functions enable mobile 802.11 client devices to conserve power and increase battery longevity.

The sections that follow describe these functions.

Data Delivery

With 802.11, there are several types of frames—management, control, and data (see Table 6-1)—differentiated by the Type field located in the control field of every frame. 802.11 stations send and receive data from higher layers—such as e-mail messages, voice packets, and website transactions—in 802.11 data frames, as shown in Figure 6-1. Multiple data frames are usually necessary to carry all the data that a particular application is sending.

Table 6-1   *Type Field Bit Specification*

bit3	bit2	Frame Type
0	0	Management frame
0	1	Control frame
1	0	Data frame
1	1	Reserved

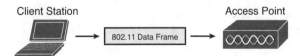

Figure 6-1   *802.11 Data Frames Carry Higher-Layer Data Between 802.11 Stations*

Note 802.11 exchanges data between stations in frames, which have a specific format for carrying information from higher layers, as well as 802.11 management and control data. For a description of different types of 802.11 frames, see the sections "MAC Frame Structures" and "MAC Frame Types," later in this chapter.

In 802.11 terminology (and in relation to the MAC layer), the payload of an 802.11 data frame is referred to as a *MAC service data unit* (*MSDU*), which is the information handed down to the MAC layer from the logical link control (LLC) layer. This is part of the layering process that takes place with communications protocols. For example, the MSDU may be an LLC information frame carrying a voice packet. The complete MAC layer frame, which includes header, frame body (payload), and FCS (frame check sequence) fields, is what 802.11 refers to as a *MAC protocol data unit* (*MPDU*). Figure 6-2 shows the distinction between the MSDU and MPDU. This terminology might not seem important to know, but it is necessary as the basis for understanding other functions, such as frame aggregation and 802.11 physical layer operations. The 802.11 physical layer, for instance, wraps the MPDU with an additional header (see Chapter 7 for more information).

Figure 6-2 *Distinction Between MSDUs and MPDUs*

Medium Access

Because multiple stations share the wireless medium, 802.11 has strict rules for stations accessing the medium. These rules apply to the transmission of all types of 802.11 frames, including data frames, control frames, and management frames.

The following are different types of medium access that 802.11 specifies:

■ **Distributed coordination function (DCF):** The DCF access method is part of the original 802.11 standard and uses a carrier sensing access method similar to Ethernet that provides distributed asynchronous (unpredictable) access to the medium.

■ **Point coordination function (PCF):** The PCF access method is also part of the original 802.11 standard, but it implements a polling function that determines when a specific client station can transmit. As a result, PCF provides synchronous (predictable) access to the medium, which supports time-bounded delivery of information. Very few vendors implemented PCF, so it is not described in this book.

■ **Hybrid coordination function (HCF):** The HCF access method was introduced to the 802.11 standard through the 802.11e amendment as an enhancement to the original DCF and PCF in order to support QoS needs.

Distributed Coordination Function

The DCF access method implements carrier sense multiple access with collision avoidance (CSMA/CA), a contention-based protocol similar to IEEE 802.3 Ethernet that requires stations to decide on their own when to access the medium, based on the presence or absence of traffic. Think of this process of accessing the medium as a meeting where everyone is polite and each person speaks only when no one else is talking. The DCF is a mandatory medium access protocol that was introduced in the original 802.11 specification. As a result, it is part of all 802.11 networks.

The DCF uses a combination of physical and virtual carrier-sense mechanisms to determine whether the medium is busy or idle. If both physical and virtual mechanisms indicate an idle medium, the station can transmit data. If not, the station must wait. Figure 6-3 illustrates the DCF process. The PHY layer provides a physical means of sensing the channel. The result of the physical channel assessment from the PHY layer is sent to the MAC layer as part of the information in deciding the status of the channel.

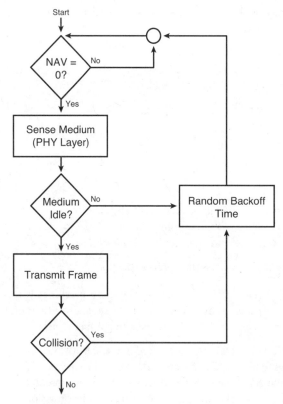

Figure 6-3 *Flowchart Illustrating the Operation of the Distributed Coordination Function*

The MAC layer carries out the virtual carrier sense protocol based on reservation information found in the Duration field of all frames. This information announces (to all other stations) a station's impending use of the medium. The MAC layer monitors the Duration field in all MAC frames and places this information in the station's NAV (network allocation vector) if the value is greater than the current NAV value. The NAV operates like a timer, starting with a value equal to the Duration field value of the last frame transmission sensed on the medium and counting down to zero.

As a condition to accessing the medium, the MAC layer checks the value of its NAV. If the NAV equals zero and the PHY layer indicates a clear channel (that is, received signal strength indication [RSSI] is below a specific threshold), the station can transmit a frame. Just before sending a frame, a station calculates the amount of time necessary to send the frame, based on the frame's length and data rate. The station places a value representing this time in the Duration field in the header of the frame. This process reserves the medium for the sending station because the Duration field causes the MAC layers in other stations to hold off transmissions until the sending station is done sending its frame.

An important aspect of the DCF is a random backoff time for which a station must wait if it detects a busy medium. If the channel is in use, the station must wait a random period of time before attempting to access the medium. Thus, if the PHY layer indicates that the medium is not clear (that is, the RSSI threshold is above a specific threshold), the MAC layer implements a backoff algorithm, regardless of the status of the NAV. This avoids the probability of collisions among stations waiting to transmit. The period of time immediately following a busy medium is when the highest probability of collisions occurs, especially under high utilization. Multiple stations may be waiting for the medium to become idle and will attempt to transmit at the same time. Once the medium is idle, a random backoff time defers each station a different amount of time, causing stations to wait different periods of time before transmitting a frame, minimizing the chance that stations will collide.

In addition to implementing a backoff for busy medium indications, stations use the same backoff mechanism when retransmitting frames due to transmission errors. Under low utilization, stations are not forced to wait very long before transmitting their frames. If the utilization of the network is high, the protocol holds back stations for longer period of times to avoid the probability of multiple stations transmitting at the same time.

Hybrid Coordination Function

The HCF includes two medium access methods: Enhanced Distributed Channel Access (EDCA), which is an extension of DCF for accommodating multiple priority levels, and HCF Controlled Channel Access (HCCA), which is based on PCF for providing time-bounded delivery of information.

Enhanced Distributed Channel Access (EDCA)

The 802.11e amendment extended the original 802.11 DCF by defining multiple queues, with each queue pertaining to a different access category/priority (see Figure 6-4). Each queue has an EDCA function (EDCAF) that determines when a frame in a respective queue can be transmitted (in addition to the access methods defined for DCF). This time is represented as an interval referred to in the 802.11 standard as the Arbitration Interframe Space (AIFS). Each queue has a different AIFS, with the higher-priority queues having a shorter AIFS and the lower-priority queues having a longer AIFS. As a result, the higher-priority traffic is permitted to transmit before lower-priority traffic.

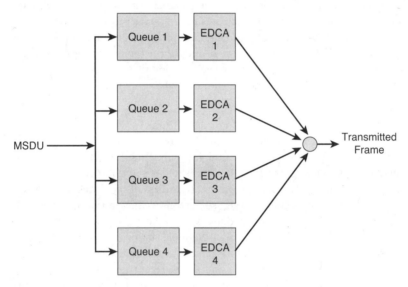

Figure 6-4   *Multiple Queues with Separate EDCA Functions*

HCF Controlled Channel Access (HCCA)

HCCA is a method that 802.11 specifies for priority-based, contention-free access to the medium. The 802.11e amendment to the 802.11 standard introduced HCCA, which includes enhancements to the PCF that was part of the original 802.11 standard (but very few vendors implemented actual products based on PCF).

With HCCA, the access point includes a hybrid coordinator (HC) that controls the transmission of frames from stations (see Figure 6-5). Instead of competing for access to the medium, all stations obey the HC during what is referred to as the *contention-free period*, which is when the HCCA is valid. A client station must receive a poll from the HC before the client station can send a data frame. For example, in Figure 6-5, Client Station A can send a data frame after receiving the poll from the HC. All other stations will refrain from sending frames until they receive a poll from the HC. For WLANs

implementing HCCA, there is an alternation of the contention-free period and a contention period. Stations use DCF during the contention-free period and the HCCA during
the contention period. This allows some stations to have asynchronous access to the
medium while minimizing the overhead of polls from the HC (that is, contention period)
and priority access to the medium at the expense of additional overhead to implement
the HCCA protocol (that is, contention-free period). This is essentially how PCF works.

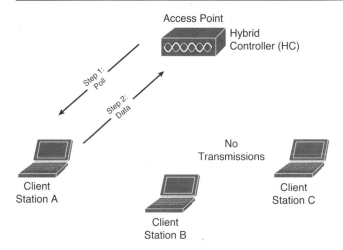

Figure 6-5 *Operation of the HCCA Protocol*

The HC, however, can also poll stations during both the contention-free period and the
contention period to reduce latency of higher-priority data transfers. This is different
from the original PCF, which allowed polling to occur only during the contention-free
period. Also, each station with HCCA can send multiple data frames for each HC poll
instead of only sending a single frame as with PCF.

Error Recovery

Because of transmission impairments, 802.11 frames can become corrupted. For example,
a station may send a data frame and, while it is en route, strong signals from a nearby
microwave oven may alter the bits in the frame. Or two stations may transmit at the same
time, despite 802.11's attempt to keep collisions from happening via the random backoff
time. Because of these problems, the MAC layer includes error recovery mechanisms.

Data Frame Acknowledgements

To recover from these situations, the 802.11 protocols incorporate the use of an
Acknowledgement (ACK) frame and Block ACK frame, as shown in Figure 6-6. If a destination station receives a directed (unicast) data frame without errors, the destination
station always sends an ACK frame to the station that sent the data frame. The receiving
stations do not acknowledge multicast frames, though. If the sending station does not

receive an ACK frame for a directed frame within a specific period of time, the sending station will assume that the corresponding data frame was corrupted and attempt to retransmit the data frame. Retransmissions will take place several times (the actual number depends on the vendor) before the sending station gives up. If the sending station is not able to successfully send the data frame and receive an ACK frame, higher-level protocols (such as TCP) may provide an additional level of error recovery.

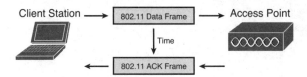

Figure 6-6   *The 802.11 ACK Frame Indicates Successful Reception of a Data Frame*

Dynamic Rate Switching

Something else that relates to data frame error control is 802.11's dynamic rate shifting. If excessive retransmissions occur, stations can operate at a lower data rate to increase the range boundary, mainly for the purpose of decreasing the signal-to-noise requirements at the receiver. The inability to successfully send a data frame (that is, no ACK frame in response) automatically prompts the sending station to lower its data rate. The receiving station will know that the data rate is lower when analyzing the 802.11 PHY layer header of the data frame, which includes data rate information.

An important point, though, is that data rate is not always a good measure of performance. The data rate is the number of data bits sent per second, but it only applies during the time that the frame is actually sent. There are lots of times when other stations are using the shared medium and possibly radio signal interference is causing delays. In addition, the 802.11 protocol periodically sends control and management frames that do not carry any information from higher layers. As a result, the actual throughput varies widely, depending on utilization, and is much lower than the data rate (often less than 50 percent lower).

Hands-on Exercise: Observing 802.11 Dynamic Rate Shifting

This exercise allows you to observe 802.11 dynamic rate shifting in action by operating a client device and moving away from an access point (where signal level decreases, causing transmission errors and corresponding reduced data rates). This will help you better understand various data rates that a client radio can support throughout the coverage area, which provides a measure of how well the client radio will perform under varying signal levels.

Perform the following steps:

Step 1.   Obtain test equipment. You need a wireless client device that indicates the association data rate. For example, you could use an 802.11n-equipped laptop. You can use the Windows wireless configuration utility or the client radio configuration software supplied by the radio vendor to observe the association data rate (sometimes referred to as "speed"). You also need an access point.

Step 2. Associate the client device with an access point. Start by positioning the client device close to the access point, such as within the same room, and prompt the client device to send 802.11 data frames. For example, you could surf the web or initiate a continuous ping against the access point's IP address. You can initiate a continuous ping by entering ping xxx.xxx.xxx.xxx -t (where xxx.xxx.xxx.xxx is the IP address of the access point) at the command prompt on the client device (if using a computer for the client device). You can terminate the continuous ping by pressing Ctrl+C on the computer's keyboard. If you do not invoke traffic from the client radio, it will likely not indicate a shift in data rate.

Step 3. Observe the association data rate as you move the client device away from the access point while the client device continues to send 802.11 data frames. Try moving far enough away from the access point so that the client device is no longer able to maintain an association with the access point. What data rate levels did you observe as you moved away from the access point?

Step 4. Repeat the preceding process for any other client radios you have. What differences do you see in how the client radio steps down to lower data rates as you move away from the access point?

As you move the client device away from the access point, the association data rate should decrease. It might not go through each data rate level, though. Each client radio behaves differently. Some client radios keep operating at higher data rates until the signal level is relatively low and then abruptly drop to lower data rates, and others gradually drop through the data rate levels as you move away from the access point.

Data Frame Aggregation

To make transmission of data over the wireless medium more efficient, the 802.11n amendment in the 802.11 standard includes data frame aggregation techniques, which concatenate two or more frames. This reduces the overhead necessary for sending the data because the concatenated frame shares the overhead necessary to send the frame (that is, it shares the same frame header and ACK frame). The concatenated frames, however, must be sent to the same destination (only when traveling from access point to client radio), have the same QoS level, and be ready for transmission at the same time. In addition, fast-moving stations may struggle with larger aggregated frames because of the extended time that the receiving station needs to process the longer frame. The moving station might be out of range before the receiving station has received the entire frame.

The following sections explain the two different types of 802.11 data frame aggregation: MSDU and MPDU.

MSDU Aggregation

MSDU aggregation bundles multiple Ethernet frames (each one a separate MSDU) requiring transmission over the WLAN and wraps them into a single frame, which contains a header and a cyclic redundancy check (CRC) field. This produces an 802.11 MPDU, as shown in Figure 6-7. MSDU aggregation is the most efficient because Ethernet headers are relatively short (compared to 802.11 headers). The receiving station acknowledges the entire aggregated frame with a single 802.11 Block ACK frame. A common security method is to encrypt the entire frame body (all MSDUs) the same. For each instance of MSDU aggregation, the source/destinations and priorities of the MSDUs must be the same.

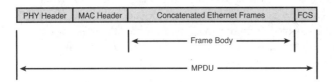

Figure 6-7   *MSDU Frame Aggregation*

MPDU Aggregation

MPDU aggregation works at the bottom of the 802.11 MAC layer by collecting and wrapping multiple MPDUs (minus the FCS field) into a single 802.11 frame, as illustrated in Figure 6-8. MPDU aggregation is not as efficient as MSDU aggregation because of the larger individual 802.11 frame headers (compared to Ethernet); however, it requires use of a Block ACK to acknowledge all of the frames. The Block ACK compiles all ACKs into a single frame in a process called block acknowledgement. After receiving the Block ACK frame, the sending station can selectively retransmit only the data frames that did not include acknowledgements.

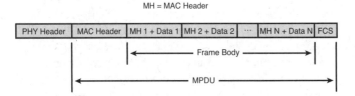

Figure 6-8   *MPDU Frame Aggregation*

Data Frame Fragmentation

The 802.11 standard includes data frame fragmentation, which is essentially the opposite of frame aggregation. A sending station uses fragmentation to divide an MSDU into smaller pieces (fragments) that are sent to the destination as separate MPDUs. Figure 6-9 illustrates this process. Each fragment consists of a MAC layer header, fragment, and FCS. The header of the frame contains a number indicating the fragment's ordered position within the complete frame. Because the sending station transmits each fragment independently, the receiving station replies with a separate acknowledgement for each fragment.

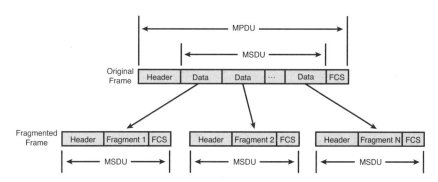

Figure 6-9 *802.11 Fragmentation Divides Data into Separate Fragments*

An 802.11 station only applies fragmentation to frames that are directed to a single destination station (that is, unicast). To avoid substantial overhead on the network, 802.11 stations do not fragment broadcast (for example, beacons) and multicast frames. The destination station reassembles the fragments back into the original sequence, using fragment numbers that the sending station places in the header of each frame. The fragment numbering starts with 0 and increases sequentially. The sending station indicates that more fragments follow by setting the More field in the frame header. The sending station clears the More field corresponding to the last fragment sent, which alerts that receiving station that there are no more fragments, and it can compile the fragments into the original data.

Even though fragmentation involves more overhead than standard aggregated frame delivery, its use can result in better performance, depending on the environment. For example, fragmentation can improve throughput in the presence of radio signal interference because the smaller fragments result in less data to retransmit if occasional transmission errors occur. The bit errors resulting from radio signal interference are likely to occasionally affect only single frames; therefore, retransmitting the corresponding smaller fragment requires less overhead than retransmitting a larger, complete frame.

Note   For details on implementing 802.11 fragmentation, see Chapter 11, "Range, Performance, and Roaming Considerations."

Encryption

The 802.11 standard includes several different methods for encrypting data that is sent over the wireless medium. These methods include the following:

- **Wired Equivalent Privacy (WEP):** WEP is the original method for encrypting 802.11 data frames. It uses static keys that make it vulnerable to compromise.

- **Temporal Key Integrity Protocol (TKIP):** TKIP is a stronger security method than WEP because it rotates encryption keys regularly.

- **CCMP:** Overall, CCMP, which uses Advanced Encryption Standard (AES), is the most secure 802.11 encryption method.

> **Note**   TKIP and CCMP utilize a 4-way handshake to establish the key for encrypting the data. (See the description of the 4-way handshake in the section "Connectivity," later in this chapter.)

Wired Equivalent Privacy

To offer frame transmission privacy similar to that of a wired network, the original 802.11 specification defined optional WEP. WEP encrypts the payload of 802.11 data frames by generating secret shared encryption keys that both source and destination stations can use to alter frame bits using RC4 encryption to avoid disclosure to eavesdroppers. This process is also known as symmetric encryption. Figure 6-10 illustrates the process that WEP follows to encrypt data.

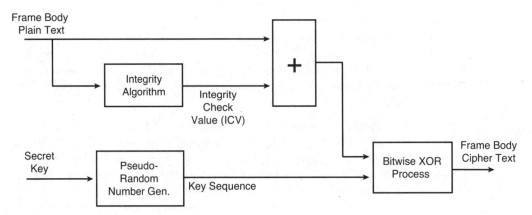

Figure 6-10   *WEP Safeguards Data Transmissions by Performing a Series of Operations Using a Secret Shared Key*

To encrypt data, WEP uses the following process:

Step 1.   At the sending station, the WEP encipherment first runs the unencrypted data located in the frame body of an 802.11 data frame through an integrity algorithm. This algorithm generates a four-octet integrity check value that is sent with the data and checked at the receiving station to guard against unauthorized data modification.

Step 2.   The WEP process inputs the secret shared encryption key into a pseudo-random number generator to create a key sequence with length equal to the plaintext and integrity check value.

Step 3.   WEP encrypts the data by bitwise XORing the plaintext and integrity check value with the key sequence to create ciphertext. The pseudo-random number generator makes key distribution much easier because only the shared key, not the variable-length key sequence, must be made available to each station.

Step 4.   At the receiving station, the WEP process deciphers the ciphertext using the shared key that generates the same key sequence used initially to encrypt the frame.

Step 5.   The station calculates an integrity check value and ensures that it matches the one sent with the frame. If the integrity check fails, the station does not hand the MSDU off to the LLC, and a failure indication is sent to MAC management.

Temporal Key Integrity Protocol

TKIP, initially referred to as WEP2, is a solution that fixes the key reuse problem of WEP (that is, periodically using the same key to encrypt data). Wi-Fi Protected Access (WPA) (version 1) is based on TKIP. The TKIP process begins with a 128-bit temporal key that is shared among clients and access points. TKIP combines the temporal key with the client's MAC address and then adds a relatively large 16-octet initialization vector to produce the key that will encrypt the data. This procedure ensures that each station uses different key streams to encrypt the data.

TKIP uses RC4 to perform the encryption, which is the same as WEP. A major difference from WEP, however, is that TKIP changes temporal keys regularly. This dynamic distribution method significantly enhances the security of the network. Another advantage of TKIP is that companies that have existing WEP-based access points and client radios can upgrade to TKIP with relatively simple firmware patches. In addition, WEP-only equipment will still interoperate with TKIP-enabled devices using WEP.

Note   TKIP is the basis for the Wi-Fi Alliance's WPA specification and the 802.11i amendment to the 802.11 standard.

CCMP

In addition to TKIP, for security the 802.11 standard includes CCMP, which is based on AES encryption and also known as WPA2. AES offers much stronger encryption. In fact, the U.S. Commerce Department's National Institutes of Standards and Technology (NIST) chose AES to replace the aging Data Encryption Standard (DES). AES is a Federal Information Processing Standard (FIPS Publication 197), which defines a cryptographic algorithm for use by U.S. government organizations to protect sensitive, unclassified information.

Note   AES is the basis for the Wi-Fi Alliance's WPA2 specification and the 802.11i amendment to the 802.11 standard.

Note   For more on choosing the most suitable security methods, see Chapter 13, "Security Considerations."

Multicasting

Most 802.11 frames are directed to a specific station. In this case, the frames are considered to be unicast and include a MAC address that designates the destination. Only the station with the corresponding MAC address will process the frame. Other stations may receive the header of the frame to determine the destination MAC address, but they do not process the frame. The 802.11 standard also supports multicasting, where the sending station can identify a group of stations that can receive and process the frame. This might include a broadcast MAC address (all 1s), which means all stations receive and process the frame, or it might include a group MAC address that corresponds to specific stations.

Figure 6-11 shows how multicast traffic is sent from a client device. An 802.11 client station (for example, Client Station A) begins a multicast delivery by sending multicast data in an 802.11 unicast data frame directed to the access point. The access point responds with an 802.11 acknowledgement frame sent to the source station if no errors are found in the data frame. Thus, initial transmission of the data from the client station to the access point includes error recovery. After receiving the unicast data frame from the client, the access point transmits the data (that the originating client wants to multicast) as a multicast frame, which contains a broadcast or group address as the destination for the intended recipients. Each of the intended destination stations receives and processes the frame; however, they do not respond with acknowledgements. As a result, 802.11 multicasting does not ensure a complete, reliable flow of data.

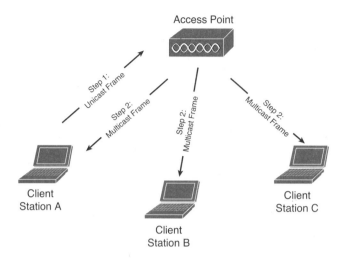

Figure 6-11   *802.11 Multicasting Operation*

Another issue with multicasting is that multicast frames might experience reduced QoS. With 802.11 networks, lower throughput definitely results when one or more of the wireless clients are using the 802.11 power saving mode. For instance, an access point buffers all multicast frames and sends them immediately following the next DTIM (delivery traffic indication message) if any one of the client devices associated with the access point has 802.11 power saving mode enabled (a likely situation). When all stations have power saving off, the access point transmits multicast frames as soon as possible and does not wait for the next DTIM.

The DTIM interval, which you configure in the access point, indicates when the DTIM occurs. A DTIM interval is a count of the number of beacon frames that must occur before the access point sends the buffered multicast frames. For example, a DTIM interval equal to one means that the multicast frames are sent after each beacon frame. A DTIM interval of two indicates that multicast frames are sent after every two beacon frames, and so on. Because each beacon frame includes a field that identifies the DTIM interval, all stations know when to wake up and receive multicast frames if they are implementing power saving mode. The default DTIM intervals of the various vendors vary, but they are usually one, two, or three. If possible, set the DTIM interval to one if implementing multicasting as an integral part of your application.

Something to consider is that client devices might experience relatively poor battery life if there is a significant amount of multicast traffic. The problem is that the combination of multicast traffic and 802.11 power saving mode makes clients stay awake longer than if there were no multicast traffic. As a result, it might be worthwhile to set the DTIM interval to a higher value if battery life becomes a problem. The optimum DTIM setting is a trade-off between throughput and power savings.

Connectivity

A client radio must first connect to an 802.11 network before sending any data. This process is automatic and involves the following actions:

Step 1.   Scanning for networks

Step 2.   Authenticating with the network

Step 3.   Associating with the access point

Step 4.   Implementing the 4-way handshake if either TKIP or CCMP is used

Once the client radio completes these steps, it can begin sending data frames.

The sections that follow explain these connectivity steps.

Scanning for Networks

Soon after an 802.11 client station is up and running, it needs to determine which 802.11 networks are within range. This is necessary to identify an access point that the client station can connect to. The client station accomplishes this discovery phase by implementing a scanning function, which includes passive or active scanning mode (or both). Figure 6-12 illustrates the differences between passive and active scanning, which are further defined in the list that follows:

- **Passive scanning:** With passive scanning, the client station tunes to each radio frequency (RF) channel, listens for a period of time, and monitors 802.11 beacon frames coming from access points (in infrastructure networks) or other client stations (in ad hoc networks). By default, each access point transmits a beacon frame every 100 milliseconds on a specific RF channel. The client station records the signal strength of the beacon frame and continues the scan of other channels. After scanning each of the RF channels, the client station makes a decision about which access point to associate with. In general, the client station chooses the access point that sent the beacon having the strongest signal. Some client radio vendors may include other parameters, such as noise levels and utilization, when making this decision.

- **Active scanning:** Active scanning involves the client station sending broadcast 802.11 probe request frames on each RF channel (or subset of channels). Access points (in infrastructure networks) and client stations (in ad hoc networks) within range respond to the probe request frame by sending a probe response frame. The probe response is very similar to a beacon frame. The station sending the probes waits on each RF channel for a period of time to receive the corresponding probe response frames coming from other stations receiving and responding to the probes. Active scanning enables client stations to receive information about nearby access points in a timely manner, without waiting for beacons; however, active scanning generates additional traffic on the network (that is, probe and response frames). Much like with passive scanning, the radio card uses the signal strength and possibly other information corresponding to the probe response frame to make decisions about which access point to associate with.

(A) Passive Scanning

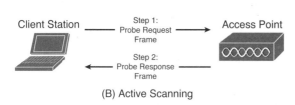

(B) Active Scanning

Figure 6-12 *Comparison of 802.11 (A) Passive Scanning and (B) Active Scanning*

Each vendor implements scanning differently, but many use both passive and active scanning. For example, the client station might initially and periodically thereafter perform a passive scan of all RF channels. Between passive scans, the client station may perform an active scan if the signal strength of the access point that the client station is connected to is declining rapidly, such as when the client station is moving away from the access point.

Hands-on Exercise: Observing 802.11 Active Scanning

This exercise allows you to observe a client radio implementing active scanning, which will help you understand the protocols and timing that support 802.11 connection and roaming processes.

Perform the following steps:

Step 1. Obtain test equipment. You need a wireless client device, such as an 802.11n- or 802.11ac-equipped laptop, and an access point. You also need a wireless protocol analyzer, such as WireShark (which is freely available) or another analyzer (see Chapter 14, "Test Tools").

Step 2. Configure the protocol analyzer to record 802.11 frame transmissions on all RF channels (within the 2.4-GHz or 5-GHz band, whichever your client device implements).

Step 3. Position the client device within close proximity, such as within the same room, to an operational access point.

Step 4. With the client device not associated to the access point, record a packet trace with the protocol analyzer (just a minute or two is enough time). What 802.11 probe requests do you see your client device sending on each of the channels? What probe responses do you see the access points sending?

Step 5. Associate the client device to the access point and record another packet trace with the protocol analyzer. What 802.11 probe requests do you see your client device sending on each of the channels now, after the client device associates with the access point? What probe responses do you see the access points sending?

Step 6. Turn off the access point (and any other access points that your test client device may be able to associate with) and repeat steps 4 and 5. What 802.11 probe requests do you see your client device sending on each of the channels now? What probe responses do you see the access points sending?

Step 7. Repeat the preceding steps with different client radios. What differences do you see in the transmission of probe requests?

If the client radio implements active scanning (which is likely), you should see the client radio periodically broadcasting 802.11 probe requests. Each client radio performs active scanning differently. When not associated with an access point, especially when no access point is within range, you will probably see the client radio sending probe request frames frequently on all channels because the radio is desperately trying to find an access point. Once associated (or after scanning all channels a few times), the client radio will probably limit the sending of probe requests (either less frequently or on fewer channels). You should always see access points within range of the client device respond to the broadcast probe request sent by the client radio with a unicast probe response directed to the client radio (unless probe responses are disabled on the access point).

Authentication

Because wireless signals generally propagate outside physically controlled areas, the 802.11 standard includes the following authentication mechanisms:

- **Open system authentication:** This is the default authentication service, and it simply announces the desire to associate with another station or access point.

- **Shared key authentication:** This optional authentication involves a more rigorous exchange of frames, ensuring that the requesting station is authentic based on knowledge of the WEP key.

- **IEEE 802.1X port-based authentication:** This enhanced authentication is provided through the use of an authentication server.

The next sections describe the operation of these authentication types.

Open System Authentication

Figure 6-13 illustrates the operation of open system authentication. A client station initiating the authentication process sends an 802.11 authentication frame directed to an access point it wants to connect to, indicating the desire to authenticate with the network. The access point responds with an 802.11 authentication frame that indicates authentication success or failure in the status code located in the body of the authentication frame.

Figure 6-13   *802.11 Open System Authentication Is a Simple Two-Step Process*

With most WLAN products, open system authentication is completely open, meaning that any client radio can authenticate successfully with the network, and the access point always indicates a successful authentication. The client device does not need to send any form of credentials. An organization may want to use open system authentication if it is not necessary to validate the identity of a sending station.

Shared Key Authentication

The optional shared key authentication approach was meant to provide a higher degree of security than does the open system approach. For a station to use shared key authentication, it must implement WEP. Figure 6-14 illustrates the operation of shared key authentication.

The shared key authentication process is as follows:

Step 1.   A client station sends an authentication frame to the access point, requesting shared key authentication.

Step 2.   When the access point receives the initial authentication frame, the access point replies with an authentication frame containing 128 octets of challenge text that the WEP services generate.

Step 3.   The client station copies the challenge text into an authentication frame, encrypts it with a shared key, and then sends the frame to the access point.

Step 4.   The access point decrypts the value of the challenge text using the same shared key and compares it to the challenge text sent earlier. If a match occurs, the access point replies with an authentication indicating a successful (or unsuccessful) authentication response.

A problem with shared key authentication is that the shared key must be distributed manually. This means that someone has to enter it into the client radios and access points (much as with implementing WEP). Also, because unencrypted and encrypted versions of the challenge text are sent, it is possible to discover the WEP key by monitoring enough of the transactions. As a result, shared key authentication should not be used in enterprise solutions.

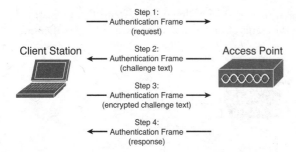

Figure 6-14   *802.11 Shared Key Authentication Involves WEP for Proving Identity*

IEEE 802.1X Port-Based Authentication

The 802.11i amendment to the 802.11 standard introduced IEEE 802.1X as an optional authentication method for WLANs. 802.1X offers an effective framework for authenticating and controlling user traffic to a protected network. 802.1X ties a protocol called EAP (Extensible Authentication Protocol) to both the wired and WLAN media and supports multiple authentication methods, such as token cards, Kerberos, one-time passwords, certificates, and public key authentication. For details on EAP, refer to IETF's RFC 2284.

Initial 802.1X communication begins with an unauthenticated supplicant (that is, client device) attempting to connect with an authenticator (that is, 802.11 access point). The access point responds by enabling a port for passing only EAP packets from the client to an authentication server located on the wired side of the access point. The access point blocks all other traffic, such as HTTP, DHCP, and POP3 packets, until the access point can verify the client's identity by using an authentication server (for example, RADIUS). Once the authentication takes place, the access point opens the client's port for other types of traffic.

The following are specific interactions that take place among the various 802.1X elements:

Step 1.   The client device sends an EAP-start message. This begins a series of message exchanges to authenticate the client.

Step 2.   The access point replies with an EAP-request identity message.

Step 3.   The client sends an EAP-response packet containing the identity to the authentication server.

Step 4.   The authentication server uses a specific authentication algorithm to verify the client's identity. This could be through the use of digital certificates or other EAP authentication type.

Step 5.   The authentication server sends either an accept message or a reject message to the access point.

Step 6.   The access point sends an EAP-success packet (or reject packet) to the client.

Step 7.   If the authentication server accepts the client, the access point transitions the client's port to an authorized state and forwards additional traffic.

> **Note**   For details on implementing 802.1X port-based authentication, see Chapter 13.

Associating with the Access Point

After authentication is successful, the client station must associate with the access point to complete the connection process. Association is necessary to synchronize the client station and access point with important information, such as beacon interval and supported data rates. The client station initiates the association by sending an association request frame containing elements such as service set identifier (SSID) and supported data rates to the access point (see Figure 6-15). The access point responds by sending an association response frame containing an association ID along with other information about the access point.

Figure 6-15   *802.11 Association Is the Final Step in Connecting to the WLAN*

An association establishes a mapping between the station and the 802.11 network. After association, 802.11 data frames can be sent between the client station and the access point (the one that handled the authentication and association process).

Hands-on Exercise: Observing the 802.11 Connection Process

This exercise allows you to observe a client radio connecting to an access point, which provides insight for troubleshooting connection issues with WLANs.

Perform the following steps:

Step 1.   Obtain the test equipment. You need a wireless client device, such as an 802.11n- or 802.11ac-equipped laptop, and an access point. You also need a wireless protocol analyzer, such as WireShark (which is freely available) or another analyzer (see Chapter 14).

Step 2.   Configure the access point for open system authentication.

Step 3.   Configure the analyzer to record 802.11 frame transmissions on only the RF channel that the access point is set to. This helps reduce extraneous frames that the analyzer displays by filtering out frames from other channels. With fewer frames, you can more easily pinpoint the 802.11 frames that are applicable to the connection process.

Step 4.   With the client radio not associated with the access point, start recording a packet trace with the protocol analyzer. A good way to ensure that the client radio is not associated with the access point is to disable the client radio.

Step 5.   While the protocol analyzer is recording a packet trace, invoke the client radio to initiate the connection process with the access point. You can do this by enabling the disabled client radio and entering any configuration data needed (for example, SSID and WPA key).

Step 6.   Continue recording the packet trace until you have confirmation that the client radio has connected to the access point. For example, observe the connection status in the Windows or vendor configuration utility for the client radio. It should indicate a connected (or "associated") status.

Step 7.   By observing the packet trace, note the occurrence of 802.11 authentication and association frames. Look at the contents of each frame to better understand the information being relayed between the client radio and the access point in the frame body of the frames. Compare what you find with the field descriptions explained in this chapter and what is explained in the 802.11 standard. For example, do you see the SSID in the association frame?

Soon after initiating the connection process, you should see the client radio send an authentication frame to the access point to initiate authentication. The access point should respond with an authentication frame. Soon after that, the client radio should send an association request frame to the access point, and the access point should respond with an association response frame. This completes the connection process. If you do not see the applicable authentication and association frames, the client radio is likely having trouble connecting to the access point.

If the client station moves, the quality of the signals between the access points and the client station may weaken. As a result, client stations continue scanning periodically and re-associate with other access points as needed. As shown in Figure 6-16, a client station may be initially connected to the network through Access Point (AP) A. As the client station moves closer to AP B, the signal quality between the client station and AP A begins to weaken, while the signal quality between the client station and AP B strengthens. Vendors utilize different signal quality metrics to determine when the re-association process occurs, but at some point (before the client station isn't able to communicate with AP A), the client station initiates the re-association process by sending an 802.11 re-association request frame to AP B. AP B responds with a re-association response frame indicating a successful re-association, and then the client station sends an 802.11 disassociation frame to AP A. AP A forwards any buffered 802.11 frames to AP B so that they can be delivered to the client station. After this process completes, the client station and AP B can begin exchanging 802.11 data frames.

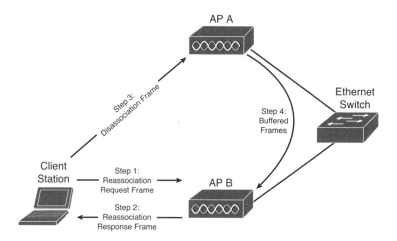

Figure 6-16 *The 802.11 Re-association Process Enables Client Stations to Roam*

4-Way Handshake

If either TKIP or CCMP is used for security, the access point initiates a 4-way handshake with the client radio immediately after the association has completed. If no security or WEP is used, the 4-way handshake is not implemented. The purpose of the 4-way handshake is to establish a common key that will be used to encrypt data. If using enterprise-based WPA, this encryption key is based on information (for example, master keys) provided by a server, along with the MAC addresses and random numbers (nonces) associated with the access point and client radio (which is exchanged during the handshake). If using the pre-shared key form of WPA, the user is prompted to enter a passphrase (instead of interacting with a server), which is then combined with the MAC addresses and nonces. Periodically (for example, every five minutes) or when a client radio roams to a different access point, the 4-way handshake is implemented again with different parameters (for example, different access point MAC address and different nonces). As a result, the actual encryption key will change over time, making using it more secure than using static encryption.

Timing and Synchronization

The 802.11 specification defines several spacing intervals that govern when a station can transmit certain types of frames. Figure 6-17 illustrates some of these intervals. Understanding these intervals can help you better design a WLAN system. The following sections describe some of the 802.11 interframe space (IFS) intervals.

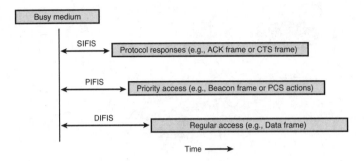

Figure 6-17 *The SIFS, PIFS, DIFS and EIFS Represent Various 802.11 Interframe Spacing*

Short IFS

The Short IFS (SIFS) is the shortest of the interframe spaces, providing the highest priority level by allowing some frames to access the medium before others. The following frames use the SIFS interval:

■ ACK (acknowledgement) frame

■ CTS (clear-to-send) frame

■ The second or subsequent MSDU of a fragment burst

These frames require expedient access to the network because they are associated with preceding frames. When a station receives an 802.11 data frame, for example, the station can respond immediately with the corresponding ACK frame because it can be sent during the SIFS and does not have to wait until the DIFS. As a result, a station can use the SIFS for some frames to maintain control of the medium because other stations must defer for longer than the SIFS before attempting access to the medium.

The 802.11 standard specifies a SIFS of 16 microseconds for 802.11a, 802.11g, and 802.11n, which is as short as possible while leaving enough time for demodulation/ decoding and MAC layer processing. If frame aggregation is not possible, perhaps because frames are addressed to different destinations, 802.11n reduces overhead of the individual frames by reducing the interframe spacing. This is referred to as the RIFS (reduced interframe space). The result is much more efficient and faster operation, but it is applicable only to purely 802.11n networks (that is, with no 802.11a, 802.11b, or 802.11g clients).

PCF IFS

The PCF IFS (PIFS) is the interval that stations operating under the point coordination function use to gain access to the medium. This provides priority over frames sent by the distributed coordination function. These stations can transmit contention-free traffic if they sense that the medium is idle. This interval gives point coordination function-based stations a higher priority of access than DCF-based (CSMA) stations for transmitting frames. The following equation defines the PIFS interval:

PIFS = aSIFSTime + aSlotTime

DCF IFS

All stations operating according to the distributed coordination function use the DCF IFS (DIFS) interval for transmitting data frames and management frames. This spacing makes the transmission of these frames lower priority than PCF-based transmissions. The following equation defines the DIFS interval:

DIFS = aSIFSTime + 2(aSlotTime)

Extended IFS

All DCF-based stations use the Extended IFS (EIFS) rather than DIFS to defer sending a frame if a transmission results in a bad reception of a frame due to an incorrect FCS value. This interval provides enough time for the receiving station to send an ACK frame. The EIFS helps prevent transmitting over the ACK frame sent by hidden nodes because the node cannot decode the Duration field and set the NAV properly. The following equation defines the EIFS interval:

EIFS = aSIFSTime + ACKTx + DIFS

where ACKTx is the time required to transmit an ACK frame at the lowest possible PHY data rate.

RTS/CTS

As an optional feature, the 802.11 standard includes the RTS/CTS (request-to-send/clear-to-send) function to add enhanced access control to the medium. If you enable RTS/CTS on a particular station, the station then refrains from sending an 802.11 data frame until the station completes an RTS/CTS handshake with another station. Figure 6-18 describes how the RTS/CTS process works.

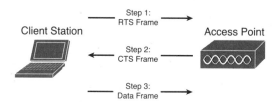

Figure 6-18 *Exchange of 802.11 Frames During an RTS/CTS Operation*

A station (client or access point) that needs to send an 802.11 data frame initiates the RTS/CTS process by sending an 802.11 RTS frame to another station. The RTS frame includes a duration value in the frame's header that is equal to the time for the RTS/CTS sequence to complete and for the sending station to transmit its data frame. The station receiving the RTS responds with an 802.11 CTS frame with a Duration field value equal to the amount of time that the sending station will need to transmit the data frame. The sending station must receive the CTS frame before sending an 802.11 data frame. All other stations copy the Duration field value found in the CTS frame into their respective NAV timers, which effectively causes other stations to hold off from accessing the medium while the station initiating the RTS transmits its data.

The RTS/CTS handshaking provides positive control over the use of the shared medium. The primary reason for implementing RTS/CTS is to minimize collisions among hidden stations (see Figure 6-19). This occurs often when client devices and access points are spread throughout a building. Imagine having two 802.11 client devices (Station A and Station B) and one access point. Station A and Station B cannot hear each other because of high attenuation (for example, substantial range), but they can both communicate with the same access point. Because of this situation, Station A can begin sending a frame without noticing that Station B is currently transmitting (or vice versa). This is likely to cause a collision between Station A and Station B to occur at the access point. As a result, both Station A and Station B would need to retransmit their respective packets, which results in higher overhead and lower throughput.

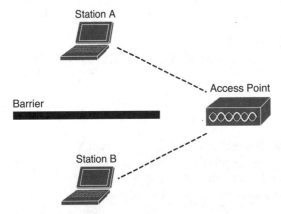

Figure 6-19   *RTS/CTS Overcomes Issues Related to Hidden Nodes*

If either Station A or Station B activates RTS/CTS, however, the collision does not happen. Before transmitting, Station B sends an RTS frame to the access point and receives a CTS frame from the access point in response. The Duration field in the CTS (which Station A also receives) causes Station A to hold off long enough for Station B to transmit the frame. Thus, the use of RTS/CTS reduces collisions and increases the performance of the network if hidden stations are present.

The increase in performance using RTS/CTS is the net result of introducing overhead (that is, RTS/CTS frames) and reducing retransmissions. If you do not have any hidden nodes, then the use of RTS/CTS only increases the amount of overhead, which reduces throughput. A slight hidden node problem may also result in performance degradation if you implement RTS/CTS. In this case, the additional RTS/CTS frames cost more in terms of overhead than you gain by reducing retransmissions. Also, keep in mind that client devices may move through the facility, which changes distribution of hidden nodes. Thus, the decision to implement RTS/CTS is somewhat difficult to determine.

Note   For details on implementing RTS/CTS, see Chapter 11.

Power Management

The 802.11 standard defines optional power saving modes that enable client stations to conserve battery power. These modes are as follows:

- **Spatial multiplexing power save (SMPS):** With SMPS, a client station can power down all but one radio to conserve battery power statically or dynamically. To initiate static SMPS mode, the client station sends a special 802.11 management frame to the access point, indicating that it is entering static single-radio mode. The access point then knows to only send data to the client station via a single spatial stream. The client station and the access point continue to operate over a single stream until the client station notifies the access point that it is powering up additional radios.

  To initiate dynamic SMPS mode, the client station also sends a special 802.11 management frame to the access point, indicating that it is entering dynamic single-radio mode. A difference with dynamic mode, however, is that a client station can quickly enable all its radios temporarily to receive data frames over all spatial streams. The access point gives the client station a heads up that incoming frames are imminent by sending an 802.11 RTS frame to the client station. The client station powers up all its radios and sends an 802.11 CTS frame to the access point to acknowledge that the client station is ready to receive the data frames. After the client station receives the frames, it can power down its radios again.

- **Power save multi-poll (PSMP):** The PSMP mode enables client stations to inform the access points to buffer data frames corresponding to specific QoS levels until the client station requests that they be sent. The triggers for sending the buffered frames are specific types of frames sent by the client station. This is useful, for example, to conserve battery power in wireless IP phones during active calls. The client station (that is, wireless IP phone radio) would inform the access point to buffer frames corresponding to the voice packets and indicate that a voice packet sent from the phone to the access point be a trigger for the access point to forward data frames containing voice packets. In addition, PSMP allows the client station to schedule the delivery of frames buffered at the access point. This reduces contention between client stations and the access point, which reduces power requirements.

Note   See Chapter 16, "Installing and Configuring a Wireless LAN," for details on configuring MAC layer functions.

802.11 MAC Frame Structures

The previous sections in this chapter refer to some of the 802.11 frames to explain the operation of various MAC layer functions. This section describes the structure and purpose of each of these 802.11 frames (and others).

The 802.11 standard specifies an overall MAC frame format, as shown in Figure 6-20. After forming the applicable frame, the MAC layer passes the frame's bits to Physical Layer Convergence Protocol (PLCP), starting with the first bit of the Frame Control field and ending with the last bit of the frame check sequence (FCS). See Chapter 7 for more information.

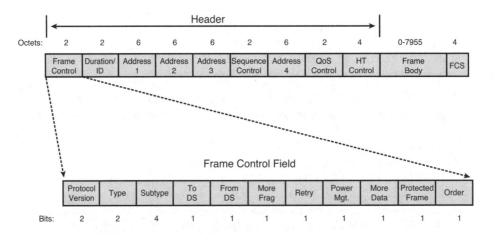

Figure 6-20   *802.11 MAC Frame Format*

The subsequent sections define the MAC frame fields.

Protocol Version Field

The protocol version is zero; therefore, the Protocol Version field always contains 0. IEEE will add version numbers in the future if a newer version of the standard is fundamentally incompatible with an earlier version.

Type Field

The Type field is indicated by the bits shown in Table 6-1.

Note   All reserved bits are transmitted as value 0.

Subtype Field

The Subtype field defines the function of the frame. Table 6-2 shows a sampling of 802.11 frames that have different functions based on this field.

Table 6-2 *Sample of 802.11 Frame Subtypes*

Type	Subtype	Frame Function
00(Management Type)	0000	Association request
	0001	Association response
	0010	Re-association request
	0011	Re-association response
	0100	Probe request
	0101	Probe response
	0110-0111	Reserved
	1000	Beacon
	1001	Announcement traffic indication map (ATIM)
	1010	Disassociation
	1011	Authentication
	1100	Deauthentication
	1101	Action
	1110	Action no ACK
	1111	Reserved
01(Control Type)	0000-0110	Reserved
	0111	Control wrapper
	1000	Block ACK request
	1001	Block ACK
	1010	Power-save (PS) poll
	1011	Request to send (RTS)
	1100	Clear to send (CTS)
	1101	Acknowledgement (ACK)
	1110	Contention-free (CF) end
	1111	CF end + CF ACK
10(Data Type)	0000	Data
	0001	Data + CF ACK

Type	Subtype	Frame Function
	0010	Data + CF poll
	0011	Data + CF ACK + CF poll
	0100	Null
	0101	CF ACK
	0110	CF poll
	0111	CF ACK + CF poll
	1000	QoS data
	1001	QoS data + CF ACK
	1010	QoS data + CF poll
	1011	QoS data + CF ACK + CF poll
	1100	QoS null
	1101	Reserved
	1110	QoS CF poll
	1111	QoS CF ACK + CF poll
11 (Reserved)	0000-1111	Reserved

To DS Field

The single-bit To DS field is set to 1 in any frame destined for the distribution system in an infrastructure WLAN. It is 0 for all other transmissions, such as in an ad hoc WLAN.

From DS Field

The single-bit From DS field is set to 1 in any frame leaving the distribution system in an infrastructure WLAN. It is 0 for all other transmissions, such as in an ad hoc WLAN. Both the To DS and From DS fields are set to 1 if the frame is being sent from one access point through the distribution system to another access point.

More Frag Field

The single-bit More Frag field is set to 1 if another fragment of the same MSDU follows in a subsequent frame. For example, a station sending three data frames containing fragments corresponding to the same MSDU will set the More Frag field to 1 in the first two data frames and to 0 in the third and final data frame. The receiving station then knows that the last data frame contains the last fragment, which prompts the receiving station to reassemble the complete data.

Retry Field

If a station sends a data frame that is a retransmission of an earlier frame, the single-bit Retry field is set to 1. It is 0 for all other transmissions. The reason for retransmission could be that the errors in the transmission of the first frame resulted in an unsuccessful FCS.

Power Management Field

The bit in the Power Management field indicates the power management mode that the sending client station will be in after the current frame exchange sequence. The MAC layer places a 1 in this field if the station will be in a sleep mode (802.11 defines this as power saving mode). A 0 indicates that the station will be in full active mode. A receiving station can use this information to adjust transmissions to avoid waking up sleeping stations. Frames originating from the access points always have this field set to 0.

More Data Field

An access point sets the More Data field to 1 if any of the following conditions are met:

- The access point is sending a directed frame to a client station in power saving mode, and the access point has additional frames buffered for the station.

- The access point is sending an ACK to a station implementing QoS with APSD enabled, and the access point has additional frames to send to the station.

- The access point is sending a broadcast or multicast data frame, and the access point will send additional broadcast or multicast frames during the same beacon interval.

Protected Frame Field

A 1 in the Protected Frame field tells the receiving station that the frame body of the frame is encrypted. The field is set to 0 for all other types of transmissions.

Order Field

The Order field is set to 1 in any data frame being sent using the strictly ordered service class, which tells the receiving station that frames must be processed in order.

Duration/ID Field

In most frames, the Duration/ID field contains a duration value, depending on the type of frame sent. In general, each frame contains information that identifies the duration of the next frame transmission. For example, the Duration/ID field in data and ACK frames specifies the total duration of the next fragment and acknowledgement. Stations on the network monitor this field and hold off transmissions based on the duration information. In a PS poll frame, this field represents the association identifier of the client station sending the PS poll frame.

Address 1, 2, 3, and 4 Fields

The Address fields contain different types of addresses, depending on the type of frame being sent. These address types may include the basic service set identification (BSSID), source address, destination address, transmitting station address, and receiving station address. IEEE standard 802-1990 defines the structure of the addresses, which are all 48 bits in length.

The addresses can be either individual or group addresses. There are two types of group addresses: multicast addresses, which associate with a group of logically related stations, and broadcast addresses, which refer to all stations on a given LAN. A broadcast address consists of all 1s.

802.11 defines the following address types:

- **Destination address (DA):** The DA is the MAC address of the final destination for the MSDU and is contained in the frame body of the MAC frame.

- **Source address (SA):** The SA is the MAC address of the entity that initiated the MSDU transmission.

- **Receiver address (RA):** The RA is the MAC address of the access point that is to receive the frame next. It is present in the Address 1 field of all frames.

- **Transmitter address (TA):** The TA is the MAC address of the immediately preceding access point sending the frame. It is present in the Address 2 field of all frames except for the ACK and CTS frames.

Table 6-3 indicates the contents of the various address fields, depending on the situation.

Table 6-3 *Contents of MAC Frame Address Fields*

To DS	From DS	Address 1	Address 2	Address 3	Address 4
0	0	Destination address	Source address	BSSID	N/A
0	1	Destination address	BSSID	Source address	N/A
1	0	BSSID	Source address	Destination address	N/A
1	1	Receiver address	Transmitter address	Destination address	Source address

Sequence Control Field

The leftmost 4 bits of the Sequence Control field are a Fragment Number subfield, indicating the fragment number of a particular MSDU. This number starts with 0 for the first fragment and then increments by 1 for each successive transmission. The next 12 bits of this frame are the Sequence Number subfield, starting at 0 and incrementing by

1 for each subsequent MSDU transmission. Each fragment of a specific MSDU will have the same sequence number. A station shall have one or more outstanding MSDUs concurrently. On reception of a frame, a station can filter duplicate frames by monitoring the sequence and fragment numbers. The station knows the frame is a duplicate if the sequence number and fragment number are equal to the frame immediately preceding, or if the Retry bit is set to 1.

Duplicate frames can occur when a station receives a frame without errors, sends an ACK frame back to the sending station, and transmission errors destroy the ACK frame. After not receiving the ACK over a specific time period, the sending station retransmits a duplicate frame. The destination station sends another ACK frame for the retransmitted frame even if the frame is discarded due to duplicate filtering.

QoS Control Field

The QoS Control field is present in QoS data frames and identifies the traffic class or stream for the frame that is being sent. It also carries other information related to QoS operation, such as indication of the end of the service period, acknowledgement policy (normal ACK, no ACK, Block ACK, and so on), and an indication of whether an aggregate MSDU (multiple MSDUs) is present in the frame body.

HT Control Field

The HT Control field is present in control wrapper frames and QoS data frames when the Order bit is set to 1. This field contains elements that are part of high-throughput operations.

Frame Body Field

The Frame Body field provides a variable-length payload and carries information that pertains to the specific type of frame being sent. In the case of a data frame, the Frame Body field may contain LLC data, which ultimately may include a voice packet or part of a document file. MAC management and control frames, on the other hand, may include specific parameters in the frame body that pertain to the particular service the frame is implementing. If the frame has no need to carry information (for example, null data frames), this field has a length of 0. The receiving station determines the frame length from a field within the applicable 802.11 physical layer headers.

Frame Check Sequence Field

The MAC layer at the sending station calculates a 32-bit frame check sequence (FCS) by using a cyclic redundancy code (CRC) and places the result in the Frame Check Sequence field. The MAC layer uses the following generator polynomial over all fields of the MAC header and frame body to calculate the FCS:

$$G(x) = X^{32} + X^{26} + X^{23} + X^{22} + X^{16} + X^{12} + X^{11} + X^{10} + X^8 + X^7 + X^5 + X^4 + X^2 + X + 1$$

The result's highest-order coefficient is placed in the field at the leftmost bit. The receiver implements a CRC to check for transmission errors in the frame.

MAC Frame Types

To carry out the delivery of MSDUs, the MAC layer uses a variety of frame types, each of which has a particular purpose. The IEEE 802.11 specification divides MAC frames into three broad categories that provide management, control, and data exchange functions between stations and access points. The sections that follow describe some of the major frame types.

Management Frames

The purpose of 802.11 management frames is to establish and maintain communications between stations and access points. Thus, management frames provide services such as association and authentication.

The Duration field in all management frames during the contention-free period is set to (decimal) 32,768 (or hexadecimal 8000), giving management frames plenty of time to establish communications before other stations have the capability to access the medium. During the contention period (as defined by the CSMA-based distributed coordination function), all management frames have the Duration field set as follows:

- If the destination address is a group address, the Duration field is set to 0.

- If the More Frag bit is set to 0 and the destination address is an individual address, then the Duration field contains the number of microseconds required to transmit one ACK frame plus one short interframe space.

- If the More Frag bit is set to 1 and the destination address is an individual address, then the Duration field contains the number of microseconds required to transmit the next fragment, plus two ACK frames, plus three short interframe spaces.

The sections that follow define a sample of 802.11 management frames.

Association Request Frame

A station sends the association request frame to an access point if it wants to associate with that access point. A station becomes associated with an access point after the access point grants permission.

Association Response Frame

After an access point receives an association request frame, the access point sends an association response frame to indicate whether it is accepting the association with the sending station.

Re-association Request Frame

A station sends a re-association request frame to an access point if it wants to re-associate with that access point. A re-association may occur if a station moves out of range from one access point and within range of another access point. The station needs to re-associate (not merely associate) with the new access point so that the new access point knows it will need to negotiate the forwarding of data frames from the old access point.

Re-association Response Frame

After an access point receives a re-association request frame, the access point sends a re-association response frame to indicate whether it is accepting the re-association with the sending station.

Probe Request Frame

A station sends a probe request frame to obtain information from another station or access point. A client station, for instance, will broadcast a probe request when using active scanning to determine which access points are within range for possible association. Some sniffing software (for example, NetStumbler) tools send probe requests so that access points will respond with desired info.

Probe Response Frame

If a station or an access point receives a probe request frame, the station responds to the sending station with a probe response frame that contains specific parameters about itself. An 802.11 probe response frame is similar to a beacon frame, except that probe responses do not carry the TIM info and are sent only in response to a probe request.

Beacon Frame

In an infrastructure network, an access point periodically sends a beacon that provides synchronization among stations. The beacons are sent at a rate based on a beacon interval setting, which is generally 100 milliseconds (10 beacons each second) by default. This beacon rate is sufficient for most applications, but lower beacon rates may be necessary to support faster roaming, and higher beacon rates can improve power savings.

A beacon includes a timestamp that all stations use to update what 802.11 defines as a timing synchronization function (TSF) timer. Stations use this timer for various functions. If an access point supports the point coordination function, it uses a beacon frame to announce the beginning of a contention-free period. If the network is an independent BSS (that is, it has no access points), all stations periodically send beacons for synchronization purposes.

A typical beacon frame is approximately 50 bytes long, with about half of that being a common frame header and CRC field. As with other frames, the header includes source and destination MAC addresses and other information regarding the communications process. The destination address is always set to all 1s, which is the broadcast MAC address. This causes all other stations on the applicable channel to receive and process each beacon frame.

In ad hoc networks, there are no access points. As a result, one of the stations assumes responsibility for sending the beacon. After receiving a beacon frame, each station waits for the beacon interval and then sends a beacon if no other station does so after a random time delay. This ensures that at least one station will send a beacon, and the random delay rotates the responsibility for sending beacons.

There are no reservations for sending beacons, and they must be sent using the 802.11 distributed coordination function. If another station is sending a frame when a beacon is to be sent, then the access point (or client station in an ad hoc network) must wait. As a result, the actual time between beacons may be longer than the beacon interval. Stations, however, compensate for this inaccuracy by using the timestamp found within the beacon to reset their clocks after receiving each beacon.

Beacon Interval Impacts on Battery Life

My consulting firm, Wireless-Nets, Ltd., has conducted tests with 802.11 client devices that have 802.11 power saving mode enabled, along with different access point beacon intervals. By increasing the beacon interval, we have found that clients sleep longer and save more battery power. To get a better idea of the savings, we ran tests with the beacon interval set to 100 milliseconds (the default), 1 second, 2 seconds, 4 seconds, and 5 seconds. We found that beacon intervals at 1 second provided approximately a 14 percent increase in battery life of a bar code scanner under normal operation. Beacon intervals set beyond 1 second did not have a significant impact on battery life. Based on this testing, it is probably worth setting the beacon interval at around 1 second for clients implementing power saving mode where battery life is an issue. Of course, you should run your own tests with specific devices that you plan to deploy. Just be certain that implementing longer beacon intervals (and corresponding time between beacons) does not negatively impact roaming and delivery of multicast frames.

Hands-on Exercise: Observing 802.11 Beacons

This exercise allows you to observe the transmission and contents of beacons from an access point, which helps you better understand the basis for WLAN functionality.

Perform the following steps:

Step 1.   Obtain test equipment. You need an access point and a wireless protocol analyzer, such as WireShark (which is freely available) or another analyzer (see Chapter 14).

Step 2.   Configure the access point to broadcast the SSID in beacons. For some access points, this might be the only option. As a result, you might not see any configuration setting for this. Check the manual for your access point.

Step 3. Configure the analyzer to record 802.11 frame transmissions on only the frequency band (2.4 GHz or 5 GHz) that the access point is implementing.

Step 4. After powering up the access point, record a packet trace (one or two minutes is enough time) with the protocol analyzer.

Step 5. Observe the packet trace and look at the details of one of the access point beacons. Also, note the time period between the beacons. Can you find the SSID in the frame body of the beacon frame? What else is included in the frame body of the beacon, and what does it tell you about the configuration of the WLAN? Compare what you find with the 802.11 frame field descriptions in this chapter and what is explained in the 802.11 standard.

Step 6. Configure the access point to not broadcast the SSID in beacons (if supported by your access point), and repeat steps 4 and 5. Do you see the SSID in the beacon frame body?

The period between the beacons should comply with the beacon interval setting in the access point, which is usually 100 milliseconds by default. With SSID broadcasting enabled, you should see the SSID in the frame body of the beacon frame. With SSID broadcasting turned off, you should not see the SSID in the beacon frame (it will appear as "null"). In addition to the SSID, you should see lots of information in the frame body of the beacon regarding the access point, such as the beacon interval and supported rates. Some beacons may also contain a traffic indication map indicating which stations (in power saving mode) have frames buffered at the access point.

ATIM Frame

In an ad hoc WLAN, a station with frames buffered for other stations sends an announcement traffic indication message (ATIM) frame to each of these stations during the ATIM window, which immediately follows a beacon transmission. The station then transmits these frames to the applicable recipients. The transmission of the ATIM frame alerts stations in sleep state to stay awake long enough to receive their respective frames.

Disassociation Frame

If a station or an access point wants to terminate an association, it sends a disassociation frame to the opposite station. A single disassociation frame can terminate associations with more than one station through the broadcast address of all 1s.

Authentication Frame

A station sends an authentication frame to a station or an access point that it wants to authenticate with. The authentication sequence consists of the transmission of one or more authentication frames, depending on the type of authentication being implemented (open system or shared key).

Deauthentication Frame

A station sends a deauthentication frame to a station or an access point with which it wants to terminate secure communications.

Action Frame

The action frame was introduced into the 802.11 standard to enable adding more frame types within the limited space available for additional management frames subtypes. The frame body of an action frame includes codes that identify many different frame types that support various functions, such as QoS and high-throughput operation.

Action No ACK Frame

This frame has the same use as the action frame, except that the action no ACK frame does not require that the receiving station send an acknowledgement.

Management Frame Body Contents

The 802.11 standard describes elements that reside in the frame body of management frames. For a complete list, refer to the most current 802.11 standard.

The following are some of the most common information elements:

■ **Authentication Algorithm Number:** This field is present in authentication request/ response frames and specifies the authentication algorithm that the authenticated stations and access points are to use. The value is either 0 for open system authentication or 1 for shared key authentication.

■ **Authentication Transaction Sequence Number:** This field is present in authentication/ response frames and indicates the state of progress of the authentication process.

■ **Challenge Text:** This field is in authentication frames and contains the challenge text of a shared key authentication sequence.

■ **Association ID (AID):** This field is in association/re-association response frames to provide a 16-bit identification assigned by the access point for a client station corresponding to a particular association.

■ **Status Code:** This field is in association/re-association response frames to indicate the status of a particular operation. Examples of status are as follows: successful, unspecified failure, association denied because the access point is unable to handle additional associated stations, and authentication rejected due to timeout waiting for next frame in the sequence.

■ **Reason Code:** This field is in disassociation and deauthentication frames to indicate (via a numbered code) why a station is generating an unsolicited disassociation or deauthentication. Examples of the reasons are previous authentication no longer valid and disassociated due to inactivity.

- **Beacon Interval:** This field, which is present in beacon frames, represents the amount of time between beacon transmissions. Before a station enters power saving mode, the station needs the beacon interval to know when to wake up to receive the beacon (and learn whether there are buffered frames at the access point).

- **Listen Interval:** This field is in association and re-association frames and indicates how often a station will wake to listen to beacon frames.

- **Traffic Indication Map:** This field, which is in beacon frames, specifies the stations having MSDUs buffered at the access point. An access point periodically sends the TIM within a beacon to identify which stations using power saving mode have data frames waiting for them in the access point's buffer. The TIM identifies a station by the association ID that the access point assigned during the association process.

- **Capability Information:** This field is in beacon and other frames to announce capability information about a particular station. For example, a station can identify its desire to be polled in this element.

- **Timestamp:** This field is in beacon and probe response frames and is a time value entered by a sending station when it transmits the frame. After receiving a beacon frame, a station uses the timestamp value to update its local clock. This process enables synchronization among all stations that are associated with the same access point.

- **Service Set Identifier (SSID):** This field is in association/re-association request, probe request/response, and beacon frames. The SSID identifies a specific WLAN. Before associating with a particular WLAN, a station must have the same SSID as the access point. By default, access points include the SSID in the beacon frame to enable client stations to find the WLAN. Some access point vendors have an option to disable the SSID from being broadcast in beacon frames to reduce security issues.

- **Supported Rates:** This field is in most frames and identifies all data rates a particular station can accept. This value represents the data rate in 500-Kbps increments. The MAC layer has the capability to change data rates to optimize performance of frame transmissions.

Note The 802.11 standard defines a basic service set load element that is transmitted in beacons and probe responses transmitted by the access points. The element advertises the number of clients connected to the access point and a measure of utilization of the access point. With this information, clients scanning available access points can make a more informed decision on which access point to associate with.

There are many other elements that 802.11 frames carry in the frame body. For a complete list, refer to the most recent version of the 802.11 standard.

Control Frames

802.11 control frames provide functionality to assist in the delivery of data frames. This includes functions such as acknowledgements and RTS/CTS.

The sections that follow define some of the 802.11 control frames.

Control Wrapper Frame

The control wrapper frame replicates legacy 802.11 control frames by wrapping the original frame and adding an HT Control field, which is necessary for 802.11n and 802.11ac operation.

Block ACK Request Frame

The Block ACK request frame is sent from a source station to a destination station to request that the destination station acknowledge a specific block of frames.

Block ACK Frame

To avoid sending an acknowledgement for each frame, a single Block ACK frame is sent from the recipient of the frames to the source of the frames to acknowledge the successful reception of multiple frames.

Power-Save Poll Frame

If a station receives a power save poll (PS poll) frame, the station updates its network allocation vector (NAV), which is an indication of time periods during which a station will not initiate a transmission. The NAV contains a prediction of future traffic on the medium.

Request-to-Send Frame

A station may send a request-to-send (RTS) frame to another station to negotiate the sending of data frames. The value of the Duration field, in microseconds, is the amount of time the sending station needs to transmit the frame, plus one CTS frame, plus one ACK frame, plus three short interframe space (SIFS) intervals.

Clear-to-Send Frame

After receiving an RTS frame, a station sends a clear-to-send (CTS) frame to acknowledge the right for the sending station to send data frames. Stations always pay attention to the duration information and respond to an RTS frame, even if the station was not configured to initiate RTS frame sequences. The value of the Duration field, in microseconds, is the amount of time from the Duration field of the previous RTS frame, minus the time required to transmit the CTS frame and its SIFS interval.

Acknowledgement Frame

A station that receives an error-free frame must send an ACK frame to the sending station to acknowledge the successful reception of the frame. The value of the Duration field, in microseconds, is equal to 0 if the More Fragment bit in the Frame Control field of the previous data or management frame is set to 0. If the More Fragment bit of the previous data or management frame is set to 1, the Duration field is the amount of time from the Duration field of the previous data or management frame minus the time required to transmit the ACK frame and its SIFS interval.

Contention-Free End Frame

Contention-free end (CF end) designates the end of a contention period that is part of the point coordination function. In these frames, the Duration field is always set to 0, and the receiver address (RA) contains the broadcast group address.

CF End + CF ACK Frame

The CF end + CF ACK frame acknowledges the contention-free end announcement of a CF end frame. In these frames, the Duration field is always set to 0, and the RA contains the broadcast group address.

Data Frames

The main purpose of data frames is to carry information, such as MSDUs, to the destination station. The duration value in data frames is the amount of time necessary to transmit the frame and receive an acknowledgement. This causes other stations to hold off accessing the medium while the data frame is being sent. The payload size of the data frame body can be up to 7,955 bytes, which means that most information requires multiple data frames to carry the entire load. In fact, streaming video demands a continuous flow of data frames to transport the moving pictures.

Some WLAN vendors use null data frames, which contain an empty Frame Body field, to carry special control information to another station. For example, wireless clients commonly use a null data frame sent to the access point to indicate a change in sleep state by setting the power management bit in the frame control field appropriately. This most often occurs after a wireless client implementing power saving mode has been awake and receiving buffered frames from the access point. The null data frame tells the access point to start buffering frames again for that client station because the client is going back to sleep.

Another use of null data frames is for active scanning. The client station sends a null data frame to the access point to indicate sleep state prior to performing active scanning, which is the process of looking for access points on different channels for the purpose of possible roaming. The access point then buffers frames for the client station while the client scans other radio frequency (RF) channels. While on another channel, the client cannot receive frames from the access point.

Once the client station comes back to the associated access point channel, the client sends another null data frame to the access point with the power management bit reset to indicate that the client is ready to receive frames again. This maneuver somewhat fools the access point into thinking the client is in sleep mode; however, it works well to reduce frame retransmissions while the client is busy scanning other channels.

> **Note**   For more information about the 802.11 MAC layer, refer to the most current IEEE 802.11 standard.

Interoperability

802.11n and 802.11ac WLANs use protection mechanisms to compensate for legacy devices not being able to decode frames sent at the higher 802.11n/ac speeds. At 802.11n rates, for instance, some legacy devices cannot decode the Duration field in 802.11n data frames, which can cause timing problems, collisions, and resulting decreases in performance. The protection mechanisms keep legacy devices from transmitting while an 802.11n device is sending a data frame. This involves a CTS-to-self mechanism used by 802.11n/ac client radios when any legacy devices are associated with any access point on the same channel as the 802.11n/ac device.

For example, with CTS-to-self, an 802.11n device transmits a short CTS frame addressed to itself. The CTS frame does not need to be addressed to any other device on the network because the main idea is to just get a CTS frame in the air to convey timing information that blocks legacy devices from transmitting for the time the 802.11n device needs to send its data frame. The CTS frame is sent using a data rate that the legacy devices can receive and decode. This reduces collisions, but it also adds overhead in the form of a CTS frame (with an additional legacy preamble) for every data frame transmission. As a result, you must implement only 802.11n/ac devices to achieve the maximum throughput from 802.11n/ac WLANs.

Hands-on Exercise: Observing 802.11 Frames Resulting from Typical User Traffic

This exercise allows you to observe the transmission of 802.11 frames that represent typical user traffic, which gives you a better understanding of how a WLAN operates.

Perform the following steps:

Step 1.   Obtain the test equipment. You need a wireless client device, such as an 802.11n- or 802.11ac-equipped laptop, and an access point. You also need a wireless protocol analyzer, such as WireShark (which is freely available) or another analyzer (see Chapter 14).

Step 2.   Configure the analyzer to record 802.11 frame transmissions on only the RF channel that the access point is set to. This helps reduce extraneous frames that the analyzer displays by filtering out frames from other channels. With fewer frames, you will be able to more easily pinpoint the 802.11 frames that are applicable to the connection process.

Step 3.   Start recording a packet trace with the protocol analyzer.

Step 4.   Use typical wireless applications, such as browsing the web or sending e-mail, from the client device. After several minutes of using applications, stop the recording of the packet trace.

Step 5.   Observe the packet trace recording and look for the transmission of 802.11 data frames that occur between the applicable client device and access point. Observe and analyze the sequence of 802.11 frames. For example, you might see the protection mechanisms (CTS-to-self frames) if there are legacy client devices associated with the WLAN. You might also see frames that you might not be familiar with. Compare what you find with the frame descriptions explained in this chapter and in the 802.11 standard.

In addition to the regular beacons, you should predominantly see a series of 802.11 data frame transmissions between the client radio and the access point, which of course is carrying information pertaining to the application. When you are browsing the web, the majority of data frames will likely be going from the access point to the client radio. Other applications might behave differently. If you have any legacy radios associated with the WLAN, you should see the corresponding CTS-to-self frames, as described in this chapter.

Summary

The 802.11 MAC layer provides a variety of functions, such as data delivery, network connectivity, timing and synchronization, and power management. To support these functions, the 802.11 protocol defines a series of MAC layer frames that have a defined frame type and format. Actual data represented by MSDUs are sent in the frame body of 802.11 data frames. Other types of frames convey information for setting up and maintaining a client radio's connection to the WLAN.

Chapter 7

IEEE 802.11 Physical (PHY) Layers

This chapter will introduce you to:

- 802.11 Physical Layer Architecture

- 802.11 Physical Layer Functions

- Legacy 802.11 Physical Layers

- High-Throughput (802.11n)

- Very High-Throughput 6 GHz (802.11ac)

The 802.11 standard defines multiple physical layer specifications. An 802.11 station implements one of these physical layers, which interfaces with the common 802.11 Medium Access Control (MAC) layer. Similar to the 802.11 MAC layer, the physical layers have undergone revisions since the ratification of the initial 802.11 standard. The most current 802.11 physical layer today resulted from the 802.11ac amendment to the 802.11 standard, and several physical layers based on other amendments to the standard, including 802.11n and the ones considered legacy versions (for example, 802.11a, 802.11b, and 802.11g, which are still in use). As a result, this chapter covers the legacy physical layers in addition to the one based on the 802.11n and 802.11ac amendments.

802.11 Physical Layer Architecture

The architecture of the 802.11 physical layer (see Figure 7-1) consists of the physical layer convergence procedure (PLCP) sublayer and the physical medium dependent (PMD) sublayer. The sections that follow describe the purpose of each sublayer.

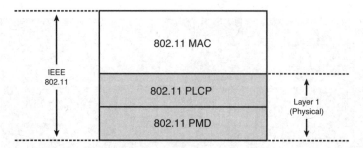

Figure 7-1   *The PLCP Sublayer Minimizes the Dependence of the MAC Layer on the PMD Sublayer by Mapping MAC Protocol Data Units into a Frame Format Suitable for Transmission by the PMD*

PLCP Sublayer

The MAC layer communicates with the PLCP sublayer through what the standard refers to as the physical layer service access point (SAP). Through the SAP, the PLCP accepts MAC protocol data units (MPDUs) from the MAC layer. See Chapter 6, "IEEE 802.11 Medium Access Control (MAC) Layer," for details on what constitutes the MPDU. At the physical layer, the MPDU units are called PLCP service data units (PSDUs). When the MAC layer instructs, the PLCP prepares a PSDU for transmission by appending fields around the PSDU (see Figure 7-2). The transmitter and receivers need the information in these fields to perform their respective functions. The 802.11 standard refers to this composite frame as a PLCP protocol data unit (PPDU). The frame structure of a PPDU provides for asynchronous transfer of MPDUs between stations. As a result, the receiving station's physical layer must synchronize its circuitry to each individual incoming frame. The PLCP also delivers incoming frames from the wireless medium to the MAC layer.

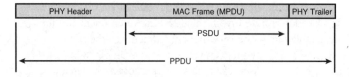

Figure 7-2   *The 802.11 PLCP Prepares a PPDU for Transmission by Appending Fields to the PSDU*

PMD Sublayer

Under the direction of the PLCP, the PMD sublayer does the actual transmission and reception of 802.11 frames. To provide this service, the PMD interfaces directly with the wireless medium (that is, the air) and provides modulation and demodulation of the frame transmissions. The PLCP and PMD communicate with each other to govern the transmission and reception functions.

Note The following sections of this chapter cover the PLCP and PMD for each specific 802.11 physical layer (PHY) in more detail:

"Frequency-Hopping Spread Spectrum PHY"

"Direct-Sequence Spread Spectrum PHY"

"Infrared PHY"

"Orthogonal Frequency-Division Multiplexing PHY (802.11a)"

"High-Rate Direct-Sequence Spread Spectrum PHY (802.11b)"

"Extended-Rate PHY (802.11g)"

"High-Throughput PHY (802.11n)"

"Very High-Throughput 6-GHz PHY (802.11ac)"

802.11 Physical Layer Functions

The general operation of the 802.11 physical layer includes carrier sense, transmit, and receive functions. This applies to all physical layer types, except that they perform these functions differently and offer varying levels of performance. The next sections define each of these primary functions.

Carrier Sense Function

The physical layer implements a carrier sense operation by directing the PMD to check whether the medium is busy or idle. This involves activating a receiver that receives and demodulates radio frequency (RF) signals at specific frequencies. The PLCP performs the following sensing operations if the station is not transmitting or receiving a frame:

- **Detection of incoming signals:** The PLCP within the station will sense the medium continually. When the medium becomes busy, the PLCP will read in the PLCP preamble and header of the frame to attempt synchronization of the receiver to the data rate of the signal.

- **Clear channel assessment:** The clear channel assessment operation determines whether the wireless medium is busy or idle. The PMD measures the energy on the medium that exceeds a specific level, which is the energy detection (ED) threshold. If the medium is idle, the PLCP will send an "idle" notification to the MAC layer. If the medium is busy, the PLCP will send a "busy" notification to the MAC layer. The MAC layer can then make a decision whether to send a frame.

Transmit Function

The PLCP switches the PMD to transmit mode after receiving notice from the MAC layer indicating a start of transmission. The MAC layer sends the number of octets that need to be transmitted and the data rate instruction along with this request. The PMD responds by sending the preamble of the frame along with the remaining physical layer header and MSDU.

The transmitter sends the physical layer preamble and header at the lowest standard data rate to provide a specific common data rate at which the receiver listens. After sending the header, the transmitter changes the data rate of the transmission to what the header specifies. After the transmission takes place, the PLCP sends a configuration to the MAC layer, shuts off the transmitter, and switches the PMD circuitry to receive mode.

Receive Function

If the clear channel assessment discovers a busy medium and valid preamble of an incoming frame, the PLCP monitors the header of the frame. If the PLCP determines that the physical layer header is error free, the PLCP sends a receive indication to the MAC layer to provide notification of an incoming frame. The PLCP sends the information it finds in the frame header, such as the number of octets and data rate.

The PLCP sets an octet counter based on the value in the PSDU Length Word field in the header. This counter keeps track of the number of octets received, enabling the PLCP to know when the end of the frame occurs. As the PLCP receives data, it sends octets of the PSDU to the MAC layer. After receiving the final octet, the PLCP sends a receive end indication to the MAC layer to indicate the final octet of the frame.

Legacy 802.11 Physical Layers

The 802.11 standard includes a number of physical layer definitions that have evolved over the years since the initial ratification of the 802.11 standard in 1997. The following sections describe the physical layers of the 802.11 standard that are referred to as legacy standards. Some of them are still in wide use today, but some of them have become obsolete.

Frequency-Hopping Spread Spectrum PHY

The Frequency-Hopping Spread Spectrum (FHSS) physical layer was part of the original 802.11 standard published in 1997. Very few wireless LANs (WLANs) in use today use this version of the standard; however, it is worth including here as a comparison/baseline for the versions of the standard that follow. The existing FHSS networks are sometimes found in hospitals, where a lot of the FHSS systems were deployed. Few if any vendors continue to sell 802.11 FHSS equipment.

The 802.11 FHSS physical layer uses FSSS to deliver 1-Mbps and 2-Mbps data rates in the 2.4-GHz band. Figure 7-3 illustrates the format of an FHSS PPDU. In general, the preamble enables the receiver to prepare clocking functions and antenna diversity before the actual content of the frame arrives. The header field provides information about the frame, and the whitened PSDU (PLCP service data unit) is the MPDU the station is sending.

Figure 7-3 *Fields in an FHSS PPDU*

The following are the FHSS PPDU fields:

- **SYNC:** This field consists of alternating 0s and 1s, alerting the receiver that a potentially receivable signal is present. A receiver will begin to synchronize with the incoming signal after detecting the SYNC.

- **SFD (Start Frame Delimiter):** The content of this field is always the 0000110010111101 bit pattern, which defines the beginning of a frame.

- **PLW (PSDU Length Word):** This field specifies the length of the PSDU in octets. The receiver uses this information to determine the end of the frame.

- **PSF (PLCP Signaling):** This field identifies the data rate of the whitened PSDU portion of the frame (either 1 Mbps or 2 Mbps). The preamble and header of the PPDU are always sent at 1 Mbps, but the remaining portions of the frame can be sent at different data rates, as indicated by this field. The PMD, however, must support the data rate.

- **HEC (Header Error Check):** This field contains a 16-bit cyclic redundancy check (CRC) result based on the CRC-16 error-detection algorithm. The generator polynomial for CRC-16 is $G(x) = x^{16} + x^{12} + x^5 + 1$. The physical layer does not determine whether errors are present within the PSDU. The MAC layer checks for errors based on the frame check sequence (FCS). CRC-16 detects all single- and double-bit errors and ensures detection of 99.998 percent of all possible errors. Most experts think that CRC-16 is sufficient for data transmission blocks of 4 KB or less.

- **Whitened PSDU:** The PSDU is the MPDU being sent and can range from 0 to 4,095 octets in length. Before transmission, the physical layer whitens the PSDU by stuffing special symbols every 4 octets to minimize DC bias of the data signal. The PSDU whitening process involves the use of a length-127 frame-synchronous scrambler and a 32/33 bias-suppression encoding algorithm to randomize the data.

The FHSS PMD performs a frequency-hopping function and frequency shift-keying modulation technique. The 802.11 standard defines a set of FHSS channels that are evenly spaced across the 2.4-GHz band. The number of channels depends on geography. For example, the number of channels for North America and most of Europe is 79. The FHSS-based PMD transmits PPDUs by hopping from channel to channel according to a particular pseudo-random hopping sequence that uniformly distributes the signal across the operating frequency band. Once the hopping sequence is set in an access point, stations automatically synchronize to the correct hopping sequence. The 802.11 standard defines a particular set of hopping sequences. The sequences avoid prolonged interference with one another. This enables designers to collocate multiple PMDs to improve performance. The hop rate is adjustable, but the PMD must hop at a minimum rate that regulatory bodies within the country of operation specify. For the United States, FHSS must operate at a minimum hop rate of 2.5 hops per second.

The FHSS PMD transmits the binary data at either 1 Mbps or 2 Mbps, using a specific modulation type for each, depending on which data rate is chosen. The PMD uses two-level Gaussian frequency shift-key (GFSK) modulation for transmitting data streams at 1 Mbps. The concept of GFSK is to vary the carrier frequency to represent different binary symbols. Thus, changes in frequency maintain the information content of the signal. Noise usually affects the amplitude of the signal, not the frequency. As a result, the use of GFSK modulation reduces potential interference.

The input to the GFSK modulator is either a 0 or 1 coming from the PLCP. The modulator transmits the binary data by shifting the transmit frequency slightly above or below the center operating frequency (Fc) for each hop. To perform this operation, the modulator transmits on a frequency using the following rules:

Transmit frequency = Fc + fd for sending a 1 bit

Transmit frequency = Fc − fd for sending a 0 bit

In the equation, Fc is the operating center frequency for the current hop, and fd is the amount of frequency deviation. The value of fd is greater than 110 KHz. The 802.11 specification explains how to calculate exact values for fd, but the nominal value is 160 KHz.

The FHSS PMD uses four-level GFSK modulation for transmitting data streams at 2 Mbps. Stations implementing the 2-Mbps version must also be able to operate at 1 Mbps for the entire MSDU. For 2-Mbps operation, the input to the modulator is combinations of 2 bits (00, 01, 10, or 11) coming from the PLCP. Each of these 2-bit symbols is sent at 1 Mbps, meaning each bit is sent at 2 Mbps. Thus, the four-level modulation technique doubles the data rate while maintaining the same baud rate as a 1-Mbps signal.

Note   Much like with two-level GFSK, the modulator transmits the binary data bits by shifting the transmit frequency slightly above or below the center operating frequency for each hop. In this case, though, the transmitter can transmit at four possible frequencies—one for each 2-bit combination. To perform this operation, the modulator transmits on the operating center frequency with a frequency deviation equal to fd. There are two values of fd that move the transmit frequency above Fc and two values of fd that move the transmit frequency below Fc. The 802.11 standard describes how to calculate the exact value of fd.

New deployments of FHSS wireless LANs are rare; however, you might still find relatively old 802.11 FHSS systems installed in some organizations, especially hospitals.

Direct-Sequence Spread Spectrum PHY

Along with FHSS, the Direct-Sequence Spread Spectrum (DSSS) physical layer was also part of the original 802.11 standard published in 1997. Some WLANs in use today still use the DSSS version, and many of WLAN client cards and access points sold today are backward compatible with DSSS.

The 802.11 DSSS physical layer uses DSSS to deliver 1-Mbps and 2-Mbps data rates in the 2.4-GHz band. Figure 7-4 illustrates the DSSS PPDU. The preamble enables the receiver to synchronize to the incoming signal properly before the actual content of the frame arrives. The header provides information about the frame, and the PSDU (PLCP service data unit) is the MPDU that the station is sending.

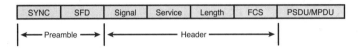

Figure 7-4   *Fields in a DSSS PPDU*

The following are the DSSS PPDU fields:

- **Sync:** This field consists of alternating 0s and 1s, alerting the receiver that a potentially receivable signal is present. A receiver begins to synchronize with the incoming signal after detecting the Sync.

- **SFD (Start Frame Delimiter):** This field defines the beginning of a frame. The bit pattern for this field is always 1111001110100000, which is unique for DSSS PLCPs.

- **Signal:** This field identifies the type of modulation that the receiver must use to demodulate the signal. The value of this field is equal to the data rate divided by 100 Kbps. The only two possible values for the June 1997 version of 802.11 are 00001010 for 1-Mbps DSSS and 00010100 for 2-Mbps DSSS. The PLCP preamble and header are both always sent at 1 Mbps.

- **Service:** The 802.11 specification reserves this field for future use; however, a value of 00000000 means 802.11 device compliance.

- **Length:** The value of this field is an unsigned 16-bit integer that indicates the number of microseconds to transmit the MPDU. The receiver uses this information to determine the end of the frame.

- **FCS (Frame Check Sequence):** Much like with the FHSS physical layer, this field contains a 16-bit CRC result based on CRC-16 error detection algorithm. The generator polynomial for CRC-16 is $G(x) = x^{16} + x^{12} + x^5 + 1$. The CRC operation is done at the transmitting station before scrambling.

- **PSDU:** The PSDU is the MPDU being sent.

The operation of the DSSS PMD translates the binary representation of the PPDUs into a radio signal suitable for transmission. The DSSS physical layer performs this process by multiplying a radio frequency carrier by a pseudo-noise (PN) digital signal. The resulting signal appears as noise if plotted in the frequency domain. The wider bandwidth of the direct sequence signal enables the signal power to drop to lower levels without loss of information. As with FHSS, the DSSS physical layer operates in the 2.4-GHz frequency range, depending on regulatory authorities in different parts of the world. The 802.11 standard specifies operation of DSSS on up to 14 channel frequencies (see Table 7-1).

In the United States, only Channels 1 through 11 are authorized. Channels are each 22 MHz wide.

Table 7-1   *Specific DSSS Channel Frequencies*

Channel Number	Frequency (GHz)
1	2.412
2	2.417
3	2.422
4	2.427
5	2.432
6	2.437
7	2.442
8	2.447
9	2.452
10	2.457
11	2.462
12	2.467
13	2.472
14	2.484

The general idea of DSSS is to first digitally spread baseband data frame (PPDU) and then modulate the spread data to a particular frequency. The transmitter spreads the PPDU by combining the PPDU with a PN code (sometimes referred to as a chip or spreading sequence) via a binary adder. The specific PN code for 802.11 DSSS is the following 11-chip Barker sequence, with the leftmost bit applied first to the PPDU:

+1, −1, +1, +1, −1, +1, +1, +1, −1, −1, −1

The output of the binary adder is a DSSS signal that has a higher-rate signal than the original data signal. A 1-Mbps PPDU at the input, for example, will result in a signal with 11-Mbps rate at the output of the adder. The modulator translates the baseband signal into an analog signal at the operating transmit frequency of the chosen channel.

DSSS is different from code-division multiple access (CDMA). CDMA operates in a similar fashion; however, it uses multiple orthogonal spreading sequences to enable multiple users to operate at the same frequency. The difference is that 802.11 DSSS always uses the same spreading sequence, but it enables users to choose from multiple frequencies for concurrent operation.

A balanced modulator modulates the digitally spread PPDU by combining it with a carrier set at the transmit frequency. The DSSS PMD transmits the PPDU at 1 Mbps or 2 Mbps using different modulation types, depending on which data rate is chosen. For 1 Mbps (basic access rate), the PMD uses differential binary phase shift-keying (DBPSK) modulation. The input to the DBPSK modulator is either a 0 or 1 coming from the PLCP. The modulator transmits the binary data by shifting the carrier signal's phase.

For 2-Mbps transmission (enhanced access rate), the PMD uses differential quadrature phase shift-keying (DQPSK) modulation. In this case, the input to the modulator is combinations of 2 bits (00, 01, 10, or 11) coming from the PLCP. Each of these 2-bit symbols is sent at 1 Mbps, resulting in a binary data rate of 2 Mbps. Thus, the four-level modulation technique doubles the data rate while maintaining the same baud rate as a 1-Mbps signal. This makes effective use of the wireless medium.

Infrared PHY

The 802.11 infrared (IR) physical layer was part of the initial 802.11 standard published in 1997. No known 802.11 IR networks are in use today, however. Over the years, 802.11 IR lost support within the 802.11 Working Group, and the IR physical layer did not advance to higher performance as did the physical layers based on radio waves. Because of this, and the inability of IR light to pass through walls, the 802.11 IR physical layer lost support. As a result, the 802.11 IR physical layer is not covered in this book.

Orthogonal Frequency-Division Multiplexing PHY (802.11a)

The IEEE 802.11 orthogonal frequency-division multiplexing (OFDM) physical layer delivers 6-Mbps to 54-Mbps data rates in the 5-GHz band. The OFDM physical layer, commonly referred to as 802.11a, was once targeted to become the basis for high-speed WLANs. The 802.11a amendment to the standard was ratified in 1999, but products were not available until late 2001, which was long after 802.11b (another amendment ratified in 1999) networks began to proliferate and dominate the market. As a result, very few 802.11a WLANs have actually been deployed.

Note The benefits of OFDM are high spectral efficiency, resiliency to radio signal interference, and lower multipath distortion. The orthogonal nature of OFDM allows subchannels to overlap, which has a positive effect on spectral efficiency. The subcarriers transporting information are just far enough apart to avoid interference with each other, theoretically.

Figure 7-5 illustrates the format of an OFDM PPDU.

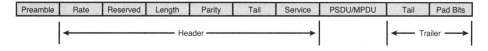

Figure 7-5 *Fields in an OFDM (802.11a) PPDU*

The following are the OFDM PLCP frame fields:

- **Preamble:** The preamble enables the receiver to acquire an incoming OFDM signal and synchronize the demodulator. The preamble consists of 12 symbols. Ten of them are short for establishing AGC (automatic gain control) and the coarse frequency estimate of the carrier signal. The receiver uses the long symbols for fine-tuning. With this preamble, it takes 16 microseconds to train the receiver after first receiving the frame.

- **Rate:** This 4-bit field identifies the data rate at which the content of the frame body is sent: 6, 9, 12, 18, 24, 36, 48, or 54 Mbps.

- **Reserved:** This field is set to 0.

- **Length:** This field identifies the number of octets in the frame.

- **Parity:** This field is 1 bit, based on positive (even) parity and on the first 17 bits of the frame (Rate, Reserved, and Length fields).

- **Tail:** This field must be set to all 0s.

- **Service:** This field consists of 16 bits, with the first 7 bits as 0s to synchronize the descrambler in the receiver and the remaining 9 bits (all 0s) reserved for future use (and set to 0s).

- **PSDU:** The PSDU (PLCP service data unit) is the payload from the MAC layer being sent.

- **Tail:** This field consists of 6 bits (all 0s) appended to the symbol to bring the convolutional encoder to zero state.

- **Pad Bits:** This field contains at least six bits, but it is actually the number of bits that make the Data field a multiple of the number of coded bits in an OFDM symbol (48, 96, 192, or 288).

The PLCP Preamble and Signal fields are convolutional encoded and sent at 6 Mbps using BPSK no matter what data rate the Signal field indicates. A data scrambler using a 127-bit sequence generator scrambles all bits in the data field to randomize the bit patterns in order to avoid long streams of 1s and 0s.

Note   Some 802.11a chipset and module suppliers use proprietary techniques to combine OFDM channels for applications requiring data rates that exceed 54 Mbps.

The operation of the 802.11a PMD translates the binary representation of the PPDUs into a radio signal suitable for transmission. The 802.11 OFDM PMD performs these operations by dividing a high-speed serial information signal into multiple lower-speed subsignals that the system transmits simultaneously at different frequencies in parallel. The operating frequencies for the 802.11a OFDM layer vary, depending on the regulatory of the applicable country where the WLAN will operate. Table 7-2 identifies the authorized channels in the 5-GHz band.

Table 7-2 *Unlicensed National Information Infrastructure (UNII) 5-GHz Channel (20-MHz) Allocations for OFDM in the United States (Refer to Local Regulatory Bodies for Other Countries)*

Channel Number	Center Frequency (GHz)
U-NII 1 Band	
36	5.180
40	5.200
44	5.220
48	5.240
U-NII 2 Band	
52	5.260
56	5.280
60	5.300
64	5.320
U-NII 2 Extended (Worldwide) Band	
100	5.500
104	5.520
108	5.540
112	5.560
116	5.580
132	5.660
136	5.680
140	5.700
144	5.720
U-NII 3 Band (primarily U.S. only)	
149	5.745
153	5.765
157	5.785
161	5.805
165	5.825

> **Note**   The U-NII 1 band (Channels 36–48) and U-NII 3 band (Channels 149–165) do not require use of dynamic frequency selection (DFS); on the other hand, both U-NII 2 bands do require DFS.

The 802.11 OFDM physical layer uses a combination of BPSK, QPSK, and QAM, depending on the chosen data rate (see Table 7-3). Data rates of 6 Mbps, 12 Mbps, and 24 Mbps are mandatory for all 802.11a-compliant products.

Table 7-3   *802.11a OFDM Modulation Techniques*

Data Rate (Mbps)	Modulation
6	BPSK
9	BPSK
12	QPSK
18	QPSK
24	16-QAM
36	16-QAM
48	64-QAM
54	64-QAM

OFDM is not a form of spread spectrum. Instead, OFDM splits an information signal across 52 separate subcarriers within a 20-MHz channel. Four of the subcarriers are pilot subcarriers that the system uses as a reference to disregard frequency or phase shifts of the signal during transmission. A pseudo-binary sequence is sent through the pilot subcarriers to prevent the generation of spectral lines. The remaining 48 subcarriers provide separate wireless pathways for sending the information in a parallel fashion. OFDM divides groups (symbols) of 1, 2, 4, or 6 bits, depending on data rate chosen, and converts them into complex numbers representing applicable constellation points. An inverse FFT (fast Fourier transform) combines the subcarriers before transmission.

High-Rate Direct-Sequence Spread Spectrum PHY (802.11b)

The 802.11 High-Rate Direct-Sequence Spread Spectrum (HR-DSSS) physical layer is a rate extension to the initial 802.11 DSSS standard. HR-DSSS, commonly referred to as 802.11b (ratified in 1999 along with 802.11a), includes complementary code keying (CCK) and operates in the 2.4-GHz band to achieve additional data rates of 5.5 Mbps and 11 Mbps. The HR-DSSS is backward compatible with 802.11 DSSS implementations.

Figure 7-6 illustrates the format of an HR-DSSS (802.11b) PPDU.

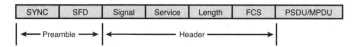

Figure 7-6 *Fields in an HR-DSSS (802.11b) PPDU*

The following are the HR-DSSS (802.11b) PLCP frame fields:

- **Sync:** This field consists of alternating 0s and 1s to alert the receiver that a potentially receivable signal is present. A receiver begins to synchronize with the incoming signal after detecting the Sync field. A shorter alternate Sync field can be used in implementations to minimize overhead and maximize throughput. The short Sync field consists of 56 scrambled bits.

- **SFD (Start Frame Delimiter):** This field defines the beginning of a frame. The bit pattern for this field is always 1111001110100000, which is unique for DSSS PLCPs.

- **Signal:** This field identifies the type of modulation that the receiver must use to demodulate the signal. The value of this field is equal to the data rate divided by 100 Kbps. The following are mandatory data rates specified by HR-DSSS:

  - **1 Mbps:** 00001010

  - **2 Mbps:** 00010100

  - **5.5 Mbps:** 00110111

  - **11 Mbps:** 01101110

The PLCP preamble and header are both always sent at 1 Mbps.

- **Service:** Bit 2 of the Service field indicates whether the transmitter frequency and the symbol clocks derive from the same oscillator. Bit 7 is used in conjunction with the Length field to eliminate ambiguity when converting the number of octets to corresponding transmit time for data rates greater than 8 Mbps. For example, at 11 Mbps, the Length field value equals the number of octets times 8, divided by 11, and rounded up to the next integer. Bit 7 of the Service field will be 0 if the rounding takes less than 8/11 and 1 if the rounding is equal to or greater than 8/11.

- **Length:** The value of this field is an unsigned 16-bit integer that indicates the number of microseconds to transmit the MPDU. The receiver uses this information to determine the end of the frame.

- **FCS (Frame Check Sequence):** Similar to the FHSS physical layer, this field contains a 16-bit CRC result based on CRC-16 error detection algorithm. The generator polynomial for CRC-16 is $G(x) = x^{16} + x^{12} + x^5 + 1$. The CRC operation is done at the transmitting station before scrambling.

- **PSDU:** The PSDU is the MPDU being sent.

The operation of the HR-DSSS PMD translates the binary representation of the PPDUs into a radio signal suitable for transmission. The HR-DSSS PMD is the same as DSSS PMD, except for a different modulation type necessary to deliver higher data rates. For 1 Mbps and 2 Mbps, the HR-DSSS PMD uses the Barker spreading sequence, which is the same for 802.11 DSSS implementations. HR-DSSS uses CCK to provide the spreading sequences for the 5.5-Mbps and 11-Mbps data rates. The HR-DSSS PMD uses the channel plan shown in Table 7-1.

CCK uses an I/Q modulation architecture with a spreading code 8 chips long at a chipping rate of 11 million chips per second. Each symbol (group of data bits) transmitted is represented by a particular CCK spreading code. Each chip of the spreading code is complex (that is, it has more than two possible phases). The spreading codes are known as complementary codes based on Walsh-Hadamard functions.

Extended-Rate PHY (802.11g)

The 802.11g amendment ratified in 2003 extends the data rates in the 2.4-GHz band to 54 Mbps through the use of OFDM (same as 802.11a) and is backward compatible with the initial DSSS and HR-DSSS (802.11b) physical layers. 802.11g defines several PPDU formats. One of them, referred to as ERP-OFDM, is the same used by the 802.11a OFDM physical layer. Another one, called DSSS-OFDM, includes a similar frame structure as the DSSS physical layer, but it transports ERP-OFDM PPDUs. This enables backward compatibility and avoids the need for protection mechanisms. The ERP physical layers use the same frequency plan shown in Table 7-1.

High-Throughput (802.11n)

The 802.11n amendment, which specifies MIMO (multiple-input multiple-output) technology to extend data rates into the hundreds of megabits per second in the 2.4-GHz and 5-GHz bands, was ratified in 2009. 802.11n is backward compatible with 802.11a and 802.11b/g. Because of the much higher data rate and flexibility of 802.11n, most new deployments today in the 2.4-GHz band are based on 802.11n.

MIMO Concepts

Legacy WLANs communicate through a single spatial stream and a single antenna. MIMO enables transmission over two or more spatial streams with multiple transmitters and receivers. This makes 802.11n WLANs more robust and resilient to transmission impairments, such as multipath propagation, and provides much higher data rates and corresponding throughputs.

Transmit Beamforming

A basic form of 802.11n MIMO (referred to as transmit beamforming) uses more than one transmitter at the sending station to improve the signal at the receiving station. Figure 7-7 illustrates this concept.

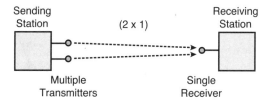

Figure 7-7 *Transmit Beamforming Includes More Transmitters Than Receivers*

In this 2×1 example, the two signals sent by separate transmitters (on separate antennas) will likely arrive at the receiver antenna with a phase difference between the signals, which impacts signal strength at the receiver. The receiver provides feedback regarding the phase difference to the sending station, which can then adjust the phase of the signals at the transmitter in a way that better aligns the phases of the signals at the receiver in order to maximize the signal at the receiver. As a result, transmit beamforming increases SNR and data rate. This, however, requires feedback from the receiver, which is done by 802.11n devices (not the legacy devices). For example, transmit beamforming does not work if the access point is 802.11n and the client device uses 802.11g.

A problem with transmit beamforming is that movement of either the source station or the receiving station (even walking speeds) will change the phase between the signals, which requires the receiver to continually provide feedback. Also, 802.11n transmit beamforming is possible only when sending unicast frames, not broadcast or multicast frames. The access point sends beacons via broadcast delivery; therefore, the ranges of the client devices are limited to beacons being sent without beamforming. Client devices cannot operate beyond the range of the beacons. Therefore, transmit beamforming only increases the data rates within this maximum range.

It is also possible for 802.11n MIMO to provide gains in throughput by having fewer transmitters than receivers. In a 1×2 configuration, for example, the two receivers both receive the same single transmitted signal and perform complex calculations that result in higher effective signal strength at the receiver. Because legacy devices have a single transmitter, this method works with legacy devices. In fact, legacy clients can have up to a 30 percent improvement in performance when connecting to an 802.11n access point, assuming the 802.11n access point implements multiple receivers.

Spatial Multiplexing

To dramatically improve throughput, 802.11n MIMO implements spatial multiplexing, which allows separate data streams (referred to as spatial streams) to be sent between the sending and receiving stations. Figure 7-8 illustrates this concept. In this 2×2 example, there are two transmitters at the sending station and two receivers at the receiving station, and each transmitter/receiver pair operates independently. 802.11n specifies a maximum of four transmitters at the sending station and four receivers at the receiving station (4×4 configuration), which offers maximum throughput. The improvement in throughput beyond 3×3, though, is not significant.

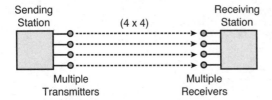

Figure 7-8 *Spatial Multiplexing Increases the Number of Spatial Streams*

> **Note**   In spatial multiplexing notation such as A×B, A represents the number of transmit streams, and B represents the number of receive streams.

Hands-on Exercise: Understanding Performance Impacts of Increasing 802.11n Spatial Streams

This exercise helps you understand how increasing the number of spatial streams can improve performance and range. It is not possible to change the spatial streams on all 802.11n access points, so check yours before getting too far with this exercise.

Perform the following steps:

Step 1.   Configure an 802.11n wireless client device to test performance against a point located on the wired network. For example, you can run a throughput test from the client device against an online performance tester, such as the one at http://performance.toast.net. The main idea is to measure performance for comparison purposes as you test different spatial stream configurations.

Step 2.   Configure an 802.11n access point to have 1×1 spatial streams (with data rates that will change automatically) and run a performance test with the 802.11n client device associated to the access point. Ideally, run the test with the client device relatively far from the access point where performance is somewhat low. This should allow you to see a difference when increasing the spatial streams.

Step 3.   Configure the 802.11n access point to have the maximum spatial streams, such as 2×3. Repeat the performance test with the client device and access point at the same location as the previous test. What change in performance do you see as compared to when the access point was configured with 1×1 spatial streams?

Step 4.   If you can change the access point to additional spatial streams, try each combination while repeating the performance test. How does the change in performance correspond with the spatial stream settings?

You should notice an improvement in performance as you increase the spatial streams. Keep in mind that other environmental elements, such as radio signal interference, may impact the results. For example, some interference may arise when testing a greater number of spatial streams, which could result in lower (rather than higher) performance. Therefore, it is a good idea to repeat the throughput tests a few times for each configuration and perform the tests as close together as possible for each configuration that you are comparing.

Note   A receiver can have more antennas than spatial streams. If so, the receiver will have an order of diversity (which improves signal strength) equal to the difference between antennas and spatial streams.

Channel Bonding

Legacy WLANs operate over 20-MHz channels, but 802.11n can operate over 20-MHz or 40-MHz channels. This feature is configurable when deploying 802.11n WLANs. 802.11n uses channel bonding to join two 20-MHz channels into one that is 40-MHz wide, which provides much higher data rates (theoretically double). Channel bonding is best if done in the 5-GHz band because the 2.4-GHz band does not have enough room for effective frequency reuse.

The 20-MHz channels have a small amount of reserved spectrum at the top and bottom of the channel to reduce adjacent channel interference. When bonding two adjacent 20-MHz channels, 802.11n combines the channels in a way that makes use of the reserved spectrum. As a result, channel bonding increases the data rate slightly more than double.

Hands-on Exercise: Understanding Performance Impacts of 802.11n Channel Bonding

This exercise helps you understand how channel bonding impacts performance.

Perform the following steps:

Step 1.   Configure a 5-GHz 802.11n wireless client device to test performance against a point located on the wired network. For example, you can run a throughput test from the client device against an online performance tester, such as the one at http://performance.toast.net. The main idea is to measure performance in a way for comparison purposes as you test 20-MHz and 40-MHz channels.

Step 2.   Configure a 5-GHz 802.11n access point on a particular channel initially with a 20-MHz channel width (with data rates that will change automatically) and run a performance test with the 802.11n client device associated to the access point. Ideally, run the test with the client device relatively far from the access point where performance is somewhat low. This should allow you to see a difference when changing the channel width.

Step 3.   Configure the 802.11n access point to have a 40-MHz channel width and repeat the performance test with the client device and access point at the same location as the previous test. What changes in performance do you see compared to when the access point was set to 20-MHz channel width?

You should notice an improvement in performance as you increase the channel width to 40 MHz. As with the previous exercise on spatial streams, environmental elements such as radio signal interference, however, may impact the results. Therefore, you should repeat each test a few times for each configuration and perform the tests of different configurations as close together as possible. Also, because a higher channel width mainly only increases the capacity of the channel, you may not see any difference in performance if the throughput testing you are doing does not consume much capacity.

802.11n Modulation

Much like 802.11a and 802.11g, 802.11n uses OFDM in both the 2.4-GHz and 5-GHz band but increases the number of data subcarriers for each radio transceiver in each 20-MHz channel from 48 to 52. This increases the data rate to 65 Mbps per spatial stream. Each radio can be set to eight different data rate selections. It is possible to use up to four radios (that is, four separate spatial streams), which provides maximum data rates of 65 Mbps (one stream), 130 Mbps (two streams), 195 Mbps (three streams), and 260 Mbps (four streams). For 40-MHz channels, 802.11n makes use of 108 subcarriers, which results in maximum data rates of 135 Mbps (one stream), 270 Mbps (two streams), 405 Mbps (three streams), and 540 Mbps (four streams). 802.11n allows different modulation for different spatial streams (unequal modulation), which enables a larger set of possible data rates. This is not practical to implement in most applications, however, because of required feedback channels to identify which spatial streams must use each of the different modulation methods.

Tables 7-4, 7-5, 7-6 and 7-7 identify the modulation types that 802.11n uses at various data rates, based on the number of spatial streams for 20-MHz channels and 800-nanosecond guard interval. The guard interval is a quiet period between each OFDM symbol transmission to minimize intersymbol interference caused by multipath environments. The guard interval allows time for symbols taking longer paths to arrive at the receiver. The 800-nanosecond guard interval allows for path differences of approximately 800 feet.

Table 7-4   *802.11n Modulation Techniques for One Spatial Stream (20-MHz Channel)*

Data Rate (Mbps)	Modulation
6.5	BPSK
13.0	QPSK
19.5	QPSK
26.0	16-QAM

Data Rate (Mbps)	Modulation
39.0	16-QAM
52.0	64-QAM
58.5	64-QAM
65.0	64-QAM

Table 7-5   *802.11n Modulation Techniques for Two Spatial Streams (20-MHz Channel)*

Data Rate (Mbps)	Modulation
13.0	BPSK
26.0	QPSK
39.0	QPSK
52.0	16-QAM
78.0	16-QAM
104.0	64-QAM
117.0	64-QAM
130.0	64-QAM

Table 7-6   *802.11n Modulation Techniques for Three Spatial Streams (20-MHz Channel)*

Data Rate (Mbps)	Modulation
19.5	BPSK
39.0	QPSK
58.5	QPSK
78.0	16-QAM
117.0	16-QAM
156.0	64-QAM
175.5	64-QAM
195.0	64-QAM

Table 7-7   *802.11n Modulation Techniques for Four Spatial Streams (20-MHz Channel)*

Data Rate (Mbps)	Modulation
26.0	BPSK
52.0	QPSK
78.0	QPSK
104.0	16-QAM
156.0	16-QAM
208.0	64-QAM
234.0	64-QAM
260.0	64-QAM

Tables 7-8, 7-9, 7-10, and 7-11 identify the modulation types that 802.11n uses at various data rates, based on the number of spatial streams for 40-MHz channels.

If multipath is not a problem, 802.11n makes available a shorter guard interval of 400 nanoseconds. This increases the data rates slightly. For 20-MHz channels (400-nanosecond guard interval), the maximum data rates are 72 Mbps (one stream), 144 Mbps (two streams), 216 Mbps (three streams), and 288 Mbps (four streams). For 40-MHz channels (400-nanosecond guard interval), the maximum data rates are 150 Mbps (one stream), 300 Mbps (two streams), 450 Mbps (three streams), and 600 Mbps (four streams).

Note   See Tables 7-1 and 7-2 for 802.11n operating frequencies.

Table 7-8   *802.11n Modulation Techniques for One Spatial Stream (40-MHz Channel)*

Data Rate (Mbps)	Modulation
13.5	BPSK
27.0	QPSK
40.5	QPSK
54.0	16-QAM
81.0	16-QAM
108.0	64-QAM
121.5	64-QAM
135.0	64-QAM

Table 7-9 *802.11n Modulation Techniques for Two Spatial Streams (40-MHz Channel)*

Data Rate (Mbps)	Modulation
27.0	BPSK
54.0	QPSK
81.0	QPSK
108.0	16-QAM
162.0	16-QAM
216.0	64-QAM
243.0	64-QAM
270.0	64-QAM

Table 7-10 *802.11n Modulation Techniques for Three Spatial Streams (40-MHz Channel)*

Data Rate (Mbps)	Modulation
40.5	BPSK
81.0	QPSK
121.5	QPSK
162.0	16-QAM
243.0	16-QAM
324.0	64-QAM
364.5	64-QAM
405.0	64-QAM

Table 7-11 *802.11n Modulation Techniques for Four Spatial Streams (40-MHz Channel)*

Data Rate (Mbps)	Modulation
54.0	BPSK
108.0	QPSK
162.0	QPSK
216.0	16-QAM
324.0	16-QAM
432.0	64-QAM
486.0	64-QAM
540.0	64-QAM

Interoperability

Initial backward compatibility of 802.11n with legacy devices is important because of the large base of 802.11b and 802.11g client devices. As a result, 802.11 addresses interoperability with legacy devices. The 802.11n mixed-mode operation is applicable when there are any 802.11a, 802.11b, or 802.11g client devices that will associate with the wireless network.

The problem is that legacy devices cannot understand the signal that 802.11n transmits. As a result, 802.11n (in mixed) first transmits a preamble and header (see Figure 7-9) that all legacy devices can understand and at a data rate that the legacy devices can receive. This informs the legacy devices that an 802.11 transmission is taking place, which causes the legacy devices to hold off and avoid transmitting (which could cause a collision). The 802.11n transmitter follows the "legacy" PLCP header with an 802.11n preamble and signal field at 802.11n rates and applicable number of spatial streams. In addition to the protection mechanisms implemented by the MAC layer, the additional legacy preamble and signal field reduces throughput when 802.11n is operating in mixed mode.

| Legacy Preamble | Legacy Header | 802.11n Preamble | 802.11n Header | PSDU/MPDU |

Figure 7-9   *Fields in an HT-OFDM (802.11n) PPDU Operating in Mixed Mode*

Very High-Throughput 6 GHz (802.11ac)

The 802.11ac amendment extends data rates to the gigabits-per-second range in the 5-GHz band and is backward compatible with 802.11a and 802.11n (5 GHz). Because of the much higher data rate of 802.11ac, new deployments in the 5-GHz band today are based on 802.11ac, especially for applications requiring very high performance. The following sections describe the primary changes that 802.11ac brought to the 802.11ac physical layer.

RF Channel Bandwidth

802.11ac allows access points to be configured with the following RF channel bandwidths that extend well beyond that of 802.11n: 80-MHz (mandatory) and 160-MHz (optional), which provide substantial increases in data rate. Each 80-MHz channel is composed of two adjacent 40-MHz channels. For instance, each of the U-NII 1 and 2 bands (see Table 7-2) can support one 80-MHz channel because each band is 80-MHz wide, the U-NII 2 extended band can support three 80-MHz channels, and the U-NII 3 band can support one 80-MHz channel. Each 160-MHz channel includes two 80-MHz channels that are contiguous (next to each other) or noncontiguous (not next to each other). As a result, the U-NII 1 and 2 bands (combined) can support one 160-MHz channel, and the U-NII 2 extended band can support one 160-MHz channel. The U-NII 3 band does not support use of 160-MHz channels. In addition, it's possible to comprise a 160-MHz channel using two

80-MHz channels chosen from different bands (for example, one from the U-NII 1 band, and one from the U-NII 3 band). The implementation of 160-MHz channels provides the greatest data rates, but it is limited to environments, such as homes, where there is no need for multiple access points (since reuse of the 160-MHz channels with neighboring access points causes inter–access point interference problems).

Multi-User MIMO

802.11ac supports up to eight spatial streams, which is double that of 802.11n. In addition, 802.11ac makes use of multi-user MIMO (optional), which enables simultaneous communications between an access point and multiple client devices. In order to accomplish this, 802.11ac uses Space Division Multiple Access (SDMA), where streams are separated by space (not time or frequency). For example, two clients may be located on opposite sides of an access point. In this case, the access point can use multi-user MIMO to transmit information to both clients at the same time and frequency without interference assuming the signals are kept separated by space (for instance, transmitted directionally from the access point to the two clients without any overlap of the signal in any given space). This can significantly increase the capacity of the access point due to the simultaneous communications. In addition, it could increase the performance of using 160-MHz channels in implementations having multiple access points (since the use of space to separate simultaneous communications will likely decrease inter-access point interference). The use of multi-user MIMO, however, requires the client devices to be equipped with 802.11ac transceivers that implement the optional multi-user MIMO. As a result, it may be a few years before enterprises begin implementing it.

Note   802.11ac extends the level of 802.11n QAM coding to 256-QAM.

Interoperability

Because of differences in 802.11ac (such as wider RF channel bandwidth), 802.11ac implements several features that enable it to coexist and interoperate with legacy (802.11a and 802.11n 5 GHz) equipment. For example, 802.11ac extends 802.11n by including an RF header that implements both 802.11a and 802.11n modulation. This ensures that 802.11a and 802.11n 5 GHz devices can hear 802.11ac transmissions, which informs the non-802.11ac devices to avoid transmitting for a period of time while the 802.11ac device is transmitting.

Note   For more information about the 802.11 physical layer, refer to the most current version of the IEEE 802.11 standard.

Summary

The 802.11 standard defines multiple physical layer standards. FHSS and DSSS, which provide 1-Mbps and 2-Mbps operation, were part of the initial 2.4-GHz standard ratified in 1997. The 802.11b amendment ratified in 1999 extended the data rate of 2.4-GHz DSSS up to 11 Mbps. Also in 1999, the 802.11a amendment defined operation in the 5-GHz band using OFDM for operation up to 54 Mbps. The 802.11g amendment ratified in 2003 also extended data rates up to 54 Mbps in the 2.4-GHz band using OFDM. 802.11n was ratified in 2009 and uses MIMO technology to extend data rates in both the 2.4-GHz and 5-GHz bands up to hundreds of megabits per second, depending on the number of transmitters and receivers that the devices implement. 802.11ac, ratified in 2013, increases potential data rates to the gigabit per second range in the 5-GHz band. In order to interoperate with legacy systems, 802.11n is backward compatible with 802.11a, 802.11b, and 802.11g. 802.11ac is backward compatible with 802.11a and 802.11n (5 GHz).

Chapter 8

Planning a Wireless LAN Deployment

This chapter will introduce you to:

- Project Management Principles
- Wireless LAN Deployment Planning Steps
- Evaluating the Outcome of the Project

When deploying a wireless LAN (WLAN), it is important to plan and execute the project using applicable steps for requirements definition, design, installation, testing, and operational support. A poorly planned wireless network deployment generally leads to inconsistent delivery of services. This chapter provides an overview of the steps to complete when deploying a WLAN.

> **Note** A common case study about a fictitious company (Acme Industries) begins with Case Study 8-1 in this chapter and surfaces periodically throughout this chapter and following chapters in this book to provide real examples of key steps for planning, designing, installing, testing, and supporting a wireless LAN.

Project Management Principles

In most cases, organizations accomplish work in functional groups, which perform parts of an operation that are continuous and repetitious. As the system administrator for a client/server system, for example, you might perform daily backups of databases. This task, and others, is part of the operation of a system management function. Projects are similar to functional operations in several ways:

- They are performed by people.

- They are constrained by limited resources.

- They should be planned, executed, and controlled.

Projects, however, are temporary endeavors that people undertake to develop a new service or product. Therefore, you should classify network deployments as projects because each one has a definite beginning and end.

The Project Management Institute (PMI) defines project management as follows:

- It is the art of directing and coordinating human and material resources throughout the life of a project.

- Project management primarily consists of planning, monitoring, and controlling the execution of a project.

- Planning involves identifying project goals and objectives, developing work plans, budgeting, and allocating resources.

- Project monitoring and control ensure that the execution of the project conforms to the plan by periodically measuring progress and making corrections to the project plan, if necessary.

Note   PMI offers a certification titled Project Management Professional (PMP) that you can earn through work experience, education, and successful completion of the PMP examination. The PMP certification ensures that you have mastered the skills necessary to manage a project of any type. Many corporations are beginning to recognize the importance of PMP-certified professionals. You should consider completing the PMP certification process as part of your continuing professional education. Learn more about PMI from its website, www.pmi.org.

The use of sound project management principles results in many benefits, such as the following:

- Clarification of project goals and activities

- Better communication among project team members, executives, and the customer

- Accurate projections of resource requirements

- Identification and reduction of risks

- More effective resolution of contingencies

Such benefits help an organization complete a quality wireless system implementation on time and within budget.

An important part of project management is planning. You need to dedicate ample time at the beginning of a project to thinking about what could go wrong and to visualizing solutions that will keep the project on the right track. Specifically, project planning is a process consisting of analysis and decisions for the following purposes:

- Directing the intent of the project

- Identifying actions, risks, and responsibilities within the project

- Guiding the ongoing activities of the project

- Preparing for potential changes

In the planning stage of a WLAN deployment project, visualize the goals you have for implementing the network and the actions necessary to maximize a successful outcome. In most cases, you will need to determine the requirements and any necessary products before you can complete the project plan.

Case Study 8-1: Acme Industries Begins a Wireless LAN Deployment

Acme Industries is a fictitious company, with corporate headquarters and a manufacturing plant in Dayton, Ohio. Acme Industries, which has five distribution centers located throughout the United States, designs and builds a popular line of widgets. As the company produces the widgets, it ships them to the distribution centers for temporary storage. When resellers and retail stores order the widgets, the company can ship them to the requester from the nearest distribution center. Profits for this $800-million-per-year company were fairly high last year; therefore, the company has been looking seriously at investing some of the profits to improve efficiencies of its workforce.

The CFO for Acme Industries, Bob, went on a fishing trip, and a friend talked about how his university had just finished the implementation of a new (802.11n/802.11ac) WLAN that supports wireless access for students with laptops. Bob recalled that his manufacturing company is experimenting with WLANs, but the company still depends primarily on wired Ethernet networks for connectivity.

After returning from the fishing trip, Bob immediately notified his director of information systems, Chris, to plan the deployment of WLANs throughout the company.

Refer to case studies that resurface throughout the remainder of this book to better understand the process of deploying a WLAN for Acme Industries.

Wireless LAN Deployment Planning Steps

When planning a WLAN deployment, you should produce a project plan that includes the following steps:

Step 1.   Define the project scope.

Step 2.   Develop a work breakdown structure.

Step 3.	Identify staffing.
Step 4.	Create a schedule.
Step 5.	Develop a budget.
Step 6.	Evaluate risks.
Step 7.	Analyze feasibility.

The order of these steps is not too important; however, you should define the project scope at the beginning to provide a basis for the other items. Treat the project plan as a living document that you update as more information, such as detailed requirements and design, becomes available.

Step 1: Defining the Project Scope

The project's scope provides a basis for future project decisions. The project scope gives a project team top-level direction, allowing an accurate development of remaining planning elements and execution of the project. For each project, you should prepare a project scope that has at least the items described in the following sections.

Project Charter

The project charter formally recognizes the existence of the project, identifies the general business need that the project is addressing, and gives a basic description of potential solutions. At this point, you need to gather some information from managers and potential users, but the requirements phase of the project will define more details of the needs. A manager external to the project generally creates the charter and names the person who will be the project manager, but the company may assign the project manager to create the charter. The project charter should provide the project manager with the authority to apply people and material resources to project activities. For WLAN projects, the project manager is generally someone from the IT organization.

Assumptions

The project team should state assumptions for unknown or questionable key factors that could affect the project. For example, a product vendor might tell you that a new wireless device will be available on a specific date. If the success of the project depends on the availability of this product, you should identify its availability as an assumption. This will assist you when evaluating project risks.

Constraints

Constraints limit the project team's options in completing the project. Common constraints are funding limits, technical requirements (such as a mandate to implement 802.11n and 802.11ac access points), availability of resources, type and location of project staff, and schedules. Be sure to fully define constraints to keep the visualized outcome of the project within an acceptable scope.

For more details on creating a project scope for a WLAN deployment project, refer to Case Study 8-2.

Case Study 8-2: Acme Industries Develops a Project Scope for a Wireless LAN Project

As the first step for planning the project, Chris, the director of information systems for the fictitious company Acme Industries, developed a project scope to ensure that everyone will be focusing on the same basic goals throughout the project. Chris met with Bob, the CFO of Acme Industries, to clearly understand his perspective of the project. Chris asked questions that probed business problems and addressed the constraints that will limit the project. Chris met with Violet, the distribution center director of Acme Industries, to gain a basic understanding of the issues and needs of the warehouse staff. Chris met with Acme's vice president of manufacturing to understand the basic needs of the manufacturing plant. Of course, Chris also met with several of the information systems staff concerning their views on the proposed project.

After gathering this information, Chris prepared a project scope. The following are the main points of the document:

- **Project charter:** The purpose of this project is to deploy a WLAN that results in significant return on investment (ROI) within the corporate headquarters, distribution centers, and manufacturing plant. The warehouse staff currently uses paper-based methods to manage all aspects of the warehouse, resulting in inefficient use of labor and higher delays than competitors when processing orders for customers. A wireless automatic identification and data capture (AIDC) system is a solution that would decrease delays in getting parts to customers by enabling the warehouses to keep more accurate records of parts in stock, shorten order-picking time, and speed up the shipping-preparation process. The AIDC system will need to interface with the company's existing warehouse management system to feed management and reporting systems already in place. All parts of the company (corporate headquarters, manufacturing plant, and distribution centers) can benefit from the use of wireless phones, but cell phone coverage inside the buildings is limited.

- **Assumptions:** The company is assuming that there will be a positive outcome of a feasibility study for the WLAN deployment. Chris will prepare the feasibility study as part of the project planning process. It must indicate an ROI that is acceptable to upper management before the funding and deployment can go forward.

- **Constraints:** Acme Enterprises can allocate up to $500,000 during the first year to implement the system. There are no restrictions on the selection of hardware and software for this project; however, the information systems group has a strong preference for implementing an 802.11n-/802.11ac-compliant network.

Step 2: Developing the Work Breakdown Structure

Part of planning a WLAN deployment is defining the tasks necessary for completing the project. This involves realizing applicable steps, such as requirements analysis, design, and installation, which are common to any system solution. It also involves planning a series of tasks that produce the end solution with minimal time and money.

Using a work breakdown structure (WBS) is a good way of planning the tasks and tracking the progress of the project. A WBS has a tree-like structure and identifies the tasks that the team members will need to perform and the products they must deliver. The first level of the WBS should indicate major phases, followed by lower layers that identify tasks and subtasks. The WBS also provides a basis for other planning elements, such as staffing and schedules.

What level of detail should the WBS include? At a minimum, specify enough detail so that it is possible to determine the length of time to complete and estimate the cost of each phase and task. This will make it possible to more accurately plan the project. You can get into more detailed planning just before getting started with the actual tasks.

The following sections provide an overview of the project phases that a WBS should address:

- Requirements definition phase

- Design phase

- Implementation phase

- Operations and maintenance phase

Requirements Definition Phase

The requirements definition phase of a WLAN deployment reviews and evaluates the needs of the users of the WLAN and existing systems. This provides the basis for making decisions when designing the solution. If you do not do a good job of defining the requirements, the solution might not meet the needs of users. For smaller networks, the requirements gathering process could be as simple as spending a couple days thinking about requirements and preparing a two- or three-page document that defines them. Larger systems, however, will likely demand a more involved process because of a broader base of users and systems.

The requirements definition phase of the deployment should include the following tasks:

- **Elicit user needs:** Spend time talking with representatives from all functional groups that the WLAN will serve. For example, in a hospital, interview the department heads of the emergency department, radiology, and so on.

- **Elicit existing system information:** Survey the existing wired network infrastructure, servers, and communications equipment rooms. Also identify all servers and applications that the WLAN will provide access to.

- **Analyze requirements:** The gathering of user needs may not define all requirements. If there are any missing elements, determine the most effective requirements. Users, for example, will likely not know what level of encryption is necessary to protect them from applicable threats. As a result, you might need to "fill in" some of these requirements based on experience with previous projects or advice from consultants.

- **Document the requirements:** Describe all requirements in a document so that there is a record of what the solution needs to support. The requirements should be explained in enough detail so that someone designing the network will have very few if any questions.

- **Obtain requirements approval:** All applicable functional groups of the company should indicate acceptance of the requirements. It is generally best to have a formal process where the head of each functional group signs the requirements document indicating approval.

Note   For more on defining WLAN requirements, see Chapter 9, "Defining Requirements for a Wireless LAN."

Design Phase

The design phase of a WLAN deployment determines how the WLAN will satisfy requirements, which includes defining the architecture, optimum location for access points, configuration settings, and so on. The design should specify an open architecture that provides maximum support for existing and future applications and ability to migrate to newer technologies as they become available.

The design phase is generally split into the following parts:

- **Preliminary design:** In some cases, you might have to perform a preliminary design as a basis for initial budgeting and work planning. The preliminary design provides just enough details as the basis for determining the cost of the deployment. For example, the preliminary design might include the conductance of a wireless site survey to determine the number of access points that the company must install to provide adequate levels of signal coverage. In addition, the preliminary design may involve determining the network architecture to better understand all components needed.

- **Detailed design:** The detailed design defines all aspects of the solution. The resulting design specification should have enough detail so that someone not involved in the design can install the network without needing further consideration of design elements.

The design phase of the deployment should include the following tasks:

- **Perform a wireless site survey:** Before installing a WLAN, it is crucial to first perform a wireless site survey to identify existing wireless networks and radio signal interference that may impact the operation of the WLAN and determine optimum locations of access points necessary for covering all facilities.

- **Define the system architecture:** This involves choosing a well-tested network model that indicates how the necessary components will interact and effectively support requirements.

- **Consider technical aspects of the solution:** It is important to spend some time considering the details of the design, such as performance and roaming solutions, radio frequency attributes (for example, 2.4-GHz versus 5-GHz frequencies), and security solutions. In addition, it's important to determine whether an existing wired network will support the number of anticipated wireless access points and applications.

- **Select products:** Select all products and materials necessary for implementing the network and create a bill of materials. In some cases, you might have already selected the products as part of your company's existing policies. In general, select products based on capability to satisfy requirements (technology, form factor, security technologies, and so on), product availability, level of vendor support, and price.

- **Define component configurations:** This includes determining the optimum settings for all hardware and software, based on the chosen system architecture, performance and roaming solutions, radio frequency attributes, security solutions, and products. In addition to following the tips provided in this book, it is advisable to review applicable white papers offered by the product vendors that you have selected.

- **Verify the design:** The design of a WLAN is often complex, especially for larger facilities, such as hospitals, and when there are requirements to support large numbers of users or high-end applications such as voice. Consider the following approaches for verifying the design: simulation, physical prototyping, pilot testing, and independent assessment. (See Chapter 17, "Testing a Wireless LAN," for more details.)

- **Document the design:** This documentation is a valuable reference when installing the system and also when supporting the system. The design specification includes diagrams that illustrate the hardware and software needed to realize the solution, description of the component configuration settings, and a bill of materials that identifies all necessary hardware, software, and cabling for implementing the WLAN. Be certain to update any documentation prepared throughout the design with any changes made after verifying the design.

- **Obtain design approval:** The last step before procuring the components is to obtain approvals for the design. A qualified representative (with possible advice from an independent consultant) should approve the design. After the approval, consider the design documentation as a baseline that can be changed only by following the company's change control procedures.

> **Note** For more details on designing a WLAN, see the following chapters in this book:
> - Chapter 10, "System Architecture Considerations"
> - Chapter 11, "Range, Performance, and Roaming Considerations"
> - Chapter 12, "Radio Frequency Considerations"
> - Chapter 13, "Security Considerations"
> - Chapter 14, "Test Tools"
> - Chapter 15, "Performing a Wireless Site Survey"

Implementation Phase

The implementation phase of a WLAN deployment consists of physically installing the system components and running tests to verify proper operation. It might also involve developing software that interfaces wireless client devices to databases or application software.

The implementation phase of the deployment should include the following tasks:

- **Procure components:** Obviously, before installing components, you need to purchase them and have them delivered to either a staging location or an installation. Before doing this, be sure to check on the amount of time it takes for the manufacturer or supplier to ship the components. In some cases, the provider might have components in stock that can be shipped within a few days. However, it may take several months if the vendor must first manufacture the components. The latter might be the case for larger orders. Be sure to account for this lead time in the schedule when planning installation dates.

  When procuring components, you need to understand warranties and maintenance agreements the vendors offer. Most vendors offer excellent warranties and also have maintenance agreements at an additional charge.

  Here are some questions you should ask vendors:

  - How long is the product covered?

  - When does the warranty begin?

  - What are the limitations of the coverage?

  - How should the product be returned if it becomes defective?

  - Does the vendor provide onsite or offsite maintenance?

  Before actually ordering the components, you should plan where the components will be stored after delivery. For small implementations, this may not be significant, but for larger projects, it is crucial. Be sure to plan locations to which the components should be delivered, storage locations while waiting for installation, methods for moving components from the delivery point to the storage area, and methods for moving the components from the storage area to the point of installation.

Note   Be sure to include an adequate level of sparing when purchasing network components. (Ask your chosen vendor for recommendations on sparing levels.) Even though vendors provide warranties on the hardware, they might not be able to respond fast enough with a replacement component if one fails. Spares should be kept near the operational site to provide fast replacement of faulty network components. Of course, sparing will add cost to the project, but this must be weighed against potential downtime that will occur if a unit fails.

- **Develop application software:** It might be necessary to develop software for a WLAN, especially when integrating wireless client devices to existing databases and application software. The requirements, for example, may call for the use of hand-held data collectors to perform inspections throughout a manufacturing plant. Users may scan a bar code at a particular point and answer question prompts on the data collector. This application would likely require custom software that interfaces the client device to the existing database or application software running on a server. In these cases, programmers must fully understand wireless impairments, such as radio signal interference, coverage holes, and so on, to include appropriate error recovery mechanisms in the software routines. A WLAN can be transparent to the user, but only if the programmer takes into account issues related to wireless connectivity.

- **Configure components:** This task includes configuring all equipment settings for controllers, access points, and such to provide optimum performance, signal coverage, security, and supportability for satisfying requirements. This generally involves writing a document that describes these settings.

- **Install a pilot system:** To reduce risks in larger system deployments, think about starting with one or more pilot sites to test the solution with a limited number of users. The feedback from users during the pilot testing will often uncover problems with the design. Keep in mind that it is much less expensive to fix a problem with the design before installing the system throughout the entire company. The deployment of a pilot is especially important when using new technologies (for example, 802.11n and 802.11ac) or if the design is complex, such as when security solutions include 802.1X-based authentication.

- **Install the company-wide system:** The installation includes mounting access points, installing controllers, running cabling, and configuring the system. If the design is done effectively, the installation should be a smooth process. For example, the design should specify where to mount the access points. It is generally best to place the access points as high as possible, but be practical. Warehouses have high ceilings; however, avoid mounting the access points so high that you need expensive equipment to reach them. Also, strongly consider using Power over Ethernet (PoE) to run electricity to the access points. This avoids the time and costs of installing electrical outlets throughout the facility. In many cases, especially for larger deployments, it is usually best to write a request for proposals (RFP) and contract the company-wide installation of access points with a firm that specializes in installing WLANs.

■ **Perform verification testing:** After completing the installation, be sure to fully test for proper operation and signal coverage. The testing may indicate the need to move some access points and possibly use different configuration settings. Ideally, perform verification testing of the completed system installation, with actual applications if available. Also, plan on performing the tests during worst-case times. For example, it would be most beneficial to test the signal coverage in an airport during the day, when the airport is active, not in the middle of the night, when very few, if any, people are present in the terminals and concourses. The verification testing should conclude with a report that describes the testing completed, issues found, and recommended resolutions.

■ **Document the installation:** After completing the installation, do not forget to carefully document what was done. Documentation should include a diagram depicting the location of installed access points and applicable configuration settings. You will certainly need this documentation to physically find the access points in the future, assuming that you were really good at concealing them. In addition, the configuration information will be necessary to monitor, troubleshoot, and upgrade the WLAN in the future.

Note   For more details on implementing WLANs, see the following chapters in this book:
■ Chapter 16, "Installing and Configuring a Wireless LAN"
■ Chapter 17, "Testing a Wireless LAN"

Operations and Maintenance Phase

The operations and maintenance phase of a WLAN deployment includes various functions, such as system administration, network monitoring, maintenance, troubleshooting, and reengineering, to ensure that the network continues to run smoothly. It is important to plan the operations and maintenance functions and carefully transfer the network from the implementation phase to a production system, which is when the operations and maintenance functions begin.

Note   The operations and maintenance phase of WLAN deployment is often more expensive than implementing the network (costs for hardware, software, and services). Therefore, you should define enough details of the support elements to provide a realistic ongoing budget.

The operations and maintenance phase of WLAN deployment should include the following tasks and functions:

■ **Define support procedures:** Most companies do not have effective WLAN support procedures in place before beginning a WLAN deployment. In some cases, companies have small WLANs and some experience setting them up and responding to support calls, but the deployment of WLANs throughout the company has not been great enough to warrant establishing applicable support procedures. Most support in these situations is done in an ad hoc manner. Before finalizing a WLAN implementation, however, be certain to have procedures for administering, monitoring, and maintaining the network.

■ **Prepare support staff:** This will likely require interviewing the support staff regarding their experience in WLANs. Often, especially for companies with no existing WLANs, the support staff will require training on all support procedures. Definitely ensure that this training is done before the WLAN becomes operational and available to users.

■ **Train users:** The training of users and support staff is extremely important. Training strengthens the interface between the system and the users, which improves ROI. With wireless access to laptops for general network access, the training will likely not need to be extensive. You will probably just need to announce that the wireless network is available and identify the corresponding network name. The implementation of some applications, such as wireless IP phones or inventory control, will probably require more extensive training, such as a live class, where an instructor can demonstrate use of the application.

■ **Transfer the network to operations and maintenance:** This is where the deployment project ends and operational support begins. While implementing the network, the project team provides support for the network, such as the creation of initial user accounts, and troubleshooting and repair actions. Be sure to clearly transfer support of the network from the project team to applicable support functions. This clearly marks the end of the project and ensures that users having problems with the system will call upon the right people for assistance. Be certain as part of the transfer that the operational support staff have copies of network documentation, such as designs and support plans.

For more details on creating a WBS for a WLAN deployment, see Case Study 8-3.

Case Study 8-3: Acme Industries Develops a Work Breakdown Structure for a Wireless LAN Deployment Project

Chris, the director of information systems for the fictitious company Acme Industries, is in the process of planning the project. After putting together the project scope (see Case Study 8-2), Chris has drafted the following WBS:

1. Requirements definition phase:

1.1 Elicit needs from corporate headquarters

1.2 Elicit needs from manufacturing plant

1.3 Elicit needs from distribution centers

1.4 Document requirements

1.5 Approve requirements (gain consensus among all departments)

2. Design phase:

    2.1 Perform wireless site surveys (all buildings)

    2.2 Define system architecture (entire network)

    2.3 Consider performance and roaming solutions

    2.4 Consider radio frequency attributes

    2.5 Consider security solutions

    2.6 Select products

    2.7 Define configuration settings (access points, controllers, etc.)

    2.8 Verify design (through independent assessment)

    2.9 Document design

3. Implementation phase:

    3.1 Procure/stage components

    3.2 Develop bar code devices interface software

    3.3 Configure components (controllers, access points, etc.)

    3.4 Install/test pilot system: 3rd floor, corporate headquarters

    3.5 Install/test pilot system: Dayton distribution center

    3.6 Install/test production system (all locations)

    3.7 Document installations

4. Operations and maintenance phase:

    4.1 Review/modify existing support procedures

    4.2 Prepare/hire support staff

    4.3 Train users on AIDC system

    4.4 Transfer network to operations and maintenance

This WBS ensures that time is spent eliciting needs from each of the primary user groups: corporate headquarters, manufacturing plant, and distribution centers. Chris plans to involve the managers from each of these groups and key potential users. Some of this was done while developing the project scope, but not at the level of detail necessary for fully defining the needs. Approval of the requirements will entail having the heads of each department sign the requirements document indicating agreement with the requirements.

The design phase will begin with a thorough wireless site survey of all buildings, including corporate headquarters (a four-story building), a manufacturing facility that adjoins the corporate headquarters building, and each of the distribution centers. The design will then continue with defining the system architecture for the entire network and take into account several technical considerations. The design also includes selecting products and defining configuration settings for all components. Chris will then have an independent consultant review the design and provide feedback on whether the design satisfies requirements and whether there are any areas in the design to improve.

Chris will designate space in one of the distribution centers (the one in Dayton near corporate headquarters) to store network components prior to the installation. The deployment will include installing pilot WLANs in one of the distribution centers (located in Dayton) and on the third floor of corporate headquarters where the information systems department resides. This provides an opportunity to easily test the applications and technologies before rolling out the system to the entire company.

Chris's help desk and support staff have existing operational support procedures for wired networks, but they will need to review the procedures and make them applicable to WLANs. With the updated procedures, Chris will train the existing support staff and possibly hire additional staff, if necessary. Because the AIDC system is fairly complicated, the deployment project will include training distribution center users on the AIDC system.

Note   For more details on managing and implementing WLAN operational support, see the following chapters in this book:

- Chapter 18, "Managing a Wireless LAN"
- Chapter 19, "Troubleshooting a Wireless LAN"

Step 3: Identifying Staffing

Staff are the people you need to perform the activities identified in the WBS. The goal of resource allocation, as with most other planning activities, is to assign people who maximize the success of the project while minimizing the cost and time to complete the project. As you identify the resources, you need to confirm their availability and schedule them to ensure that they are ready when needed.

The following describes the team member positions of a WLAN deployment project:

- **Project manager:** The team should have one project manager who manages, directs, and is ultimately responsible for the entire project. This person coordinates the people and resources, ensuring that all objectives of the project are met on time and within budget. The project manager should have experience and education in managing projects, have excellent communication skills, be familiar with WLAN concepts, and be familiar with the users' environments.

- **User representative:** The team should have one or more user representatives who portray the interests of the users of the network and aim the project team in the right direction when determining requirements. The user representatives should be very familiar with the user population and be able to honestly speak for the users.

- **Analysts:** Analysts gather information and define the needs of the users and the organization. The analysts should have good interviewing skills and be able to translate user and organizational needs into system requirements.

- **Engineers:** Engineers provide the technical expertise necessary to fulfill the objectives of the project. Engineers should be part of analyzing needs, but primarily they should work on designing solutions that satisfy requirements. Therefore, engineers should be very familiar with wireless technologies and products. If needed, engineers can also assist with developing wireless software and installing and configuring network components.

- **Implementation manager:** The implementation manager directs the implementation phase of the network, which mostly includes installing and configuring the components.

- **Implementers:** The implementers are the software engineers and technicians who develop application software and install and test the network.

- **Operations and maintenance representative:** The project team should have an operations and maintenance representative to coordinate the project with existing network support organizations, ensuring that the implementation integrates well with the existing network infrastructure and support mechanisms. Therefore, the operations and maintenance representative should have a good knowledge of the existing network and should understand current network support mechanisms.

How many staff should you have on the team? There are no accurate rules because the level of staffing depends on the complexity of the company that the WLAN will serve, the scope of the project, schedule constraints, and the experience of the people you have available to perform the work. For smaller projects, very few people might fill the role of all project team members. For example, the project team for a single-story 10,000-square-foot office building may include only one person who acts as project manager, user representative, analyst, engineer, and so on. In other cases, several team members might be needed to complete the project activities. If you are planning to deploy a voice over WLAN solution, for example, for a 500-bed hospital, you will probably need a handful of people.

See Case Study 8-4 for more details on identifying staffing for a WLAN deployment.

Case Study 8-4: Acme Enterprises Identifies Staffing for a Wireless LAN Deployment

Chris, the director of information systems for Acme Industries, has spent some time reviewing the WBS (see Case Study 8-3) to determine the staffing necessary for the project. Chris was able to assign people from the information systems department except for the implementers who will be installing the access points throughout the entire company. Chris can use internal resources for installing the pilot systems, however.

The following is the staffing that Chris has identified:

- **Project manager:** Ted, one of Acme's network administrators, will manage the deployment project. Ted has experience managing wired network deployments and is a certified Project Management Professional (PMP). Ted will take on planning the remainder of the deployment.

- **System analyst:** Henry, one of Acme's system administrators, will handle all aspects of the requirements definition phase. Henry has been working for the company for nearly 10 years and has a good understanding of the user needs throughout all the departments and functional groups.

- **User representative:** Violet, Acme's distribution center director, will be available to review user requirements as needed.

- **Engineer:** Frank, one of Acme's network engineers, will complete the tasks associated with the design phase. Frank is new to the company and implemented a large 802.11n/802.11ac network at his previous company.

- **Implementation manager:** John, Acme's network manager, will manage the hardware installation, component configuration, and software development.

- **Implementer (hardware installation):** Ted will outsource the installation of access points and associated cabling to a network installation company after completing the design phase of the project.

- **Implementer (component configuration):** Frank, the Acme Industries engineer who will design the WLAN, will configure the WLAN controllers, access points, and authentication system. In addition to having experience deploying 802.11n network at his employer before coming to Acme Industries, Frank has CCIE, CWNA, and CWSP certifications.

- **Implementer (software development):** Evelyn, Acme's database developer, will develop the interface software between the warehouse client devices and the company's warehouse management system to support the AIDC that the company is planning to deploy.

- **Implementer (verification testing):** Ted will outsource the verification testing of the WLAN to an independent firm after completing the installation of the system.

- **Operations and maintenance representative:** Susan, Acme's network support manager, will assist with preparing operations and maintenance for the WLAN. This includes developing or modifying existing procedures for supporting the WLAN and specifying the training necessary to prepare the support staff. Susan is very new to the company.

Step 4: Creating a Schedule

The schedule indicates the element of timing in a project, making it possible for the project manager to coordinate work activities. The schedule and WBS are the basis for selecting and coordinating resources and the primary tools for tracking project performance.

A schedule should contain the following information:

- Names of the phases and tasks listed on the WBS

- Starting date, duration, and due date of each task

- Relationships between phases and tasks

The project manager should create the schedule by first recording the phase names listed in the WBS and assigning someone to be responsible for each phase (and possibly individual tasks). The next step, working with the responsible team members, is to determine the starting date, duration, and due date for each task. If you cannot determine these characteristics for each task, consider further division of the task into subtasks to accommodate a more accurate assessment of timing. You should also indicate the relationships between tasks using precedence relationships. In other words, show conditions that must be met (such as the completion of a particular task) before starting each task.

A project team must often deal with unrealistic schedules; therefore, there might not be enough time to complete a quality implementation. In this case, you might want to consider decreasing the scope of the project or hiring external resources.

See Case Study 8-5 to learn more about creating a schedule for a WLAN deployment.

Case Study 8-5: Acme Enterprises Develops a Schedule for a Wireless LAN Deployment

After being selected as the project manager for the WLAN deployment for the fictitious company Acme Industries, Ted is continuing with project planning. Chris, the director of information systems for Acme Industries, has already created the project scope (Case Study 8-2), created the WBS (Case Study 8-3), and identified project staffing (Case Study 8-4). After reviewing these documents, Ted met with all project team members and created a schedule in the form of a Gantt chart.

Step 5: Developing a Budget

The budget is the key financial element of a WLAN deployment. It indicates the cost of deploying the system, which upper management must usually approve before you can proceed with the project. The company may approve the budget for deploying the entire system, or it may want to install the network in phases. For example, a university may limit the installation of a WLAN to the eating establishments the first year and continue with the deployment throughout classrooms when more funding is available. Regardless of whether the company phases the installation, you should determine the budget for deploying the entire system and then scale it back if the organization can initially afford only a portion of the deployment.

Note   To minimize budget overruns, ensure that a process is in place for handling changes and enhancements that upper management and users voice after the project is under way. This process must include provisions for assessing the impacts on the project resources, schedule, and cost before proceeding with the changes.

Preliminary Requirements and Design

To figure costs for a project, you need to perform a preliminary design to identify the major system components. The preliminary design must provide enough detail to approximate the cost of implementing and supporting the system. Later stages of the design phase will further define the components and configurations necessary to implement the system. As part of the preliminary design, it is very important to perform a wireless site survey to determine the effects of the facility on the propagation of radio waves. This will help you calculate the number of access points necessary to cover the entire facility (and technical risks associated with deploying the WLAN).

Note   When identifying costs, be sure to include everything that the project will require for the implementation and operational support of the system. Remember that sustaining the system after it becomes operational will require continual funding.

Before determining the costs of a WLAN, you need a preliminary sketch of the requirements and design to know what components form the basis of the solution. Requirements at this point should at least describe the overall application. A network that only provides Internet access versus one that supports widespread use of wireless IP phones results in widely varying costs.

To help you prepare a foundation for assessing the costs of deploying a WLAN, here are some questions related to the requirements and design:

- What applications will the WLAN support?

- How many client devices (laptops, wireless IP phones, and so on), printers, and other devices will the WLAN serve directly?

- How many client radios do you need (beyond what are already integrated into client devices)?

- How many existing client devices are equipped with radios? What version of 802.11 do they support (that is, 802.11a, 802.11b, 802.11g, 802.11n, or 802.11ac)?

- How many access points do you need to cover the facility?

- Do you need to install new cabling and switches to connect the access points to the wired network? Is yes, how many ports do you need to implement?

- Do you need to develop wireless software that interfaces client devices to databases or servers?

- What services do you plan to outsource?

Hardware and Software Costs

The cost of hardware and software components is a large part of a WLAN deployment budget. When planning the deployment, you may already know what manufacturer you want to use for the components, especially if your company has an existing contract with one, such as Cisco, or a preliminary design may provide manufacturer information. Obtain cost quotes from reputable resellers, such as those recommended by the manufacturer of the components you plan to use. After completing the detailed design, you may decide to use a different manufacturer for a particular component. In that case, you will need to update the budget accordingly.

Hardware and software costs for a WLAN deployment apply to the following components:

- **Client devices:** The wireless applications that you choose to implement may require purchasing client devices. A hospital, for example, may want to deploy a WLAN to support wireless patient monitoring. As a result, the corresponding WLAN deployment budget will likely need to include costs for new wireless patient monitors.

- **Client radios:** Take an inventory of the existing client radios and determine the number of radios and required form factors that you will need to purchase. Most mobile client devices have the option of ordering them equipped with internal 802.11 radios, which might be less expensive than ordering the radios separately. If you want to take advantage of proprietary enhancements, however, you might need to order a different radio for each client (one that matches the manufacturer of the access points, if possible). In that case, avoid purchasing the client devices with internal 802.1l radios. If you have an existing 802.11b/g WLAN, you can get by with not replacing the corresponding radios in the existing client devices, but for best performance, you should replace the 802.11b/g radios with 802.11n or 802.11ac radios as soon as possible.

- **Access points:** It is highly advisable to perform a wireless site survey to determine an accurate count of the access points you will need to cover the facility. With this total number of access points and the prices of the access points, you can determine the total cost. If it is not possible to perform a site survey before the budgeting process (which might be the case if funding for even the site survey is pending until the budget is available), you can approximate the number of access points for an indoor WLAN (a typical office building) based on one access point for every 30,000 square feet for data-only applications. This assumes a range between client radios and access points of approximately 100 feet. The WLAN may or may not be able to achieve this range, however, depending on construction of the facility, sources of radio signal interference, performance requirements, and so on. In addition, you may need considerably more access points for voice- or location-based applications. For an outdoor wireless mesh network in a typical city environment, factor in 45 to 55 mesh nodes per square mile. Keep in mind that these are rough estimates. Again, conducting a wireless site survey is the best way to determine the number of access points.

- **Wireless controllers:** The number of wireless controllers depends on the chosen architecture of the WLAN. If you are deploying the standalone access point architecture, you do not need any controllers. If the architecture is controller based, you need one or more controllers, depending on the performance and reliability requirements. To determine the ideal number of controllers, refer to recommendations from the chosen manufacturer of the access points.

- **Antennas:** Most access points come with low-gain omnidirectional antennas, which usually suffice for most WLAN deployments. However, consider using higher-gain directive antennas for more control over the propagation of radio waves, especially for access points located near the edge of the facility (for security purposes) or when needing to cover a long, narrow area. If it is possible to replace the client radio antennas, consider doing so with higher-gain antennas to raise the equivalent isotropically radiated power (EIRP) of the signal from the client radio to the access point. This can help extend the range of the client devices.

- **Repeaters:** In rare situations, you may find that repeaters are beneficial for extending the range of a WLAN. In those cases, include the costs for the applicable number of repeaters.

- **Bridges:** The preliminary design may indicate the need for bridges, and you will need to include the costs for the applicable types and numbers of them. For example, you may need to specify the need for wireless point-to-point bridges to provide connectivity between two adjacent buildings.

- **Switches:** Survey the existing switches and determine whether there are sufficient ports to support the WLAN access points. Many companies can get by with using existing Ethernet switches to provide the electronics for the distribution system; however, be sure that these switches are rated at 1 Gbps or better for 802.11n or 802.11ac. If ports are needed, include costs for the corresponding switches.

- **PoE equipment:** Based on the preliminary design, include costs for the types and numbers of PoE devices that are necessary to provide electrical power to the access points. In some cases, even if existing switches are available, you might need to include costs of adding PoE equipment.

- **Cabling:** Include the cost for cables that will be necessary to connect the access points to the switches. Some facilities may have existing unused cable distributed throughout the facility, so perform a survey to determine whether any of the unused cabling can support the WLAN deployment. If needing to provide costs for the installation of cabling, include costs for conduit or cable trays (which adds significant costs) if required by the facility owner.

- **Application software:** Include costs for all application software, which may include software that runs on the client device, databases, and operating systems (and applicable servers).

- **Authentication systems:** If the WLAN will include 802.1X authentication, you might need to budget for components that provide certificate provisioning and authentication services. The necessary components and cost depends on your existing authentication system. For example, you may already have an authentication system that the WLAN client devices can use, which will result in primarily labor costs to configure the system for the new clients. A survey of the existing system and the preliminary design will indicate the types and numbers of authentication system components that you might need.

- **Tools:** If your company will be undertaking any parts of the design, implementation, or operations and maintenance of the WLAN, consider what tools might be necessary. When performing a wireless site survey, for example, you need a device that measures signal strength and possibly a spectrum analyzer to determine the impacts of potential radio signal interference. See Chapter 14 for more on the tools you may need to purchase.

■ **Warranties:** The majority of manufacturers provide a basic warranty for hardware and software. Include costs for extended warranties, though, if they apply.

Be sure to include an adequate number of component spares in the budget. It is generally sufficient to budget for a 10 percent sparing level for client radios and access points, but check with the manufacturer for its specific recommendations on the number of spares. In some situations, especially for higher-priced components, such as wireless controllers and authentication servers, you might not need to include any spares, especially if the system design includes adequate redundancy, such as data backup and server failover functions.

Deployment Services Costs

Deployment services include the work done by the project manager, implementers, and others associated with the project. This budget should address all aspects of the WBS. (For a description of WBS elements, see the section "Step 2: Developing the Work Breakdown Structure," earlier in this chapter.) Ordinarily, the budget needs to include only costs for services that contractors perform, not costs for employees of the company deploying the WLAN. Some companies, however, require the budget to include the cost of services for each person associated with the project, including employees. In this situation, the cost may be stated as a number of hours or a percentage of a person's total time at work. The cost of employee involvement may also involve explaining how participation in the WLAN deployment will impact the person's other projects. The inclusion of service cost of all project members, regardless of whether they are contractors, is a good idea because it provides the most accurate depiction of the cost of deploying the WLAN.

When budgeting for deployment services costs, consider the following elements:

■ **Requirements definition costs:** These costs include services for eliciting needs of users and existing systems, analyzing requirements, and documenting the requirements. In addition to including the cost for the people actively defining the requirements, take into account the time and impact of the people the analysts will be interviewing when gathering the needs.

■ **Design costs:** These costs include performing a wireless site survey, defining the system architecture, considering various technical aspects of the system, comparing/ selecting products, defining component configurations, verifying the design, and documenting the design. These costs include labor costs of the engineers and purchase of any design tools such as network simulators.

■ **Software development costs:** In some cases, a deployment may require the development of application software or an interface that interfaces the client devices to a database or an application running on a server. In this case, you will likely need to provide costs in the budget for having a contractor develop the software. If you develop the software internally, be sure to also include the costs for applicable software development kits and possibly compilers.

- **Installation and testing costs:** These costs include services for procuring components, configuring and installing components (such as access points, controllers, and cabling), performing verification testing, and documenting the installation.

- **Operations and maintenance preparation costs:** These costs include services for defining support procedures and preparing/training support staff. You should figure on needing at least a couple weeks of services to develop support procedures. You will probably also need to create a training course with several class sessions to teach the procedures to the support staff. It would be most economical to hold a single class session, but it is not generally possible to have all support staff attend a single class because that would probably leave no one supporting the existing system. So plan on having at least three classes that support staff attend in shifts. You can get cost quotes for this type of training from various training companies, or you can develop the training internally.

- **User training costs:** If you are purchasing commercially available applications, such as a warehouse management system, user training may be part of the standard package, or you may have to budget for it separately. Check with the applicable application software vendor for pricing. Bear in mind that custom applications will likely require development of custom training, which can be done internally or outsourced to a contractor.

In addition to the preceding considerations, do not forget to include costs for the project manager, which might be for the entire project or specific phases of the project. Also include the costs of others, such as the implementation manager and representatives for users and operations and maintenance. Be certain to include all travel and training expenses relevant to the design phase, too.

Ongoing Operations and Maintenance Costs

After the system is operational, it will cost money to keep it running properly. Therefore, you should include costs in the budget for covering the applicable operations and maintenance services.

The following costs are associated with operating and maintaining the system:

- **Support costs:** After transferring the WLAN to operational support, the costs involve all functions needed to operate and maintain the network. This includes people who configure client devices for accessing the network, resolve user problems (that is, help desk calls), and periodically troubleshoot and reconfigure the network. When considering how many administrators and resulting costs are necessary, think about the number of users, geographic layout of the network, and experience level of the support staff. Consider making use of existing staff for supporting the network or, if necessary, outsourcing the support tasks to a contractor.

■ **Electricity costs:** The electronic devices within the WLAN, such as computers, access points, controllers, and so on, all require electricity; therefore, include approximate costs for the electricity. This is mostly important for larger WLAN deployments because of the greater number of access points. You can obtain electrical power requirements from the manufacturer of the components and check with your power utility company (or the organization in your company that pays the electric bill) for details on the cost of electricity. For smaller networks, the cost of electricity is negligible.

For an example of creating a budget for a WLAN deployment, see Case Study 8-6.

Note   Keep in mind that during the planning stages of a project, the initial budget is an estimate. After completing the requirements and design stages, the team might need to adjust the budget to reflect more precise information.

Case Study 8-6: Acme Enterprises Develops a Budget for a Wireless LAN Deployment

Ted, a project manager for the fictitious company Acme Industries, has been planning the deployment of a WLAN. Ted is now putting together the budget for the project. As a basis for the budget, Ted tasked Frank, the engineer for the project, to perform a wireless site survey and create a preliminary design. Ted also spoke with the rest of the team members to understand costs of all hardware/software, deployment services, and ongoing operations and maintenance functions.

The following are the key elements that impact the budget:

Hardware and Software Costs

■ All parts of the company (corporate headquarters, manufacturing plant, and distribution centers) are planning to use wireless IP phones. Eventually, the system will include up to 100 phones, but this initial project will deploy only 25 phones. Therefore, Ted will include costs for 25 phones in the budget.

■ The AIDC system will support 25 bar code scanners (5 per distribution center). Ted will include the costs of these scanners in the budget. Each scanner comes equipped with an 802.11n radio at no extra charge.

■ The wireless LAN will support 50 laptops and 75 desktop computers. Some of these client devices already have 802.11g radios, but Ted plans to replace the radios with ones that are compliant with 802.11n/ac. As a result, the budget must include costs for 125 802.11n/ac radios for these devices. In addition, Ted will budget for 10 spare 802.11n/ac radios.

■ After completing the wireless site survey, Frank found that 125 access points are necessary to fully cover the facilities (corporate headquarters, manufacturing plant, and five distribution centers). The budget will need to include cost information for these access points plus 10 spares.

- Frank feels that, based on the preliminary design, there's a need for seven wireless controllers (one in each warehouse and two in the combined corporate headquarters and manufacturing plant building). Ted will include the costs of these controllers in the budget. To support an 802.1X authentication system, Frank recommends budgeting for two RADIUS servers. In addition, the deployment will use antennas that come standard on the access points and client cards.

- The company already owns one Wi-Fi tester, but Susan recommends two more. In addition to that, the budget should include the cost for purchasing a spectrum analyzer.

- Because of a recent upgrade of the wired network, there are sufficient switch ports and cabling available for all access points, but they do not support PoE. Therefore, Ted will include costs for a PoE injector for each access point (125 total).

Deployment Services Costs

- Henry, the system analyst for the deployment, will need approximately 3 weeks of his time to define the requirements.

- Frank will need 4 weeks of his time (in addition to the 1 week he already spent developing a preliminary design) to complete the detailed design, select the products, define component configuration settings, and document the design.

- The distribution centers will include a custom AIDC system that improves the efficiency of warehouse functions, such as put-away, picking, inventory control, and shipping. Evelyn has determined that this will require 60 days of time to develop and test the software interface using the software development kit available for a fee from the bar code device manufacturer. Ted will include Evelyn's time involvement and the cost of the software development kit in the budget.

- Frank will need 3 weeks of his time to configure the wireless controllers and the authentication servers.

- Ted received quotes for outsourcing the independent design assessment, installation of access points, and system verification testing and will include these quotes in the budget.

- Susan will need about 2 weeks of her time to review the existing support procedures and make applicable modifications for supporting the wireless LAN. She will also need 3 weeks to develop and deliver training for the support staff.

- Violet, the user representative for the project, will assign someone within her distribution center division to develop and deliver the user training for the AIDC system. Violet is estimating that this will require several weeks of one of her staff's time.

Ongoing Operations and Maintenance Costs

■ Because of the additional workload that the WLAN will offer on the operations and maintenance staff, Susan recommends including cost in the budget for an additional staff member, someone with significant experience supporting WLANs. No one on her support staff currently has significant experience in WLAN support.

■ After talking with Acme's facility manager, Ted found that the electrical requirement of the 125 access points and other components is not significant enough to include in the budget.

■ Based on the criteria, Ted will obtain pricing for all the components and services and create a spreadsheet that includes the costs for all elements and a total.

Step 6: Evaluating Risks

When planning a WLAN deployment, you need to be sure to carefully assess and resolve risks. Otherwise, unforeseen implications will wreak havoc. By handling risks during the early phases of the deployment, you significantly increase the success of the deployment.

See Case Study 8-7 for an example of identifying and resolving risks during the planning stages of a WLAN deployment.

Case Study 8-7: Acme Enterprises Identifies Risks for a Wireless LAN Deployment

Ted, a project manager for the fictitious company Acme Industries, has been planning the deployment of a WLAN and has just finished creating the budget for the deployment (see Case Study 8-6). Ted is now going to consider potential risks. To accomplish this, he calls together all project team members to discuss the risks.

The following is a summary of the results of discussing potential risks:

■ **Clarity of project objectives:** The objectives of the project seem clear enough, as stated in the project scope (see Case Study 8-2). The requirements definition phase of the project, however, will provide much greater detail regarding the needs of users. After completing the requirements definition, the team will check the requirements against the objectives and resolve any differences before moving on with the design.

■ **Team geographical disbursement:** The project team is located in the same city, making the project easy to manage. The majority of distribution centers, though, are located in other parts of the United States. This could pose team communications problems when defining the needs of users and installing the WLAN in the remote areas. As a result, Ted will be sure to add sufficient travel costs to the budget for Henry, the system analyst for the project, to visit each of the distribution centers when gathering requirements and for the implementation manager, John, to periodically visit the distribution centers during and after the installation of the network.

■ **Project timing:** After looking at the project schedule (see Case Study 8-5), the team believes that there seems to be enough time for each phase of the project, except that the actual time needed to develop the interface between the warehouse client devices and the company's warehouse management system is not very clear. Evelyn, who will be developing the software, cannot make an accurate estimate on time until more details on the warehouse user needs are known. As a result, Ted, Evelyn, and Henry will need to reevaluate the applicable schedule soon after Henry completes the requirements. Also, Evelyn is concerned about the possible communications issues involved in Henry defining the user needs for the AIDC system and then conveying them in written form only. To gain the most accurate understanding of these needs, Evelyn and Henry will jointly interview the warehouse users.

■ **Project manager's experience:** Ted has experience managing network deployment projects but does not have much experience with 802.11n and 802.11ac WLANs. As a result, Frank, who has significant experience with deploying 802.11n and 802.11ac networks, will work closely with Ted during the execution of the project.

■ **Project team member experience:** All project team members have adequate experience to fulfill their roles, except possibly Susan, the operations and maintenance representative for the deployment. Susan is the network support manager and is new to the company. She does not yet have a full understanding of the existing systems and is just getting to know the people in her department. This poses some risk in terms of Susan being able to effectively support the project. Chris, the director of the information systems department, however, should be able to fill in the holes.

■ **Use of contractors:** This could be an issue with this project. Acme Industries has had contractors install wired networks in the past, but these contractors do not specialize in installing wireless networks. As a result, Ted will spend some time vetting suitable contractors.

■ **Potential loss of team members to other projects:** The company has had trouble in the past getting projects completed on time, mainly due to lack of staffing. After projects get started, team members are often pulled off a project to handle crises in other systems. This could be a problem with the current project. To help circumvent this, Ted will get applicable commitments from Chris to not overload the team members with other projects. Ted will also keep the team members active continuously throughout their specific portions of the project to avoid idle time that may expose them to being taken to work on other projects (and having difficulties getting them back).

■ **Level of management commitment:** The company CFO, Bob, is fully backing this project. He is the one who initially tasked Chris with starting the planning process. Bob, however, has not yet pitched the project to the company president. Therefore, there is an overall risk of the project not going forward at all. To ensure commissioning of the project, Ted and Chris will clearly define the feasibility of the project, including explaining the benefits, costs, and return on investment. This is crucial in order for Bob and ultimately the company president to make a decision on spending the money to deploy the WLAN.

■ **Availability of relevant technologies:** WLAN technologies have been in use for well over a decade, and the addition of 802.11n and 802.11ac offers substantially higher performance than with earlier versions. There are no significant issues with deploying 802.11n and 802.11ac, except that it may be necessary to use client radios and access points made by the same vendor to ensure interoperability of proprietary enhancements. Frank will keep this in mind during the design phase.

- **Complexity of the interfaces to existing systems:** Evelyn has known of complexities when interfacing mobile devices to existing applications and servers. As a result, Evelyn will take a closer look at the existing system interfaces and start determining how best to map the applications to different types of client devices. This might help when selecting which client devices to use.

Note   Periodically reevaluate risks throughout a deployment and take necessary counteractive measures.

Step 7: Analyzing Feasibility

A feasibility study helps an organization decide whether to proceed with the project based on the costs associated with the components and the expected benefits of deploying the system. Before an organization will allocate funding for a project, upper management needs to know what ROI to expect within a particular amount of time. Most companies will not invest a large amount of money, such as $50,000 or more, to deploy a wireless system without assurance that gains in productivity will pay for the system.

Upper management considers the following key factors when making a decision to move forward with a WLAN deployment:

- Costs
- Benefits
- Impacts on users
- Impacts on existing systems

Costs

Costs include money you plan to spend on hardware, software, services, tools, and travel. In addition to the money it takes to install the network, do not forget to take into consideration the ongoing costs associated with operations and maintenance. Be as accurate as possible when identifying costs. When you are not sure how much something will cost, add an extra safety margin. It is much harder to go back later and ask for more money.

Note   To understand the costs involved with deploying a WLAN, see the section "Step 5: Developing a Budget" and Case Study 8-6, earlier in this chapter.

Benefits

The benefits that a WLAN provides offset the costs of deploying the network. To make a decision to move forward with a deployment, upper management will want to see that solid benefits outweigh the costs. This might be a straightforward task, where tangible benefits, such as lower costs for staffing, are clearly more than the costs of installing and supporting the system. In other cases, benefits may not be as well defined. For example, you might want to install a WLAN for general use of wireless laptops throughout the company. It will likely be difficult to sell the system to upper management, though. Spend some time analyzing the benefits of applications that your WLAN can support and choose ones that significantly avoid costs.

Chapter 1, "Introduction to Wireless LANs," describes several benefits of wireless networks, such as mobility, the capability to install in difficult-to-wire areas, reduced installation times, fewer changes to network cabling, and productivity gains. These benefits provide cost savings that you can point to when performing a feasibility study. Review these benefits and use them as the basis for determining cost savings.

Note   Be sure to run a time study for applications that provide gains in productivity. Time actual users performing existing manual functions and compare them to using a prototype of the wireless system. This will indicate the savings in terms of efficiency gain that you should expect to receive. In addition, you can use the results to verify and validate the wireless system after completing the project.

Keep in mind that initially, user productivity might be low because users normally experience a learning curve when first using the new system. A staff of accountants, for example, might be accustomed to keeping figures on paper and in spreadsheets. A wireless system might use a centralized database, allowing the accountants to input and output data directly from a PC. This changes the way that they manage their information, causing a loss in productivity as they get accustomed to the new system. Over time, employees will become more productive using the database than they were with pencil and paper, but be sure to include the time lost as a cost.

Impacts on Users

Humans are notorious for adapting to change very slowly or avoiding it altogether. For instance, there are many benefits to replacing paper-based record systems, such as those used in hospitals and warehouses, with using handheld wireless devices that provide an electronic means via bar codes of storing and retrieving information from a centralized database. Most people cannot make this type of change very quickly, though. Therefore, upper management needs to understand how much time and training the current staff might need before realizing the benefits of the wireless system. Some people also resist change when the key concepts of the solution are not their own or if the new solution conflicts with another solution they had in mind. If these people have an impact on the success of the project, be sure to get their buy-in as early in the project as possible. Sometimes including them in defining requirements can help get their buy-in.

Impacts on Existing Systems

Systems managers will be concerned with how the new system will affect the operations and cost of the existing systems. They will ask questions such as these: Will the servers support the increase in utilization? Is there enough capacity in the network infrastructure to support the WLAN traffic? Will there need to be additional system administrators? Will there be any additional hardware or software maintenance costs? Will we need to interact with new vendors? Be ready to answer these questions when planning the project and focusing on feasibility.

Note   To justify the deployment of a WLAN, focus on initially deploying one or more applications that provide ROI of less than five years.

Making the Decision to Proceed

The final step with planning a WLAN deployment is to decide whether to proceed. As mentioned earlier, upper management will need to clearly see that the benefits outweigh the costs of deploying and supporting the network. Distribute the feasibility study and other planning documents, such as the project scope, WBS, staffing, schedule, and budget to the appropriate managers, and schedule a meeting to discuss the project. Assuming that the study convinces management that a strong ROI exists, the decision on how to proceed will be based on the availability of money to fund the project and the plans you have to resolve issues that might arise.

In some cases, managers might want to divide a project into phases and stagger the implementation over a longer period of time to accommodate the following scenarios:

- **Limited funding and no implementation issues:** If there are no implementation issues and the company is unable to fund the entire deployment, the company could agree to proceed with the entire project and spread the deployment over a time period that accommodates the future availability of money. This tends to be the most common scenario.

- **No funding issues but significant risks:** If plenty of money is available but there is concern about whether the system is necessary or if there are other risks, such as staff not having sufficient experience, the company could consider funding only the requirements definition phase of the project to better clarify the needs. The company can then distribute the requirements document to qualified system integrators, who can bid on the design and implementation phases of the project.

For an example of developing a feasibility study for a WLAN deployment, see Case Study 8-8.

Case Study 8-8: Acme Industries Develops a Feasibility Study for a Wireless LAN Deployment

Ted, a project manager for the fictitious company Acme Industries, has been planning the deployment of a WLAN (see Case Studies 8-1 through 8-7). Ted has been working with Chris, the company's director of information systems, and the rest of the team to develop a feasibility study to present to the CFO for funding approval.

The following is a description of the results of this process that will provide the basis for ensuring that there are sufficient benefits to warrant the costs of deploying the WLAN:

Costs

Ted reviewed the budget that Chris prepared (see Case Study 8-6) and included that in the feasibility study. To account for possible cost overruns, Ted added an additional 10 percent cost to the budget for contingencies.

Benefits

With this project, the primary benefits are the gain in productivity of warehouse staff using the AIDC system and the use of wireless IP phones throughout the company.

Henry, the system analyst working on the project, completed time studies with the warehouse clerks to better understand how the wireless system will improve productivity. He was able to estimate the amount of time that a warehouse clerk would save by using an AIDC-based solution for each warehouse function. This provides a basis for determining labor savings. For example, Henry found that the time it takes a clerk to perform a receive action for each item taken into the warehouse is approximately 30 seconds using the current pencil-and-paper process. The clerk must find the item number on each item and then record the item number in a journal. The use of an AIDC system for receiving each item will take only 10 seconds. This is a time savings of 20 seconds per item. The distribution centers combined receive an average of 500 items per day, resulting in a time savings of 2.8 hours per day. Based on similar analysis techniques, the total time savings per day for all the functions using the AIDC system is 8.4 hours per day, resulting in a total savings of 16,800 hours per year—significant savings. For example, based on an average pay for warehouse staff of $20 per hour, the annual labor savings for using the AIDC system would be $336,000 for the five distribution centers. Of course, the company will realize this savings only if it downsizes the warehouse staff or assigns the staff to other open positions. Also, keep in mind that the savings do not begin until after the system becomes operational. Other benefits of the AIDC system would include faster delivery times to customers and better accuracy of inventories.

Henry also looked into the benefits of using wireless IP phones and discovered the following benefits:

- Increased productivity in the distribution centers because of direct communications among warehouse clerks and administrative offices.
- Better customer service because staff are able to answer customer calls directly rather than having customers leave voice messages.
- Improved safety because employees carrying wireless IP phones can contact the appropriate services immediately if an emergency situation occurs in the manufacturing plant.

The actual dollar value of these wireless IP phone benefits was difficult to assess, but based on lessons learned from other wireless IP phone implementations, Ted strongly feels that they will be well worth the expense.

Impacts on Users

Warehouse users are accustomed to recording inventories (and such) on paper and then using data terminals located in the warehouse administration office to input the data into the company's warehouse management system. Most of the clerks have been using the existing system for years, and there may be some objection to learning an automated system. In addition, some of the clerks will worry about possibly losing their jobs in order for the company to realize the associated savings. In this situation, however, the company has been growing. The deployment of the WLAN will only require the company to reduce the number of additional clerks it had planned to hire, not terminate anyone's employment.

Impacts on Existing Systems

The existing warehouse system is terminal based, with two desktop terminals in each distribution center. The servers have had no problems keeping up with the data entry at the terminals. With the WLAN, users will access the servers directly through the wireless data collectors, and traffic will flow through the WLAN, over the company's wide-area network, and then on to the server through the Ethernet network in the headquarters building in Dayton. These servers already have connections to the Ethernet network, and they have plenty of capacity for the additional users who will be accessing the server simultaneously. There are also plenty of switch ports available for the access points.

Decision to Move Forward

Based on the feasibility study results, the company president and Bob, the company's CFO, decided to allocate the needed capital. Therefore, Bob gave approval to Chris to go ahead with the deployment of the project.

Executing the Project

After completing the planning stage of the project, the project manager can begin work activities with a kickoff meeting and can guide the project through the activities identified in the WBS. The project team should periodically hold status meetings to assess the progress to date and to make changes to the plan, if necessary, to keep the project on course. These project management actions include the following:

- Kickoff meeting

- Status checks

- Technical interchange meetings

- Progress reporting

The Kickoff Meeting

The entire project team should have a kickoff meeting to review the project plan and officially start the deployment project. This starts the team off together and avoids having people stray away from the primary objectives. At the kickoff meeting, discuss the following items:

- Project scope

- WBS

- Staffing

- Schedule

- Budget

- Risks

Periodic Activities

Periodically, the project manager should check the status of the tasks, perform technical interchange meetings, and report progress to upper management. The following list explains each of these activities:

- **Status checks:** For most WLAN deployment projects, a weekly status check is often enough to review progress. You can normally accomplish this at a project staff meeting. The project manager should at least review completed tasks and check whether the project is on time and within budget. It is also a good idea to review risk factors and take action to minimize their impact.

- **Technical interchange meetings:** Technical interchange meetings address technical issues that need attention from project team members and customer representatives. A technical interchange meeting is effective if the solution to a technical requirement or problem cannot be adequately solved by a single team member. In this case, schedule a technical interchange meeting and invite the people needed to solve the problem.

- **Progress reports:** Progress reports summarize the technical, schedule, and cost status of the project. The main idea is to show a comparison between planned and actual elements. Project managers should periodically send progress reports to upper management to keep them abreast of the status of the development.

Note It is normally best to alert management of conditions that might affect the project as early as possible. You want to allow enough time for upper management to assist in countering the problems.

Management reports should focus on current accumulative costs and the schedule status, past and present staff utilization, negative impacts on the project schedule, identification of successful and unsuccessful tasks, and major changes made to the project plan. The latter should also be thoroughly explained. The progress report should explain how the project team will counter all deficiencies.

Evaluating the Outcome of the Project

After the project is finished, the project manager should congratulate the team and review the lessons learned throughout the deployment. Gather one last time as a project team and discuss the activities that took place from the beginning of the project through the requirements, design, and installation phases. What did the team learn as a result of completing the project? You can answer this by thinking of what the successes were and why they occurred. Also identify any problems that happened that should be solved before undertaking another project.

Here are some questions the team should consider for analyzing the lessons learned:

- Does the implemented system perform as the project team and users expected it to? If not, what were the deficiencies? Have there been any other benefits that had been unforeseen?

- Did upper management continue to support the project to the end? If not, how did this impact the project?

- How can communications among the team members be improved in future projects?

- Were there any problems associated with the mechanics of product procurement? If so, how can procurement be improved?

- Was effective operational support in place before users began using the system?

- How well did training prepare users to operate the wireless applications?

- Was the project completed on schedule and within budget? If not, how can it be done better in future projects?

Before the kickoff meeting, these questions can help you get started. Be sure, though, to formulate additional questions that are more specific to your deployment.

Deploying City-wide Wi-Fi Networks

Many municipalities are in the midst of deploying municipal Wi-Fi networks that provide wireless connectivity throughout outdoor areas of a city. With signal coverage over dozens and even hundreds of square miles, these systems are expected to serve a diverse set of applications, such as wireless meter readers, public safety, traveling businesspeople, and tourists. The creation of these systems offers significant value to city governments and the public.

Because of the magnitude of these wireless systems (and considerable public attention), it is very important that cities adhere to proven methodologies geared for large-scale wireless network deployment. This means using classical system engineering with special provisions that apply to the wireless nature of the solution. The following are important steps and tips that cities should follow:

- **Requirements definition:** The deployment of any city-wide wireless network should begin with carefully analyzing requirements. Start by identifying who will be using the network and the applications they will use. For example, there may be a business need to enable wireless meter reading because it can significantly lower operating costs for the city. Also, city inspectors may strongly benefit from having wireless access to work orders to work more efficiently. Something else to consider is whether the network will provide public access to the Internet. After defining who will use the system, you need to describe additional specifications, such as supported security protocols, performance, battery backup provisions, etc. The city will need to include all this in an RFP.

- **Business analysis:** With requirements well understood, it is time to look at the ROI potential of the system once it is installed. In most cases, a city council will need to clearly see that the system will recover the costs related to deploying the network within an appreciable period of time, such as three or five years.

- **Preinstallation wireless site survey:** City-wide wireless systems operate mostly outdoors, and it is important to know what is lurking out there before getting too serious about moving forward with the deployment. The main idea is to measure wireless activity in the bands where the system will operate, such as 2.4 GHz to 2.5 GHz and 5.0 GHz to 6.0 GHz. Be sure to perform this testing at ground level, where users will access the network, and on rooftops, where backhaul components will be located. A problem is that noises in the band from 2.4 GHz to 2.5 GHz from non-Wi-Fi systems (and neighboring Wi-Fi networks, in some cases) will likely be a source of radio signal interference, and this impacts the selection of technology and mesh node density estimations. In some cases where noise levels are very high or there are significant obstacles, such as irregular buildings and structures that might cause excessive multipath, it may also be worthwhile to perform some pilot testing.

- **Mounting asset assessment:** City-wide Wi-Fi networks have mesh nodes that installers distribute throughout the city by mounting them on streetlamp and traffic light poles. Take a close look at the availability and condition of these mounting assets. Be sure that they are still in good shape and can support the weight of a mesh node. Some streetlamp poles have lots of rust and may be deemed not suitable for the installation of mesh nodes, which should be mounted near the end of the arm for maximum signal coverage along the street. Also, identify the available electrical voltages, which may limit your selection of mesh nodes. For backhaul links, which connect the mesh nodes to centrally located controllers and head ends, survey rooftops that are available for use by the city.

- **System design:** This step depends highly on requirements. A city will likely need to work with a wireless integrator, selected through a bidding process, to fully realize a solution. From the city's perspective, be sure that the integrator takes into account all application requirements, knowledge gained from the pre-installation survey, understanding of available mounting assets, and experience deploying mesh networks in city environments.

- **Acceptance testing:** After the integrator installs the system and deems it ready for use, the city should independently perform acceptance testing to determine whether the system fully meets contracted requirements. This means conducting tests to verify compliance with signal coverage area, performance, security, and operational support. This step is crucial to ensure that the system fully meets requirements and avoids future legal action between the city and the integrator.

Keep these tips in mind, and you will have a more successful experience deploying a municipal Wi-Fi network. Do not forget that these systems are based on radio waves and so require specialized testing and assurance that the resulting systems actually do what they are supposed to do.

Summary

As this chapter explains, a great deal of work is necessary to properly plan a WLAN deployment project. By applying sound project management practices, a project is sure to be a success. Spend ample time upfront to define a project scope, develop a work breakdown structure, identify staffing, create a schedule, develop a budget, evaluate risks, and analyze feasibility. The completion of these tasks provides primary elements necessary for upper management to make a decision on moving forward with the deployment. It also provides structure for the project and the basis for the first phase of the deployment, which is to define detailed requirements.

Chapter 9

Defining Requirements for a Wireless LAN

This chapter will introduce you to:

- Requirements Attributes

- Requirements Definition Steps

- Step 1: Gathering Information

- Step 2: Analyzing Requirements

- Step 3: Documenting Requirements

- Step 4: Obtaining Requirements Approval

At the beginning of a wireless LAN (WLAN) deployment, be sure to define requirements, which spell out what the WLAN needs to support. Avoid purchasing and installing components without this upfront planning. Designers will refer to the requirements when making technical decisions, such as where to install access points. This chapter explains how to fully define requirements for a WLAN.

Note A case study about a fictitious company (Acme Industries) deploying a WLAN began in Chapter 8, "Planning a Wireless LAN Deployment." This case study continues in this chapter, starting with Case Study 9-1.

Requirements Attributes

When defining requirements, be certain that they focus on true needs, not aspects of the implementation. A need is something that the WLAN must satisfy in order to achieve the benefits of the system. When deploying a WLAN, a company may be banking on the cost savings of implementing wireless IP phones. In this case, the WLAN needs to support the effective use of wireless IP phones. The requirements should not define the technologies, architecture, and so on that can support the use of wireless IP phones. There are many solutions, and stating one in the requirements limits design choices, which may result in a poor choice. It is generally best to wait until you define all requirements before designing a WLAN because different combinations of requirements lead to different solutions.

Be sure that requirements are unambiguous. They should clearly explain the needs. For example, you need to define all areas where signal coverage applies. A simple statement that signal coverage applies to a hospital building, for example, is too vague. You need to do some investigation and determine whether it is worthwhile to cover the entire building or eliminate certain areas, such as parking garages, elevators, stairwells, restrooms, storage areas, outdoor courtyards, basements, and so on.

It is also best that requirements lean toward the future. For example, if you are not expecting to implement voice telephony initially but will likely do so sometime in the future, be sure to state that in the requirements. Designers can then consider system architectures that can cost-effectively scale to the future needs.

Requirements Definition Steps

The project team should complete the following steps when defining requirements for a WLAN:

Step 1.   Gather information.

Step 2.   Analyze requirements.

Step 3.   Document the requirements.

Step 4.   Obtain approval for the requirements.

The sections that follow explain each of these steps in greater detail.

Case Study 9-1: Acme Industries Begins Defining Requirements for a Wireless LAN Deployment

Henry, the system analyst for the WLAN deployment that the fictitious company Acme Industries is undertaking, is ready to undertake the requirements definition phase of the project. Henry has been working for Acme Industries for years and knows each of the departments well. He will be gathering information as the basis for analyzing and documenting the requirements.

Refer to the case studies that appear throughout the remainder of this chapter to understand how Acme Industries defines requirements for its WLAN.

Step 1: Gathering Information

It is imperative to gather as many facts as you can related to requirements for the WLAN. This information provides the basis for each of the requirements that you will be defining during the requirements analysis. The most effective method of gathering this information is to interview various people, such as managers, potential users, and IT staff.

Consider taking these actions when gathering information:

- Interview users.

- Interview IT staff.

- Review the existing infrastructure and systems.

The sections that follow explain each of these tasks in greater detail.

Interviewing Users

Of course, potential users will be the ones using the WLAN. As a result, it is important to focus on their needs and perspectives.

The following are examples of general questions you should ask potential users, user representatives, and managers when defining the needs of a WLAN:

- What applications and functions, such as voice, location tracking, telemetry, and bar code data, does the WLAN need to support?

- What types of client devices, such as laptops, wireless IP phones, and bar code scanners, will users be operating?

- In what areas of the facility does the WLAN need to provide signal coverage?

- How many users will the WLAN need to support?

- How many users of each type of client device (and area) will use the WLAN simultaneously?

- What aesthetics requirements does the WLAN need to comply with?

- What policies and regulations does the company have that might impact the WLAN?

- What future applications will the WLAN likely need to support?

Note   For more detailed questions, see the section "Step 2: Analyzing Requirements," later in this chapter.

Interviewing IT Staff

IT staff have a wealth of information that you can use when defining requirements. Be careful, however, to differentiate needs from design solutions. IT staff may have experience with deploying WLANs and tend to discuss various solutions that relate more to design alternatives than to requirements. Try to keep the interviews focused on understanding actual requirements.

The following are examples of general questions you should ask IT staff when defining needs for a WLAN:

- What existing legacy radios (for example, 802.11a, 802.11b, or 802.11g) should the WLAN support?

- What degree of scalability does the WLAN need to support?

- What level of security does the WLAN need to support?

- What types of mobility, such as continuous movement or portability, does the WLAN need to support?

- What existing WLANs need to be part of the new WLAN deployment?

- What applications and servers do the new client devices need to interface with?

- What experience, methods, and systems are currently in place for providing operations and maintenance for the WLAN?

Note   In some cases, the process of defining WLAN requirements uncovers weaknesses in the current business processes and motivates business process reengineering, which is a realignment of the way a company operates. For example, the introduction of WLANs makes it possible to redesign paper-intensive methods into a more mobile and automated form.

Reviewing the Existing Infrastructure and Systems

In addition to interviewing people, be sure to review the existing infrastructure and systems to gain a full understanding of how they might impact the deployment of the WLAN. Be sure to review current documentation describing the existing systems. The availability of documentation varies, so you might not be able to perform a detailed review through documentation alone. In many cases, you will find it necessary to meet with the applicable IT staff or contractors who either installed the systems or are currently supporting them.

Also review the strategic information system plan, if available. This plan provides a long-term vision of the corporate information system, as well as policies and standards that the design team might need to know. In addition, the organization might have other plans, such as business and employee projections, that the team can consider. Business plans describe the future markets and strategies that the company wants to pursue, which is useful in determining the types of applications and services the users might require.

Step 2: Analyzing Requirements

After gathering information, the next step is to analyze the requirements for the WLAN. Some of the information you collect may map directly to requirements. For example, the answer to a question regarding use of legacy client radios (802.11a, 802.11b, or 802.11g) might result in an understanding that the WLAN needs to support use of client devices equipped with 802.11b/g radios. As a result, the requirements you analyze/define would indicate a need for supporting legacy devices.

In most cases, however, answers to your questions will not provide all requirements. You are often left to fill in some of the "holes," specifying requirements that make the most sense based on the known requirements. This is where you need to do some thinking and pull from experience. If you find yourself in this position, focus on choosing requirements that best enable the WLAN to provide expected benefits.

When defining requirements, focus on the following elements:

- Applications
- Client devices
- Signal coverage areas
- Utilization
- Mobility
- Security
- Scalability
- Existing infrastructure
- Integration
- Environment
- Aesthetics

The sections that follow explain each of these elements.

Application Requirements

Application requirements describe how people will use the WLAN. This includes general functions, such as e-mail, web browsing, voice telephony, location tracking, or telemetry. In addition, functional requirements should define the specific applications, such as inventory management, price marking, asset management, patient monitoring, and so on.

For each of these, consider and characterize the associated usage model, which represents how the user operates the application. For example, you should define where users will use their wireless laptops, such as offices and conference rooms, to send and receive e-mail and browse the web. This provides a basis for defining more detailed requirements, such as mobility and utilization.

Note   It is a good idea to select or develop "mobilized" software for operation over the WLAN. This is software that works in both connected and disconnected states, which is important due to the potential coverage holes that may be present.

The following are examples of questions you should answer as the basis for analyzing application requirements:

■ How does the application work?

■ Who will be using the application?

■ When and where will users use the application?

■ What types of client devices are part of the application?

■ Are there needs to utilize the WLAN to support location-based applications?

Case Study 9-2: Acme Industries Defines Application Requirements for a Wireless LAN

Henry, the system analyst for the WLAN deployment that the fictitious company Acme Industries is undertaking, is defining application requirements for the WLAN. Henry has spent some time interviewing potential users, managers, and IT staff regarding their expected use of the WLAN.

The following are the applications and usage models that Henry found to have the highest potential return on investment:

■ **E-mail and web browsing:** Users will operate 802.11-equipped laptops and smart phones to send and receive e-mail, browse the web, and interact with corporate applications from conference rooms and offices. In addition, smart phone users will likely send and receive e-mail while walking between offices and throughout the manufacturing plant and distribution centers.

■ **Voice telephony:** Users will operate wireless IP phones while in motion throughout all parts of the corporate headquarters, manufacturing plant, and distribution centers. This includes placing and receiving calls among employees located in any of the distribution centers, the manufacturing plant, and the headquarters building. In addition, users will need to place and receive calls to phone numbers outside the company.

■ **Receiving:** Users in the manufacturing plant and the distribution centers will use bar code scanners to automate the reception of parts and finished products. The user will scan an item's bar code, which contains information that identifies the item (for example, part number). The bar code data will be sent over the wireless network to the warehouse management system database, which marks the item as received and updates other applicable databases. The warehouse management system will then send details about the put-away location (for example, bin number) to the bar code scanner, which will then print a put-away label for the user to affix to the item.

- **Cross-docking:** Users in the distribution centers will use bar code scanners to perform cross-docking functions. As the distribution center receives finished products from the manufacturing plant, the user will scan the bar code on the item. The bar code traverses the wireless network back to the warehouse management system, which determines whether a customer has placed an order for that item. If yes, the warehouse management system responds with customer destination information (customer name, address, and so on). The scanner/printer prints the corresponding shipping label that the user will apply directly to the item at the loading dock. The user can then place the item in a special area on the loading dock for the shipping company to pick it up. If the warehouse management system determines that there are no orders for the product (which is rare), the warehouse management system sends the put-away details to the scanner.

- **Location-based applications:** The company has not yet chosen any applications that require using the WLAN to determine location; however, this may become necessary in the future. As a result, the requirements for the WLAN should indicate a potential need for location-based applications (and that the WLAN design should include, as an option, provisions for supporting location-based applications).

Based on the detailed interviews that Henry conducted (as compared to the preliminary discussions that Chris had done as the basis for writing the project scope), the above are the applications and usage models that the WLAN will need to support.

Client Device Requirements

You should specify the client devices (and existing client radios) to ensure that the solution accommodates them in the most effective manner. Describe anything about the client device that might impact the design of the WLAN system. For example, you might specify that users will have laptops running a Microsoft operating system with integrated 802.11n (2.4-GHz)/802.11ac (5-GHz) radios.

Be sure to specify the length of time that the client devices need to operate from a set of batteries. A mobile patient-monitoring device, for example, might need to operate for at least 72 hours, which is the typical length of an inpatient hospital stay. For a warehouse application, the battery might need to last for only one shift, typically eight hours. This information will indicate whether the WLAN components will need to perform power-save functions.

If the weight and size of the end-user device are a concern, be sure to define applicable requirements. For example, the WLAN transceiver might need to fit the comfort and usability needs of a person wearing a device all day when performing tasks. In most cases, smaller and lighter wireless devices are best.

The following are examples of questions you should answer as the basis for analyzing client device requirements:

- How many of each type of client device does the WLAN need to support?

- What radios (if any) are integrated in the client devices?

- What client radio form factors do the client devices support?

- What operating systems do the client devices have?

- How long must the client device operate on a single battery charge?

- What is the maximum weight and size of the WLAN interface cards or modules?

Case Study 9-3: Acme Industries Defines Client Device Requirements for a Wireless LAN

Henry, the system analyst for the WLAN deployment that the fictitious company Acme Industries is undertaking, is defining client device requirements for the WLAN.

Based on the application requirements (see Case Study 9-2), the following are client devices that the WLAN must support:

- **Laptops:** The company plans to use 20 existing Dell laptops with integrated 802.11n (dual-band 2.4- and 5-GHz) client cards as part of the initial WLAN deployment process. The company will eventually purchase another 30 laptops with internal 802.11n (2.4-GHz) and 802.11ac (5-GHz) radios.

- **Desktop computers:** There are 75 existing desktop computers. None of these computers have existing 802.11 radios, but the company is planning to purchase dual-band 802.11n (2.4-GHz) and 802.11ac (5-GHz) radios for these computers.

- **Wireless IP phones:** The IT department, along with managers from various departments, has decided to purchase 25 Cisco 7925G (802.11a/b/g) wireless IP phones for use on the WLAN. In the future, the company will likely purchase an additional 75 phones. The WLAN will eventually need to support a total of 100 phones. These phones have an integrated 802.11a/b/g radio and specialized power-save features when used in conjunction with Cisco access points.

- **Bar code scanners:** Another project team responsible for deploying the company's warehouse management system has decided to purchase 25 bar code scanners to support bar code applications in the manufacturing plant and distribution center. These devices have built-in 802.11n (2.4-GHz) radios and operate without charging for up to eight hours.

Signal Coverage Requirements

To determine coverage of the wireless network, figure out the area where the users will operate wireless devices to help the designer decide the number and location of WLAN access points. Users might only need connectivity in their offices and conference rooms, or they may also need connectivity inside the company cafeteria. By properly specifying the coverage area, you can ensure that the WLAN will provide coverage where needed and avoid the unnecessary expense of installing access points where coverage isn't necessary. Unless it's obvious, also identify the country where the wireless network will operate. This impacts channel planning and product availability.

Note If a minimum signal strength is known, such as −75 dBm for data applications or −67 dBm for voice telephony, specify it as a requirement for signal coverage. You must determine this minimum after taking into account performance requirements and sources of radio signal interference. Keep in mind that it is always best to conduct a wireless site survey (see Chapter 15, "Performing a Wireless Site Survey," for more information).

In addition to the obvious areas, such as offices and conference rooms, consider the following places for signal coverage:

- **Elevators:** It is often difficult to provide reliable signal coverage inside elevators, so carefully assess the need for enabling access to the WLAN from inside elevators. If deploying a voice over WLAN (VoWLAN) system in a hospital, for instance, access in elevators will likely be a requirement. Nurses and doctors are very mobile and often use elevators when rushing to care for patients. A corporate office, however, may not have critical needs to warrant usage from inside elevators.

- **Stairwells:** Stairwells are also very difficult places to provide signal coverage. The construction of the facility around the staircases usually includes fireproofing material and steel-reinforced concrete, which greatly attenuates radio waves. In most cases, you will need an access point inside each stairwell on each floor to offer adequate signal levels for voice applications. This can add up to tremendous cost. If it is absolutely necessary, however, then the benefits may exceed the high costs.

- **Restrooms:** This area may seem silly to cover, but critical organizations, such as hospitals, generally need to provide instant communications among essential people. But, in general, it is likely that needs to cover restrooms will be limited.

- **Utility rooms:** If the applications warrant, there may be need for providing signal coverage in utility rooms. For example, an IT person may need to communicate with a manager or an engineer while troubleshooting the network from inside a wiring closet.

- **Outdoor areas:** Be sure to consider all outdoor areas around the facilities. There may be parking areas, patios, courtyards, and maintenance yards where users may need to use the WLAN.

The following are examples of questions you should answer as the basis for analyzing signal coverage requirements:

- In which areas of each facility does the WLAN need to provide signal coverage?

- In what country does the WLAN need to operate?

- Does the WLAN need to provide signal coverage in elevators, stairwells, restrooms, utility rooms, basements, or attics?

- In what outdoor areas does the WLAN need to provide signal coverage?

- What minimum signal strength must the WLAN provide? (Keep in mind that this may not be known and would best be defined when performing the wireless site survey.)

Case Study 9-4: Acme Industries Defines Signal Coverage Requirements for a Wireless LAN

Henry, the system analyst for the WLAN deployment that the fictitious company Acme Industries is undertaking, is defining client device requirements for the WLAN. Along with the company's facilities manager, Henry reviewed the floor plans of the corporate headquarters, manufacturing plant, and distribution centers to better understand all areas where Acme may want to have signal coverage. He also asked users and managers where they will likely need to use the WLAN.

All offices, hallways, warehouses, the manufacturing production floor, cafeterias, break rooms, and lobbies will require signal coverage. The corporate headquarters has elevators, and based on the interviews with potential users, it will be beneficial to provide signal coverage in the elevators to maintain voice calls while roaming through the facility. Users typically use the elevators frequently throughout the day. It will not be necessary, however, to cover the stairwells because they are rarely used. In addition, there is no need to provide coverage in restrooms or any outdoor areas. The utility rooms having networking equipment, though, will need coverage so that IT staff can communicate via voice calls and access vendor websites while installing and troubleshooting network problems.

On diagrams of the buildings, Henry shaded the areas that will not have coverage, which include stairwells, restrooms, and the utility rooms that contain no networking equipment.

Utilization Requirements

The performance of a WLAN is very important. You never hear people complain that performance is too high. Low performance, however, means that users cannot do their work as quickly as they want or what they are used to. Put in the time to fully understand the performance requirements that the applications and client devices will have on the WLAN. Engineers will need to know this when implementing the WLAN.

Because of the way WLANs operate, users share the wireless medium. Users connected to the same access point, for instance, cannot transmit signals simultaneously. As a result, users must take turns transmitting, which limits the performance as the number of active users grows. This makes it important to assess the activity rate or utilization of users accessing the WLANs. A single active wireless IP phone in one particular area, for example, would not pose any issues with performance. But 20 users talking on IP phones from the same conference room would put a significant load on the WLAN. It is likely that the WLAN will not support this load unless engineers take note and carefully design the network. Each access point offers limited capacity. Thus, designers need to know the number and utilization of users in each of the areas of the facility to ensure that the WLAN is sized adequately.

> **Note**   Strongly consider requiring the WLAN to support future utilization requirements to avoid costly reengineering as activity on the network increases over time.

The following are examples of questions you should answer as the basis for analyzing utilization requirements:

- How many of each type of client device does the WLAN need to support within each major area of the facility?

- For each client device type, how often will a typical user actively operate the client device in a manner that causes transmission or reception of data?

- How large are the files that the applications send over the WLAN?

Case Study 9-5: Acme Industries Defines Utilization Requirements for a Wireless LAN

Henry, the system analyst for the WLAN deployment that the fictitious company Acme Industries is undertaking, is defining utilization requirements for the WLAN. He has already defined the number of overall client devices (see Case Study 9-3). Henry has spent more time now analyzing the use of the client devices and the information that they will need to send over the WLAN.

Henry has come up with the following elements regarding utilization that Frank, the engineer on the project, will need to know when designing the system: .

- **Headquarters building:** Users in the headquarters building will be using wireless laptops, wireless desktop computers, and wireless IP phones. All wireless laptops and the majority of desktops (all but one or two at each distribution center) will be accessing the WLAN from inside the headquarters building. Out of the 75 laptops, however, only 10 to 20 will be actively using the WLAN at any given time, but they will likely be from the same area, such as the conference rooms and training rooms. There will be other locations where users will access the network via wireless laptops and desktop computers, but they are distributed throughout the facility. Up to 40 phones may be present in the headquarters building at any given time, but only 3 to 5 should be actively placing calls at the same time. The applicable client devices are likely to be spread throughout the building and on different floors; however, there might be 15 people simultaneously using the phones in a conference room during breaks from meetings and training sessions.

■ **Manufacturing plant:** Users in the manufacturing plant will be using wireless laptops, wireless desktop computers, and wireless IP phones. Access to the WLAN, however, will be minimal. Occasionally, the manufacturing plant manager may use a wireless IP phone to place calls and use a wireless desktop to check e-mail. In addition, executives might come through the plant and need to access the WLAN using their wireless IP phone or laptop.

■ **Distribution centers:** Users at the five distribution centers will be using wireless laptops, wireless desktop computers, wireless IP phones, and bar code scanners. The use of wireless laptops and desktop computers will be minimal. The manager at each distribution center may occasionally check e-mail and access the corporate warehouse management system. A more significant utilization of the network will come from wireless IP phones and bar code scanners. At each plant, there will be 10 phones that the manager and warehouse clerks will use to communicate. This will likely result in 2 or 3 phones actively placing calls at the same time at each distribution center. Because they will be communicating with each other, the phone users will likely be far apart and in different radio cells. Each distribution center will have frequent use of bar code scanners, with up to 5 bar code scanners continuously scanning items from the same area.

Mobility Requirements

When designing a WLAN, it is important to understand the movement of users while they access the WLAN. Handoffs between access points can cause disruptions, and special care must be taken to implement solutions that avoid abrupt disconnections and dropped phone calls. When defining mobility requirements, consider whether user motion is continuous, periodic, or stationary.

The following are examples of questions you should answer as the basis for analyzing mobility requirements for each type of client device:

■ Which users or client devices will require continuous or periodic movement?

■ What are the typical paths that users will take to move continuously throughout the signal coverage area?

■ How fast will users move continuously throughout the signal coverage area?

■ Where will users need to roam and have temporary access to the WLAN?

■ Which users or client devices will require stationary access to the WLAN?

Continuous Movement

When the user or network component must have the capability to use network resources while physically moving, it is said to be in continuous movement. Examples of users in continuous movement and needing constant access to network resources include people walking between offices and conference rooms while using wireless IP phones, riding in moving vehicles or trains, and so on. Continuous movement requires the client radio to frequently re-associate with different access points as the user moves, which can be demanding as the speed increases. As a result, be sure to note the typical and maximum speed of movement, which will be important when designing an effective roaming solution.

Portable Access

Portable access means that the utilization of network resources is from temporary locations, not necessarily while the user is in transit between locations. Portability implies a temporary connection to the network from a stationary point, but the interface associated with a portable connection should be easy to move, set up, and dismantle. Examples of users requiring portable interfaces include employees responding to e-mail from conference rooms, visitors accessing the Internet, employees working from a temporary office facility, and so on. In this case, the client radio only needs to associate with the access point when the user boots the client device, which generally does not impose any roaming issues. Occasionally, there might be issues with IP address assignments, but that can be prevented with proper configuration of the client device.

Stationary Access

In some cases, users might require only stationary access to the WLAN. This is the same as periodic mobility, except that the client device will likely have a long-term association to the same access point. A desktop computer, for example, will likely require stationary access to the wireless network. The desktop will probably not be moved to different locations very often, so for all practical purposes, it is stationary. Some schools have been known, however, to mount wireless desktops on movable carts and share them among classrooms.

Case Study 9-6: Acme Industries Defines Mobility Requirements for a Wireless LAN

Henry, the system analyst for the WLAN deployment that the fictitious company Acme Industries is undertaking, is defining mobility requirements for the WLAN. He has a good understanding of the applications (see Case Study 9-2), client devices (see Case Study 9-3), and signal coverage requirements (see Case Study 9-4) and is now focusing on how users move throughout the signal coverage area. Through the interviewing process, Henry has learned a great deal about how users will roam about the facilities with client devices while using network applications.

The following are the mobility requirements for each type of client device:

- **Laptops:** The primary use of wireless laptops will require portable access from offices, conference rooms, the cafeteria, and the lobby of the headquarters building and offices within the manufacturing plant and distribution centers. There are no requirements for users to access the WLAN continuously with laptops as the users move throughout the building.

■ **Desktops:** All wireless desktops will require stationary access. The desktops may be moved from one office to another when an employee changes offices, but that rarely happens.

■ **Wireless IP phones:** The typical behavior of wireless IP phone users will be to place calls from stationary locations. For example, most calls within the headquarters building will be placed from inside the conference room or offices. Occasionally, users will operate the phones while walking between offices in the headquarters building. The use of wireless IP phones in the manufacturing plant and distribution centers, however, will primarily occur while users are continuously moving due to the nature of the work done in these areas. For example, a warehouse clerk in one of the distribution centers often needs to talk to the warehouse manager while walking through the warehouse. Also, plant managers typically need to talk to executives and parts suppliers while walking through the manufacturing plant.

■ **Bar code scanners:** The bar code scanners require portable access to the network. A warehouse clerk, for example, will walk to the loading dock and scan items as part of the receiving function. All of these scans (much like other warehouse functions) are done from a single, temporary location.

Security Requirements

Security requirements identify what the WLAN must comply with to protect information and systems so that unauthorized people do not gain access to sensitive information. The level of security depends on the severity of the consequences that the organization would face if someone were to actually gain access to the information. Of course, military and law-enforcement agencies require very high levels of security, but hospitals, universities, manufacturers, and other enterprises must also emphasize the need for wireless security.

The following sections discuss some items that are worth considering when defining security requirements.

Sensitivity of Information and Systems

Examine the sensitivity of the information that will traverse the WLAN. To do this, consider the issues that would occur if the information were to fall into the hands of unauthorized people. This is easier to do in some cases than in others.

If users will be validating credit cards over the WLAN, for example, then certainly it is easy to recognize that an unauthorized person gaining access to these credit card numbers could use them fraudulently, resulting in serious problems with customers. Of course, you would want to require the WLAN to have provisions that would keep this from happening.

A church, for example, might store only information about members of its congregation on servers connected to the WLAN. In this case, it might be difficult to determine the level of security that is necessary. Does it matter whether someone hacks into the church database and finds the names, addresses, and phones numbers of members? That might not be a big problem, but be sure to consider all information. The church database might contain bank account details for members making automatic donations. Or the pastor might use the WLAN to log in to his web-based bank account. To prevent outsiders from getting access to the bank account details of members and the pastor, the WLAN must implement effective security.

Note   In most cases, because of the sensitive nature of information and systems in general, the requirements should state that the WLAN must provide effective authentication and encryption.

Organization Security Policies

Investigate the organization's existing policies that may specify requirements for wireless security. For example, some companies have conducted security audits and have already adopted recommendations for various wireless security mechanisms, such as Extensible Authentication Protocol Transport Layer Security (EAP-TLS) for authenticating access to the network and Advanced Encryption Standard (AES) for encrypting 802.11 data frames. Other policies might define only general requirements, such as "all wireless systems must implement authentication and encryption." Be certain to review and adopt applicable elements of these policies as requirements for the WLAN. Because policy documents may be old, however, be certain to consider updating the policies before considering them as requirements.

In some organizations, actual laws mandate the protection of information. For example, since August 1996, healthcare providers have been required to comply with the Health Insurance Portability and Accountability Act (HIPAA) for medical information privacy. This strongly motivates healthcare organizations to have solid protection (that is, authentication and encryption) to ensure that patient information is not available to unauthorized people.

Network Access Privileges

Define what privileges each type of user has for accessing various systems that are part of the WLAN. Most organizations define two levels of WLAN access: authorized access and guest access. A user defined as having authorized access means that the system administrator determines that the user is authorized to access the system, which gives the user access to any of the organization's applications and servers. To access these systems, however, the user should still be required to input a username and password for the system he or she is accessing. For example, university professors would likely be given authorized and unlimited access to the university WLAN, but they would need an account set up on the specific systems that they need access to.

With guest access, users would have access to only limited resources, such as a website having specialized information (such as flight arrivals and departures in an airport) and the Internet. It is often beneficial for visitors to have guest access to the WLAN so they can use e-mail and surf the web. Ensure that the WLAN keeps guest users from accessing sensitive information.

Existing Security Mechanisms

Identify all encryption and authentication mechanisms currently in use and determine whether the WLAN must implement those mechanisms. In many cases, an organization may have deployed WLANs with somewhat outdated security technologies. As a result, you should not take it for granted that the new WLAN will need to comply with the existing security mechanisms. Designers may be able to use the existing security technologies, but better ones might be available, and plans can be made for how to migrate to the newer technologies.

The following are examples of questions you should answer as the basis for analyzing security requirements for a WLAN:

- What are the possible negative consequences of unauthorized people accessing information and systems available through the WLAN?

- What security policies does the organization have in place that the WLAN must comply with?

- What types of network access should the WLAN provide (that is, authorized access, guest access, or both)?

- What network services should guest access provide?

- What types of authentication and encryption (if any) does the existing network implement?

Case Study 9-7: Acme Industries Defines Security Requirements for a Wireless LAN

Henry, the system analyst for the WLAN deployment that the fictitious company Acme Industries is undertaking, is defining security requirements for the WLAN. Henry has spent some time interviewing managers and has a good understanding of what the WLAN must support in regard to security.

The deployment of the WLAN will provide wireless access to servers and databases containing a great deal of financial data, including the company's accounts receivable, accounts payable, and payroll accounts. These accounts contain very sensitive information, such as employee Social Security numbers. In addition, the company stores detailed order history and bank account information pertaining to customers. Unauthorized access to this data would obviously lead to severe problems. As a result, the WLAN must support effective authentication and encryption mechanisms.

The following are additional security elements that the WLAN must support:

- **Organization security policies:** The company has no existing wireless security policies. After the design is complete, the company will adopt chosen authentication and encryption for any WLANs deployed throughout the company.

- **Network access privileges:** All employees will be given access to all resources on the WLAN, but each system will require a separate username and password. For example, someone using a bar code scanner to perform a receiving operation must input an applicable username and password to use the receiving application. The WLAN must support guest access in specific areas of the headquarters building where visitors typically go, such as the lobby, cafeteria, and conference rooms. The WLAN will restrict guest access from other areas of the headquarters building, manufacturing plant, and distribution centers. Guests can have access only to the Internet, and they can have no physical access to corporate servers.

- **Existing security mechanisms:** The company currently does not implement any security mechanisms, but the information systems department has been experimenting with EAP-TLS using digital certificates. These experimental WLANs implement WPA using Temporal Key Integrity Protocol (TKIP). The use of these security mechanisms, however, is not a requirement for the new WLAN deployment.

Note   For details on WLAN security mechanisms, see Chapter 13, "Security Considerations."

Scalability Requirements

Scalability requirements indicate the capability to include additional applications and users on the wireless network beyond the initial requirements through the addition of applicable hardware and software. A WLAN generally must provide scalability to support the growing number of wireless applications being implemented in companies. For example, the initial intent of a WLAN could be only to support relatively light throughput requirements of an inventory application, but future requirements might need higher bandwidth to support voice or video information transmission.

In addition, a WLAN should have a modular design that can accommodate evolving technologies. 802.11n/802.11ac may be the norm today, but compliant enhancements or replacements may become available within the life span of the WLAN. As a result, ensure that the WLAN is capable of cost-effectively supporting the migration to new wireless technologies. Also, be certain to specify needs for a scalable wired distribution system because that plays a vital role in the ease of evolving the size of the WLAN over time.

The following are examples of questions you should answer as the basis for analyzing scalability requirements for a WLAN:

- How many users might the WLAN need to support in the future?

- What types of wireless applications might users operate in the future?

- What types of wireless client devices might users operate in the future?

- What additional technologies might the WLAN need to support in the future?

Case Study 9-8: Acme Industries Defines Scalability Requirements for a Wireless LAN

Henry, the systems analyst for the WLAN deployment that the fictitious company Acme Industries is undertaking, is defining scalability requirements for the WLAN. When Henry conducted interviews with managers, users, and information systems staff, he asked about the future needs for the WLAN to support a growing number of users, client devices, utilization, and technologies.

The following summarizes Henry's findings regarding scalability requirements:

- **Number of users:** The initial number of users will likely grow to a total of nearly 200 within the next few years.

- **Applications:** In addition to initial applications (see Case Study 9-2), the company will likely implement an 802.11-based position tracking system in the distribution centers.

- **Types of client devices:** In addition to initial client devices (see Case Study 9-3), the company might enable the use of 802.11-equipped smart phones on the WLAN within the next year.

- **Technologies:** The company does not know of any wireless technologies under development that the WLAN might need to support in the future.

Existing Network Infrastructure Requirements

Be certain to describe all existing network infrastructure that the WLAN must support. This applies to Ethernet switches, Power over Ethernet (PoE) equipment, and cable runs. These details can be found by performing a wireless site survey (see Chapter 15). If the wireless site survey will be done later during the deployment, at least describe in the requirements what is currently known about the network infrastructure and include additional details after completing the survey.

The following are examples of questions you should answer as the basis for analyzing the existing network infrastructure requirements for a WLAN:

- Where are Ethernet switches that the WLAN access points must connect to?

- What PoE equipment must the WLAN use?

- What existing optical fiber must the WLAN use?

- What existing twisted-pair wiring must the WLAN use?

Case Study 9-9: Acme Industries Defines Existing Network Infrastructure Requirements for a Wireless LAN

Henry, the systems analyst for the WLAN deployment that the fictitious company Acme Industries is undertaking, is defining existing infrastructure requirements for the WLAN. He met with several of the IT staff and found a preference to use the existing Ethernet network for interconnecting access points. In the design, they will probably establish a separate VLAN for interconnecting the access points.

Frank, the engineer responsible for designing the WLAN, has already completed a preliminary wireless site survey to determine the number of access points needed to cover all the facilities and the availability of switch ports. It appears that there will be sufficient network infrastructure available for the WLAN. As a result, Henry is indicating a preference for the WLAN to use this infrastructure to minimize deployment costs. If a detailed site survey later on indicates a need to upgrade or augment this infrastructure, then that will be dealt with during the design.

Case Study 9-10: Acme Industries Defines Integration Requirements for a Wireless LAN

Henry, the systems analyst for the WLAN deployment that the fictitious company Acme Industries is undertaking, is defining integration requirements for the WLAN. He met with IT staff to find out the information systems the client devices will need to communicate with so that designers can determine whether the WLAN needs to include functions that resolve any issues of the applications working properly.

The following summarizes the integration requirements that the WLAN will need to support:

- **Information systems:** All the company's servers run Microsoft operating systems, except for the one that hosts the warehouse management system, which is an older IBM AS/400.

- **Communications protocols:** The existing data terminals in the warehouse communicate to the AS/400 using 5250 terminal emulation, and the new wireless bar code scanners will also need to interface with the server using 5250 or some sort of middleware.

Note Some systems require nearly continuous connectivity to avoid logouts and errors. Be certain to describe conditions in which applications require such connectivity so the designers can ensure that the WLAN provides applicable support.

Environmental Requirements

Environmental requirements include physical elements in the signal coverage area that will impact the operation of the WLAN. To determine environmental requirements, look at the conditions in which the network will operate. Gather information by interviewing company facility managers and visually inspect areas where the WLAN will operate.

The sections that follow describe the various types of environmental requirements.

Building Construction and Obstacles

It is important for designers to know the construction of the buildings and other structures that fall within the signal coverage areas of the WLAN. Identify the materials in walls, which might be wood or concrete (with or without steel reinforcement). Some walls might also be lined with lead, which is common in hospital radiation therapy rooms. Also, describe whether any other structures might hinder the propagation of radio signals. This could include large file cabinets, shelves, and machinery. Be sure to take photos and include them in the requirements document.

Floor Plans

The locations of walls, beams, and other attributes of the buildings impact the propagation of radio signals, which influences the design. You should pull together the building floor plans during the requirements determination phase of the project so that they are available to designers. Be sure, however, to verify the accuracy of the diagrams. Changes to facilities are often made without updating floor plans.

Note For outdoor areas, include satellite images, aerial photographs, or applicable drawings in the environmental requirements.

Temperature and Humidity

Electronic equipment, such as access points and controllers, is sensitive to excessive temperatures and humidity. These conditions are not much of a factor when deploying a WLAN indoors, but these factors might impact the selection of equipment for outdoor installations. Access points installed outdoors might experience very low or very high temperatures and high humidity. It is critical that designers know this information so they can select components that are rated for the particular environment. Thus, always indicate the temperature and humidity ranges of the environment where the WLAN will operate, especially if the network will be installed outdoors or in any areas where temperature or humidity ranges above or below levels found in typical offices.

Durability

If designers of a WLAN will be choosing client devices that the users will operate, consider the degree of durability that the wireless client devices must possess. Be certain to specify a drop test requirement for client devices used within industrial environments, such as bar code scanners in warehouses. These details will help designers choose durable client devices to minimize costs related to replacing damaged client devices.

The following are examples of questions you should answer as the basis for analyzing environmental requirements for a WLAN:

- What materials comprise the construction of walls and floors throughout the buildings where the WLAN will operate?

- What temperature and humidity ranges will the WLAN need to operate within?

- Will access points likely need to be installed outdoors, in areas where the access points will be subjected to rain, hail, or high wind conditions?

- What degree of hardening do the wireless client devices need to support?

- In what country are you going to install the WLAN?

Case Study 9-11: Acme Industries Identifies Environmental Requirements

Henry, the systems analyst for the WLAN deployment that the fictitious company Acme Industries is undertaking, is defining environmental requirements for the WLAN. He interviewed the company's facilities manager and toured the headquarters, the manufacturing plant, and one of the distribution centers to better understand the environment in which the WLAN will operate. While walking through the facilities, Henry took lots of photos of the ceilings, walls, and obstacles, such as heavy machinery and storage racks.

The following summarizes the environmental requirements that the WLAN needs to support:

- **Building construction:** Based on previous remodeling work, Henry knows that at least some of the interior walls of the headquarters building are constructed with wood supports and drywall. He talked to the facilities manager to verify that most office walls are constructed the same, but the load-bearing walls, which run along the hallways and periodically throughout the facility, include concrete with steel reinforcement. The ceilings in the corporate headquarters and the offices within the distribution centers consist of removable tiles with ventilation ducts between the floors.

- **Obstacles:** The headquarters has typical obstacles to radio signals, such as people, desks, and so on. The manufacturing plant has large machinery that produces the widgets that the company sells and parts racks in one portion of the facility. In the distribution centers, high storage racks contain boxes of widgets, which consist of mostly plastic parts.

- **Floor plans:** The facilities manager gave Henry a copy of the building floor plans. They were fairly old, so he penciled in changes where needed. The changes consisted primarily of new walls added to the corporate headquarters. Henry also annotated the positions of the storage racks in the distribution centers and the locations of the heavy machinery in the manufacturing plant.

- **Temperature and humidity:** All buildings maintain a temperature range of 65 degrees to 85 degrees with normal humidity levels, but the loading docks at the distribution centers can get as cold as 0 degrees and as hot as 100 degrees.

- **Durability:** The client devices were already chosen prior to the deployment (see Case Study 9-3); therefore, there is no need to specify durability requirements. The designers of the WLAN will not need to choose the client devices that users will operate.

Aesthetic Requirements

Organizations that have public access, such as department stores, often require that if anything new needs to be added to the facility, it be done in a way that does not significantly impact the aesthetics of the building. Companies spend a lot of money to make their buildings' appearances fit specific purposes, and they might not tolerate, for example, the addition of antennas that destroy the ambience of a building. In addition, buildings deemed as historical might prohibit the installation of anything to walls or ceilings. Consequently, you should specify aesthetic requirements for any parts of the signal coverage areas. These requirements will prompt designers to look for alternatives that can conceal the access points and antennas or accommodate special mounting conditions.

The following are examples of questions you should answer as the basis for analyzing aesthetic requirements for a WLAN:

- Can any portion of the access point or antennas be visible to people within the coverage areas?

- What, if any, are the restrictions for mounting components, such as access points, in the ceilings of the facilities?

Case Study 9-12: Acme Industries Identifies Aesthetic Requirements

Henry, the systems analyst for the WLAN deployment that the fictitious company Acme Industries is undertaking, has talked to the executive management about aesthetic requirements for the WLAN. He has found that there are no restrictions on mounting access points in the manufacturing plant and distribution centers. The company has developed an ambience within the headquarters building that is appealing to employees and primary resellers and has positive impacts on the development and sale of widgets. Therefore, upper management prefers that the installation of the WLAN not change the appearance of the headquarters building.

Step 3: Documenting Requirements

To support the remaining phases of the deployment, be sure to clearly document the requirements. Without good documentation, requirements can become unclear as time passes and memories fade, and the handover of project information from person to person can dilute original intentions. To make matters worse, the analysts responsible for defining the requirements could leave the company and not be available during the design phase. Undocumented requirements also make it too easy for changes to occur in an uncoordinated manner during later stages of the project, making it difficult to find the correct solution.

The person responsible for defining the requirements should develop a requirements specification that addresses all requirements. The requirements specification should address the following:

- Summary of the deployment planning:

  - Project scope

  - Budget

  - Schedule

- Names and contact information of people interviewed

- List of documents reviewed

- Details regarding each of the requirements elements:

  - Applications

  - Client devices

  - Signal coverage

  - Utilization

  - Mobility

  - Security

  - Scalability

  - Existing infrastructure

  - Integration

  - Environment

  - Aesthetics

Produce a draft requirements specification and distribute it to applicable managers for review and comment.

Step 4: Obtaining Requirements Approval

After receiving feedback on the requirements specification, make any necessary changes and seek approval of the requirements. In most organizations, the director of information systems is the person who approves the requirements, depending on the size of the organization. In some cases, you might need to submit the requirements specification through a formal configuration management process, which includes a board that meets periodically to approve/disapprove major documentation related to systems, including requirements for WLANs.

After gaining approval for the requirements, it is time to revisit the planning elements. Initially, the project work breakdown structure (WBS), schedule, and budget on preliminary requirements are based on limited discussions with managers and users. After completing the requirements definition phase of the project, though, the final requirements might cast the project in a different light. For example, maybe you found during the user interviews that information security is more important than you had expected. This might mean you need to modify the WBS (and possibly the schedule and budget) and allocate more time to research security technologies and products. As another example, you might have planned to spend 3 weeks during installation setting up 150 wireless laptops, but during the interviews, you found out there will be only 75. This could enable you to cut back the schedule or reallocate the time to a task that might take longer than expected.

Case Study 9-13: Acme Industries Approves Requirements for a Wireless LAN

Henry, the systems analyst for the WLAN deployment that the fictitious company Acme Industries is undertaking, has developed a requirements specification for the WLAN and distributed it to Chris, the information systems manager, several of the key users he interviewed, many of the company's managers, and each member of the deployment team. Henry asked everyone to review the requirements and provide feedback. After incorporating some minor feedback, which did not change the primary intent of the requirements, Henry forwarded the final requirements specification to Chris, who officially approved the requirements. Based on the final requirements, Henry reviewed the planning documents (see the case studies in Chapter 8) and did not find any need to update the WBS, schedule, or budget.

Note   Try defining requirements for your own organization by referring to the steps and case studies in this chapter.

Summary

Requirements define what a WLAN needs to support and thus provide a basis for designing an effective solution. The steps for defining requirements include gathering information, analyzing the requirements, documenting the requirements, and obtaining approval for the requirements. When gathering information, interview users and IT staff and review the existing infrastructure and systems. Focus the analysis on anything that will impact the design of the WLAN, including applications, client devices, signal coverage areas, utilization, mobility, security, scalability, existing infrastructure, integration, environment, and aesthetics. After analyzing the requirements, produce a requirements specification and obtain the necessary approval before proceeding with the design phase of the project.

Chapter 10

System Architecture Considerations

This chapter will introduce you to:

- Architectural Considerations

- Wireless Access Networks

- Distribution Systems

- Voice over WLAN Systems

- Application Connectivity

The architecture of a wireless LAN (WLAN) describes the interconnection of primary components that provide major functions, including signal coverage, security, and special applications, such as voice communications. Always consider the architecture during the initial design of a WLAN to ensure that requirements are met. This chapter provides options and tips for defining an effective architecture for a WLAN system. The forth-coming chapters cover more details of the design, such as assigning access point channels and choosing encryption methods.

Note A common case study about a fictitious company (Acme Industries) deploying a WLAN began in Chapter 8, "Planning a Wireless LAN Deployment." This case study continues in this chapter, starting with Case Study 10-1.

Architectural Considerations

Before you define the architecture of a WLAN, you need to have a good understanding of the requirements. Chapter 9, "Defining Requirements for a Wireless LAN," explains how to determine these requirements. The requirements, for example, may specify a need for voice telephony, which requires a wireless architecture that has very good performance and signal coverage, fast roaming, power savings, and quality of service for consistent voice calls over the network. The need for supporting location-based applications will also shape the architecture; for example, access points may need to be installed around the perimeter of the facility and in locations that allow wireless devices to determine their locations through triangulation. If you overlook the requirements, the architecture will likely not fully satisfy the actual needs of users.

You should consider the following architectural elements when designing a WLAN system:

- **Access network:** The access network is a key part of the architecture that enables client devices to connect wirelessly to the network. Components of the access network include access points, mesh nodes, and controllers. When designing the architecture, you must choose from architectures having different configurations. In addition, it is important to specify how the architecture will provide redundancy, common access from different types of users, service to remote offices, and legacy radio migration.

- **Distribution system:** The distribution system consists of wired switches and routers that physically interconnect access points, controllers, and servers. The distribution system is an important element to consider, especially with the high performance of 802.11n and 802.11ac systems. An inadequate distribution system can significantly limit the performance of a network. From an architectural standpoint, focus on the switches and Power over Ethernet (PoE) of the distribution system. For 802.11ac networks, ensure that switches support 1 Gbps data rates.

- **Voice over WLAN (VoWLAN) system:** A VoWLAN system enables users operating wireless IP phones to place and receive calls. Components include call managers and telephone switches. When defining the architecture for larger enterprises, you need to determine where to place call processers.

- **Application connectivity:** Application connectivity includes a variety of components, such as wireless middleware and terminal emulation, that client devices and specific application software need to interface with servers and databases. The architecture should define the chosen connectivity methods, such as terminal emulation, browser based, direct database, or wireless middleware.

Wireless Access Networks

The first aspect of the architecture that you should define is the wireless access network. There are several primary access network architectures, and you must choose one as the basis for your WLAN deployment. All other design elements follow this selection and provide additional details.

The following are the primary wireless access network architectures:

- Autonomous access point architecture

- Controller-based access point architecture

- Mesh network architecture

- Ad hoc architecture

The following sections cover each of these architectures and some additional considerations for your WLAN deployment.

Autonomous Access Point Architecture

Figure 10-1 shows an architecture implementing autonomous access points that form an infrastructure WLAN. An autonomous access point is relatively intelligent and implements enough functions to allow the access point to interconnect with other access points via conventional Ethernet switches. An autonomous access point, however, has limited communications with other access points and other devices on the network. As a result, autonomous access points operate independently from each other.

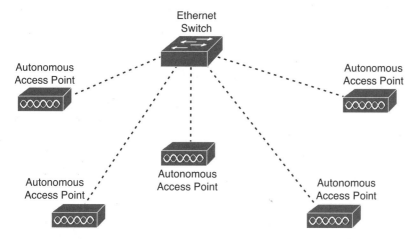

Figure 10-1 *Autonomous Access Points Offer Distributed Management and Control*

Advantages of the autonomous access point architecture include the following:

- **Possibly less expensive for smaller installations:** It might be cost-prohibitive to install a WLAN controller for a very small network, especially one that has a single access point, such as a coffee shop.

- **Less hardware to install:** Autonomous access points plug directly into a wired switch and do not require any additional equipment. This limits what you need to know to install and configure the system.

Disadvantages of the autonomous access point architecture include the following:

- **Time-consuming installation:** Someone must configure each access point manually, and this takes considerable time and often leads to misconfigurations. You must configure the access points individually by logging into each access point or using centralized management software that communicates with the access points via Simple Network Management Protocol (SNMP). This is especially time-consuming for larger networks, beyond 5 or 10 access points.

- **Time-consuming management:** When making changes to the configuration settings, such as service set identifier (SSID), you must reconfigure each access point manually (unless a centralized management utility provides this function).

- **Security issues:** There is no way to automatically disable an autonomous access point. Someone might connect a rogue access point to the wired network, which can allow open access to an unauthorized person.

Consider using the autonomous access point architecture for home and small office applications. This architecture is best if a single access point will satisfy signal coverage requirements or if the number of access points is limited (5 to 10). Contemplate the number of access points that your WLAN deployment will have and decide whether you can deal with the issues related to autonomous access points. You can generally get by with using an autonomous access point architecture if you have fewer than 10 access points.

For very small WLANs, such as a single access point covering a home or coffee shop, think about deploying an autonomous access point with built-in router functions. Figure 10-2 illustrates this approach. This solution offers a method for distributing multiple private IP addresses that share a common official IP address available from an Internet service provider (ISP).

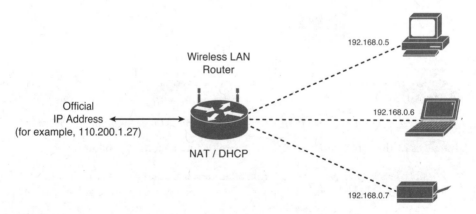

Figure 10-2 *Wireless LAN Routers Are Beneficial for Sharing a Single Official IP Address and Distributing Unique IP Addresses to Each Client Radio*

Controller-Based Access Point Architecture

Figure 10-3 shows an architecture in which controller-based access points form an infrastructure WLAN. The lightweight access points connect to a WLAN controller, which provides centralized management, security, and performance functions. The controller installs within an organization's wired network.

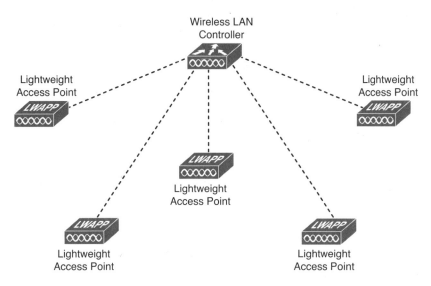

Figure 10-3 *Controller-Based Access Points Provide Centralized Management and Control*

The communication between the lightweight access points and the controller is proprietary. Cisco, for example, implements Lightweight Access Point Protocol (LWAPP), which was developed initially by Airespace (acquired by Cisco in 2005). LWAPP supports access point discovery and configuration. Cisco controller software release 5.2 and later also supports the IETF's Control and Provisioning of Wireless Access Points (CAPWAP) protocol, which provides the discovery and configuration functions as an alternative to LWAPP. In addition, LWAPP-enabled access points are compatible with CAPWAP. With CAPWAP, the network infrastructure must support layer 3 functionality because the discovery process uses IP addresses, not MAC addresses. As a result, you must configure each access point with a valid IP address (for example, through Dynamic Host Configuration Protocol [DHCP]) before the access point will join the controller. Lightweight access points use X.509 certificates to authenticate with the controller, which handles filtering and policy enforcement. This reduces the amount of processing within an access point.

Note Some controller-based networks, such as Meraki, are cloud based, where the controller is hosted on a server outside the confines of the facility.

Advantages of the controller-based access point architecture include the following:

- **Easy installation:** The controller automatically configures each access point based on a centralized configuration policy. This significantly reduces the amount of time necessary to install the access points compared to using autonomous access points.

- **Robust security:** Access points must conform to a specific security configuration to be part of the network.

■ **Effective mobility:** The controllers can track users and handle roaming functions from a centralized location without changes to the core network. This means that users and client devices do not need to re-authenticate when roaming from one access point to another, which greatly improves performance.

■ **Easily expandable:** You can install additional access points and controllers as needed to expand the network with very few configuration changes. The controller automatically configures new access points that connect to the wired network.

Disadvantages of the controller-based access point architecture include the following:

■ **Possibly cost-prohibitive for smaller organizations:** The controllers add costs to the deployment, and this might be too expensive for organizations installing smaller networks.

■ **More hardware to install:** Installers must install a controller in addition to the access points, but the time savings resulting from faster configuration of the network will likely offset the additional time needed to install the controller.

Strongly consider using the controller-based access point architecture when deploying WLANs that have more than 10 access points. The benefits of easy installation, robust security, effective mobility, and scalability result in lower implementation and support costs compared to using autonomous access points.

Include at least one controller (and possibly more) for the controller-based architecture. For larger facilities, plan on having multiple controllers distributed throughout the enterprise, depending on performance requirements. Consider placing a controller at each remote site to avoid WAN delays. It is possible to avoid having a controller at each remote site by using FlexConnect (formally called hybrid remote edge access point [HREAP]), which supports local 802.1X authentication. This significantly reduces capital expenses for controllers and associated rack space, but it can result in lower performance and reliability, depending on the WAN connection.

Note   Think about scaling the number of controllers over time as performance requirements increase.

Mesh Network Architecture

Figure 10-4 illustrates the architecture of a WLAN implementing mesh nodes. Much like access points, mesh nodes provide wireless connectivity to wireless client devices via 802.11 protocols. The mesh nodes associate with each other to create a communications path from one point in the network to another. The routing protocols are proprietary. For example, Cisco uses Adaptive Wireless Path Protocol (AWPP), which creates and maintains the wireless mesh. Most mesh network vendors offer mesh nodes (often referred to as gateways or root access points) that have a special capability in addition to a typical mesh node to provide connections to various types of wired networks or wireless backhaul equipment. Mesh networks can also take advantage of having a controller manage the configuration of the mesh node devices.

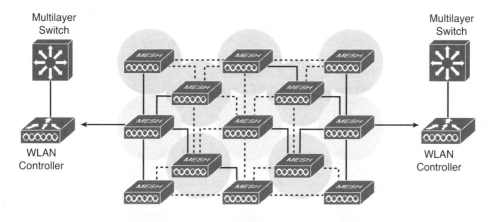

Figure 10-4 *Mesh Nodes Extend the Reach of the Wireless Network to Areas with Limited Interfaces to a Wired Network*

Advantages of the mesh network architecture include the following:

- **Reduced dependence on wired networks:** This is a strong advantage when implementing a WLAN in an area that does not have any wired network connectivity and where it is not feasible to install a wired network, such as a city or football stadium.

- **Reduced installation time:** Mesh nodes do not require a connection to the wired network. As a result, there's no need to run cables to the mesh node, which makes installation faster and less expensive.

- **Easily expandable:** After connecting a new mesh node to electrical power, it automatically meshes with the network and configures itself based on a centralized configuration profile.

Disadvantages of the mesh network architecture include the following:

- **Might reduce performance:** Communications between mesh nodes are generally slower than the communication speeds with traditional access points over wired networks. Consequently, a mesh network might introduce unacceptable delays, depending on the applications, selection of radio frequency (RF) spectrum, and number of hops between the user and the gateway.

- **Availability of electrical power sometimes not practical:** Mesh nodes are electronic components that need electrical power to operate. Venues where mesh networks are most beneficial (large open areas where it is not practical to install cabling) generally do not have readily available electrical power where you want to install a mesh node. It might be possible to use light poles for mounting the mesh nodes and tap into the lights' electrical power, but the voltages might not be sufficient. The use of solar panels can satisfy the need for electricity, but that can be costly and sometimes ineffective in places that have limited sunshine.

- **Somewhat difficult to maintain:** If a mesh node does not mesh to the rest of the network for some reason, you cannot access it remotely from a support center. Instead, someone must travel to the installation location to troubleshoot and fix the node. A firmware problem, for example, might inadvertently disable the radio in a mesh node, which eliminates its connection to the overall network. Therefore, the bad node is no longer reachable unless it is a gateway that has a wired connection or an alternate wireless connection to the network.

For larger mesh networks, such as those covering an entire city, designate some mesh nodes as gateways, which are mesh nodes with a wireless backhaul link that interfaces the mesh network to a wired network. The backhaul link is generally a point-to-point radio. Multiple mesh nodes mesh to the gateway, and the gateway provides connectivity to the wired network. A common rule of thumb is to specify approximately 1 gateway for every 10 mesh nodes.

Consider the mesh network architecture mostly for outdoor campus and city-wide deployments or other areas where it is not feasible to run wired network cabling. Large marinas, for example, can eliminate the need to install cabling along boat docks (which is rough on metallic wires). In some cases, it might be beneficial to implement a mesh network indoors, but the primary application for mesh networks is in large outdoor areas.

Ad Hoc Architecture

Figure 10-5 shows an ad hoc WLAN, which consists of client devices that communicate directly with each other. The 802.11 standard includes all protocols needed to support this form of WLAN. There are no access points, mesh nodes, or controllers in an ad hoc network.

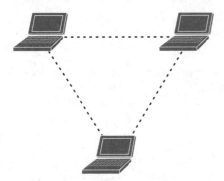

Figure 10-5 *An Ad Hoc Wireless LAN Provides Connectivity to Multiple Client Devices Within Radio Range of Each Other*

Advantages of the ad hoc network architecture include the following:

- **Inexpensive:** The only costs are for client radios. There are no costs for access points or controllers.

- **Fast and easy to set up:** You can simply configure each client radio for ad hoc networking, and the network forms automatically.

- **Possibly higher performance between users:** Transmission of data directly from one client device to another is at least twice as fast (compared to transmission in networks using access points) because in an ad hoc network, there's no need for packets to go through an access point (which has to rebroadcast packets going from one wireless client to another).

Disadvantages of the ad hoc network architecture include the following:

- **Limited connection to wired networks:** The absence of access points eliminates user connectivity to resources on a company's wired network, unless provisions are made on one or more of the client devices to interface users to the wired network.

- **Difficult to manage:** Because ad hoc networks do not connect to the wired network, support centers cannot effectively manage the WLAN. As a result, users usually have little help in solving issues.

- **Possibility of introducing security risks:** The enabling of ad hoc mode, depending on how a user configures the client device, might make the client device vulnerable to security attacks. A hacker, for example, can easily find client devices enabled for ad hoc mode by scanning the ad hoc beacons. The hacker can connect to the ad hoc network, which makes him part of the network, with possible access to the user's client device files or even the corporate network (if the client device is also connected to the wired network).

The main application of the ad hoc architecture is for creating spontaneous WLANs. In general, you should not consider ad hoc WLANs for enterprise-wide deployments. In fact, you might want to think about even banning the creation of ad hoc networks because of security issues.

2.4-GHz Versus 5-GHz

The overwhelming majority of legacy WLANs operate in the 2.4-GHz spectrum. Deployments started in the late 1990s with the initial 802.11 standard and continued with 802.11b and then 802.11g as the most popular versions throughout the 2000s. This made the choice of spectrum fairly straightforward when designing a wireless network because the majority of the client devices were equipped with 2.4-GHz radios. 802.11a networks, which use 5-GHz frequencies, have been available for a number of years, but their deployments are fairly uncommon because they do not interoperate with the more preferred and much larger installed base of 2.4-GHz client devices. This left 2.4-GHz as the primary spectrum to deploy.

With 802.11n (2.4 and 5 GHz) and 802.11ac (5 GHz only), however, you have a choice of using the 2.4-GHz or 5-GHz (or both) spectrum and also maintaining interoperability with legacy devices. As a result, with the proliferation of 802.11n and 802.11ac, the decision to deploy 2.4 GHz or 5 GHz is much tougher. 2.4 GHz is no longer the lone contender. You can get by with only 2.4-GHz 802.11n networks, but to realize top-end performance, seriously consider deploying 802.11ac 5-GHz devices.

Before making a decision on which spectrum to deploy (2.4 GHz, 5 GHz, or both 2.4 GHz and 5 GHz), look over the requirements and think about the considerations in the sections that follow to make the right choice for the deployment.

Geographic Location Considerations

Before getting too far with a deployment, consider the geographic location of the WLAN. The 2.4-GHz spectrum has regulatory acceptance throughout most of the world; however, the use of 5 GHz for WLANs is somewhat limited. Therefore, your location might require you to use only the 2.4-GHz band with 802.11n networks. This makes the choice of spectrum easier, but the resulting 802.11n network will have limited performance.

Performance Considerations

Compared to the 2.4-GHz band, the 5-GHz band has much greater bandwidth available, which leads to significantly better performance than with the 2.4-GHz band. In fact, the use of 5-GHz devices is really the only way to achieve the highest performance from wireless networks. If the highest performance is an important requirement, then certainly lean toward a pure 5-GHz deployment.

Existing Client Device Considerations

In many scenarios for the foreseeable future, client devices with 802.11b/g radios will already exist, and it will not likely be practical to replace all of them with 5-GHz 802.11ac radios. In fact, with many 2.4-GHz client devices with embedded wireless interfaces, such as bar code scanners and wireless IP phones, you cannot even change the radio. You have to purchase new client devices. As a result, for cost reasons, you will probably need to continue supporting 2.4-GHz operation, at least until it is feasible to migrate the legacy client devices to 802.11ac. After migrating all devices, you should move to 5-GHz-only operation if it is necessary to have greater performance.

Facility Size Considerations

As radio signal frequency increases, range generally decreases. Consequently, 5-GHz systems, based only on frequency, may have less range than systems operating in the 2.4-GHz band. This means that the selection of 5-GHz spectrum could require a greater number of access points, which results in higher costs. As a result, you may achieve cost benefits by deploying 2.4-GHz systems in larger facilities (unless high performance is critical). Keep in mind, however, that 5-GHz systems may have equal or even better range in some situations. The construction and shape of the facility may attenuate 2.4-GHz signals more than 5-GHz signals, which can give 5-GHz signals an edge over 2.4-GHz signals. Therefore, it is best to perform a wireless site survey to fully understand the behavior of radio signals throughout the facility before choosing which spectrum to use. See Chapter 15, "Performing a Wireless Site Survey," for more information about determining the propagation of 2.4-GHz and 5-GHz signals for a particular environment.

Radio Signal Interference Considerations

If it is not possible to reduce potential interference in the 2.4-GHz band to an acceptable level, consider deploying a pure 5-GHz system. The noise floor in the 5-GHz band is generally lower compared to the 2.4-GHz band, which allows the 5-GHz network to function at higher data rates. Figure 10-6 shows the output from a spectrum analyzer at 2.4 GHz and 5 GHz from the same location in a typical office building without an existing WLAN. Notice how much lower the noise floor is in the 5-GHz band as compared to the 2.4-GHz band. This difference of 5 dB to 10 dB has a significant impact, which would make the range and performance at this location in the 5-GHz band much better than in the 2.4-GHz band.

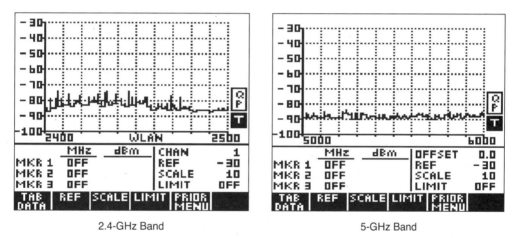

Figure 10-6 *The 2.4-GHz and 5-GHz Bands Offer Different Levels of Radio Signal Interference*

Microwave ovens, Bluetooth devices, and most cordless phones do not offer any interference to WLANs operating in the 5-GHz band. As a result, it is advantageous to implement 802.11ac networks operating in the 5-GHz spectrum. Keep in mind, however, that as 5-GHz WLANs and other devices proliferate, the potential for interference in the 5-GHz band will increase.

Hybrid Frequency Band Considerations

Legacy client radios (802.11a, 802.11b, or 802.11g) operating on an 802.11n network will lower performance for all users, similar to 802.11b users bringing down the performance of 802.11g networks. If you must support legacy devices, define an architecture that solves this problem. From an architectural standpoint, the 2.4-GHz and 5-GHz bands offer physically separate collision domains. Figure 10-7 illustrates this concept. Wireless client devices configured to associate via only 2.4-GHz frequencies operate completely separately from client devices configured to associate via only 5-GHz frequencies. Therefore, consider implementing a hybrid 2.4-GHz and 5-GHz WLAN to avoid conflicts between client devices having legacy and 802.11ac radios. This allows the 802.11ac devices to operate at maximum performance.

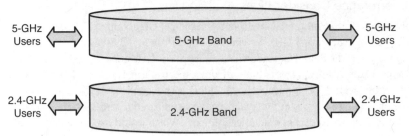

Figure 10-7 *The 2.4-GHz and 5-GHz Bands Enable the Creation of Physically Separate WLANs in the Same Area*

Common Infrastructure Considerations

In addition to implementing two physically separate WLANs (using both 2.4-GHz and 5-GHz frequency bands, as explained earlier), it is possible to divide a (2.4-GHz or 5-GHz) WLAN into separate virtual WLANs. Figure 10-8 describes this configuration. The access point in the figure is configured with two SSIDs, SSID 1 and SSID 2, which are mapped to VLAN 1 and VLAN 2, respectively. Client A and Client B associate with the access point via SSID 1, and all communications with these two clients over the network traverse VLAN 1. Client C associates with the access point via SSID 2, which forces all communications with Client C over VLAN 2.

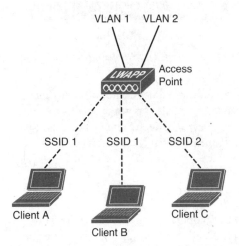

Figure 10-8 *The Mapping of SSIDs and VLANs Enables the Creation of Logically Separate Wireless LANs*

A common WLAN infrastructure is capable of supporting multiple virtual WLANs, each serving a different set of client devices and applications that have varying requirements. For example, a company might want a WLAN to support both employees and visitors. For security purposes, organizations usually want to keep employee and visitor traffic on separate networks. You can do this by implementing two separate virtual WLANs, keeping the traffic from the two user groups separate and allowing the company to apply different configuration policies to each user group.

Most vendors, such as Cisco, enable the creation of logical WLANs by allowing the configuration of multiple SSIDs, with each SSID mapped to a different VLAN. This logically divides an access point into several virtual access points, all within a single hardware platform. Multiple SSIDs allow users to access different virtual networks through a single access point. Network managers can assign different policies and functions for each SSID, increasing the flexibility and efficiency of the network infrastructure.

The following are examples of settings that commonly apply to each SSID:

- **VLAN number:** If a network uses VLANs, it is possible to assign a particular SSID to VLAN 1, and the access point group client devices using that SSID into VLAN 1. This enables the separation of wireless applications based on security and performance requirements. For example, you could enable encryption and authentication on a particular SSID to protect private applications and enable no security on another SSID to maximize open connectivity for public usage.

- **SSID broadcasting:** You can enable one particular SSID to be broadcasted and disable the broadcasting for other SSIDs, depending on security requirements. In some cases, such as visitor access applications, it is advantageous to broadcast the SSID to enable user client radios to automatically find available access points. For private applications, it is generally best to not broadcast the SSID for security purposes.

- **Maximum number of client associations:** It is possible to set the number of users that can associate via a particular SSID, which makes it possible to control usage of particular applications. This can help provide a somewhat limited form of bandwidth control for particular applications.

The benefits of a shared infrastructure are certainly cost savings and flexibility. Rather than implement two physically separate WLANs (which may not be feasible), a company can deploy one physical WLAN and satisfy all requirements. The combination of multiple applications enables the ones having lower return on investment to be part of the WLAN. Sometimes a company needs to have several applications supported together to make the costs of deploying a WLAN feasible. As a result, consider integrating applications with multiple SSIDs if there are benefits to configuring varying wireless settings for each user group or application.

Note   For details on configuring access controller settings, see Chapter 16, "Installing and Configuring a Wireless LAN."

Migration Considerations

Ideally, focus on implementing an 802.11ac-only solution. This provides the greatest performance for wireless applications because legacy client devices will not bog down the network (due to protection mechanisms), and all client devices will be able to operate at higher line speeds. An all-802.11ac solution, however, might not be feasible. Many of the existing client devices, such as laptops, might already have 802.11a/b/g/n radios, and upgrading them to 802.11ac might be cost prohibitive. Do the math to figure out the best way to go in a particular situation.

If a legacy WLAN exists, check whether it is possible to upgrade the existing access points to 802.11n or 802.11ac with firmware changes. Unfortunately, in most cases, you will need to replace the existing access point hardware. Some vendors, however, have made their 802.11n and 802.11ac access points compatible with the older wireless controllers that are already in place; so it is likely that only the access points will need to be replaced (of course, that is still a big investment).

Plan the obsolescence of your legacy WLAN. As 802.11ac products become available, the legacy devices will likely not be strongly supported. In addition, the operation of legacy devices on your 802.11ac network can bog down performance of all users. Focus on purchasing new client devices with 802.11ac and replacing existing 802.11a/b/g/n radios with 802.11ac as quickly as possible.

Redundancy Considerations

When defining WLAN architecture, you need to think about what will happen if any of the components become inoperative, and you should also include recovery provisions in the architecture. You certainly want to avoid a single point of failure. If one component, such as a controller, becomes overwhelmed or fails completely, be sure that there is enough redundancy that the WLAN will continue to operate and support users until someone can fix the problem.

Controller Redundancy

Be certain to use multiple wireless controllers for redundancy and increased performance. A single controller might be sufficient for 802.11a/b/g/n implementations, but it might become a bottleneck for the much greater volume of 802.11ac traffic. In addition, the migration to 802.11ac often ushers in mission-critical applications, and a single controller represents a single point of failure that you should avoid. As a result, ensure that the architecture of an 802.11ac WLAN includes redundant controllers.

A method for providing controller redundancy is to include a dedicated backup controller (see Figure 10-9). If one of the primary controllers fails, the controller services automatically fail over to the backup controller. This approach is fairly simple to implement, but it may be too expensive for small and medium-sized deployments.

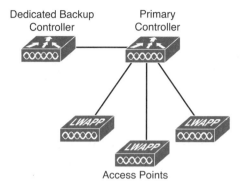

Figure 10-9 *A Dedicated Backup Controller Provides Failover Redundancy for Controller Services*

To improve controller redundancy without a dedicated backup controller, consider associating access points to different controllers in an interspersed grid approach, as shown in Figure 10-10. This allows a user to continue using the network if a specific controller has a malfunction or cannot keep up with a surge in utilization. The failure of a controller will force a user's client device radio to re-associate with a nearby access point that is connected to a different controller.

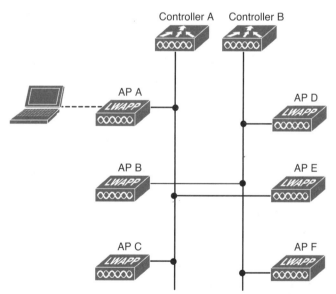

Figure 10-10 *An Interspersed Grid Approach for Wireless Controllers Improves Availability of the Wireless LAN*

For example, in the approach shown in Figure 10-10, two controllers serve different sets of access points. Controller A is the controller for access points AP A, AP C, and AP E. Controller B is the controller for access points AP B, AP D, and AP F. A client device may be initially associated with AP A. If Controller A fails for any reason, the user's client device radio will automatically re-associate with AP B, which is served by Controller B.

The primary advantage of using the interspersed grid approach for increasing redundancy of wireless controllers is that it does not require dedicated backup controllers, which reduces capital expenses for controller hardware and the rack space needed to house the controllers. The main disadvantage is that, when a controller fails, some users will probably experience a drop in performance if the alternate access point they connect to has low signal strength, which provides a correspondingly lower data rate. You can attempt to avoid this situation by increasing the density of access points (which improves the signal strength of alternate access points that users may connect to), but this might be more costly than implementing a dedicated backup controller. The interspersed grid approach for providing controller redundancy is most cost-effective if it is acceptable to have some loss in performance when a controller fails to provide service.

If a WLAN deployment includes controllers at remote sites, designate one or more controllers at the main locations as backups. This simplifies global provisioning and lowers capital expenses by reducing the number of backup controllers. Figure 10-11 illustrates this concept. If Controller A fails at Branch Office A, the centralized backup controller, which may be residing at the company's headquarters building, will take over and continue providing controller services until someone can bring the faulty controller back into service. Likewise, the centralized controller will continue providing controller services to access points in Branch Office B if Controller B fails.

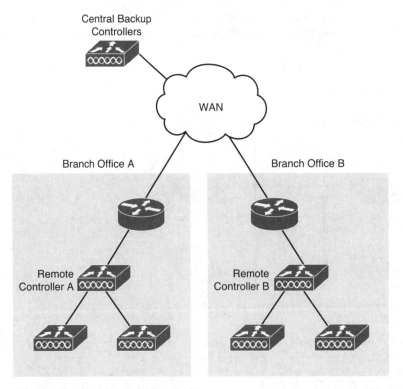

Figure 10-11 *A Centralized Controller Serves as Backup for Multiple Remote Sites*

Access Point Redundancy

To provide access point redundancy, ensure that a wireless client device located anywhere within the coverage area can connect to an alternative access point if the primary access point fails to provide service. For example, an access point might encounter firmware problems and inadvertently disable its radio. Or there might be very high utilization associated with the access point, which is not able to service any additional traffic. In these cases, some client devices will not have access to the WLAN. By specifying that the architecture include a degree of redundancy of access points, you can resolve this issue.

As shown in Figure 10-12, consider having at least two access points within range of any point within the signal coverage area. With this configuration, Client X might be initially associated with AP A. If AP A fails, Client X will automatically re-associate with AP D. Similarly, Client Y and Client Z are within range of two access points; therefore, they both have an alternative access point to connect to if one of the access points that they are associated to fails. Communication between the client device and the network continues without significant interruption. Thus, access point redundancy improves the availability of the network.

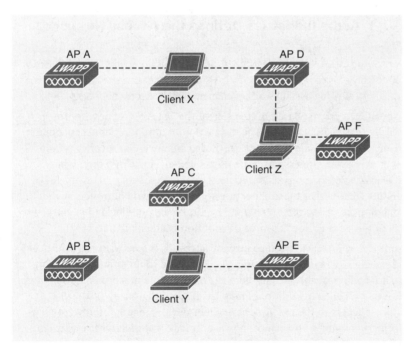

Figure 10-12 *Redundant Access Points Improve the Availability of the WLAN*

The introduction of access point redundancy can negatively impact the capacity of a WLAN, especially when operating within the 2.4-GHz band. The reason is that it is usually not possible to avoid inter–access point interference in the 2.4-GHz band when the access points are close together. There are not enough non-overlapping channels to circumvent significant inter–access point interference. This can substantially lower the capacity of the overall WLAN. As a result, consider using access point redundancy with 2.4-GHz operation if lower capacity is acceptable.

Keep in mind that lower capacity does not mean that users will experience lower performance. The implementation of access point redundancy, for example, may decrease capacity by 25 percent. A handful of users operating wireless bar code scanners will not notice any difference in performance if the network is delivering 100-percent capacity (without access point redundancy) or 75-percent capacity (with access point redundancy). The utilization of the network in this case is very likely lower than the capacity, so everyone receives high performance. A large group of wireless IP phone users, however, might notice a difference in performance because the higher utilization of the WLAN might very well exceed the reduced capacity due to the access point redundancy. In that case, one or more of the wireless IP phone users may experience choppy voice or dropped calls.

With 5-GHz operation, many non-overlapping channels are available. It is possible to tune all access points to non-overlapping channels, even if the access points are close enough together to provide redundancy. Consequently, there are very few or even no impacts on capacity when deploying redundant 5-GHz access points.

Case Study 10-1: Acme Industries Defines the Access Network Architecture

Frank, the engineer for the WLAN deployment that the fictitious company Acme Industries is undertaking, is in the process of designing the WLAN and considering the architecture of the access network. The following list summarizes elements of the access network:

- **Controller-based access points:** Based on the size of the WLAN, the best approach is to use a controller-based architecture. The installation of autonomous access points would be too time-consuming and would not provide assurance that security requirements can be met. Also, the wireless IP phone users need effective mobility, which controller-based access points can provide. After looking over the signal coverage requirements, Frank figured that the architecture will include two controllers at the headquarters building to service the users in the headquarters building and manufacturing plant and a controller at each of the five distribution centers.

- **Frequency band:** The WLAN will need to provide access to the network via both 2.4-GHz and 5-GHz frequency bands, at least initially. There are some existing 802.11b/g client devices, and it will probably be another year or so before it is possible to migrate them to 802.11n or 802.11ac. In addition, Frank has learned that many of the visitors who need guest access to the network have client devices that have only 2.4-GHz radios. To provide maximum performance, however, Frank will specify that all users operate in the 5-GHz band.

- **Multiple SSIDs:** To keep traffic between employees and visitors separate (for security purposes), Frank is specifying that the WLAN implement an SSID for employees that requires encryption and a different SSID for guest access. (The type of encryption is defined in Chapter 13, "Security Considerations.") Each SSID will be tied to a different VLAN. The VLAN for employees will provide access to all applications, and the VLAN for the visitors will only provide connectivity to the Internet. Neither of the SSIDs will be broadcasted to avoid letting others "see" the network.

■ **Redundancy:** One of the two operational controllers at the headquarters building will act as a backup (non-dedicated) for the controllers at the distribution centers and the other one at the headquarters building. For access point redundancy, Frank decided to specify that a client device located at any point within the signal coverage area will be able to connect to at least two access points. The relatively narrow spacing between access points will probably create a great deal of inter–access point interference in the 2.4-GHz band (because of the limited number of non-overlapping channels), but the majority of devices will be operating in the 5-GHz band.

Distribution Systems

A distribution system consists of a variety of components that you should take into account when defining the architecture for an 802.11n or 802.11ac WLAN. This primarily includes switches and PoE equipment. Be certain to define the architecture of a WLAN to include applicable aspects of these components.

Switch Considerations

Consider beefing up an existing wired network to support the higher capacity of 802.11n or 802.11ac. To do this, you need to predict the flow of traffic and determine whether existing switches will support the higher traffic. If not, plan on upgrading the switches. Utilize 1-Gbps connections between access points and switches to realize full capacity of the access network.

With voice applications, the access points will sometimes be operating near capacity. As a result, there may be times when the number of voice users could exceed the capacity of a particular access point, and the access point will begin dropping packets and may degrade the voice quality of all users. To prevent this situation from happening, take advantage of rate limiting on a switch. For example, the Cisco Catalyst 3750 has rate-limiting capabilities. You can set the 3710, for instance, to limit at the maximum throughput level of the access point. This will prevent the access point from dropping voice packets.

PoE Considerations

As explained in the section "Power over Ethernet" in Chapter 3, "Wireless LAN Types and Components," the following are options for providing electrical power to access points using PoE (see Figure 10-13):

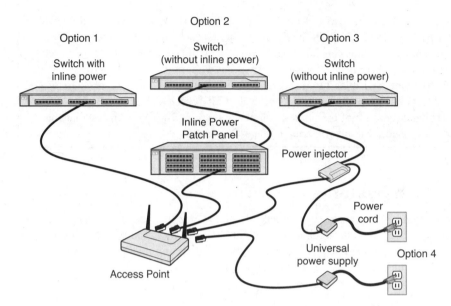

Figure 10-13 *Several Options Exist for Supporting Electrical Power to Access Points over Cabling*

- **Switch with inline power:** This is the ideal configuration for PoE because it reduces the amount of equipment and resulting complexity. If there is no existing wired network, specify an architecture that uses switches with inline power.

- **Inline power patch panel:** For many existing wired networks, the existing switches will not have inline PoE. In this case, specify the inclusion of inline power patch panels for supplying electrical power to access points.

- **Power injector:** This PoE configuration should not be considered for the majority of WLAN deployments, except for very small implementations (fewer than five access points).

To achieve maximum performance from 802.11n and 802.11ac implementations, specify an architecture that implements an enhanced version of PoE. The IEEE 802.3af standard currently defines PoE to deliver 15.4 watts, but many 802.11n and 802.11ac access points require higher power to run both 2.4-GHz and 5-GHz radios (needed for maximum performance). Strive to meet the higher power demands of access points by implementing switches with 802.3at PoE if feasible.

Depending on requirements, it might be beneficial to implement auxiliary electrical power in case of a power outage. The implementation of switches with inline PoE or inline power patch panels allows faster recovery from a power outage because it is easier to connect the PoE equipment to a single backup generator than to connect distributed electrical outlets when power injectors are in use. Just be sure that all controllers, authentication servers, and voice gateways are on the auxiliary power network so that users are able to continue using the network during power outages.

Case Study 10-2: Acme Industries Defines the Distribution System Architecture

Frank, the engineer for the WLAN deployment that the fictitious company Acme Industries is undertaking, is in the process of designing the WLAN and considering the architecture of the distribution system. The following are elements of the distribution system:

■ **Switches:** All the existing switches operate at 1 Gbps, which is sufficient for supporting 802.11n and 802.11ac connections. So, there are no requirements to upgrade the switches.

■ **PoE:** Most of the existing switches do not include inline PoE. As a result, Frank is specifying the inclusion of inline power patch panels to provide electrical power to the access points.

Voice over WLAN Systems

To support wireless IP phones, define the architecture to implement an effective voice over WLAN (VoWLAN) system. It is strongly recommended that you base the system on a well-tested architecture, preferably one that is outlined by the manufacturer of the wireless IP phones that you plan to use. For example, if you plan to use Cisco 7925 wireless IP phones, Cisco offers the following deployment architectures:

■ Single–site architecture

■ Multisite WAN with centralized call processing

■ Multisite WAN with distributed call processing

The following sections cover each of these architectures.

Single-Site Architecture

Figure 10-14 illustrates the single-site architecture, which consists of a call-processing agent (Cisco CallManager) located at a single site that has a WLAN for carrying voice traffic. Any calls that interface outside the WLAN must use the PSTN (public switched telephone network). This is the ideal model for a single campus or a site that has fewer than 30,000 phone lines. The primary benefit of this architecture is that it is relatively easy and inexpensive to deploy. For example, there is no need for a WAN to interconnect users to the call-processing agent. All call control and voice traffic occur over a common local infrastructure.

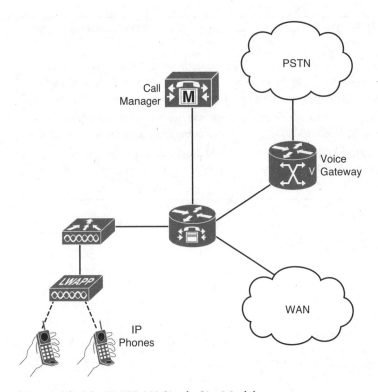

Figure 10-14   *VoWLAN Single-Site Model*

Tips for deploying the single-site model architecture include the following:

- **Analyze calling patterns of your company:** The single-site model is best when most of the calls stay within the same site or when calls are destined to PSTN users outside the company.

- **Include G.711 codecs for all endpoints:** This reduces the processor consumption for transcoding signals, which allows the processor to be available for other functions.

- **If there is no need for H.323 functionality, use Media Gateway Control Protocol (MGCP) gateways for the PSTN:** This simplifies the dial plan configuration.

Multisite WAN with Centralized Call Processing

Figure 10-15 illustrates the architecture model for Cisco VoWLAN systems that have multiple sites with centralized call processing. This model includes a single call-processing agent at a centralized site. As a result, the call-processing packets must flow over the WAN equipped with quality of service (QoS). Therefore, a WAN outage will disrupt calls within each site. The WAN must support speeds of at least 768 Kbps per connection. The WAN can use just about any technology, such as leased lines, Frame Relay, and Asynchronous Transfer Mode (ATM). It is best to use this architecture if there are more than 30,000 phone lines.

When deploying the multisite model architecture with centralized call processing, focus on strengthening the reliability of the WAN. The following are recommended methods that you can implement for improving the reliability:

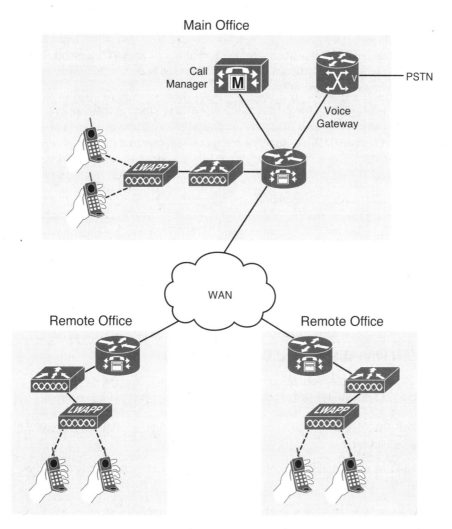

Figure 10-15   *VoWLAN Multisite WAN Model with Centralized Call Processing*

- **Redundant IP WAN links in the branch router:** This low-cost strategy enables the system to continue working if one of the WAN links goes down. It cannot survive the loss of a branch router, however. As a stronger solution, consider deploying redundant branch routers.

- **Survivable Remote Site Telephony (SRST):** This approach alone provides high reliability for only voice services, not data. In this case, the wireless IP phones rehome to call-processing functions available in the local router if a WAN failure occurs. When the WAN is operational, the branch office connects over the WAN to CallManager at the central site. The WAN carries the voice traffic, call signaling, and data traffic. If the WAN fails, the wireless IP phones register with the branch router, which allows calls to take place internally within the branch office and routes external calls over the PSTN. In this case, the phones display the message "Unified CM fallback mode" to the user. Some of the advanced phone features are grayed out and not available because of the limitations of the PSTN network. When the WAN is reestablished, the wireless IP phones at the branch office automatically reregister with CallManager at the central site.

- **SRST with ISDN backup for data:** In addition to using SRST, you can interface the branch router to an Integrated Services Digital Network (ISDN) connection to provide data backup. If this is done, be certain to configure the ISDN connection to not allow SCCP traffic from the wireless IP phones from entering the ISDN interface. This keeps signaling from the wireless IP phones from reaching CallManager at the central site.

- **Data and voice ISDN backup:** With this approach, SRST is not used. Instead, the branch router provides a backup connection to the ISDN, which maintains voice traffic, call signaling, and data flowing between the branch and central office if the primary WAN goes down. This approach, however, is effective only if the bandwidth requirements of the voice traffic are equal to or less than the ISDN bandwidth allocation. In addition, the interface between the branch router and the ISDN must implement Cisco's QoS for network infrastructures.

Multisite WAN with Distributed Call Processing

Figure 10-16 illustrates the architecture model for Cisco VoWLAN systems that have multiple sites with distributed call processing. This model involves a call-processing agent, such as CallManager, at each site. As a result, disruption of the WAN does not disrupt all calls. This model best serves a maximum of six large sites with a maximum of 30,000 phone lines total.

In addition to tips and strategies provided for the other models earlier, consider implementing the following:

- **Gatekeepers:** A gatekeeper is an H.323 device that provides call admission control and E.164 dial plan resolution. To provide high reliability of the gatekeeper, use Hot Standby Router Protocol (HSRP) gatekeeper pairs, gatekeeper clustering, and alternate gatekeeper support. In addition, use multiple gatekeepers to provide redundancy within the network.

- **Session Initiation Protocol (SIP) proxies:** Ensure adequate redundancy for the SIP proxies and that the SIP proxies have the capacity for the call rate and number of calls required in the network.

■ **Call-processing agents:** It is possible to use different processing agents at each site. Table 10-1 provides recommendations for which Cisco processing agent to use, based on requirements.

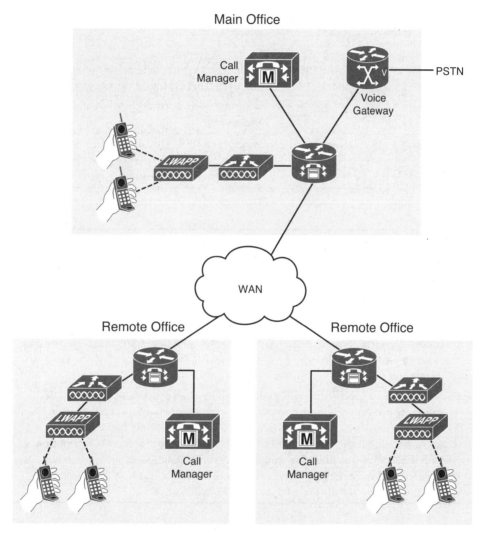

Figure 10-16 *VoWLAN Multisite WAN Model with Distributed Call Processing*

Table 10-1   *Recommended Call-Processing Agents*

Call-Processing Agent	Recommended Size	Comments
Cisco Unified CallManager Express (CME)	Up to 240 phones	For small remote sites. Capacity depends on Cisco IOS platform.
Cisco Unified CallManager	50 to 30,000 phones	Small to large sites, depending on the size of the Cisco Unified CallManager cluster. Supports centralized or distributed call processing.
Legacy PBX with VoIP gateway	Depends on PBX	Number of IP WAN calls and functionality depend on the PBX-to-VoIP gateway protocol and the gateway platform.

Case Study 10-3: Acme Industries Defines the VoWLAN System Architecture

Frank, the engineer for the WLAN deployment that the fictitious company Acme Industries is undertaking, is in the process of designing the WLAN and considering the architecture of the VoWLAN system. After careful deliberation, Frank decided to implement the VoWLAN system with a multisite WAN with centralized call processing (with the call-processing agent located at the headquarters building). A multisite architecture is necessary because of the requirement to support the distribution centers, which are located in different parts of the United States.

A major choice was to specify centralized or distributed call processing. Frank favored the centralized approach due to lower costs. This means that all call processing from the distribution centers will flow over the WAN to the headquarters building. There was some concern about the reliability of the WAN that interconnects the distribution centers with the headquarters building and manufacturing plant building, but Frank found that the reliability of the existing WAN is sufficient. To add a degree of protection, however, Frank will specify the use of redundant IP WAN links.

Note   For details on cell edge design for VoWLAN systems, see Chapter 12, "Radio Frequency Considerations."

Application Connectivity

As described in the section "Application Connectivity Software" in Chapter 3, there are several approaches for connecting client devices to servers and databases. The selection of which connectivity approach to use depends on the specifics of the application, such as server type, where the application software resides, and so on. The following sections explain the advantages and disadvantages of each application connectivity approach to help you decide which one makes most sense for the architecture of a particular WLAN.

Terminal Emulation Considerations

Terminal emulation provides an interface to an application running on a host server, such as UNIX or an IBM AS/400 (see Figure 10-17). Through a terminal or a client device running terminal emulation software, a user can interact with the application. The application actually runs on the server, and the terminal is fairly "dumb" and merely displays prompts from the application and provides a means for a user to enter data. Terminal emulation has been around for decades. In the early days, terminals were mostly dedicated hardware that connected to the network through a terminal server; a terminal had a screen and keyboard and no real processing power. Today, most terminals are client computers running terminal emulation software that makes the computer behave like a terminal. There are several different terminal emulation types, such as VT100 for UNIX and 5250 for AS/400s.

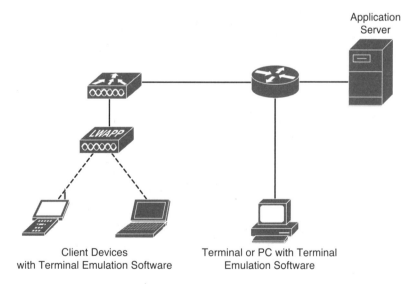

Figure 10-17 *Terminal Emulation Enables a User to Interface with an Application Running on an Application Server*

Terminal emulation provides the following advantages:

- **Lower presumed initial costs:** Terminal emulation can seem less expensive initially than other approaches if you consider only the costs of the terminal emulation software. Customers often make this mistake when cost-justifying a WLAN implementation. They are not aware that other elements, such as potential host application modifications and support issues, can increase the cost of a terminal emulation–based system. As a result, it is important that a solution provider fully assess the costs associated with terminal emulation before proposing a solution to the customer.

- **Central application software control:** With terminal emulation, all application software is updated only on the host, not on the individual appliances. All users automatically get the advantages of changes to the application without needing updates to the software on the appliance. This makes configuration management much easier, especially when there are hundreds of appliances.

- **Common technical expertise:** If the end-user organization has an existing terminal/host system, then the company will likely have the core competency to implement terminal emulation–based wireless systems.

Terminal emulation provides the following disadvantages:

- **Legacy code changes:** Most host-based application screens have been written to fit a standard desktop terminal screen. When integrating a wireless terminal, programmers must often rewrite the host application code to present screens small enough to fit in the smaller displays of the wireless terminals. If printing is necessary from the end-user device, programmers will also need to embed the print streams of the particular printer in the application on the host. The problem is that it is not always practical to modify the host application software. For example, the vendor supplying the application software may not permit such changes to be made. In this case, the solution provider is severely limited in adding new functionality to the application.

- **Inflexible programming environment:** When developing or modifying the application on the host, the terminal emulation specifications (for example, VT200, 5250, and 3270) limit the control of the end-user device from the host-based application. This often constrains what programmers can do when adding functionality.

- **Limited support for migration to client/server systems:** Terminal emulation software does not interface directly to databases, making it unsuitable for client/server implementations. Thus, terminal emulation enables users to access only the screens that the host application provides.

- **Difficulty in supporting the end-user devices:** With standard terminal emulation, there is no effective way to monitor the performance of the wireless appliances, making it difficult to troubleshoot wireless network problems. In addition, terminal emulation protocols were designed to operate over wired networks, not wireless networks that are prone to loss of connections due to radio frequency (RF) interference and inadequate coverage from time to time. As a result, wireless terminals can lead to erratic information being stored in the application software or databases when transactions are not fully completed due to loss of connectivity over the wireless network.

- **Significant effect on wireless networks:** With terminal emulation, all screens and print streams must traverse the wireless network, affecting the performance of the overall system. In addition, terminal emulation uses TCP to maintain a connection with the host, and TCP does not operate efficiently over wireless networks.

The implementation of terminal emulation over wireless networks was common throughout the 1990s; today, companies are now replacing many of these host-based systems with client/server systems. Client/server systems consist of a client software element that generally runs on the end-user devices and a database located on a server. The migration from terminal/host systems to client/server is eliminating the need for terminal emulation. Instead, customers need other forms of connectivity software, as explained in the following sections. Consider other forms of connectivity to support interoperability with client/server systems.

Browser-Based Connectivity Considerations

Browser-based connectivity is similar to terminal emulation, except users operate a web browser to use applications located on a web server. In fact, browser-based connectivity is a modern form of terminal emulation. Figure 10-18 illustrates this approach. In most cases, organizations need a WLAN to support browser-based connectivity when deploying an intranet.

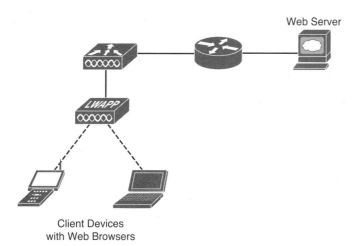

Figure 10-18 *Browser-Based Connectivity Enables a User to Interface with a Web Application Located on a Web Server*

Browser-based application connectivity provides the following advantages:

- **Common open interface:** The common open interface to applications and information leverages skills needed to develop applications for wireless users.

- **Central application software control:** With intranet-based connectivity, all application software is updated only on the web server, not the individual end-user devices. As with terminal emulation, all users will automatically take advantage of changes to the application without needing updates to the software on the end-user device.

- **Strong support for client/server systems:** Intranet-based connectivity software (that is, a web browser) offers a thin-client front end to an application residing on the server.

Browser-based application connectivity provides the following disadvantages:

- **Extensive web page changes:** As with terminal/host systems, most existing websites have pages that are designed to occupy larger desktop screens. As a result, existing pages must be rewritten to work effectively on the smaller screens of wireless end-user devices. Developers must pay close attention to usability issues with smaller screens.

- **Potential effect on wireless network performance:** Web-based connectivity can consume large amounts of limited wireless bandwidth, depending on the type of application. For example, the browser on an appliance may point to a web page containing large graphic files that must be sent from the server to the appliance. Most intranet-based implementations might also use TCP to maintain a connection with the host. As mentioned earlier, TCP does not operate efficiently over wireless networks.

Many end-user companies in the logistics supply chain are deploying intranets and Internet-based applications. It is likely that these end users will benefit from access to these applications via mobile devices such as cell phones, PDAs, data collectors, and portable computers. As a result, consider developing web browser interfaces for their end-user devices.

Direct Database Considerations

Direct database connectivity is quite different from terminal emulation and browser approaches. Direct database connectivity, for instance, interfaces application software running on the user's client device with a database that is located on a server (see Figure 10-19).

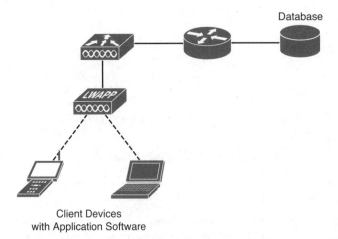

Figure 10-19 *Direct Database Connectivity Enables a User to Operate an Application That Interfaces with a Database*

Direct database interfaces provide the following advantages:

- **Flexible programming environment:** Direct database connectivity enables a programmer to interact directly with database records rather than be limited to what the application software on the host provides (as is the case with terminal emulation). This provides a great deal of control for a solution provider to add functionality to an application.

- **Moderate amount of programming needed to interface new appliances with existing applications:** With direct database connectivity, developers must often create a program that runs on the appliance to interface with the existing database. This requires the developer to understand how to write software that interfaces with the specific display, keyboard, scanner, and peripherals of the applicable end-user device.

- **Distributed application software control:** New releases of application software must be installed on each of the end-user devices when deploying upgrades to the application. This can be a tedious task if there are more than just a few end-user devices. One method that helps overcome this problem is to store the current version of the end-user device application software on a server and have the application software running on the appliance compare its current version with the one located on the server. If the one on the server is a newer release, the application software on the end-user device can automatically download and install the newer version of software over the wireless network. In addition, modifications to the central database structure might require changes to the application software on the appliance. Care must be taken to ensure that these application changes are made to guarantee that the application works properly.

- **Good support for client/server systems:** Direct database connectivity fits well into the client/server system model, enabling programmers to develop front-end applications that run on the appliance.

Direct database interfaces provide the following disadvantages:

- **Application size limited to the amount of appliance memory:** With direct database connectivity, the end-user device must have sufficient storage for the application software.

- **Wireless network impacts:** With direct database connectivity, only the database inquiries and data records must traverse the wireless network, making efficient use of the wireless network performance in terms of data transfers. All print streams and screen interfaces can be handled within the end-user device. Most direct database implementations, however, use TCP to maintain a connection with the host. As mentioned earlier, TCP does not operate efficiently over wireless networks.

Because of the poor performance of TCP over wireless networks, you should avoid the direct database form of connectivity if possible. If no other approach, such as wireless middleware, will work, be sure to fully test the application. You need to be sure that the application can recover effectively from slow performance (as compared to the performance in higher-speed wired networks) and potential loss of connectivity.

Wireless Middleware Considerations

Wireless middleware includes a broad set of features that provide effective connectivity of client devices, servers, and databases over WLANs. Figure 10-20 shows a WLAN architecture with wireless middleware. To take advantage of the services offered by wireless middleware, you install middleware client software on each wireless client device. This client software interfaces with the middleware software located on a middleware server. All traffic between the wireless client devices and the various application, database, and web servers goes through the wireless middleware server. The middleware server maintains effective connections with the various servers.

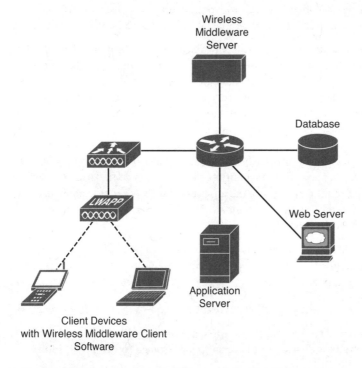

Figure 10-20   *Wireless Middleware Provides Enhanced Connectivity Among a Variety of Client Devices, Servers, and Databases*

Wireless middleware can provide these features/advantages:

- **Intelligent restarts:** With wireless networks, a transmission might be cut at midstream due to interference or operation in fringe areas. An intelligent restart is a recovery mechanism that detects when a transmission has been cut. When the connection is reestablished, the middleware resumes transmission from the break point instead of at the beginning of the transmission. This process is sometimes referred to as session persistence.

- **Optimization techniques:** Many middleware products include data compression at the transport layer to help minimize the number of bits sent over the wireless link. Some implementations of middleware use header compression, where mechanisms replace traditional packet headers with a much shorter bit sequence before transmission.

- **Effective migration to client/server networks:** Through middleware software, an end-user device can be enabled to communicate with both host-based applications and databases residing on servers. The capability of wireless middleware to interface with a wide variety of end systems enables the migration from terminal/host to client/server systems, without affecting end-user device functionality.

- **Data bundling:** Some middleware is capable of combining (bundling) smaller data packets into a single large packet for transmission over the wireless network. This is especially beneficial to help reduce transmission service costs of wireless WANs. Because most wireless data services charge users by the packet, data bundling results in a lower aggregate cost.

- **Store-and-forward messaging:** Middleware often performs message queuing to guarantee message delivery to users who might become disconnected from the network for a period of time. Once the station comes back online, the middleware sends the stored messages to the station.

- **Screen scraping and reshaping:** The development environment of some middleware products permits the developer to use visual tools to "scrape" and "reshape" portions of existing application screens to more effectively fit within the smaller display of data collectors.

- **Application development tools:** Some middleware packages include tools for developing applications that operate independently from the end-user device and host application. This allows a company to add application functions to legacy systems.

- **Operational support mechanisms:** Some middleware products offer utilities and tools to monitor the performance of wireless end-user devices, enabling MIS personnel to better troubleshoot problems.

Wireless middleware provides the following disadvantages:

- **Higher initial costs:** The wireless middleware software and associated hardware platform is relatively expensive compared to other forms of application connectivity. Wireless middleware list prices range from $5000 to $15,000 per server plus additional license fees for each end-user device. The solution provider must clearly cost-justify the benefits of purchasing a wireless middleware-based solution for customers.

- **Lack of standards:** There are many proprietary wireless middleware products, each offering a different form of operation and development/integration environment. This often requires developers to learn a somewhat foreign form of programming. Also, end users must often use only end-user devices that have been integrated into the chosen middleware software.

Strongly consider implementing wireless middleware if there are needs for effective in-motion roaming and support of multiple client device types and applications. There is lots of variance in the feature sets of different middleware products, however, which makes it difficult to decide which vendor to choose. You should start the selection process by analyzing the application's environment and then define which middleware features are most important. Be sure to identify all types of end systems that will be part of the applications and ensure that the middleware has the appropriate hooks. For example, the middleware will likely need to incorporate 5250 terminal emulation if there is a need to interface with AS/400 applications. Just as important as the end systems are the mobile client devices. Bear in mind that middleware vendors produce client software for a limited number of device types. If there's a need to support a specific smart phone, for instance, ensure that the middleware includes client software for that device. The middleware client is generally not portable because of the need to match the applicable operating system, screen size, and keyboard.

Case Study 10-4: Acme Industries Defines the Application Connectivity Architecture

Frank, the engineer for the WLAN deployment that the fictitious company Acme Industries is undertaking, is in the process of designing the WLAN and considering the architecture of the application connectivity architecture. Based on integration requirements (see Case Study 9-10), the system must support interfaces to the warehouse management system residing on an IBM AS/400, which requires 5250 terminal emulation for the bar code scanners. Frank is thinking about using the 5250 terminal emulation that is built in to the bar code scanners to interface the scanners to the warehouse management system because it seems to be the least cost and easiest alternative to implement.

A problem, however, is that the warehouse management system was designed to work with desktop terminals that have much larger screens than the bar code scanners. The use of terminal emulation on the bar code scanners, which have very small screens, will require users to do a great deal of scrolling around the tiny screen to find data inquiries and input fields. This will be extremely frustrating and time-consuming for users. It is possible to rewrite some of the warehouse management system code through a developer's customization kit, but that will require months of development and related expenses.

Frank decided to use wireless middleware that offers a screen-reshaping feature and several enhancements for communications over WLANs, such as intelligent restarts and data optimization.

Summary

Before getting into the details of a WLAN design, consider the architectural elements, which include the wireless access network, distribution system, VoWLAN system, and application connectivity.

Alternatives for the wireless access network include autonomous access point, controller-based access point, and mesh network architectures. For most full-scale WLANs, the controller-based architecture, which includes a controller that manages the access points, is best because it offers easy installation, robust security, effective mobility, and expandability. The autonomous access point architecture, which does not contain a controller, is more suited for smaller WLANs. Mesh networks do not require physical cabling between access points; they are best for large outdoor installations or any area where data cabling is not feasible to install. The alternatives for frequency band are 2.4 GHz and 5 GHz. Lean toward selecting 5 GHz for enabling the highest performance, and use 2.4 GHz for supporting legacy devices (802.11a, 802.11b, and 802.11g). Be sure to consider factors such as geographic location, performance requirements, existing client devices, facility size, and potential radio signal interference. Also, possibly define multiple SSIDs for supporting different user groups and incorporate a degree of redundancy in the architecture for controllers and access points.

For the distribution system, consider specifying 1-Gbps switches to support the higher throughput of 802.11n and 802.11ac access points. Also, to achieve the highest possible performance, include specifications for an enhanced, higher-power (18.5-watt) version of PoE. If the WLAN will support wireless IP phones, determine the most effective architecture, which can be a single-site architecture or a multisite WAN with either centralized or distributed call processing. Options for application connectivity include terminal emulation, browser based, direct database, and wireless middleware. In most cases, wireless middleware provides the optimum solution.

Chapter 11

Range, Performance, and Roaming Considerations

This chapter will introduce you to:

- Range Versus Performance
- Range Considerations
- Performance Considerations
- Roaming Considerations

When designing a wireless LAN (WLAN), take care to ensure that the WLAN will satisfy requirements for signal coverage, performance, and roaming. Problems related to these items often crop up when supporting a WLAN, generally due to designers not considering all relevant elements of the design. This chapter provides insights and addresses important elements you should consider to avoid these problems.

Range Versus Performance

It would be great if WLANs had unlimited range and performance. If they did, the job of designing a WLAN would be much easier. There would be no need to consider the multitude of design elements to ensure that there is enough signal coverage and capacity to support applications. Unfortunately, due to the constraints of physics, definite range and performance limits apply.

In addition, something that complicates WLAN design is that range and performance are sometimes indirectly proportional. By increasing some design elements (for example, transmit frequency or data rate), the performance will increase but range will decrease (if all other design parameters, environment, and so on are constant). In other cases, changing design elements, such as transmit power and antenna gain, will increase performance and range. As a result, you must be familiar with how changing various design elements impacts range and performance to design an effective WLAN.

In addition, you need to have a solid understanding of the WLAN requirements related to performance, signal coverage, and the operating environment before you get started with the design. You need to know the requirements in order to determine which elements are most important and worthwhile to change.

Note   The associated data rate between a client radio and an access point generally increases as the client radio becomes closer to the access point, which results in higher throughput closer to the access point.

Range Considerations

To satisfy signal coverage requirements, you need to install access points in optimum locations, determined by the results of a wireless site survey, as explained in Chapter 15, "Performing a Wireless Site Survey." This involves completing propagation tests that determine the range of the access points based on specific minimum signal levels sufficient to support required client devices and applications. 802.11n and 802.11ac systems provide much better range and performance than legacy 802.11a, 802.11b, and 802.11g networks, but you can do some fine-tuning. To maximize range and reduce the total number of access points, carefully consider the following design elements:

- Signal coverage requirements

- Radio frequency bands

- Transmit power settings

- Transmission channel settings

- Data rate setting

- Antennas

- Amplifiers

- Repeaters

- Physical obstacles

- Radio signal interference

Signal Coverage Requirements

You need to review requirements that define the environment where the WLAN will operate and areas where signal coverage is needed. This will give you a feel for the importance of maximizing the range. If the WLAN must provide signal coverage over a large open area where it is not feasible to install access points, for example, the use of higher-gain antennas and possibly amplifiers may prove worthwhile.

Note For details on how to determine signal coverage requirements, see Chapter 9, "Defining Requirements for a Wireless LAN."

Radio Frequency Bands

As part of the design, you can choose to use 2.4-GHz or 5-GHz (or both) bands. Communications theory explains that (with all other things constant), an increase in transmission frequency causes a decrease in range of the signal. As a result, the higher transmit frequencies of the 5-GHz band should provide shorter range than the lower 2.4-GHz band. In practice, the use of the 5-GHz band, though, might or might not provide shorter range. In fact, sometimes a 5-GHz system provides the same or even greater range as compared to a 2.4-GHz system. This might occur, for example, if the noise in the 2.4-GHz band is considerably higher than in the 5-GHz band (which is often the case). The resulting signal-to-noise ratio (SNR) values of the 5-GHz system, despite a decrease in signal strength due to higher operating frequencies, might be higher due to much less noise in the 5-GHz band.

Figure 11-1 illustrates a case where the range of a 2.4-GHz access point and a 5-GHz access point are the same. At the client device (laptop) associated with the 2.4-GHz access point, the signal level is –70 dBm, and the noise is –85 dBm. This results in SNR of 15 dB, which of course indicates a specific level of performance. Because of higher operating frequency, the signal at the client device associated with the 5-GHz access point is significantly lower, at –80 dBm (an arbitrary number chosen for illustration purposes only). Because of the much lower noise level (–95 dBm) in the 5-GHz band, the SNR for the 5-GHz system is also 15 dB, which would likely provide similar performance as the 2.4-GHz system. This indicates that the 2.4-GHz and 5-GHz systems have the same range, which is a probable outcome, depending on difference in noise levels between the 2.4-GHz and 5-GHz bands. Therefore, be certain to take into account the actual environment where a WLAN will operate when choosing 2.4-GHz or 5-GHz bands based on range requirements and expectations.

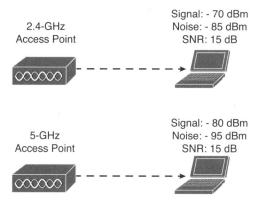

Figure 11-1 *A Case Where the Range Is the Same for 2.4-GHz and 5-GHz Systems*

Transmit Power Settings

For a constant performance level, increasing the transmit power of an 802.11 radio increases range. As the transmit power increases, communications at a particular data rate, such as 12 Mbps, will be possible at greater ranges. The reason for this is that increasing transmit power improves the SNR at points farther away from the radio. The range expands to cover areas where increases in the transmit power cause the SNR at points farther away to be at or above the minimum signal values needed for reliable operation. This higher SNR allows the end radios to receive communications at these farther points where they might not have been able to before.

Figure 11-2 illustrates this point. With the access point tuned to 10 dBm, the SNR at Location A is 15 dB, which for this example we will assume is the signal strength necessary for reliable communications at 12-Mbps data rates. At Location B, the signal level is −76 dBm due to free space loss, attenuation, and so on, which results in a 9 dB SNR. Therefore, at Location B, the access point tuned to 10 dBm will support something less than 12 Mbps. If you increase the access point transmit power to 16 dBm (a 6-dB increase), the signal level at Location B will increase by 6 dB, to −70 dBm. This makes the SNR at Location B equal to 15 dB, which allows reliable 12-Mbps operation. As a result, increasing the transmit power has made it possible to extend the range for a specific data rate.

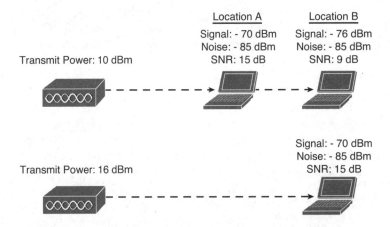

Figure 11-2   *Transmit Power Increases Provide Greater Range by Increasing Signal Strength*

This increase in range, however, impacts the communications in only one direction, which is the outward path relative to the radio with increased transmit power. The increase of transmit power of an access point, for example, only improves the range of the communications path from the access point to the client radios. To improve the overall communications of 802.11 signals, which occur in both directions between the access point and client radios, you need to increase the transmit power of the client radios as well. In fact, it is usually not useful to increase the transmit power of the access points because the client radios are almost always operating at much lower transmit power. As a result, it will likely be worthwhile to increase the transmit power only of the client radios. The signals going from the access points to the client radios are already relatively strong. The increase in client radio transmit power alone will improve the range of the overall communications in this case.

An advantage of using transmit power changes to improve range is that there are no expenses for additional hardware. A problem, however, is that it might not be possible to increase the transmit power on the client radios (the devices that would likely need a boost in power) because they might already be set by default to the highest power. Also, if you have little control over the client devices operating on the network, as is the case with public networks, you might not have the ability to change the transmit power of some or all of the client radios.

Note   Some WLAN vendors have proprietary features that cause the client radios to automatically change to a specific transmit power, based on the data rate set in the access point.

Transmission Channel Settings

Within each of the 802.11 frequency bands, specific operating channels span from the lower-frequency end of the band to the higher-frequency end of the band. These channels use different transmission frequencies; however, there is negligible impact on range from using the lower-frequency channels versus the higher-frequency channels because increases in frequency reduce the range (and vice versa). For example, choosing Channel 1 rather than Channel 11 in the 2.4-GHz band has no significant impact on range. There is not enough spread in the frequencies across the band to make a notable difference in range.

The choice of transmission channel settings does, however, make a difference in range if it is possible to choose a channel to avoid radio signal interference. An access point, for example, may be set to Channel 11, but you might notice from a spectrum analyzer that there is significant interference in the upper part of the band (including Channel 11). The lower part of the band, Channels 1 through 3, may be relatively free from interference. By changing the access point to channel 1, it is possible to improve the SNR throughout the area, which improves range. For example, the noise levels relative to channel 1 might be 6 dB lower than what it had been for channel 11. As a result, the signal level can be 6 dB lower and still constitute acceptable SNR. Figure 11-3 illustrates this concept.

As with transmit power, changing the transmission channel to improve range does not cost anything in terms of new hardware. In addition, with infrastructure WLANs (ones with access points), there is no need to make changes to client radios. As a result, transmission channel changes can be made on networks where you may have little or no control over the client radio settings. Keep in mind, however, that there are a limited number of non-overlapping channels available (especially in the 2.4-GHz band), and radio signal interference may change over time. For example, with larger WLANs, you might have significant inter–access point interference if you only set access points to lower-frequency channels to avoid the interference present in the higher-frequency channels.

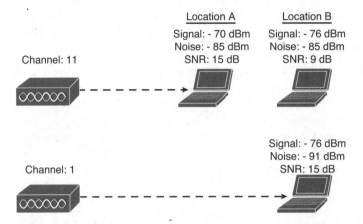

Figure 11-3   *Transmission Channel Changes Can Provide Greater Range by Lowering Noise Levels*

Data Rate Settings

At first, it might seem that data rate settings impact only the performance of a WLAN. The data rate settings, however, have an indirect impact on range. As a general rule, with all else constant, an increase in data rate causes a decrease in range. Therefore, data rate and range are indirectly proportional. The reason for this is that higher data rates require higher received signal strength at the radio for the receiver to decode the 802.11 signal. Companies that make access points and client radios publish the received signal strengths that support various data rates.

Be careful when adjusting the data rate setting in access points and client radios. By default, access points and client radios usually have their data rate setting configured as "auto" so that they will rate shift as needed to maintain associations with users. This is usually the best setting for general use. Most access points also allow the data rate to be set to specific values, such as 12 Mbps. If it is desirable to maximize range, consider setting all access points and client radios to low data rates. Just be sure that data rates are set high enough to provide adequate levels of performance.

Something to realize is that, based on the 802.11 standard, the setting in the access point applies only to the data rate that the access point uses, not the rate the wireless clients use. For example, setting the access point to 54 Mbps causes the access point to transmit all data frames at 54 Mbps. In this situation, wireless clients set to auto still continue to use higher data rates if possible. To extend range by forcing lower data rates, set both access points and user radio cards to the lower data rate configurations. This ensures that the data rates are the same in both directions.

Note   Some WLAN vendors have proprietary features that cause the client radios to automatically change to a specific data rate, based on the data rate set in the access point. This is a proprietary feature not defined by the standard, so you must use products from the same (or compatible) vendor in order to realize this feature.

Hands-on Exercise: Analyzing Impacts on Range Using Different Data Rate Settings

This exercise allows you to experience the impacts that different date rate settings have on range between a client device and an access point. While observing the connection status of a wireless client device and an access point, you will determine the maximum range that provides a connection at different data rates.

Perform the following steps:

Step 1. Obtain test equipment. You need a wireless client device and an access point to complete this exercise.

Step 2. Disable adaptive transmit power control on the access point, if applicable.

Step 3. Associate the client device with the access point, with the access point and client radio configured for the maximum fixed data rate.

Step 4. Initiate a continuous TCP/IP ping between the client device and the access point to generate regular traffic between the client radio and the access point. This is necessary for the client radio to accurately monitor the connection state of the client radio.

Step 5. Position the client device close to the access point and begin walking away from the access point with the client device along a defined path until the connection is lost.

Step 6. Observe the connection state as you walk away from the access point until the connection is lost. You can observe this in the Windows (or vendor-specific) wireless client utility or by monitoring the continuous pings. If the pings continue successfully, the connection status is "connected." If the pings discontinue, the connection status is "disconnected."

Step 7. Note the location/range where the connection was lost.

Step 8. Repeat steps 5 and 6 multiple times with the access point and client radio configured to progressively lower fixed data rates. For example, after performing the test with the higher data rate setting, you might want to perform a second test by choosing a data rate somewhere in the middle between the lowest and highest data rates. As a third test, you could set the access point and client radio to the lowest fixed data rate. In each test at a different data rate, note the range along the predefined path where a connection is lost. What differences in range do you see for the various data rate settings?

As you lower the data rate settings, the range should increase where the connection is lost between the access point and the client device. The reason for this is that, as explained earlier, 802.11 radios have better receive sensitivity at lower data rates, which allows the radios in the client device and access point to be farther apart.

Antennas

The factory-default antennas that come with an access point usually have low gain (around 2 dBi). If an access point has removable antennas, replacing the default antennas with higher-gain omnidirectional or directional antennas boosts range. For example, replacing a standard 2 dBi antenna with a 6 dBi omnidirectional antenna effectively adds 4 dB to the signal strength throughout the coverage area. As shown in Figure 11-4, adding this gain improves the signal strength at Location B enough to maintain 15 dB SNR as compared to only 9 dB by using the standard 2 dBi antenna. Therefore, the increase in antenna gain has provided greater range for a specific data rate that corresponds to 15 dB SNR.

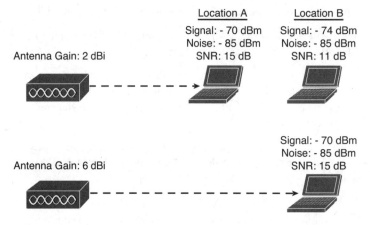

Figure 11-4   *Higher-Gain Antennas Boost Range by Increasing Signal Strength*

Note   Keep in mind that some access points do not have removable antennas, which of course precludes you from using different antennas to increase range.

Installing a higher-gain antenna on an access point improves range from the access point to the client radios and from the client radios to the access point. This is different from increasing transmit power on only the access point, which would increase range only for the communications going from the access point to the client radios. The reason that a higher-gain antenna improves range in both directions is that the higher gain of the antenna improves both transmission and reception of radio waves. Therefore, the installation of higher-gain antennas can provide significant increases in range without requiring changes to the client radios.

In addition to using higher-gain antennas, antenna diversity can also help extend range in both directions because it minimizes multipath propagation. Diversity is an important part of 802.11n and 802.11ac, and various vendors sell 802.11n and 802.11ac access points and client radios that have different levels of diversity. If your intent is to maximize range, choose components that have high levels of diversity.

An advantage of using higher-gain antennas or diversity is that these changes impact range in both directions. As a result, you may be able to get by with changing the antenna configuration on only the access point, avoiding the need to alter each client radio. The cost of upgrading the antennas, however, might be considerable (possibly $50 to $100 or more per access point). Therefore, the cost might be prohibitive in larger networks.

Be sure to test different antenna gain and diversity with actual propagation testing in the target operating environment to determine the lowest overall cost of deploying the network. For example, you might find that using standard 2 dBi antennas may require 100 access points and using 6 dBi antennas might reduce the number of access points to 80. The additional cost for 6 dBi antennas in this example would probably be $4,000 to $8,000 ($50 to $100 each for 80 access points). This additional cost is likely much less than the cost of the 20 additional access points that you would need to purchase if you went with the standard 2 dBi antennas. As a result, in this example, it would be worth the additional cost for the 6 dBi antennas—assuming that the goal is to maximize range.

The trouble with increasing antenna gain for purposes of extending range is that you will likely place the access points farther apart (to reduce the number of access points and reduce costs). This results in a larger 802.11 collision domain, which limits the capacity of the WLAN. More client devices end up connecting to fewer access points.

Note   For more details on antennas, see Chapter 3, "Wireless LAN Types and Components."

Amplifiers

Using an amplifier is a way of increasing range. Much like increasing the transmit power on an access point (or a client radio), an amplifier boosts the signal strength throughout the coverage area, as illustrated in Figure 11-5. In addition, amplifiers have receive gain, which amplifies the incoming signals coming from the client devices. Therefore, the signal-strength-increasing behavior of an amplifier is similar to that of an antenna.

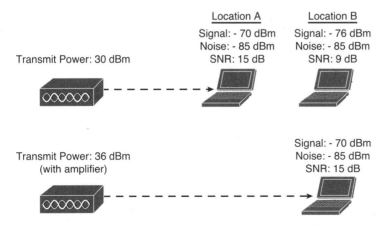

Figure 11-5 *Amplifiers Improve Range by Increasing Signal Strength*

> **Note**   When using amplifiers, be certain to follow your country's regulations that define the use of radio frequency (RF) amplifiers.

Most WLAN amplifiers are rated at a specific transmit power, such as 200 mW, and a specific receive gain, such as 15 dB. Amplifiers with higher transmit power produce greater range for communications going from the access point to the client radios. The receive gain will increase the range for communications going from the client radios to the access point. Therefore, be sure to consider both transmit power and receive gain of the amplifier. Of course, it is a good idea to do some propagation testing with amplifiers to determine their actual impact on range.

Companies such as Hyperlink and RF Linx sell amplifiers for WLANs. These amplifiers are designed to install between the antenna and the access point. As a result, you can use an amplifier only if it is possible to remove the access point antenna.

> **Note**   For more details on amplifiers, see Chapter 3.

Repeaters

A WLAN repeater is meant to reside between access points and client radios and regenerate the signals it receives. As a result, a repeater increases the range between access points and client radios (see Figure 11-6). A repeater might double the range, but it can significantly reduce the capacity of the WLAN because the repeater retransmits data frames it receives. This causes a duplication of data traffic, which reduces the overall capacity by up to 50 percent. This could be a problem if performance is important. Also, a repeater requires electrical power, which might be costly to install. Because a repeater does not connect to the distribution system, Power over Ethernet (PoE) is not an option.

> **Note**   For more details on repeaters, see Chapter 3.

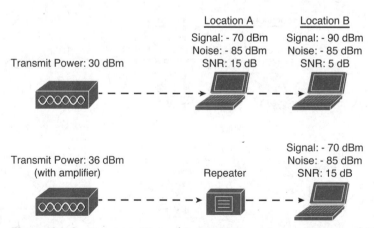

Figure 11-6   *Repeaters Extend Range Between Access Points and Client Radios*

Physical Obstacles

Physical obstacles may be present within the operating environment of a WLAN, and these obstacles offer varying amounts of attenuation. To improve range in some areas, consider installing access points in locations that avoid obstacles. If possible, consider moving some obstacles, if possible, to improve range by effectively improving the signal strength throughout the applicable areas.

For example, signal coverage may be needed in an office where there are ceiling-high filing cabinets along one of the walls in the office. These cabinets will likely highly attenuate RF signals. As a result, it would be wise to position one or more access points to cover the office so that the signals do not travel through the cabinets.

Note   For more details on obstacles and RF signal propagation, see Chapter 2, "Radio Wave Fundamentals."

Radio Signal Interference

As discussed earlier in this chapter, a way of avoiding existing interference is to use frequencies where there is less interference, such as using the 5-GHz frequency band or turning the access point to channels having lower interference levels. By reducing radio signal interference, you can increase the range between access points and client radios, as illustrated in Figure 11-7. Another similar way of improving range is to remove the source of interference. For example, it might be possible to decrease the noise levels by 6 dB in the 2.4-GHz band by stopping the use of 2.4-GHz cordless phones (and possibly switching to 5-GHz or 6-GHz phones instead). Also, you could use RF shielding to reduce noise. Special RF shielding paint and wallpaper offer high degrees of attenuation (80 dB). Of course, the elimination of interference sources may not be feasible, but it is at least something to consider.

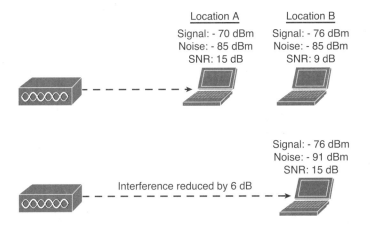

Figure 11-7   *Lowering Radio Signal Interference Increases Range*

Note   For more details on radio signal interference, see Chapter 4, "Wireless LAN Implications."

Extending Municipal Wi-Fi Mesh Indoors

Most municipalities require Wi-Fi signal coverage in 90 percent of outdoor areas and 70 percent inside homes and businesses. For indoor places, the coverage is generally required just inside the exterior wall of the facility, on the first and second floors. To meet overall coverage requirements, the trend is to install Wi-Fi mesh nodes on city-owned assets, such as streetlamp poles and traffic lights. This generally offers good coverage outside through-out the city, but indoor coverage is generally not sufficient without careful planning.

Indoor signal propagation suffers because the exterior walls of facilities offer significant attenuation. In addition, the transmit power of user devices operating inside the buildings is usually relatively weak. The transmit power of the mesh nodes is much higher, but this only affects the downlink communications path, from the mesh node to the user device. It does not do much good when the user devices have much lower transmit power. In this case, the ability for the communications link to operate is based on the weaker uplink signal, which limits range.

Because of varying wall attenuation and the relatively weak transmit power of user devices operating inside facilities, signal propagation indoors is not reliable and is difficult to verify. You cannot depend on getting inside an appropriate sample of facilities to test signal propagation and tweak the positioning of the mesh nodes to improve coverage. Most of the indoor locations are private homes and businesses, and a large number of them are not likely going to let you in to do testing.

As a result, when designing a municipal Wi-Fi network, it is highly recommended to specify the use of indoor customer premises equipment (CPE), which offers a stronger uplink signal to compensate for the attenuation of the walls. The use of indoor CPE will make signal coverage inside buildings much more reliable and satisfy requirements. I have found that about 50 percent of the homes and businesses in cities actually require CPE to provide acceptable indoor coverage, but a blanket requirement for all indoor locations to use CPE may be beneficial.

CPE is installed inside a facility, near one of the exterior walls, and is associated via Wi-Fi with the nearest mesh node. CPE also provides a separate Wi-Fi or Ethernet connection inside the facility. With a Wi-Fi connection, users will likely have much greater indoor Wi-Fi coverage than the municipal network requirements specify. Each indoor location will have the equivalent of a Wi-Fi router installed inside the building. With an Ethernet connection, users will need to connect a laptop or PC directly to the CPE device or plug in an external Wi-Fi router or access point.

It is important to properly set user expectations regarding indoor coverage of a wireless municipal network and the need for CPE. Many potential users are accustomed to using Wi-Fi hotspots where signal coverage is good without CPE devices. A municipality can avoid frustrating users by educating them early on during the deployment of the network. Users need to realize that without indoor CPE, they will not have reliable Wi-Fi signal coverage.

Performance Considerations

When WLANs first became available in the early 1990s, primary applications were wireless bar code solutions for needs like inventory control and retail price marking. Data transfers for these types of applications do not demand very high performance. In fact, 1 Mbps data rates are generally sufficient to handle the transfer of relatively small bar codes for a limited number of users.

Today, enterprises are deploying WLANs for larger numbers of users with needs for corporate applications that involve large file transfers and wireless telephony. In addition, there are often needs for supporting a high density of users in a smaller area, such as a conference room. The need for higher data rates and techniques to improve performance of WLANs is becoming crucial for supporting these types of applications. To get the needed performance when designing a WLAN, consider the following elements:

- Throughput versus data rate
- Radio frequency bands
- Transmit power settings
- Transmission channel settings
- Data rate settings
- Antennas
- Amplifiers
- Radio signal interference
- Channel width settings
- Signal coverage
- Fragmentation settings
- Request-to-send/clear-to-send (RTS/CTS) settings
- Bandwidth control mechanisms
- Microcell deployment strategies

Throughput Versus Data Rate

The data rate of a signal is based on the time it takes to send information and overhead data bits when transmitting. Therefore, the aggregate data rate (throughput) is actually much lower because of delays between transmissions. Data rate mostly affects the delay performance of a WLAN. The higher the data rate, the lower the delay when sending data from one point to another. As a result, higher data rates can increase the capability to support a larger number of users. Data rate alone is not a good measure of the performance of a system, though. You also need to consider the effect of overhead bits, waiting times to access the medium, and the format of the data being sent.

Actual throughput is a much better indicator of the performance of a WLAN because it provides an indication of the time it takes to send information. Throughput is the flow of information over time. It is important to not confuse throughput with 802.11 data rate, which is the speed that the data bits in individual 802.11 data frames are sent. Because there is idle time between 802.11 data frames and retransmission due to noise, the throughput is always lower than the data rate. Throughput, however, provides a more accurate representation of the delays that users experience because they are concerned with how fast information is sent, not about 802.11 frames. It is possible to have a very high 802.11 data rate and still have throughput that is relatively low. This can occur, for example, when the user is close to an access point but there are many other users actively accessing the WLAN from the same access point or when there is substantial radio signal interference present. In these cases, the WLAN carries the information at a much slower rate. As a result, be sure to focus on specifying throughput, not 802.11 data rates, as the basis for performance.

> **Note**   When a laptop is unplugged from an electrical outlet and running on batteries, the client device operating system will likely cause the client radio to enter power saving mode. As a result, throughput may drop by as much as 50 percent. To ensure that throughput is not affected when running on batteries, configure the operating system to not invoke client radio power management.

Radio Frequency Bands

As mentioned earlier in this chapter, you can choose to use 2.4-GHz or 5-GHz bands—or both. In addition to the impact this selection has on range, the choice of frequency band also affects performance. The 5-GHz band includes much more spectrum (and more channels) than the 2.4-GHz band. There are many more overlapping channels in the 5-GHz band than in the 2.4-GHz band. In addition, the 5-GHz band is usually relatively free from RF interference sources. As a result, the 5-GHz band offers much greater capacity. Keep in mind, however, that the 5-GHz band, as explained earlier, might provide less range than 2.4-GHz deployments.

Transmit Power Settings

For a constant range, increasing the transmit power of an 802.11 radio increases performance in the outward direction. As the transmit power increases, communications at a particular location will be possible at greater data rates. The basis for this is that increasing transmit power improves the SNR at a particular location, which allows the receiving radio to decode signals at higher data rates.

For example, as shown in Figure 11-8, increasing the transmit power of the access point by 6 dB causes a 6-dB increase in the signal strength and corresponding SNR throughout the coverage area. In the case shown in Figure 11-8, the client device associated with the access point set to higher transmit power has SNR of 21 dB, which is significantly higher than it would be if the transmit power of the access point were set to a lower level. The higher signal level (and SNR) allows the client device to receive 802.11 signals at higher data rates.

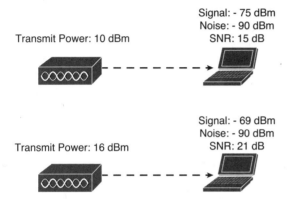

Figure 11-8 *Transmit Power Increases Provide Higher Data Rates at Specific Points Due to Corresponding Increases in SNR*

This increase in data rate applies to the communications in only one direction, which is the outward path relative to the radio with increased transmit power. The increase in transmit power of an access point, for example, only improves the data rate of the 802.11 data frames being sent from the access point to the client radios. To improve the overall communications of 802.11 signals, you may need to increase the data rate settings on the access points and the client radios. As discussed previously in this chapter, client radios may have considerably less transmit power than the access points. Therefore, you will likely need to increase the transmit power on the client radios to see any improvement in data rates.

Transmission Channel Settings

As with range improvements, transmission channel settings can impact performance if it is possible to select a channel that avoids radio signal interference. Figure 11-9 illustrates an example of this concept, where testing has shown that the noise level for Channel 1 is 5 dB lower than the noise level for Channel 11. Because of the lower radio frequency interference corresponding to Channel 1, the resulting SNR for channels at the client device is 15 dB, which enables the applicable client radio to process 802.11 signals at a higher data rate.

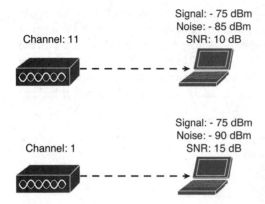

Figure 11-9   *Transmission Channel Changes Can Provide Greater Performance by Lowering Noise Levels*

Data Rate Settings

If you need to deploy a high-performance WLAN, consider configuring data rate settings to higher fixed values. This forces operation at a higher specific data rate and avoids transmissions at lower data rates, which would negatively impact overall performance. Keep in mind, however, that using higher data rate settings will significantly reduce range. Also, as explained earlier in this chapter, data rate settings impact communications in only one direction. For example, setting an access point to 54 Mbps causes the access point to transmit all data frames at 54 Mbps, but the client radios may transmit at different data rates, depending on their data rate settings. As a result, you must configure the data rate settings in client radios (which might not be feasible) to realize benefits of using higher fixed data rate settings to improve performance.

Note   Check administration logs to verify that client devices are connecting to the network at desired rates.

Antennas

The use of higher-gain antennas increases communication performance in both directions between access points and client radios. For example, as Figure 11-10 illustrates, if you replace a standard 2-dBi antenna with one having 6 dBi, the signal level and corresponding SNR at the client radio at a specific location will increase. The higher signal level and SNR allows the radio in the access point and client radio to decode signals at higher data rates. Increasing antenna diversity has a similar effect on performance. Also, you should test different antenna gain and diversity with actual propagation testing in the target operating environment to determine the lowest overall cost of deploying the network.

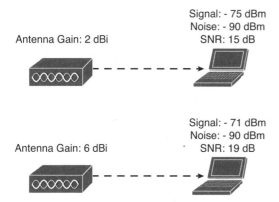

Figure 11-10 *Higher-Gain Antennas Boost Performance Throughout the Coverage Area*

Amplifiers

In addition to improving range, an amplifier can also increase performance. Because an amplifier increases the signal strength and corresponding SNR throughout the coverage area, a client radio at a specific point is able to decode the 802.11 signals at a higher data rate. For example, as shown in Figure 11-11, without an amplifier at the access point, the signal strength and SNR at the client device are −75 dBm and 15 dB, respectively. After installing an amplifier on the access point, the signal strength and SNR at the client device increase to −69 dBm and 21 dB, respectively. As a result, in this example, the client radio is able to support reception of data frames at a higher rate than without the amplifier because of the higher signal level and SNR. Also, because of the amplifier's receive gain, the access point will also be able to receive 802.11 signals from the client radio at a higher data rate.

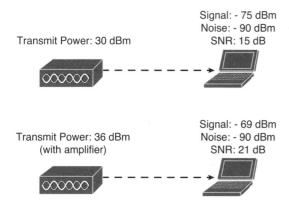

Figure 11-11 *Amplifiers Improve Performance Throughout the Coverage Area*

Radio Signal Interference

By reducing radio signal interference, it is possible to increase performance at specific points within the coverage area. For example, in the scenario shown in Figure 11-12, a reduction of noise levels by 6 dB (possibly by eliminating the operation of other radio equipment) will raise the SNR at points throughout the coverage area by 6 dB. This enables the access points and client radios to successfully decode 802.11 signals at higher data rates.

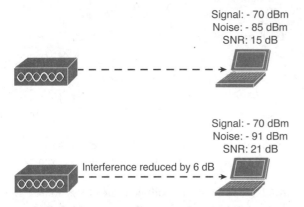

Signal: - 70 dBm
Noise: - 85 dBm
SNR: 15 dB

Signal: - 70 dBm
Noise: - 91 dBm
SNR: 21 dB

Interference reduced by 6 dB

Figure 11-12 *Lowering Radio Signal Interference Increases Performance at Specific Locations*

Channel Width Settings

The 802.11n standard provides two different channel width settings, 20 MHz and 40 MHz, and the 802.11ac standard extends this by offering 80-MHz and 160-MHz channel widths. The wider channels support much higher performance. For 2.4-GHz implementation, however, it is not wise to configure 40-MHz channels. As discussed in other parts of this book, there is not enough spectrum in the 2.4-GHz band to support multiple 40-MHz channels without significant inter–access point interference. As a result, if you choose to implement the 2.4-GHz band, the only practical option is 20-MHz channels.

The 5-GHz band, however, has a much greater amount of spectrum, with plenty of room for wider channels. Therefore, seriously consider configuring the network for 40-MHz channels (if 802.11n) or 80-MHz or 160-MHz channels (if 802.11ac). It might not be possible to implement 40-MHz channels if the network must accommodate legacy 2.4-GHz client devices. A way of still taking advantage of 40-MHz channels in this case, as expressed in other parts of this book, is to configure legacy radios to connect to the WLAN over 2.4 GHz (with 20-MHz channels) and have only 802.11ac (or 5-GHz, 802.11n) devices connect via 5 GHz (with 40-MHz or wider channels).

Signal Coverage

As the basis for providing good performance, it is important to have adequate signal coverage throughout the required coverage areas. In areas that have weak signal coverage, the signal level and corresponding SNR will be relatively low. The 802.11 radios might still be able to decode the signals and successfully communicate, but the data rate may be fairly low. To ensure that signal coverage is good enough, perform a proper wireless site survey, as described in Chapter 15.

Fragmentation Settings

The use of 802.11 fragmentation can increase the reliability of 802.11 data frame transmissions in the presence of radio frequency interference, which improves the throughput of the network. When sending smaller frames, corrupted bits in the frame due to radio frequency interference are much less likely to occur. If a frame does receive corrupted bits, the source station can retransmit the frame quickly.

The fragment size value can typically be set manually on access points and client radios to between 256 and 2048 bytes. This value is user controllable. In fact, you activate fragmentation by setting a particular frame size threshold (in bytes). If the frame that the access point is transmitting is larger than the threshold, it will trigger the fragmentation function. If the packet size is equal to or less than the threshold, the access point will not use fragmentation. Of course, setting the threshold to the largest value effectively disables fragmentation.

A good way to find out whether you should activate fragmentation is to monitor the WLAN for retransmissions. If very few retransmissions are occurring, do not bother implementing fragmentation. The additional headers applied to each fragment will likely dramatically increase the overhead on the network, which will actually reduce throughput. If you find a relatively high percentage of retransmissions (greater than 5 percent) and the presence of radio signal interference or weak signal levels is likely causing the retransmissions, try using fragmentation. This can improve throughput if the fragmentation threshold is set to the optimum value, which is where the throughput is maximum.

If the retransmission rate is relatively high, start by setting the fragmentation threshold to around 1,000 bytes and then tweak it until you find the best results. After invoking fragmentation, follow up with testing to determine whether the number of collisions is reduced and that the resulting throughput is better. You should try a different setting or discontinue using it altogether if the throughput drops (even if you have fewer retransmissions).

The issue with using fragmentation to improve performance is that interference driving the retransmission rate may change over time or as users roam throughout different portions of the signal coverage area. On one day, for example, the presence of significant radio signal interference may cause the retransmission rate to be around 20 percent. In this case, you may find that a fragmentation threshold of around 800 bytes maximizes throughput. On another day, the interference may go away, resulting in a drop in the retransmission rate to only 1 percent or 2 percent. If you don't change the fragmentation threshold, throughput may actually drop because the cost of additional overhead resulting from the fragmentation mechanism is not providing much benefit in terms of reducing the retransmission rate.

> **Note**   For more details on the 802.11 fragmentation mechanism, see Chapter 6, "IEEE 802.11 Medium Access Control (MAC) Layer."

RTS/CTS Settings

The use of 802.11 RTS/CTS can increase the reliability of 802.11 data frame transmissions in the presence of hidden nodes, which improves the throughput of the network. Much like analyzing the need for fragmentation, a way to gauge whether RTS/CTS will help throughput is to monitor the WLAN for retransmissions. If the retransmission rate is low (under 5 percent), do not implement RTS/CTS. The additional frame transmissions needed to implement RTS/CTS will likely dramatically increase the overhead on the network, which will actually reduce throughput.

If the retransmission rate is high, and you find a large number of collisions with users that are relatively far apart and likely out of range of each other (that is, hidden nodes are present), try enabling RTS/CTS on the applicable client radios. After activating RTS/CTS, test to determine whether the number of retransmissions is lower and the resulting throughput is better. Because RTS/CTS introduces overhead, disable it if you find a drop in throughput, even if you have fewer collisions. After all, the goal is to improve performance.

Of course, keep in mind that user mobility can change the results. A highly mobile user may be hidden for a short period of time, perhaps when you perform the testing, and then may be closer to other stations most of the time. If retransmissions are occurring between users within range of each other, the problem may be a result of radio signal interference. In that case, fragmentation might help.

In most cases, initiating RTS/CTS in the access point is fruitless because the hidden station problem does not exist from the perspective of the access point. All stations having valid associations are within range and not hidden from the access point. Forcing the access point to implement the RTS/CTS handshake will significantly increase the overhead and reduce throughput. Focus on using RTS/CTS in the client radios to improve performance.

> **Note**   For more details on the 802.11 RTS/CTS mechanism, see Chapter 6.

Bandwidth Control Mechanisms

To provide consistent performance for all users, it might be necessary to implement bandwidth control mechanisms, which divide the total capacity of the network into smaller sizes made available to each user. For example, as shown in Figure 11-13 (a case without bandwidth control), a single user (Client A) may download a very large file that requires a few minutes (or even hours), consuming nearly all the capacity of the network. As a result, other users, such as Clients B and C, may have very little or no throughput. Such uncontrolled use of the network can aggravate users and significantly reduce the effectiveness of the network. A solution to this is to use bandwidth control and configure the access points (or other applicable components) to provide each user a throughput limit, such as

250 Kbps each. This level of performance, based on the total users and utilization of the network, forces users to share the total capacity of the WLAN in a manner that ensures sufficient performance for everyone.

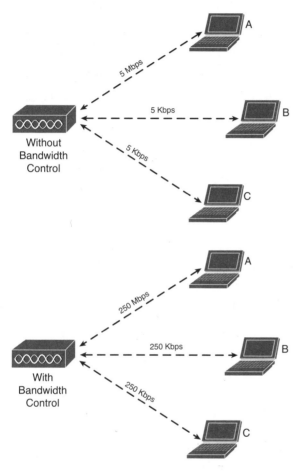

Figure 11-13 *Bandwidth Control Provides Consistent Performance for All Users*

Microcell Deployment Strategies

If WLAN requirements call for extremely high performance, consider using a high density of access points. This involves turning down the transmit power of all access points and client radios, which forces access points to be much closer together (and avoid interfering with each other). This "microcell" architecture makes the physical area collision domains smaller than with conventional access point density. The microcell architecture leads to much higher performance because there are fewer client devices connecting to each access point. This allows each client device radio to consume a greater percentage of the access point's capacity and avoid collisions with other radios. Therefore, performance can be much greater.

An issue with using higher access point density to improve performance is that it leads to a great number of access points. Of course, this means that the deployment will cost more— possibly considerably more. To reduce the need for increasing the density of access points, first consider all other less-expensive options covered previously in this chapter.

Note Your organization will likely not realize the true potential of 802.11n or 802.11ac until you are able to migrate away from legacy (802.11b and 802.11g) devices and implement a pure 802.11n or 802.11ac network. Of course, this requires that all wireless client devices must implement 5-GHz frequencies.

Determining Wireless LAN Capacity

One way of sizing up a WLAN is to install the access points and see what happens. This approach does not require much investment in time and brain power; however, you may not really know the maximum capacity until users start to complain. For example, you might install a WLAN to enable users in an office to access Internet services. After you commission the system, only a handful of users may be active at any given time. Within six months, the number of active users may increase to 50, and you might start to hear users complaining about slow performance. This is an indirect sign that access points are operating at capacity. Of course, this result assumes that there are no other bottlenecks, such as sluggish servers or slow Internet service provider (ISP) connections.

Another method of sizing a WLAN is to gather up a bunch of people armed with wireless client devices and have them hammer on the network. Just keep adding more and more active users until performance starts to decline to a level that is not acceptable. The maximum capacity could be the point at which users experience more than a five-second delay when loading a particular web page, for example. This approach provides fairly accurate results, but it is often not feasible. The difficulty is finding enough people and client devices to perform the testing. In most cases, this type of testing is just too expensive.

Simulation programs, such as OPNET, run on a computer and imitate a WLAN under different situations. With simulation, you can artificially characterize WLAN components, such as access points, client radios, and users. A simulation calculates resulting throughput, which gives you a good idea of how many users can be active on the network. By adjusting the number of users, you can estimate how many users the access points can handle and the resulting per-user performance. A strong advantage of simulation is that it can be done before purchasing and installing a WLAN. Simulation tools are rather costly, however, with prices in the tens of thousands of dollars. In addition, you will probably have a steep learning curve before becoming proficient at developing the simulation models. This can make the simulation option out of reach for most companies. Results are also only as good as the utilization level estimates.

Roaming Considerations

WLAN requirements generally call for the ability of users to roam with wireless client devices throughout the coverage area. Each client radio roams differently, depending on proprietary protocols that the vendor has incorporated into the radio. The type of wireless application that a client device is using also impacts the ability to roam. As a result, it is crucial that you test the roaming capability of all client devices before finalizing the design of a WLAN.

When designing a WLAN, consider the following elements that impact roaming:

- Roaming levels
- Wireless IP phone roaming
- Mobility settings

Roaming Levels

As a basis for designing a WLAN that provides effective roaming, it is important to first understand basic roaming concepts. For WLANs, roaming takes place at several levels. As shown in Figure 11-14, roaming can take place at layer 2 or layer 3. As a user moves about the coverage area, the client radio automatically hands off from one access point to another, as needed to support communications. This is layer 2 roaming, sometimes referred to as access point roaming. In addition, the client device might need to roam from one subnet to another, which is layer 3 roaming.

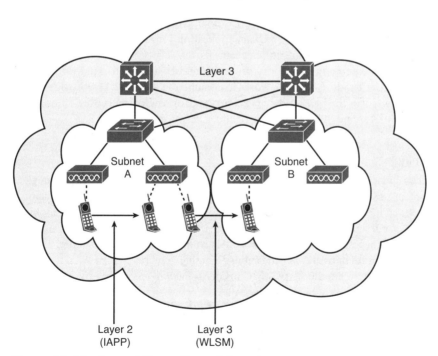

Figure 11-14 *Layer 2 Versus Layer 3 Roaming*

Access Point Roaming

Through the collaboration of WLAN vendors, the Inter–Access Point Protocol (IAPP) specification is a common roaming protocol that enables users (client radios) to move throughout a facility while maintaining a connection to the network via multivendor access points. Interoperability tests and demonstrations show that IAPP works with a variety of access points. The Wi-Fi Alliance includes interoperable roaming as a requirement for receiving Wi-Fi certification.

The IAPP specification builds on the capabilities of the IEEE 802.11 standard, using the distribution system interfaces of the access point that 802.11 provides. IAPP operates between access points, using User Datagram Protocol (UDP) and the Internet Protocol (IP) as a basis for communications. IAPP defines two basic protocols: the Announce Protocol and the Handover Protocol. The Announce Protocol provides coordination between access points by performing the following functions:

- Informing other access points about a new active access point
- Informing the access points of network-wide configuration information

The Handover Protocol informs an access point that one of its stations has re-associated with a different access point. The old access point forwards buffered frames for the station to the new access point. The new access point then updates filter tables to ensure that MAC-level filtering (bridging) will forward frames appropriately.

The finalization and proliferation of IEEE 802.11r and 802.11k amendments to the 802.11 standard have positive impacts on access point roaming. 802.11r provides seamless roaming between access points. The main application for 802.11r is for providing effective roaming for VoIP and security mechanisms. 802.11r provides functions for determining QoS and performing security protocol handshakes before handoffs occur to avoid delays after handoff. 802.11k works in conjunction with 802.11r, providing information to discover the best available access point for handoff purposes. Consider incorporating 802.11r and 802.11k into VoIP and security applications.

Subnet Roaming

As a wireless client device roams from one IP subnet to another, the client device might need to obtain a valid IP address for the new subnet. The client device can make use of DHCP to obtain the IP address, but this is not always effective when supporting mobility. DHCP is not designed to renew addresses when crossing subnet boundaries. As a result, it might be necessary to configure a WLAN to operate on a single subnet. This might work in a private network, but the subnet roaming issue resurfaces when the client device needs to roam to another network. Consider using wireless middleware for applications that are affected by subnet roaming issues.

Some companies might want to implement multiple IP subnets across a common WLAN for various reasons, such as to make network management easier, facilitate location-based services, and decrease the spread of broadcast packets throughout the network.

For instance, a company might want to deliver specific information to users based on their location in a specific building. By designating different subnets throughout the WLAN, the location of the user can be found and content can be delivered to the user based on his or her location. An airport, for example, could use location information to deliver a map of the applicable concourse or terminal, indicate flight information, and provide the locations of ticket counters. The system could also deliver advertisements from concessions located in the general area.

With multiple subnets, mobile users must be able to seamlessly roam from one subnet to another while traversing a facility. As users roam across subnets, though, there must be a mechanism at layer 3 to ensure that a user device configured with a specific IP address can continue communications with applications. Some controller-based WLAN implementations, such as Cisco using layer 3 services, however, can solve this via a feature called Proxy ARP, where a wireless client device can roam from an initial anchor controller to a foreign controller while maintaining the IP address originally assigned via the anchor controller. This is possible even though the foreign controller is operating on a different subnet than the anchor controller.

If the wireless solution you choose does not implement Proxy ARP, consider Mobile IP, which solves layer 3 roaming problems by allowing the mobile user to use two IP addresses. One address, the home address, is static. The second address, the "care-of" address, changes at each new point of network attachment and can be thought of as the user's position-specific address.

The home address enables the mobile node to continually receive data relative to its home network, through the use of a network node called the *home agent*. Whenever the user is not attached to the home network, the home agent receives all the packets sent to the mobile user and arranges to deliver them to the mobile user's current point of attachment, which is its care-of address. Whenever a Mobile IP user moves, it registers its new care-of address with its home agent. This makes it possible for the home agent to keep up with the whereabouts of the mobile user. The home agent sends any packets it receives for that user to the applicable care-of address.

To implement Mobile IP, you need two major components: a Mobile IP server and Mobile IP client software. The Mobile IP server fully implements the Mobile IP home agent functionality, providing mobility management for the mobile users. The Mobile IP server can generally also keep track of where, when, and how long users use the roaming service. That data can then provide the basis for accounting and billing.

The requirement for client-side software makes Mobile IP impractical for some applications. For example, public networks demand open connectivity for users, which makes it difficult to deploy solutions that require client software. Of course, the task of installing software on user devices before enabling roaming is too cumbersome. Another problem with Mobile IP is that it is somewhat vendor specific. To ensure interoperability among multivendor Mobile IP clients and servers, definitely do some upfront testing.

Wireless ISP Roaming

With Wi-Fi hotspots, there is very limited roaming among wireless ISPs. The Wi-Fi Alliance tried developing standards to make wireless ISP roaming seamless, but the effort disbanded due to significant incompatibility among different access controllers. In general, standards for roaming from one Wi-Fi wireless ISP to another are nonexistent. As a result, you must negotiate teaming agreements with other ISPs when deploying widespread Wi-Fi hotspots and create a custom access control system that is common among all applicable ISPs.

Wireless IP Phone Roaming

One of the applications that roaming impacts a great deal is wireless telephony. If you plan to have wireless IP phones operating on a WLAN, ensure that the WLAN you design supports effective roaming. A voice user must be able to move about the facility, and the system will need to allow roaming at both layer 2 and layer 3. Without smooth roaming, users will experience dropped calls.

Layer 2 roaming takes place when a wireless IP phone moves out of range of an access point and re-associates with a different access point. Because this type of roaming occurs frequently as users move about a facility, such as a warehouse or hospital, be certain that layer 2 roaming is fast (ideally less than 100 milliseconds). This mid-call roam time is the amount of time that elapses after the last RTP packet is seen from the current access point and the first RTP packet is seen from the access point that the wireless IP phone associates with.

When selecting wireless IP phones, be certain that they support fast roaming. Cisco 7925 wireless IP phones, for instance, are specially designed to make layer 2 roaming fast enough to avoid dropped calls. For example, a Cisco 7925 phone will initiate a re-association process with a different access point if the phone does not receive three consecutive beacons from the existing access point and if its unicast frame to the access point is not acknowledged. The 7925 also periodically scans for better access points and maintains a list of potential access points. A decision to roam is made on signal strength and signal quality metrics. The quality metric makes use of information provided by each access point in its beacon regarding the utilization of the access point. As a result, the phone can avoid attempting to re-associate with access points that have high utilization and may not be able to effectively support voice traffic. With these mechanisms, the 7925 is generally able to complete layer 2 roaming within 100 milliseconds.

The addition of layer 3 roaming might cause substantial delays and dropped voice calls. This depends on the wireless solution you implement, especially if it does not implement enhanced features for voice roaming. You might therefore need to consider avoiding having wireless IP phones perform mid-call layer 3 roaming. In this case, if possible, define a single subnet for the entire WLAN. This will completely avoid layer 3 roaming.

If this is not feasible, at least minimize the possibility of layer 3 mid-call roaming. For example, you might have a different subnet on each floor of a hospital. When performing the wireless site survey, ensure that signals from one floor do not overlap to such an extent that the wireless IP phones will roam to the floor above (or below) while the user is walking through a particular area.

Mobility Settings

Many WLAN product vendors enable you to indicate the degree of mobility of each station so that the access point can optimize roaming algorithms. If you set up a station as being "mobile," the roaming protocols will enable the station to re-associate as it moves from one access point to another. If set to "mobile" mode, stationary devices, such as wireless desktops, might experience a short episode of radio signal interference and falsely re-associate with a different access point. As a result, stationary roaming modes usually take this into consideration.

Note   Avoid the use of automatic/adaptive channel control on access points when implementing wireless IP phones. Frequently changing channels will cause the phones to roam frequently, which generally results in a higher and undesirable call drop rate.

Summary

It is important to pay close attention to aspects of WLAN design that impact range, performance, and roaming. Bear in mind that sometimes range and performance are indirectly proportional. You need to have a good idea of whether range or performance is more essential before getting too far with the design. If focusing on maximizing range, consider signal coverage requirements, radio frequency bands, transmit power settings, transmission channel settings, data rate, antennas, amplifiers, repeaters, physical obstacles, and radio signal interference. If performance is more important, consider radio frequency bands, transmit power settings, transmission channel settings, data rate settings, antennas, amplifiers, physical obstacles, radio signal interference, channel width settings, signal coverage, fragmentation settings, RTS/CTS settings, multicasting mechanisms, and microcell deployment strategies. To optimize roaming in cases where mobility is imperative, think about the various levels of roaming, special considerations for wireless IP phones, and mobility settings.

Chapter 12

Radio Frequency Considerations

This chapter finishes explaining design considerations related to radio frequency elements that are not covered in other chapters. This includes the following topics:

- Frequency Band Selection

- Transmission Channel Settings

- Difficult-to-Cover Areas

- Radio Signal Interference Reduction

Frequency Band Selection

802.11 supports operation in the 2.4-GHz and 5-GHz bands. Each of these bands is in a completely different part of the radio frequency (RF) spectrum. As a result, operation in one band does not interfere at all with the other. This allows the designer to choose one of the bands or both as the basis for an 802.11 WLAN deployment. To implement 2.4 GHz, 5 GHz, or both, you must ensure that the access points and corresponding client devices have radios that implement the chosen frequencies.

2.4-GHz Frequency Band

For 802.11 WLANs, the 2.4-GHz band has been in use since the initial release of the 802.11 standard in 1997. The most common legacy WLANs (802.11b and 802.11g) use this band. This 2.4-GHz band is roughly 100 MHz wide, which can occupy three non-overlapping transmission channels. This restricts the overall performance capacity in a particular area to what these three non-overlapping channels can support. In addition, because of the limited bandwidth, it is not practical to implement 40-MHz transmission channels when using 802.11n. Because of these limitations, you should focus on using the 2.4-GHz band to primarily support legacy client devices.

5-GHz Frequency Band

The 5-GHz band was first introduced into the 802.11 standard in the 802.11a amendment in 1999. Because of delays in releasing 802.11a-compliant products, WLANs in the 2.4-GHz band continued to proliferate and consume the majority of market share. Because of much greater bandwidth and effective use of wider channels in 802.11n and 802.11ac, 5-GHz WLANs are well suited for today's growing need for higher performance. Therefore, you should strongly consider implementing the 5-GHz band.

Note   For specific band channel frequencies, see Chapter 7, "IEEE 802.11 Physical (PHY) Layers."

Transmission Channel Settings

The access points in a WLAN need to be set to specific RF transmission channels, which the client radios will use when communicating with the access points.

Manual Channel Settings

To deploy an effective wireless network, the adjacent access points within range of each other should be set to different, non-overlapping channels. This minimizes contention between users and the additional overhead of beacons coming from multiple access points, while improving performance. With 2.4-GHz WLANs, these channels are 1, 6, and 11 (see Figure 12-1). In the 5-GHz band, the individual channels do not overlap, so you are free to use any of them.

When choosing access point channels, start by properly planning the optimum installation location for each access point. It is important to have enough access points to provide adequate signal coverage throughout the facility, but you shouldn't overdo it. Make sure that access points are far enough apart as needed (depending on performance requirements) so that you will be able to assign non-overlapping channels to access points that are within range of each other. Therefore, it is crucial to perform a wireless site survey before assigning access point channels. For example, it's a good practice to ensure that the signal strength for an access point covering a particular area is 20 dB or higher than the signal strength associated with other neighboring access points.

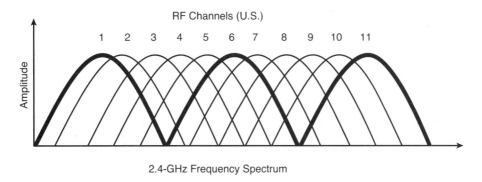

Figure 12-1 *Non-overlapping Channels in the 2.4-GHz Band Include Channels 1, 6, and 11*

Single-Level Facilities

For WLANs with a single access point, such as WLANs in small offices, hotspots, and homes, it is theoretically possible to set the access point to any one of the channels. Therefore, in the United States, you could set the access point to channel 1, 2, 3, 4, 5, 6, 7, 8, 9, 10, or 11. In practice, however, it is best to choose the channel based on the channel settings of WLANs operating nearby and possibly other interference. For instance, Wireless-Nets, Ltd., has performed widespread scans of large municipalities, such as San Francisco and Los Angeles, and found that approximately 75 percent of 2.4-GHz access points are set to channel 6, which is a common factory default channel. Many small companies and homeowners purchase and set up WLANs without changing any of the default factory settings. As a result, these default channels (predominately channel 6) end up being the most common channels in use.

To avoid interference with neighboring networks, it is very likely that you will need to set your access points well away from channel 6, which means channel 1 or 11. Greater than two access points might pose a problem because ideally you need to make use of channel 6 to satisfy use of non-overlapping channels. It might be possible, though, to use channel 6 on the access points toward the center of the facility or away from the side of the facility nearest the location of the neighboring interfering network. The attenuation that the walls of the facility provides generally reduces external interference to acceptable levels. Figure 12-2 illustrates this concept.

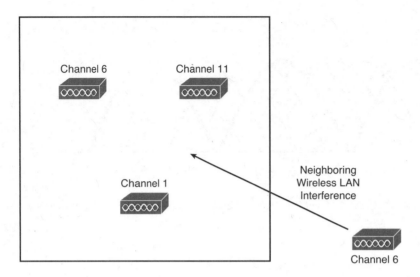

Figure 12-2 *Assignment of Transmission Channels That Avoids Interference from Neighboring Wireless LANs*

Keep in mind that the operating environment for your WLAN may be different. Always perform a wireless site survey to fully understand potential sources of RF interference to provide the basis for making intelligent decisions on access point channel settings. For example, you might find that there is more interference from neighboring networks on channel 1, which means that you should avoid the use of channel 1 (instead of channel 6) near the perimeter of the facility.

With single-floor facilities, the access points will be spread relatively far apart, making channel assignment relatively straightforward. You can easily use a drawing to identify the position of your access points in relation to each other and assign each access point a channel. The key with larger networks is to make certain channels are assigned in a way that minimizes the overlap of signals. Just ensure that all access points within range of each other are set to channels that do not overlap. It may not be possible to have absolutely no overlap in channel usage, but keeping the channel reuse as far apart as possible will improve overall capacity of the network and resulting performance.

In terms of throughput, there is not much of a problem with adjacent access points set to the same channel if the utilization of the network is low. The addition of 802.11 beacon broadcasts from a properly designed network with a limited number of access points with common channel settings has insignificant impact on performance (but it could be a problem where the network is not designed correctly, resulting in beacons from an excessive number of access points). Nevertheless, keep in mind that having the access points set to the same channel will sometimes confuse client radios, which leads to roaming problems. In addition, setting access points near each other to the same channel will degrade capacity, and performance will be significantly lower as traffic on the network increases. Therefore, it is best to stick with the design rule of assigning non-overlapping channels.

Multilevel Facilities

The deployment of a WLAN in a multifloor facility is similar to a single-floor deployment, except that you must also factor in the propagation of 802.11 signals through the floors of the facility where you are deploying the wireless network. Every building is different, so it is a good idea to do some testing and determine how much the floors actually attenuate radio signals. Keep in mind that 2.4-GHz and 5-GHz signals propagate differently through the same materials, so you should perform testing with the frequencies you plan to deploy. Definitely test both 2.4-GHz and 5-GHz frequencies. Perform this testing at the beginning of a wireless site survey so that you have a better idea of how to position test access points based on the interfloor signal propagation.

You should complete the following steps when analyzing interfloor signal propagation:

Step 1. **Assess the construction of the facility.** Walk through the building to observe and understand the construction between the floors. You might need to consult with the building manager and possibly peek above the ceiling tiles. Make notes about the general construction, such as wood, concrete, steel, etc. Identify areas where the construction varies because you should perform testing in each area where the interfloor construction is significantly different.

Step 2. **Activate an access point.** Do this toward the center of the building, away from exterior walls, so that you have room to see the impacts of interfloor propagation. Ideally, position the access point where there are floors above and below the access point location (for example, the second level). All you need to do is supply power to the access point and ensure that it is configured with the same radio (2.4 GHz or 5 GHz) and transmit power that you plan to install. As in wireless site survey testing, you will be measuring the access point beacons as the basis for signal strength. Be sure to mark the position of the test access point on the building diagrams.

Step 3. **Measure interfloor signal propagation.** The main idea here is to see how well the signal propagates through the floors in the areas above and below the access point. For example, with the use of the building diagrams, go to the floor above the test access point and measure the signal strength just above and around the test access point. Also take measurements on the floor below the access point. In most large buildings, acceptable signal propagation generally does not occur beyond the floor immediately above and below the access point, but you should check higher and lower floors, too, just in case the construction allows better-than-average propagation. Move the access point to other areas of the facility where the interfloor construction is very different and repeat the testing.

Step 4. **Characterize the interfloor propagation.** Make notes regarding the diameter of the interfloor signal propagation (on the floors above and below the access point) for each of the areas tested. Be sure to take into account the minimum signal level that constitutes acceptable signal coverage. You will need to keep this information and use it for spacing access points when completing a wireless site survey.

Note   Some test tools, such as AirMagnet Survey, have special features that allow you to record interfloor signal coverage and generate applicable coverage maps. These tools are very beneficial, especially when performing a site survey of a large facility with varying interfloor construction.

If the signals that propagate through to an adjacent level of the building are below the noise floor, you can assign channels on each level, the same as with separate single-level facilities. The bleed-through of signals on adjacent floors will not significantly impact communications. If the signals that propagate through to adjacent floors have relatively high signal power (at or above the noise floor), stagger the spacing of the access points on each floor in a manner that reduces the number of access points necessary to cover the facility. This also makes better use of limited non-overlapping channels.

Figure 12-3 illustrates the effective channel assignments for a multifloor facility with access points using omnidirectional antennas. Access points AP-1 and AP-2 provide coverage on the third level, and partial coverage on level 2 immediately below them. AP-3 provides coverage on the second level in addition to partial coverage on levels 1 and 3. AP-4 and AP-5 cover the first level while also partially covering the second level. This configuration takes advantage of interfloor signal propagation, which can reduce the number of access points and associated costs of the system. In addition, the alternate assignment of transmission channels minimizes inter–access point interference. The reuse of channels 1 and 11 is likely far enough apart to avoid problems. To extend coverage horizontally and include additional floors vertically, be sure to keep the reuse of channels as far apart as possible.

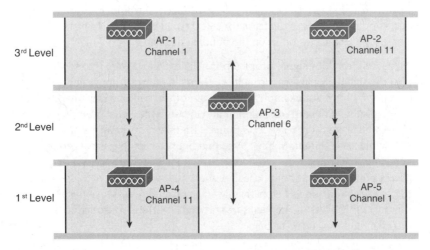

Figure 12-3   *Optimum Location of Access Points and Channel Assignments in Multifloor Facilities*

Adaptive Channel Settings

Most enterprise access points have an optional mechanism, often referred to as adaptive mode (referred to as radio resource management in Cisco networks) that automatically changes the channel in access points based on the current radio activity at each access point location, as illustrated in Figure 12-4. The controller analyzes each access point's received noise and utilization and makes a decision to change the access point's channel if doing so will significantly improve communications. Activating this feature makes sense in a highly dynamic environment, such as in congested areas like cities. Neighboring WLANs and sources of radio signal interference come and go throughout the day, so setting specific static channels one day will likely not be best in the near future.

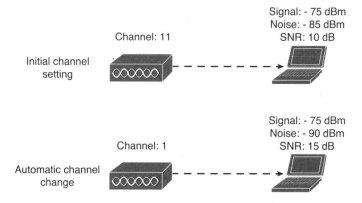

Figure 12-4 *Adaptive Channel Operation*

When determining whether to use adaptive channel settings, take into account that it can disrupt voice communications over the WLAN. The changing of the channel forces the associated client radios to effectively hand off (that is, roam) to the new channel, even if the client device is stationary. As a result, an access point that decides to change channels causes substantial latency, due to the roaming, which might drop voice calls going through that particular access point.

Note See Chapter 11, "Range, Performance, and Roaming Considerations," to understand various impacts of different transmission channel settings.

Difficult-to-Cover Areas

For some areas, such as elevators, stairwells, and parking garages, you will find it very difficult to provide adequate levels of signal coverage. In these cases, be certain to perform thorough propagation testing to best understand the alternatives for access point installation locations.

Signal Coverage in Elevators

In many WLAN deployments, access to the network from inside elevators is often necessary, and this poses issues for radio signal propagation. For example, nurses and doctors using wireless IP phones must be able to continue communicating over the phones while traveling between floors. If you discover needs for providing coverage inside elevators, investigate the issues and implement a well-tested solution.

Many elevator shafts are surrounded by metal, which offers a high degree of attenuation to radio signals. Even elevators that appear to be constructed with wood might still have metal frames, which significantly attenuate radio waves. Of course, the problem with high attenuation is that signal levels coming in and out of the elevator are relatively weak, requiring careful positioning of access points to ensure that signal coverage is adequate.

Another problem with roaming is that the wireless client devices in the elevator must hand off to different access points as the elevator moves between the floors. Two- or three-story buildings usually have relatively slow-moving elevators, and they do not go very far. As a result, roaming is usually not an issue for smaller buildings. You will likely experience more roaming problems in taller buildings, where elevators service many floors. A 30-story building, for instance, might have an elevator that travels much faster, with speeds similar to those of automobiles racing along a highway. In this case, the relatively high speed results in roaming-related issues.

For example, a person actively using a wireless application might enter an elevator on the first floor and punch the button for the twenty-third floor. As the elevator zooms out of range of the initial access point (maybe around the third floor), the wireless client device begins to hand off to an intermediate access point as the elevator makes its way up to the twenty-third floor. If the handoff takes too long, the elevator will pass the intermediate access point before it has time to successfully complete the re-associating process. In fact, the client device probably will not complete a handoff to another access point until the elevator comes to a stop at the twenty-third floor. Of course, this causes a disruption in the flow of information between the client device and the network, which causes VoIP calls to drop and other applications to fail.

To counter the attenuation problems with elevators, it is usually best to install an access point near the elevator door on each floor (or possibly on every other level). You should complete specific testing when performing the site survey, however, to confirm the optimum spacing of access points.

Initially perform the following steps to better understand the attenuation problem and gain insight into where you will need to install access points:

Step 1.   Power up an access point just outside the elevator door at the elevator landing on the first level.

Step 2.   Measure the signal level inside the elevator with the door shut while the elevator is parked at each floor (including the first level) and as the elevator moves between the various floors.

Step 3.   Analyze the signal data and determine where signal coverage is above and below the minimum acceptable signal level.

With this data, establish the optimum placement of access points. For example, if the access point on the ground level provides acceptable coverage inside the elevator parked on the second level (but not the third level), you can probably install access points at the landings of every other floor, such as floors 1, 3, 5, and so on, as shown in Figure 12-5. If the coverage at the second floor is not adequate (but it's okay on the first floor and at least the first half of the way up to the second floor), you should install an access point on the landing of each floor.

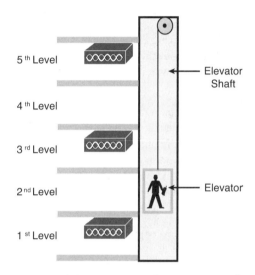

Figure 12-5 *Location of Access Points for Covering an Elevator*

There is a rare possibility that an access point installed at the landing of a particular floor will not provide adequate signal coverage inside the elevator while parked at that same floor with the elevator door closed. If this occurs, consider installing an antenna at the top or bottom of the elevator shaft if possible or use a leaky coax approach for providing signal coverage throughout the elevator shaft. A leaky coax solution involves installing specially designed cabling (coax cable with holes) along the interior of the entire elevator shaft. This might seem like an easy fix for the attenuation (and possibly roaming) problem, but there are many issues.

For example, the leaky coax approach might cause performance troubles on the network, especially for wireless IP phone applications. The long coax cable acts as an antenna for a single access point, which offers a single collision domain throughout a large portion of the facility. This limits the number of users who can use the network. In addition, many companies and organizations will not allow the installation of cable inside the elevator shaft due to safety regulations. This approach also requires specially equipped installation crews (there are not many who can scale elevator shafts) and substantial coordination with facility owners. Therefore, it is probably best to stick with the conventional approach of using access points, if possible.

Do not forget to address potential roaming issues. As with the attenuation problem, you should perform tests to determine the magnitude of the roaming problem as the basis for considering possible solutions. Once you have access points installed in a manner that satisfies signal coverage criteria, make use of the target applications while traveling on the elevator from the bottom floor to the top floor. If this results in unacceptable disruptions in communications, consider implementing roaming enhancement software that provides session persistence from companies such as NetMotion and Bluesocket.

Signal Coverage in Stairwells

As with elevators, it is common that organizations need signal coverage in elevators to support users roaming throughout a building. Instead of taking elevators, users may use stairwells to save time and get additional exercise throughout the day. In addition, elevators are often not available for use during fire emergencies, forcing people to take stairs to exit the building.

Stairwells often have construction that includes special metal reinforcement materials and fireproofing that introduces significant attenuation to radio waves. Therefore, you need to perform sufficient signal propagation testing to fully understand how radio waves propagate through the stairwells. Place a test access point near the doorway just outside the stairwell (for example, in the hallway) and measure the signal levels throughout the inside of the stairwell at the same floor of the access point and floors above and below where the test access point is located. If the stairwell has a door, be certain to close the door when testing to examine the worst-case scenario.

In most cases, you will probably find through testing that the installation of an access point on each floor, just outside the entrance to the stairwell, is necessary to sufficiently cover a stairwell. This is especially true if the entrance to the stairwell has a closed construction with doors at the entrance on each floor. If the stairwell has no doors and is relatively open, you will probably find that an access point is needed only on every other floor. In rare cases, you might find that the stairwell highly attenuates radio signals, and you end up needing to install access points inside the stairwell areas, possibly at the landing of each floor.

Signal Coverage in Parking Areas

In some cases, an organization may require signal coverage in parking areas. This can be a challenge in parking garages because the construction of walls and ceilings is usually steel-reinforced concrete, which highly attenuates radio signals. In fact, based on testing that Wireless-Nets, Ltd., has performed, the walls and ceilings inside parking garages act as a complete barrier to 802.11 signal propagation. This means that each area of the parking garage that is surrounded by concrete will likely need an access point. For large multifloor garages, this can be cost-prohibitive. As with any other difficult-to-cover area, always perform signal propagation testing in parking garages to fully understand the situation.

In outdoor parking areas, there are generally only a few obstructions, such as trees, but you must ensure that the access point antennas are high enough to avoid allowing the automobiles in the parking lot to attenuate the 802.11 signals. This requires positioning the access point antennas at a height that allows radio signals to propagate over the tops of the automobiles. For example, you could mount the access point antenna on a pole or on the roof of a sufficiently tall building. The antenna height depends on the types of vehicles parking in the lot and other obstructions.

If signal coverage is needed inside vehicles, take into consideration the signal losses that a vehicle introduces. The degree of attenuation can be 3 dB to 10 dB, depending on the type of vehicle and the direction the radio waves cut through the vehicle. Perform testing as needed to best understand the applicable losses.

Radio Signal Interference Reduction

When testing a WLAN, you might find that interference is an issue. You should consider the following tips for reducing radio interference problems:

- **Analyze the potential for RF interference:** Do this before installing the WLAN by performing a wireless site survey. Also, talk to people within the facility and learn about other RF devices that might be in use. You need to arm yourself with information that will help when deciding what course of action to take to reduce the interference.

- **Prevent the interfering sources from operating:** Once you know the potential sources of radio signal interference, you may be able to eliminate them by simply turning them off. This is the best way to counter interference; however, it is not always practical. For example, you cannot usually tell the company in the office space next to you to stop using cordless phones; however, you might be able to disallow the use of Bluetooth-enabled devices or microwave ovens where your 802.11 users reside.

- **Provide adequate WLAN coverage:** A good practice for reducing impacts of RF interference is to ensure that the WLAN has strong signals throughout the areas where users will reside. If signals get too weak, interfering signals will be more troublesome. Of course, this means doing a thorough wireless site survey to determine the most effective number and placement of access points.

- **Set configuration parameters properly:** Tune access points to channels that avoid the frequencies of potential interfering signals. This might not always work, but it is worth a try. For example, microwave ovens generally offer interference in the upper portion of the 2.4-GHz band. As a result, you might be able to avoid microwave oven interference by tuning the access points near the microwave oven to channel 1 or 6 rather than 11.

- **Deploy 5-GHz WLANs:** Most potential for interference today is in the 2.4-GHz band. If you find that other interference-avoidance techniques do not work well enough, consider deploying a 5-GHz WLAN. In addition to avoiding RF interference, you will also receive much higher throughput.

Designing an Effective Cell Edge for VoWLAN Systems

To design an optimal WLAN for voice over WLAN (VoWLAN) systems, consider the following guidelines pertaining to the cell edge (which are based on implementing Cisco wireless IP phones):

Step 1. Plan on having a cell overlap of 20 to 30 percent.

Step 2. Specify a cell boundary of –67 dBm to minimize packet loss.

Step 3. Specify a separation between adjacent AP channels of –86 dBm to minimize co-channel interference from other access points on the same channel.

Step 4. Make use of static data rates to avoid delays associated with changing data rates. A series of retransmitted data frames normally results before switching to lower data rates when auto data rates are enabled, and this sometimes introduces delays that cause dropped calls.

Be sure to look at the vendor guidelines for deploying non-Cisco solutions because they might be different depending on the characteristics of the wireless IP phones that you plan to use.

Summary

When designing a WLAN, you must determine the optimum frequency band selection and transmission channel settings. The 2.4-GHz band is the most common in use today, but because of limited performance, you should strongly consider use of the 5-GHz band. This is especially important for maximizing the potential of 802.11 networks. The selection of transmission channels involves choosing non-overlapping channels for adjacent access points, which reduces inter–access point interference and improves performance. Coverage of multilevel buildings requires you to fully understand interfloor signal propagation and take into consideration interactions between access points on different floors. In addition, some areas of the facility, such as elevators, stairwells, and parking areas, require special attention.

Chapter 13

Security Considerations

This chapter will introduce you to:

- Security Elements
- Encryption
- Authentication
- Rogue Access Point Detection
- RF Shielding
- Wireless Security Policies

The security of a wireless LAN (WLAN) is very important, especially for applications hosting valuable information. For example, networks transmitting credit card numbers for verification or storing sensitive information are definitely candidates for emphasizing security. In these cases and others, it's important to proactively safeguard the network against security attacks. This chapter helps you understand how to make your wireless network secure.

Security Elements

As part of defining effective security for a WLAN, be certain to have a good understanding of the requirements. Chapter 9, "Defining Requirements for a Wireless LAN," explains how to determine these requirements. For example, the requirements may specify the need for encryption and authentication and even mandate the use of a specific encryption or authentication type.

The following are security elements that you should consider when designing a WLAN system:

- **Encryption:** Encryption scrambles the data bits of an 802.11 frame to keep unauthorized people from seeing the actual information content of the frame. You need to choose an encryption type that provides an adequate level of protection.

- **Authentication:** Authentication ensures that client devices connecting to an access point are authorized to access protected resources. This is necessary to provide solid security.

- **Rogue access point detection:** Sometimes employees or hackers may purposely or mistakenly plant a rogue access point that provides open access to protected resources. Methods must be in place to locate and eliminate rogues.

- **Radio frequency (RF) shielding:** Consider using RF shielding paint and window film to highly attenuate radio waves and minimize spillage of signal coverage outside controlled areas.

- **Security policies:** Define security policies, such as encryption/authentication methods, that best satisfy requirements.

Encryption

To prevent people from stealing information being sent wirelessly from one location to another, it is important to encrypt the data. In the most basic form, encryption is done with a common key at the sending and receiving stations. Figure 13-1 illustrates this concept. At the sending station, the client radio encrypts the data before sending it over the air medium. The client radio at the receiving station receives the encrypted data and decrypts it using the same key used for encryption. Other encryption technologies, as explained later in this chapter, use different keys at the sending and receiving stations.

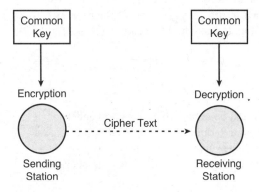

Figure 13-1 *Encryption Produces Ciphertext, Which Is a Scrambled Form of the Actual Information Content of the Frame*

It is possible to implement encryption of data at either layer 2 (data link layer) or layer 3 (network layer), or both at the same time. As shown in Figure 13-2, layer 2 encryption takes place only between the client radio and the access point; on the other hand, layer 3 encryption provides protection between the client device and the application server location. When supporting users from remote locations, such as from homes, airports, and hotels, strongly consider using layer 3 encryption, which is often implemented through virtual private network (VPN) client software running on the client device and a VPN server operating from within a secure corporate network. For example, a user connecting to a Wi-Fi hotspot (which is not secure) can connect to corporate applications through a VPN connection, which encrypts all data flowing from the client device to the application. For access to the WLAN within a corporation, consider using layer 2 encryption. In this case, a VPN is not necessary if the corporate network is secure against a hacker physically accessing the corporate network. The client radio implements the layer 2 encryption natively.

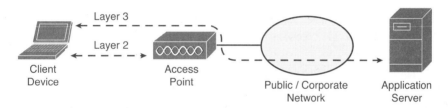

Figure 13-2   *Encryption Applies to Either Layer 2 or Layer 3 of the Network*

As described in Chapter 6, "IEEE 802.11 Medium Access Control (MAC) Layer," the following are types of layer 2 encryption available for WLANs:

- Wired Equivalent Privacy (WEP)

- Temporal Key Integrity Protocol (TKIP)

- CBC-MAC Protocol (CCMP)

See Chapter 6 for information about these protocols.

Note   802.11n and 802.11ac require CCMP on all encrypted links.

Understanding Public Key Cryptography

Public key cryptography uses asymmetric keys, with one key that is private and another one that is public. The private key is (as the name implies) kept secret; the pubic key can be known by anyone. This enables more effective encryption and authentication mechanisms. A set of public and private keys match from a cryptographic standpoint. For example, the sending station can encrypt data using the public key, and the receiver uses the private key for decryption. The opposite is also true: The sending station can encrypt data using the private key, and the receiving station decrypts the data using the public key.

If the goal is to encrypt data, the sending station will use a public key to encrypt the data before transmission. The receiving station uses the matching private key to decrypt the data upon receipt. Each station keeps its private key hidden to avoid compromising encrypted information.

Public key cryptography works effectively for encrypting data because the public key can be made freely available to anyone wanting to send encrypted data to a particular station. A station that generates a new private key can distribute the corresponding public key over the network to everyone without worry of compromise. Therefore, the public key can be posted on a web server, sent unencrypted across the network, and so on. Some security protocols, for example, may distribute a new WEP key periodically to a station by encrypting it first with the receiving station's public key. The receiving station uses its secret private key to decrypt the encrypted WEP key and then begin using the new WEP key for encrypting data frames.

In addition to protecting information from hackers, stations can use public key cryptography to authenticate themselves to other stations or access points. This may be necessary before an access point or controller allows a particular station to interface with a protected side of the network. Likewise, the client can authenticate the access point in a similar manner.

A station authenticates itself by encrypting a string of text within a packet using its private key. The receiving station decrypts the text with the sending station's public key. If the decrypted text matches some predetermined text (for example, the station's name), the receiving station knows that the sending station is valid. The encryption of a particular string of text acts as a digital signature.

Authentication

802.1X defines a framework of standards and IETF specifications that explain how network client devices (supplicants) authenticate with a port on the network. In the case of a WLAN, the port is an access point (authenticator), which acts like a security gate to the network. Before completing the authentication process, the access point does not let any user traffic from the client device through to the protected side of the network. A client device that needs to connect to the network must first go through an authentication process, as illustrated in Figure 13-3, which includes sending credentials (for example, password or digital certificate) through the access point to an authentication server. The authentication server responds with an authorization to the access point, which then either allows or disallows the client device to communicate with the protected network resources. If the client device is not granted access to the protected side of the network, the access point may enable guest access to limited resources.

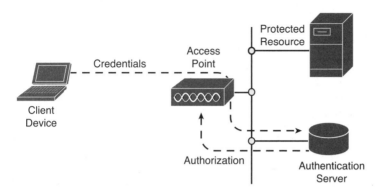

Figure 13-3 *Authentication Involves Authorization of Credentials*

EAP Methods

802.1X alone does not provide authentication mechanisms. When using 802.1X, you need to choose an Extensible Authentication Protocol (EAP) method, such as EAP Transport Layer Security (EAP-TLS) or EAP Tunneled Transport Layer Security (EAP-TTLS), that defines how the authentication takes place.

The software supporting the specific EAP method resides on the authentication server and within the operating system or application software on the client devices. The access point acts as a "pass-through" for 802.1X messages, which means you can specify any EAP method without needing to upgrade an 802.1X-compliant access point. As a result, you can update the EAP authentication method as newer types become available and your requirements for security change.

802.1X has become the industry standard for authentication, and you would be wise to include it as the basis for your WLAN security solution. Windows operating systems support 802.1X natively, and some vendors support 802.1X in their 802.11 access points.

The following is a summary of the various EAP methods:

- **Cisco Lightweight Extensible Authentication Protocol (LEAP):** Cisco LEAP is primarily supported only on Cisco client cards, and there is a charge associated with the supplicant software licenses. In addition, Cisco LEAP is easy to crack with the freely available ASLEEP tool available from hacker websites. An enterprise should strongly consider not using Cisco LEAP because of its security weaknesses.

- **EAP-Flexible Authentication via Secure Tunneling (EAP-FAST):** EAP-FAST is a replacement for Cisco LEAP (because of security weaknesses of LEAP) and is fairly secure.

- **EAP-Protected EAP (EAP-PEAP):** EAP-PEAP is fairly secure and is supported on a wide range of client cards. There is no cost for the supplicant software. The server authenticates to the client using a certificate, and the client authenticates to the server using a username and password.

- **EAP-Tunneled Transport Layer Security (EAP-TTLS):** EAP-TTLS is very secure and is supported on a wide range of client cards; however, it is not native to Microsoft Windows. There is a cost associated with installing third-party supplicant software on the client devices. EAP-TTLS is beneficial where there is a need to support legacy client-side authentication mechanisms, which are sent from the client to the server through a secure tunnel. In addition, EAP-TTLS does not require client certificates, which can ease deployment.

- **EAP-Transport Layer Security (EAP-TLS):** EAP-TLS is very secure and is supported on a wide range of client cards. It is native to Microsoft Windows, and there is no cost associated with the supplicant software. EAP-TLS is generally regarded as the most secure EAP method. The server authenticates to the client by using a certificate, and the client authenticates to the server by using a certificate. This provides effective mutual authentication. As a result, an enterprise should strongly consider implementing EAP-TLS. Keep in mind, however, that you need a method for issuing certificates, which can be done in-house or through a third party.

Note   To download the 802.1X standard, go to www.ieee802.org/1/pages/802.1x.html.

Authentication Servers

The following is a summary of the various authentication servers available for an EAP-TLS system:

- **Cisco Secure Access Control Server (ACS):** ACS is Cisco's solution for a RADIUS-based authentication server, which is often preferred by companies that have Cisco wireless networks and deploy 802.1X-based authentication systems. Cisco ACS can be run on Cisco Secure Network Server (SNS). Cisco ACS is a relatively expensive solution, with the approximate cost being $8,000 to $10,000 per ACS server; at least two servers are needed for redundancy.

- **Microsoft Internet Authentication Service (IAS):** IAS is part of Windows 2003 Server. In Windows Server 2008, IAS is replaced with Network Policy Server (NPS). When an IAS server is a member of an Active Directory domain, IAS uses the directory service as its user account database and is part of a single-sign-on solution. The same set of credentials is used for network access control (authenticating and authorizing access to a network) and to log on to an Active Directory domain. If your organization already has widespread deployment of Microsoft Windows Server, strongly consider implementing IAS.

- **FreeRADIUS:** This is a widely deployed free implementation of a RADIUS server that runs on UNIX. The server is fairly stable but generally requires extensive integration costs and experience with UNIX-based systems. This is a significant issue with organizations currently focusing more on Microsoft Windows-based systems.

Other RADIUS server implementations require investment in server software, such as Juniper's Steel-Belted Radius.

Guest Access

In addition to supporting users authorized to use protected applications and servers, it is often beneficial for a WLAN to support guest access to public resources, such as the Internet or a local web server. For example, a customer may visit your corporate head-quarters and need to access the Internet to check e-mail. Or guest access at an airport might allow passengers to access a local web server that provides flight information.

Figure 13-4 shows the architecture of a WLAN that supports guest access. An autho-rized user (for example, employee) can complete the authentication process over the secure service set identifier (SSID) by producing acceptable credentials during the authentication process. The employee is allowed access to the protected network over the protected VLAN. A visitor does not have valid credentials to authenticate with the protected network. The visitor can, however, connect to the guest SSID, and the access point will connect the visitor with the guest network via the guest VLAN. In this manner, the different VLANs provide sufficient protection against visitors (or hackers) getting access to protected resources.

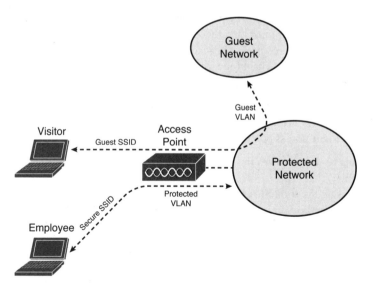

Figure 13-4 *Guest Access Expands the Use of a Wireless LAN to Visitors*

When implementing guest access, consider forcing visitors to accept the terms of use and agree to be liable for any activities or security incidents that result from inappropri-ate use of the network. Be sure to limit guest access to only those resources that can be safely provided to the public. It is also a good idea to log guest activity over the net-work.

Rogue Access Point Detection

A critical security concern is the possibility that rogue wireless access points may be present on the corporate network. A rogue access point is one that the company does not authorize for operation. The trouble is that rogue access points often do not conform to WLAN security policies, and when they don't, they enable an open, insecure interface to the corporate network from outside the physically controlled facility.

Employees have relatively free access to a company's facility, which makes it possible for them to inadvertently (or mischievously) install a rogue access point. An employee, for example, may purchase an access point at an office supply store and install it without coordinating with the IT organization to support wireless printing or access to the network from a conference room. Developers working on wireless applications may connect an access point to the corporate network for testing purposes.

In most cases, employees installing these types of access points do not understand the security issues involved. These scenarios often lead to access points not conforming to adequate security practices. As a result, the corporate network is left wide open for a casual snooper or criminal hacker to attack. To avoid this situation, implement security policies that mandate conformance with effective security controls and coordination with the IT organization before installing access points.

A hacker can install a rogue access point to provide an open, insecure interface to a corporate network. To do this, the hacker must directly connect the access point to an active network port within the facility. This requires the hacker to pass through physical security, which is easy to do in most companies. Thankfully, though, it is unlikely that someone would go to this trouble unless the company has resources worth the trouble and risk.

There is really no effective way to eliminate the possibility of a rogue access point from cropping up on your network. As a result, you must implement processes and mechanisms to constantly monitor for rogue access points as part of your ongoing security assessments.

One method of detecting rogues involves the use of wireless sniffing tools (for example, AirMagnet or NetStumbler) that capture information about access points that are within range of where you are using the tool. This requires you to walk through the facility to capture the data. With this method, you can scan the entire facility, but this can be very time-consuming for larger companies with many buildings or that span a large geographic area. Also, capturing data in this fashion is valid only at the time of capture. Someone could activate a rogue seconds after you turn off the sniffing device, and you will not have any idea that it is present. Still, it is often the most common and least-expensive method of finding rogues. It just takes a lot of time and effort.

If you find an access point that looks suspicious, consider it to be a rogue and then try locating it by using homing techniques. To do this, walk in directions that cause the signal strength of the access point's beacons to increase. It's helpful to use a directional antenna to find the direction to the device. Eventually, you will narrow the location to a particular room, which often means you must do some looking. In some cases, the "rogue" will simply be an active access point that it not connected to the corporate network. This does not cause any security harm. When you find a rogue that actually interfaces to the corporate network, immediately shut it off.

The ideal method of detecting rogue access points is to use a central console attached to the wired side of the network for monitoring. This eliminates the need to walk through the facility. For example, Cisco lightweight access points scan for all Wi-Fi activity and inform the controller of any suspicious access points. If a nonmanaged access point is found, the approximate location is plotted on a floor plan map. This is an effective way to spot rogues, but those that are not within range of a managed access point will go undetected. Also, such systems can be relatively expensive, and they do not work unless you either have or plan to install a WLAN. Rogue access points can be a problem even if the company does not have a WLAN. If funding is limited or you do not have a WLAN, using a wireless sniffing tool to manually search the facility periodically will likely be your best alternative.

RF Shielding

The application of shielding in the form of specialized wall paint substantially attenuates RF signals, which improves wireless security and performance. Indoor WLANs transmit RF signals that often propagate outside the physically controlled area of a building (a security risk), and RF signals originating from outside the facility penetrate the walls and interfere with the operation of the WLAN (resulting in performance reduction). As a result, consider applying a RF shield around the perimeter of the building.

An RF shield highly attenuates RF signals going out of and coming into a building, resulting in significant improvements in security and performance. Serious wireless product developers have been shielding rooms for years to provide a "quiet" chamber (Faraday cage) for testing wireless products in the absence of external RF signals. The implementation of a Faraday cage requires specialized construction of the walls of a room, which makes the approach not feasible for most WLANs. It is rarely cost-effective, obviously, to rebuild the walls to enclose an entire building in a Faraday cage.

The use of special RF shielding paint and window film is a good alternative for protecting larger rooms and even buildings. There are several varieties of paint and window film available, with attenuation ranging from 40 dB to 80 dB for the frequencies that WLANs use. You just paint the walls and apply film to the windows, and this additional attenuation does a good job of shielding the building.

An additional 80 dB of attenuation substantially reduces the possibility that someone outside the shielded area can connect to or even detect the wireless network located inside the facility. For example, a WLAN may exist inside your building with an access point near an exterior wall. In this situation, with no RF shielding applied, the signal levels propagating just outside the building near the access point will likely be around –50 dBm, which is high enough for a client device located outside the building to detect and connect to the wireless network. With most indoor WLANs, this poses a security risk because an unauthorized person sitting in the parking lot can easily "see" the network. This opens the door to various security attacks.

If you apply 80-dB wall paint in this scenario, the signals measured from the same outside location will drop to approximately –130 dBm, which is well below the receive sensitivity of an 802.11/Wi-Fi client device radio. The outcome is that the client device outside the facility will not be able to detect or connect to the network. Therefore, the application of shielding gives your building "skin" that offers a layer of security on top of existing security mechanisms, such as encryption and authentication.

A similar improvement occurs regarding the reduction in RF interference. Imagine, for instance, that a neighbor has a WLAN. The signal level of the neighboring WLAN measured inside your facility may be as high as –40 dBm (assuming that the access point is really close). With 80-dB wall paint applied, the signal levels from the neighboring WLAN will drop to approximately –120 dBm, which is below the receive sensitivity of 802.11/Wi-Fi client devices. Consequently, the shielding eliminates typical RF interference originating from outside the building, which allows your WLAN to operate at higher performance levels. In addition, the attenuation of external signals helps preclude the origination of denial-of-service (DoS) attacks from outside the building.

Consider the following when implementing RF shielding:

- **Define security requirements:** Applying RF shielding paint can be fairly costly, so seriously think about whether you need it. Determine the possible damage that could occur if someone from outside the building detected and connected to your WLAN. Certainly encryption and authentication go a long way in providing sound security, but you would be surprised by how well seasoned hackers can outsmart even the better security mechanisms. You should perform a security assessment with emphasis on penetration testing to determine whether a security risk from outside the building exists.

- **Determine impacts of RF interference:** If your WLAN must provide optimum performance, the reduction of external RF interference through shielding may be valuable. Assess existing RF interference through the use of a spectrum analyzer and identify the magnitude of signals originating from outside the facility. It gets a bit tricky to predict the real impacts of this interference on performance, so you probably need to do some capacity testing, using the actual network with and without the anticipated levels of external interference. Keep in mind that you will likely not benefit from reducing external interference if there are substantial sources of RF interference originating from inside the building (unless you isolate the interference by shielding interior walls). If you cannot bear a DoS attack on the WLAN, shielding may be a good solution regardless of the existing interference.

- **Consider the cost of applying the shielding:** A gallon of RF shielding paint can cost $450, which is about 20 times the cost of standard wall paint. Based on security requirements and the impacts of existing RF interference, you must determine whether the cost of repainting the perimeter of the building (or room, for smaller applications) is worthwhile. As with standard paints, a gallon of RF shielding paint will cover about 600 square feet. Multiple coats may be necessary, however, to achieve maximum attenuation.

- **Apply the shielding:** You can easily apply shielding paint and window film. Paint application is completed with standard rollers and brushes, and cleanup is often done with just water. Window film is generally a peel-and-stick application. Be certain to follow the manufacturer's instructions to ensure proper use.

After implementing the shielding, perform testing inside and outside the building to confirm signal attenuation results. This may also be a good time to rerun penetration tests to ensure that your facility is "bulletproof."

Note To maximize security, consider operating access points at relatively low power and positioned with directional antennas that limit radio waves from propagating outside required coverage areas.

Wireless Security Policies

With a wireless network, you must consider security policies that will protect resources from unauthorized people. Consider the following recommendations:

- **Activate 802.11 encryption:** WEP has weaknesses that make it inadequate for protecting networks containing valuable information. Some good hackers out there can crack into a WEP-protected network using freely available tools. The problem is that 802.11 does not support the dynamic exchange of WEP keys, leaving the same key in use for weeks, months, or even years. For encryption on enterprise networks, aim higher and choose WPA, which is now part of the 802.11i standard. Just keep in mind that WPA (like WEP) only encrypts data traversing the wireless link between the client device and the access point. That may be good enough if your wired network is physically secured from hackers. If not, such as when users are accessing important information from Wi-Fi hotspots, you need more protection.

Note Utilize WPA2 (CCMP) when deploying 802.11n or 802.11ac networks to better support higher performance.

- **Use IPsec-based VPN technology for end-to-end security:** If users need access to sensitive applications from Wi-Fi hotspots, you can use a VPN system to provide sufficient end-to-end encryption and access control. Some companies require VPNs for all wireless client devices, even when they are connecting from inside the secured walls of the enterprise. A "full-throttle" VPN solution such as this offers good security, but it becomes costly and difficult to manage when there are hundreds of wireless users (mainly because of the need for VPN servers). As a result, consider implementing 802.11 encryption when users are operating inside the enterprise and VPNs for the likely fewer users who need access from hotspots.

Note   Some controller-based solutions, such as Cisco, implement encryption between an access point and a controller.

- **Establish the WLAN on a separate VLAN outside the firewall:** A firewall can help keep hackers located on the VLAN associated with the wireless network from having easy access to corporate servers located on different, more secured VLANs (which are not accessible from the wireless network). In this manner, the wireless network is similar to a public network, except you can apply encryption and authentication mechanisms to the wireless users.

- **Ensure that firmware is up-to-date in client cards and access points:** Vendors often implement patches to firmware that fix security issues. On an ongoing basis, make it a habit to check that all wireless devices have the most recent firmware installed.

- **Ensure that only authorized people can reset the access points:** Some access points revert back to factory default settings (that is, no security at all) when someone pushes the reset button. This makes the access point a fragile entry point for hackers to extend their reach into the network. As a result, provide adequate physical security for the access point hardware. For example, do not place an access point within easy reach. Instead, mount access points out of view, such as above ceiling tiles, if possible. Some access points do not have reset buttons and allow you to reset the access point via an RS-232 cable through a console connection. To minimize the risk that someone will reset an access point in this manner, be sure to disable the console port when initially configuring the access point.

- **Disable access points during nonuse periods:** If possible, shut down access points when users do not need them. This limits the window of opportunity for a hacker to use an access point as a weak interface to the rest of the network. To accomplish this, you can simply pull the power plug on each access point; or you can deploy Power over Ethernet (PoE) equipment that provides this feature in a more practical manner via centralized operational support tools.

- **Assign strong passwords to access points:** Do not use default passwords for access points because they are also well known, making it easy for someone to change configuration parameters on the access points. Be sure to alter these passwords periodically. Ensure that passwords are encrypted before being sent over the network.

- **Do not broadcast SSIDs:** You can avoid having user devices automatically sniff the SSID in use by the access point. Most operating systems and monitoring tools automatically sniff the 802.11 beacon frames to obtain the SSID. With SSID broadcasting turned off, the access point does not include the SSID in the beacon frame, making most SSID sniffing tools useless. This is not a foolproof method of hiding the SSID, however, because someone can still monitor 802.11 association frames (which always carry the SSID, even if SSID broadcasting is turned off) with a packet tracer. At least shutting off the broadcast mechanism will limit access and keep casual snoopers off your network.

■ **Reduce propagation of radio waves outside the facility:** Through the use of directional antennas and RF shielding, you can direct the propagation of radio waves inside the facility and reduce "spillage" outside the perimeter. This not only optimizes coverage, it also minimizes the ability for a hacker located outside the controlled portion of the company to eavesdrop on user signal transmissions and interface with the corporate network through an access point. It also reduces the possibility of someone jamming the WLAN from outside the perimeter of the facility. In addition, consider setting access points near the edge of the building to lower transmit power and reduce the range outside the facility. This testing should be part of the wireless site survey.

■ **Control the deployment of WLANs:** Ensure that all employees and organizations within the company coordinate the installation of WLANs with the appropriate information systems group. Forbid the use of unauthorized access points. Mandate the use of approved vendor products for which you have had a chance to verify appropriate security safeguards. Maintain a list of authorized radio network interface card (NIC) and access point MAC addresses that you can use as a basis for identifying rogue access points.

These recommendations give you a basis for forming a solid security policy. When deciding on which techniques to implement, however, be sure to consider actual security needs.

Summary

The security of a WLAN is very important. If security isn't a priority, a hacker may be able to access sensitive information on your network. By implementing encryption and authentication mechanisms, however, it is possible to hide data being sent over the WLAN and control access to the network. Consider using layer 2 encryption, such as TKIP (WPA1) or CCMP (WPA2), to protect data transmissions between client radios and access points. Layer 3 encryption, such as a VPN, can protect the data across the entire network, which is advantageous when users will be connecting to a WLAN from home and public hotspots. To control access, the 802.1X framework offers effective authentication. Choose an EAP method, such as EAP-TLS, to provide the actual authentication. The ongoing monitoring of rogue access points and use of shielding paint can also strengthen the security of your wireless network.

Chapter 14

Test Tools

This chapter will introduce you to:

- Tool Considerations
- Spectrum Analyzers
- Signal Coverage Testers
- Wireless Protocol Analyzers

Test equipment is essential when implementing and supporting a wireless LAN (WLAN). Because radio waves are invisible and somewhat unpredictable, you need the right tools when initially designing a network, performing site surveys, verifying the installation, and troubleshooting the network. This chapter provides an overview of these tools and helps you determine which ones you need.

Tool Considerations

The various tools deploying WLANs have many features, and it is easy to get confused. To help make the right decisions about which tools to use, first think about which part of the deployment you will be involved with. For instance, consider what type of network you will be working with, such as indoor only or outdoor city-wide, because that impacts the features you need in tools. If your network is going to operate mostly outdoors, for example, it is advantageous for the signal coverage test tool to interface with a GPS for location information.

Identify what parts of the deployment you are working on. In some cases, you might be doing everything, such as design, site surveys, troubleshooting, and so forth. Or you might be focusing on only part of the deployment, such as site surveys. Also, consider how often you will be using the tools. You may need tools just to complete a single site survey for a small deployment. In that case, a freely available tool (for example,

NetStumbler) may be best. If you will need the same tools repeatedly for different projects (or a single large deployment), it is probably worth purchasing commercial tools because they have broader functionality and time-saving features.

The following are the types of tools you need for various parts of a deployment:

- **Spectrum analyzer:** Enables you to visualize radio frequency (RF) signals present within the frequency spectrum, which is helpful when performing wireless site surveys or troubleshooting a WLAN

- **Signal coverage tester:** Measures signal strength and noise when performing a wireless site survey, verifying signal coverage after the installation of access points, or troubleshooting WLANs

- **Wireless protocol analyzer:** Displays 802.11 frames being transmitted between client radios and access points, which is helpful when troubleshooting WLANs

Spectrum Analyzers

A spectrum analyzer is a crucial tool for assessing radio signal interference. The display of a spectrum analyzer shows the amplitude (usually in dBm) of all signals over a particular range of frequencies. The displayed amplitudes represent a combination of signals coming from data traffic on wireless networks and interfering signals coming from other sources. A spectrum analyzer allows you to "see" RF signals, which makes it possible to determine the significance of radio signal interference sources. Therefore, a spectrum analyzer is valuable when performing wireless site surveys and troubleshooting poor performance.

Spectrum analyzers come in several different form factors. Berkeley Varitronics sells a spectrum analyzer that comes in dedicated tablet and small handheld form factors. Other spectrum analyzers include software that runs on a laptop and interfaces with a spectrum sensor. For example, Fluke's AirMagnet solution interfaces with a special AirMagnet sensor through a USB port, and MetaGeek uses a sensor that is housed in a USB dongle.

The sections that follow describe some common features found in spectrum analyzers.

Real-Time Fast Fourier Transform

The real-time fast Fourier transform (FFT) shows the power in the RF spectrum based on frequency. To produce the real-time FFT, a spectrum analyzer sweeps a selected frequency band and displays associated signal amplitudes in dBm. Most analyzers sweep the band rather quickly—generally within 1 second. As a result, the real-time FFT is a continuous display of power amplitudes as they occur over time. To analyze real-time FFT data, it is important that a spectrum analyzer have recording capability. With that, you can go back and look at real-time FFT values at different times to see whether there are any trends.

The following are various display modes for a real-time FFT display:

- **Max:** This mode displays a trace of the amplitude of the signal power found during the last sweep of a selected frequency band. In this mode, the signal values corresponding to different parts of the spectrum change as time advances.

- **Max hold:** This mode displays the maximum amplitude reached for particular frequencies. The signal values in this mode do not change unless a signal value is higher than a previous signal value.

- **Average:** This mode displays a statistical average of the signals at various frequencies.

You càn use these modes together to get a general idea of the signals occupying the spectrum of interest. Figure 14-1 shows the output of a spectrum analyzer displaying the max signal trace for the 2.4-GHz band. This represents the signal amplitudes at an instant in time (within the previous second) from 2.4 GHz to 2.5 GHz. In this example, the spectrum is fairly active in the lower and upper portions of the band, with signal amplitudes reaching as high as –50 dBm. The middle part of the band is fairly quiet, with signal amplitudes around –90 dBm. By observing this signal trace, you can see that it appears that significant interference lies in the lower and upper parts of the band; however, keep in mind that this display is an instant in time, and the interfering signals at different frequencies may get weaker (or stronger) as time progresses. By observing the max signal trace over time, you can better assess the situation. If the interfering signals are present the majority of the time, the interference may impact the operation of a WLAN.

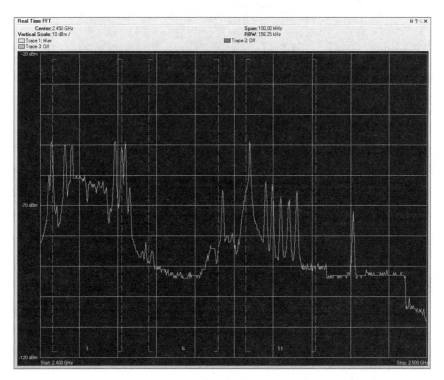

Figure 14-1   *Real-Time FFT Output Trace from AirMagnet Spectrum Analyzer*

FFT Duty Cycle

The real-time FFT display alone has limited usefulness when analyzing potential for radio signal interference because it is difficult to objectively analyze the percentage of time (referred to as the duty cycle) that a signal is present. As the duty cycle increases, the negative impact on the WLAN increases too because the interference is present more often and is keeping wireless client devices and access points from accessing the air medium. Many spectrum analyzers provide an FFT duty cycle plot, which displays the percentage of the time that the measured signal power is at least a specific level above the noise floor. For example, setting the cutoff level at 20 dB will cause the analyzer to display the percentage of time that the signal power is 20 dB or more above the noise floor.

Figure 14-2 shows the output of a spectrum analyzer displaying the FTT duty cycle signal trace for the 2.4-GHz band during the same time that the real-time FFT trace in Figure 14-2 was recorded. This is very useful when assessing the impact of the signals on a WLAN. A FTT duty cycle of less than 10 percent is generally acceptable because the interference is only reducing the overall capacity of the WLAN by less than 10 percent.

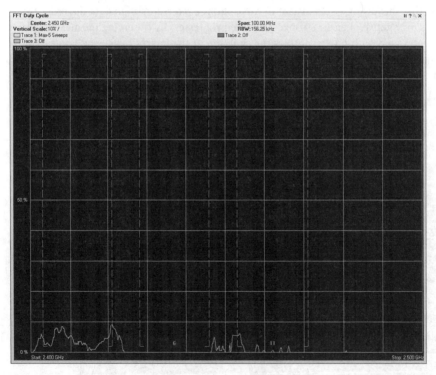

Figure 14-2   *FFT Duty Cycle Output Trace from AirMagnet Spectrum Analyzer*

Swept Spectrogram

Another useful feature of most spectrum analyzers is the swept spectrogram, which displays a combination of the data from the real-time FFT and FFT duty cycle over a period of time. The sweep spectrum allows you to visualize patterns of interference over time. Figure 14-3 shows the output of a spectrum analyzer displaying a sweep spectrogram for the 2.4-GHz band. Labels have been added to Figure 14-3 to indicate the types of interfering sources that were active at various times. The horizontal axis is frequency, and the vertical axis is time. Each horizontal line indicates the signal power level at various frequencies (as recorded over the previous sweep, which is generally one second), using different colors for various signal amplitudes.

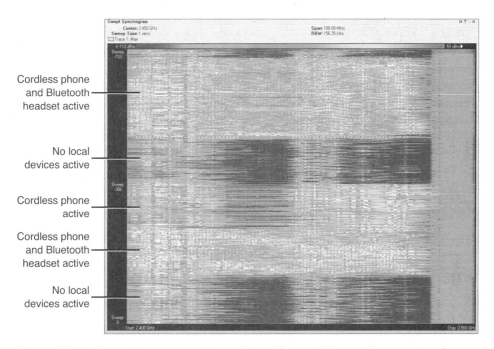

Figure 14-3 *Swept Spectrogram Output Trace from AirMagnet Spectrum Analyzer*

Active Devices

Some spectrum analyzers display a list of active devices that the analyzer has discovered based on spectrum patterns. This is helpful when determining the sources of the interference. The analyzer automatically looks at the recorded traces and filters them based on stored traces for various types of devices, such as cordless phones and Bluetooth devices. In addition, the analyzer generally makes it possible to see details regarding specific interfering sources, such as duty cycle and max amplitudes.

Recording Spectrum Data

Plan on recording and analyzing spectrum images before installing a WLAN so that you can assess the impact on the network. In addition, gather information regarding the RF devices that are currently in use. Tour the facility and physically look for potential interfering sources, such as microwave ovens, cordless phones, and Bluetooth devices. Also, talk to people in the facility and question them on how often they use these devices. All this will help you understand the data recorded by the spectrum analyzer.

Before recording spectrum data, be certain to turn off any active wireless devices that are not part of the normal environment. For example, be certain to power down the test access point you may be using when performing a wireless site survey, the Wi-Fi and Bluetooth radios in your mobile phone, and any other wireless devices, such as Bluetooth headsets that you or others on the test team may be using. That way, these radio signals will stay out of the way when you are analyzing the potential for interference.

Keep in mind, however, that an interfering source must be operating for it to impact network performance. As a result, you should look for active potential sources of interference that are part of the normal environment when recording spectrum data. If there is a microwave oven in a break room, for example, operate the oven while recording the spectrum data and observe the FFT duty cycle. You may find that a microwave oven occupies the entire spectrum (duty cycle of 75 percent, for instance), which could cause a substantial drop in performance of the WLAN in the general vicinity of the microwave oven. In the case of this microwave oven, though, consider how often it is in use during normal operations. It may be acceptable if the microwave oven is used only once or twice a week or if there are not any critical wireless users within 30 feet or so of the microwave oven.

Signal Coverage Testers

A signal coverage tester (sometimes referred to as a site survey tool) includes a signal meter designed to measure the signal strength and signal-to-noise ratio (SNR) of access point beacons and other 802.11 frames and average noise. As with spectrum analyzers, signal coverage testers come in a variety of form factors. AirMagnet Survey and Ekahau Site Survey sell software that runs on a laptop and interfaces with an 802.11 PC Card or USB dongle. Berkeley Varitronics sells a signal coverage tester that is a dedicated handheld device.

Heat Maps

The primary function of a signal coverage tester is to measure signals and generate a heat map, as shown in Figure 14-4. A heat map displays various colors that indicate certain signal strength, SNR, and noise values. A heat map helps you visualize areas that have signal coverage. As discussed in Chapter 15, "Performing a Wireless Site Survey," heat maps are beneficial when performing propagation testing prior to installing a WLAN. In addition, heat maps are useful after installing a WLAN to verify signal coverage.

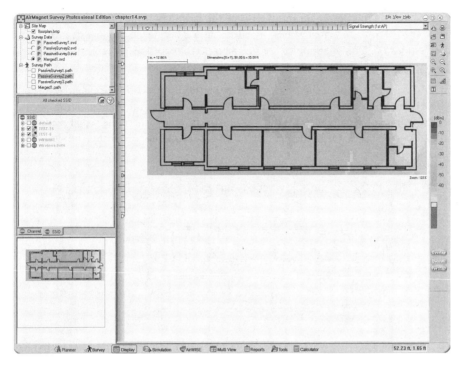

Figure 14-4   *Heat Map Generated by AirMagnet Survey PRO*

When setting up a signal coverage tester, it is possible to import a floor plan of the facility for the tool to use to identify signal values measured at discrete points in the facility. 802.11 signal coverage testers measure signals in both 2.4-GHz and 5-GHz frequency bands. After collecting the data, the coverage tester generates a heat map based on measured values throughout the facility and predicts signal values in areas not tested to produce a heat map over the entire facility. Generally, a few measurements in each room and approximately every 10 feet along hallways are enough data to create a fairly accurate heat map.

Most tools allow you to record signal information and later filter the data. For example, a tool may collect signals from all access points in the area, but you may only want to know the signal coverage applicable to a specific service set identifier (SSID). In addition, most tools allow configuration of the heat map to display signal strength or SNR, so that it is possible to interpret the signal coverage in different ways. A calibration function is also usually available that enables you to put limits on the maximum signal strength or SNR that represents signal coverage. This is an important feature for calibrating the displayed data to compensate for various factors, as explained in Chapter 15.

Positioning

To generate a heat map, the tool must know the position (relative to the floor plan) where the signal readings are taken. This is normally done using a manual "point-and-click" method, where you point the mouse pointer on your laptop to the position where you are located on the floor plan and then click the mouse button. This causes the coverage tester to record the signal values (signal strength, noise level, and so on) at that applicable position. You continue to use this method to record measurements throughout the facility, and the site survey tool records the values.

Figure 14-5 shows the use of the point-and-click method for recording signal data. The little man on the right in one of the rooms in the floor plan indicates the position of the mouse pointer, which represents the location in the room where the signal reading/recording is being taken. Once the mouse button is clicked, the tool stores the signal data at that specific point.

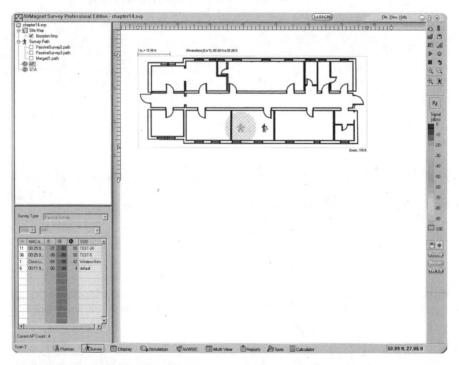

Figure 14-5 *Point-and-Click Positioning in AirMagnet Survey PRO*

When testing outdoors, positioning is much easier because the coverage tester can generally receive position information from a GPS. In this case, the tool automatically records signal information periodically and associates the data with the position information from the GPS that corresponds with the correct position on a map. For example, AirMagnet Survey PRO interfaces with a GPS and Microsoft MapPoint for position and mapping functions. With GPS position information, you can easily walk or drive through the area being tested without needing to manually identify position.

Passive Versus Active Modes

Some coverage testers operate passively and measure/record the signal strength of beacons and noise floor levels to determine the SNR. In passive mode, such a tool does not connect to an access point or transmit any data. The coverage tester simply scans all selected RF channels and channel widths in the 2.4-GHz and 5-GHz bands and listens for beacons.

In passive mode, coverage testers have a scan time value that by default is long enough to receive at least a single beacon (based on a default beacon interval of 100 milliseconds) from the access points on each channel. This causes the scanning of all channels to take several seconds. As a result, be sure to take readings with the point-and-click method after standing still for a few seconds at the appropriate location.

To minimize the overall scan time, consider configuring the coverage tester to scan on the channels that you are interested in recording. For example, when performing propagation testing with a test access point while performing a wireless site survey, you may have only two applicable RF channels (one for the 2.4-GHz band and one for the 5-GHz band). In this case, you could limit the scanning to only the two channels.

Note Some coverage testers incorporate multiple wireless adapters and can scan multiple channels at the same time, which reduces scan times.

Some coverage testers include an active mode as an alternative way of collecting coverage data. In active mode, the tester associates with and communicates with an access point that you designate. This allows the tester to generate actual performance results in addition to signal strength and SNR values. Most testers in active mode display association data rates, throughput, and packet retry rates. This data, however, might not be very accurate if other loads on the network (that is, traffic from other devices) are not taken into account.

Simulation

Some coverage testers provide simulation functions where it is possible to change the configuration of the WLAN that you have tested to see how the changes might impact coverage. For example, you can use AirMagnet Survey PRO to collect signal data using a test access point in a facility and then use the simulation feature to change transmit power, antenna gain, and other parameters that impact signal coverage. This allows you to easily visualize these changes, which can help when designing a network.

Free Signal Coverage Tester: NetStumbler

NetStumbler is a freely available signal coverage tester. It is software that runs on a laptop and interfaces with an 802.11 PC card. As a signal coverage tester, NetStumbler has limited functionality (for example, it does not generate heat maps), but it does include a signal meter that identifies various signal values. Figure 14-6 shows a screenshot of NetStumbler's main screen. Here you can see the signal values, including signal, noise, and SNR, and other details for each access point. It is possible to record these values for later viewing.

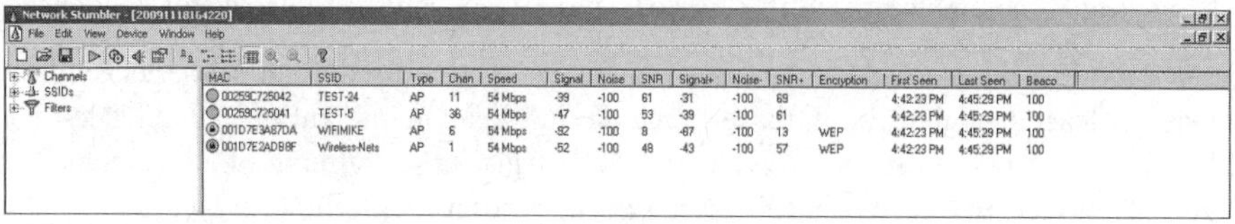

MAC	SSID	Type	Chan	Speed	Signal	Noise	SNR	Signal+	Noise-	SNR+	Encryption	First Seen	Last Seen	Beaco
00259C725042	TEST-24	AP	11	54 Mbps	-99	-100	61	-31	-100	69		4:42:23 PM	4:45:29 PM	100
00259C725041	TEST-5	AP	36	54 Mbps	-47	-100	53	-39	-100	61		4:42:23 PM	4:45:28 PM	100
001D7E3A670A	WIFIMIKE	AP	6	54 Mbps	-92	-100	8	-67	-100	13	WEP	4:42:23 PM	4:45:29 PM	100
001D7E3AD88F	Wireless-Nets	AP	1	54 Mbps	-52	-100	48	-43	-100	57	WEP	4:42:23 PM	4:45:29 PM	100

Figure 14-6 *Main Screen of NetStumbler*

Note   You can download the freely available NetStumbler from www.netstumbler.com.

NetStumbler is easy to set up on a laptop. Just download the software, install it on a laptop, and select your specific 802.11 card from the Device pull-down menu. NetStumbler works with many different vendor radio cards, but check the NetStumbler website for cards that are specifically supported and any limitations that might apply.

Wireless Protocol Analyzers

A wireless protocol analyzer captures airborne 802.11 signals and decodes the applicable frames. This allows you to analyze the structure and sequencing of 802.11 frames. For example, Figure 14-7 shows the output of a protocol analyzer. The 802.11 frames are in sequential time order, and for each frame, there is information regarding the frame, such as capture time, source/destination, basic SSID (BSSID), and a description. When you select a frame, such as the beacon frame (frame 603) in Figure 14-7, the analyzer displays details about the frame. The details include all applicable 802.11 attributes, such as the frame control field values and the contents of the frame body. The majority of wireless protocol analyzers are software that runs on a laptop and interfaces with an 802.11 PC Card or USB dongle.

When troubleshooting a WLAN, use a wireless protocol analyzer to capture and analyze the packets to see whether you can isolate the root cause of the problem. A wireless 802.1X client device on the wireless network, for example, may appear connected to the network, but the user may not be able to access network resources. After reviewing the packet trace, you may see (by observing the VLAN tagging in the appropriate packets) that the client device is actually connected to the guest network instead of the corporate network. This would point to a problem with the client's 802.1X supplicant.

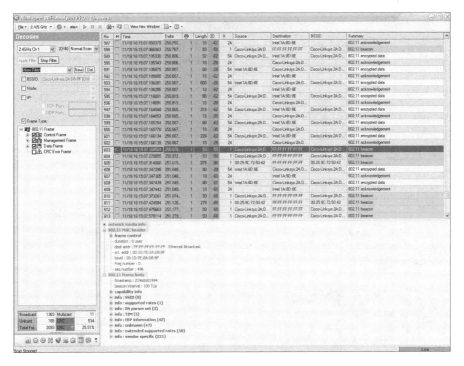

Figure 14-7 *Packet Capture and Decode Screen in AirMagnet WiFi Analyzer PRO*

Wireless packet analysis requires a solid understanding of the 802.11 standard and other protocols. Also, some vendors add proprietary functions that may cause confusion when reviewing the flow of packets. Even though this might make life difficult when trouble-shooting, concentrate on studying the packet traces captured by a protocol analyzer to learn the details of how wireless networks work.

Filtering Frames

To determine the operation of a WLAN relevant to what you are troubleshooting, it is often necessary to apply filters that limit the types of frames to the ones you are interested in seeing. Otherwise, you may be trying to find a few frames amid hundreds or thousands of frames. For example, if you are troubleshooting a client device radio connecting to the network, you should set a filter to record only frames being transmit-ted on the applicable RF channel and exclude beacons. That keeps the traffic to a mini-mum, and you can find the associated connectivity frames (such as 802.11 association and authentication frames) more easily. If you want to see the contents of 802.11 data frames (which may include details you need to see, such as higher-layer protocol fields), be sure to turn off encryption or configure the analyzer with the corresponding encryp-tion key.

Recording Traces

You need to run a protocol analyzer during the time needed to capture the 802.11 frames you are interested in seeing, and then you can record the trace for later viewing. This allows you to rerun the trace and step through it at your leisure or after capturing some other traces that might apply to the troubleshooting.

Be sure that recording the packet traces does not violate any privacy regulations, however, especially in hospitals where HIPAA (Health Insurance Portability and Accountability Act) rules apply.

Free Protocol Analyzer: WireShark

WireShark is freely available software that interfaces with an 802.11 client card and passively sniffs 802.11 packets being transmitted within a WLAN. Figure 14-8 shows the WireShark capture screen. Like AirMagnet Analyzer PRO, WireShark displays each 802.11 frame in time sequence and shows the contents of frames.

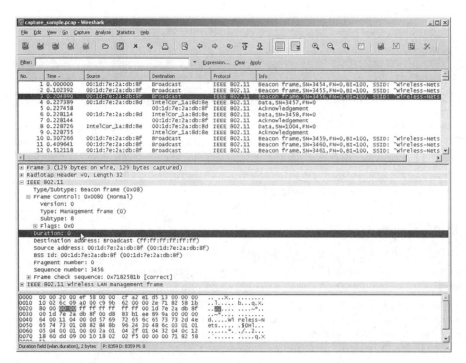

Figure 14-8 *Packet Capture and Decode Screen in WireShark*

Note   You can download the freely available WireShark from www.wireshark.org.

WireShark software is easy to install, but a problem you will likely run into is that WireShark may not display any packets after starting a capture using your existing 802.11 client card, especially if running in Windows. The issue is that many of the 802.11 cards do not support promiscuous mode. In this case, you can try turning off promiscuous mode (from inside WireShark), but you will see only (at best) packets being sent to and from the computer running WireShark.

If you have trouble getting WireShark to work with existing client cards, consider purchasing an AirPcap, which is a USB-based 802.11 radio designed to work effectively with WireShark. It comes with drivers tuned to WireShark and operates very well. An external antenna is also included with AirPcap, which increases the listening capability of the tool.

Before capturing packets, configure WireShark to interface with an 802.11 client device; otherwise, you will get a "No capture interface selected!" alert when starting a packet capture. To select an interface, click the Capture menu, choose Options, and select the appropriate interface.

Be certain to monitor the correct RF channel. For example, if the wireless network is set to Channel 1 for the traffic you are interested in, configure WireShark to monitor Channel 1. To do this, click the Capture menu, choose Options, and click Wireless Settings. The menu Advanced Wireless Settings will appear, and in it you can change the channel.

Consider filtering the packet capture to reduce clutter when analyzing packet traces. For example, if you are troubleshooting a particular client device connecting to the network, you can set a filter that excludes all packets except those associated with the IP address (or MAC address) of the client you are troubleshooting. To set a filter, click the Capture menu, choose Options, and click WireShark. Capture Filter will appear, and in it you can set various filters.

To start the packet capturing process, click the Capture menu and choose Start. WireShark will continue capturing and displaying packets until the capture buffer fills up. The buffer is 1 MB by default. This size is generally good enough, but to change it, click the Capture menu, choose Options, and adjust the Buffer Size value accordingly.

When you are done capturing packets, click the Capture menu and choose Stop. Alternatively, you can set the capture run length (in packets or minutes), and the capture will automatically stop when that length has been met. You will be prompted to save the capture for later viewing.

The packet capture will display the details of each packet as it was transmitted over the WLAN. For example, in Figure 14-8, the top panel of the window identifies each packet's source and destination nodes, protocol implemented, and information about each packet.

You can select a specific packet to display more details. The one selected in Figure 14-8, packet 3, is an 802.11 beacon frame. The middle panel displays information about this packet, and you can choose a specific field of the packet (such as the Duration field shown in the figure), and the contents of that field are displayed in hex and ASCII format in the bottom panel. As a result, you are able to analyze the flow and view each field (including data field payloads) of all packets.

WireShark offers tools that can help diagnose problems. After capturing packets, click the Analyze menu and choose Options. A window may indicate errors, which you can investigate to find the problem. Similarly, under the Statistics menu, there are several statistical functions that may help pinpoint the problem.

For more information about WireShark, see the help function inside WireShark or review the WireShark User Guide.

Summary

When deploying a WLAN, you need a set of tools. A spectrum analyzer allows you to visualize the spectrum to spot sources of potential radio signal interference. Several spectrum analyzer plots, such as real-time FFT, FFT duty cycle, and sweep spectrogram, provide valuable information that serves as the basis for analyzing the spectrum. A signal coverage tester includes a signal meter that measures signal strength and noise and displays heat maps indicating signal coverage throughout a facility. This signal information is useful when performing a wireless site survey or troubleshooting the network. A wireless protocol analyzer displays details of the actual 802.11 frames that are sent between client stations and access points, and this information is beneficial when troubleshooting the network.

Chapter 15

Performing a Wireless Site Survey

This chapter will introduce you to:

- Wireless Site Survey Considerations

- Reviewing Requirements

- Selecting Site Survey Tools

- Obtaining Floor Diagrams

- Inspecting the Facility

- Assessing the Existing Network Infrastructure

- Identifying Potential Radio Signal Interference

- Defining Signal Values for Acceptable Signal Coverage

- Identifying Optimum Access Point Antenna Installation Locations

- Writing an RF Site Survey Report

A wireless site survey is critical when designing a wireless LAN (WLAN) because it determines the optimum locations for access point antennas. A previous site survey completed for an 802.11a/g network will generally not suffice for an 802.11n/ac network. The coverage patterns of 802.11ac radios, for instance, can be very different than for 802.11a. 802.11n and 802.11ac use multiple-input multiple-output (MIMO) and do a better job of handling multipath propagation, which results in better coverage in some parts of a facility; however, the use of 5-GHz frequencies may reduce range in some areas. As this chapter explains, you should complete a thorough wireless site survey based on 802.11n (2.4-GHz) and 802.11ac technology to ensure that you design the network correctly.

Wireless Site Survey Considerations

Not all facilities need to perform a wireless site survey. For example, there is little need to perform a wireless site survey for a WLAN that covers a small (150-square-foot) room with only one or two users. In this case, a single access point will provide more than enough signal coverage. For most facilities, however, there is considerable need for performing a wireless site survey. Business office buildings, hospitals, airports, and manufacturing plants have multiple walls and floors over expansive areas. Such facilities require multiple access points to cover the entire area, which can be determined accurately only after performing a wireless site survey. Without a survey, users often end up with inadequate coverage and suffer from low performance in some areas.

Be certain to consider the facility when planning a site survey. The amount of time needed to perform a site survey varies greatly by the size and complexity of the facility. A large office building with 22 floors may require only a few days to complete the survey if each floor has a similar layout and construction. A complex hospital with the same floor area as the 22-story office building, though, might require several weeks to complete the survey, if most floors and wings of the hospital have different layouts and construction.

The following are elements that you should consider when performing a wireless site survey:

- **Review requirements:** Before completing a wireless site survey, it is crucial to have a good understanding of the requirements, such as client device types and signal coverage areas.

- **Select tools:** You need to use various tools, such as a spectrum analyzer, signal meter, and test access point, to perform radio signal interference and propagation testing.

- **Obtain floor diagrams:** Floor diagrams are necessary for identifying the coverage areas, test results, and access point installation locations.

- **Inspect the facility:** Walk through the facility to learn about possible mounting locations for access points (for example, above ceiling tiles or on beams) and any significant obstacles. This will make the testing go much more smoothly.

- **Assess the existing network infrastructure:** Inspect the existing communications rooms, switches, and WAN to determine available capacity to support the WLAN.

- **Identify potential radio signal interference:** Scan all applicable frequency bands to see if there are any sources of radio signal interference that might impact the operation of the WLAN.

- **Define signal values for acceptable signal coverage:** This requires analysis of the target client devices and determination of the minimum received signal strength and signal-to-noise ratio (SNR).

- **Identify optimum access point antenna installation locations:** Perform propagation testing to understand the behavior of radio signals throughout the facility, based on the minimum received signal strength and SNR that constitutes signal coverage. Use the results of this testing to identify antenna installation locations.

- **Write an RF site survey report:** The wireless site survey generates a great deal of information. Therefore, document the results of the wireless site survey for later reference.

The following sections in this chapter cover these elements in more detail.

Note   Before performing a wireless site survey, review Chapter 11, "Range, Performance, and Roaming Considerations," and Chapter 12, "Radio Frequency Considerations."

Reviewing Requirements

Focus on requirements that impact signal coverage. For example, the maximum range between a client device and the access point decreases as the data rate and resulting performance increase. Therefore, you need to know the target data rates (and throughput) to correctly interpret survey results. Also, client devices may have relatively low transmit power, which must be considered when using most site survey tools.

The various types of requirements impact the wireless site survey in different ways:

- **Applications:** The types of applications drives the performance that users will need, which provides the basis for the minimum signal values that you need to use when defining signal coverage. Be certain to note whether the WLAN will need to support data, voice, and location-based applications because this impacts how you perform the survey and interpret the results.

- **Client devices:** The radios in the client devices have a significant impact on the range of the WLAN. It is important to know the radio receiver sensitivity, operating frequencies, and antenna type of each client radio to determine the minimum signal values for signal coverage.

- **Signal coverage areas:** To determine the optimum placement of antennas, you must know where signal coverage is needed throughout the facility. Carefully assess needs for coverage in all areas. Do not forget to determine whether you need coverage in places like elevators, stairwells, and restrooms.

- **Utilization:** The utilization of the WLAN may indicate the need for more than one access point in common areas. For example, a conference room may need to support 10 users simultaneously using wireless IP phones. Therefore, be certain to identify areas where high utilization is needed by determining the number of devices that need to use each application.

- **Mobility:** A high degree of mobility demands access points positioned in a manner that ensures overlapping signal coverage. Therefore, identify where users need to roam throughout various parts of the facility.

- **Security:** Security mechanisms do not significantly impact signal coverage or performance of the network, at least in regard to performing a wireless site survey. Some security requirements, though, may state that it is necessary to avoid signal coverage in some areas, such as outside the facility. In this case, you need to know where to minimize signal coverage to determine the best installation locations for antennas.

- **Scalability:** You must know how the organization plans to grow the use of the network over time to make wise decisions about where to install access points. For example, at first there may only be a need to support fairly low-performance applications, and placement of 2.4-GHz access points may suffice. If the organization will likely use higher-end applications such as voice in the future, placement of the access points may need to be based on using the 5-GHz spectrum (which generally has shorter range than the 2.4-GHz spectrum).

- **Environment:** The construction and layout of the facility can greatly impact the propagation of radio waves. Therefore, always define environmental requirements before getting started with the wireless site survey. This will provide valuable insight when determining optimum placement of access points.

- **Aesthetics:** In some cases, the organization may require concealment of the WLAN components, such as access points and antennas. You must be aware of this during the site survey to make appropriate decisions about mounting the components.

> **Note**   For more details on determining requirements for a WLAN, see Chapter 9, "Defining Requirements for a Wireless LAN."

Selecting Site Survey Tools

To perform a wireless site survey, you need the following tools:

- **Test access point:** This access point should conform to the 802.11n (2.4-GHz) and 802.11ac standards. While performing active propagation testing, you will be moving this access point to different parts of the facility to obtain a thorough understanding of the propagation of radio signals throughout the facility. The access point does not need to connect to the wired network. It merely needs to transmit 802.11 beacons.

- **Test antenna:** This antenna connects to the test access point. Choose an antenna type that best fits the environment. In most cases, use a standard omnidirectional antenna for indoor facilities (3 dB or 6 dB). If there are requirements to avoid signal coverage in certain areas, you may need to use directional antennas that are aimed away from the applicable avoidance area. Experiment with different antenna types that result in the antenna/access point density that either meets or exceeds capacity requirements.

Note   When testing, you should elevate the antennas close to where you plan to install the access point. Because the antennas are often connected directly to (or integrated within) the access point, you must also elevate the access point. Consider using a tripod with a telescoping pole that can raise the antenna/access point to approximately 10 feet, which is generally high enough for most facilities. To power the access point, you can use a battery with a PoE output. Be sure that the tripod is stable after raising the access point; attaching the battery to the base of the tripod helps. For higher access point mounting/testing heights, you may need to utilize a lift truck to raise the antenna/access point (and battery) if ceilings are higher than 10 feet and there's a need to mount the access points higher. This is likely the case in warehouses and outdoor areas.

■ **Signal meter:** This is usually part of general wireless site survey tools and measures the signal strength and SNR of the test access point's beacons when performing propagation testing. It should be capable of displaying the dBm value of the signal or provide a numeric value that you can covert to dBm (generally through a table provided by the tool vendor). NetStumbler is an example of freely available signal meter software that interfaces to an 802.11 radio, but most commercial site survey tools include a signal meter in addition to methods of recording signal values on imported floor plans. Be aware that the signal indicator in Microsoft Windows is not sufficient for measuring the signal strength because it does not identify the actual dBm value, which is needed to determine whether the signal strength meets or exceeds the minimal signal level that satisfies signal coverage requirements.

■ **Spectrum analyzer:** This tool measures and analyzes all signals occupying the radio spectrum that the WLAN will use. You need to use this tool to assess the potential for radio signal inference that may impact the operation of the WLAN.

■ **Miscellaneous tools.** To make an access point easy to move about the facility, you can mount it on a telescopic pole attached to a cart with a battery and DC/AC converter. Otherwise, you need to haul around an extension cord and spend time looking for places to plug in for power.

Note   For more details on test tools, see Chapter 14, "Test Tools."

Obtaining Floor Diagrams

Floor diagrams of the buildings are crucial when performing a wireless site survey during the testing and when identifying the optimum locations for antennas. It is a good idea to request these diagrams in advance and have them when planning the survey. The diagrams will give you an idea of the magnitude of the project. Sometimes it might take a while to obtain the diagrams because the organization may need to get them from contractors or subcontractors who constructed the buildings.

Most building diagrams are maintained in AutoCAD, but site survey tools usually cannot accept that format. Therefore, ask for the diagrams in a form that your site survey tool accepts. If the image format diagrams do not work in your tool, you should be able to use a screenshot tool, such as Snagit, to covert the images. If professional building diagrams are not available, you may be able to obtain approximate floor plans from administrative staff, who often create the floor plans using graphics tools, such as Microsoft PowerPoint, when creating fire escape plans, which are often present on hallway walls. If electronic versions of the fire escape diagrams are not available, you should be able to use a digital camera to photograph fire escape diagrams and use them for the floor plan included within the site survey tool.

Inspecting the Facility

The goal of a visual inspection of a facility is to identify elements needed and the optimum installation locations for access point antennas. Walk through the facility to verify the accuracy of the facility diagrams. In addition, note any potential attenuation barriers that may affect the propagation of radio frequency (RF) signals. For example, identify obstacles to radio signals that floor plans generally do not show, such as metal racks and partitions. Note possible locations for mounting access points and antennas, such as above ceiling tiles or on pillars, and identify the locations of elevators and stairwells.

On the floor plans, indicate all areas where signal coverage is needed, such as offices, hallways, stairwells, utility rooms, bathrooms, break rooms, patios, parking garages, and elevators. Identifying where users will not need wireless coverage is also important to avoid wasting time testing unnecessary areas. Keep in mind that you can decrease the number of access points and reduce equipment costs if you can limit the roaming areas.

Also, start getting an idea of where it is possible to mount the access points. Make notes about the ceiling to indicate whether it has removable tiles or open access to pipes and ventilation ducts. The easiest places to mount access points are above ceiling tiles because there is a common rigid metal structure present to mount the access points. Access point vendors have mounting kits for attaching access points to these structures.

Assessing the Existing Network Infrastructure

Most organizations have an existing wired network infrastructure that can support the interconnection of access points. Therefore, be certain to carefully assess the existing wired infrastructure and identify what additions and improvements are needed to upgrade the infrastructure to support an 802.11n and 802.11ac WLAN.

Communications Rooms

Communications rooms are needed to install Ethernet switches and terminate WAN connections. These rooms range from full-sized air-conditioned communications centers to small utility room closets. In some cases, especially in older buildings where there are limited rooms for networking equipment, organizations often install equipment boxes for containing switches. In all cases, be certain to lock all communications rooms or boxes.

Visit the communications rooms and identify their locations on building floor plan diagrams. Ideally, there should be a communications room on each floor of the facility to stay within the 100-meter Cat 5 cable length limitations. It might be most feasible, though, to share a communications room located on a different floor, particularly for smaller buildings and cases where the number of access points on a particular floor is limited and cable runs will not exceed 100 meters.

Switches and Power over Ethernet

While visiting the communications rooms, note the vendor and model of each switch. Also identify available switch ports and Power over Ethernet (PoE) interfaces for each floor. Do not take it for granted that all available ports are available for use with the WLAN, however. Be sure to check with the appropriate representative from the IT group to see if there are any plans for any of the available ports.

Keep in mind that preferably the switch ports should be rated at 1 Gbps and the PoE should comply with the higher-power 802.3at PoE standard. This affords maximum 802.11n and 802.11ac performance. It may be possible to get by with 100-Mbps switch ports and legacy PoE with some access point models (with lower performance), but you should upgrade to 1 Gbps and 802.3at as soon as possible.

WAN

A large organization may have a WAN for connecting multiple buildings. In most such cases, the WAN uses optical fiber to support higher-speed communications. Determine the structure, capacity, and termination points for the WAN. In addition, identify any unused fiber that can be allocated to handling WLAN traffic between buildings. Typically, the existing WAN is sufficient to handle the additional traffic generated by a WLAN, but you may need to activate or install additional fiber, depending on the situation. A common example of this is when needing to connect an access point in a smaller building located next to a main facility. In this case, it is probably most feasible to connect the access point to a switch in the main complex via a fiber cable and use fiber-optic transceivers, which can greatly exceed the 100-meter distance limitation of Cat 5 cable.

Identifying Potential Radio Signal Interference

The presence of radio signal interference can impact the signal coverage of a WLAN. Therefore, carefully assess all existing RF devices and their likelihood of impacting the operation of the WLAN. Prepare an inventory of the frequencies of all RF devices, such as cordless phones and microwave ovens, and identify areas where they are typically in use. In addition, perform testing to determine the magnitude of the potential interference. Use a spectrum analyzer configured to record signals in the following frequencies to fully assess the spectrum in which the WLAN will operate:

- 2.400 GHz to 2.500 GHz

- 5.150 GHz to 5.350 GHz

- 5.470 GHz to 5.725 GHz

- 5.725 GHz to 5.850 GHz

Be sure to run all spectrum tests with other test equipment—such as the test access point used for propagation testing—turned off. From the spectrum analyzer, note the average noise (noise floor) and any significant devices and associated frequencies that have high duty cycle values.

As the next section explains, the noise floor impacts the signal levels needed to provide acceptable signal coverage. Most wireless site survey tools display the noise floor value either in numeric or graphical form. Figure 15-1, for example, includes a screenshot from AirMagnet Spectrum Analyzer that indicates the noise floor with a horizontal line across the spectrum graph. In this example, the noise floor is approximately –93 dBm. This graph also indicates the noise power of the sources of interference found by the analyzer (in this case, cordless phones).

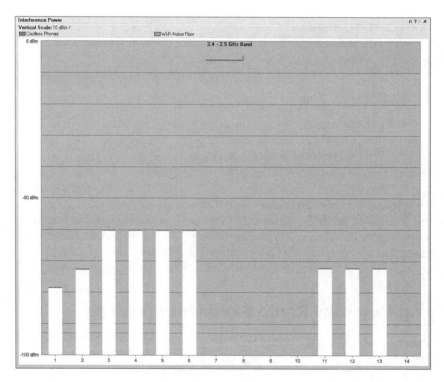

Figure 15-1 *Example of Noise Floor and Interference Power Recorded by AirMagnet Spectrum Analyzer*

The signal amplitude of the interference shown in the analyzer output in Figure 15-1 is as high as −60 dBm. This is relatively high, but the actual impact on the operation of the WLAN depends on the channel utilization of the interference. This is the percentage of time that the interference is present in the spectrum (sometimes called the "duty cycle"). As the channel utilization of the interfering devices increases, the available capacity of the WLAN decreases. This is only applicable, though, if the WLAN is configured to use the same part of the radio spectrum (and with the same area) where the existing interfering devices are operating. Therefore, it is best to use an analyzer to identify the channel utilization of the interference sources. Figure 15-2 shows a channel utilization chart produced by AirMagnet Spectrum Analyzer that was recorded in the same area as the chart in Figure 15-1. In this case, the channel utilization of the sources of interference (cordless phones) is approximately 2 percent, which is not significant. This means that 98 percent of the capacity of the spectrum is available for the WLAN. Therefore, even though relatively high interfering signals were found, there will likely be no noticeable impact on the operation of the WLAN.

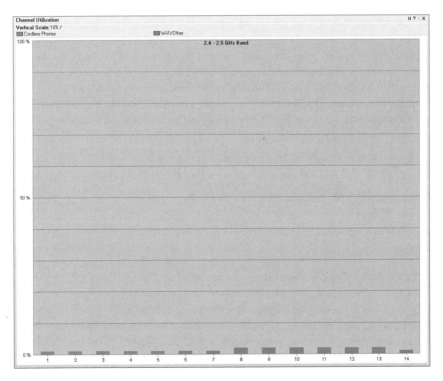

Figure 15-2 *Example of Channel Utilization Recorded by AirMagnet Spectrum Analyzer*

Note For more details on radio signal interference, see Chapter 4, "Wireless LAN Implications."

Defining Signal Values for Acceptable Signal Coverage

Signal coverage is acceptable if it enables client devices located anywhere in the defined coverage area to have two-way communication with an access point at or above required performance levels. To do this, you must ensure that the access point antennas are installed at locations that ensure a minimum received signal strength and SNR. Because the communication is two way, this applies to the received signal strength and SNR at the client radio and the access point.

Minimum Received Signal Strength

All 802.11 radios require that the received signal have a minimum received signal strength (often called receiver sensitivity). An 802.11 radio needs this minimum level to demodulate the signal. Therefore, the signal must be at or above the minimum receiver sensitivity to be considered a covered area. Bear in mind that receiver sensitivity varies depending on the data rate and specific vendor implementation of the radio. See the data sheets of the client radios you plan to deploy for the relevant receiver sensitivity values. Choose the minimum received signal strength based on the minimum data rates that you want to support to meet performance requirements. For example, requirements might specify 130-Mbps data rates. By looking at the data sheet for a specific access point or client radio, you might find that a minimum –70 dBm signal strength is required to support 130-Mbps data rates using 20-MHz channels in the 2.4-GHz band.

> **Note**   Consider guidelines offered by the vendor of the client devices you're planning to deploy for minimum signal coverage requirements. For example, a wireless IP phone will likely require a minimum RSSI of –67 dBm.

Minimum SNR

The minimum received signal strength alone is not sufficient for defining signal coverage. To facilitate acceptable signal coverage, it is important that the received signal also be above the noise floor by a specific margin. This margin is defined as SNR (in dB), which is the signal level (in dBm) minus the noise level (in dBm). The minimum SNR that you should use for defining signal coverage depends on the variability of the noise and the signal in the building where you are deploying the WLAN. Applications that are more sensitive to these fluctuations, such as wireless IP phones, require a higher SNR. In practice, the minimum SNR needed for supporting most applications is 15 dB to 25 dB. For example, Cisco recommends at least 25 dB for supporting wireless IP phones.

Keep in mind that an acceptable SNR does not necessarily mean that signal coverage is acceptable. There are cases, for example, where the noise floor may be –100 dBm, and the SNR is 15 dB, which results in a signal level of –85 dBm. This may be lower than the receiver sensitivity needed to support the desired data rate, which means that signal coverage is not acceptable at the applicable location. Just be sure that both signal strength and SNR are above their respective minimum values before deeming an area as having acceptable signal coverage.

Uplink Versus Downlink Signal Values

In a WLAN, communication takes place in both directions between the client radio and the access point as the user browses the Internet, sends and receives e-mail, or talks to someone on a wireless IP phone. This communication includes an uplink path from the client to the access point and a downlink path from the access point to the client. For example, when a user opens a browser, the client device sends a URL page request through the uplink path to the access point. Then the web page is sent through the access point to the client over the downlink path.

Access points periodically send beacon frames, which travel on the downlink path from the access point to the client devices. Most wireless site survey tools receive these beacons and display the signal strength and SNR associated with the beacon frames received at the test tool (see Figure 15-3). Do not consider these measured values to accurately represent signal coverage, however. The signal levels are only in relation to the 802.11 beacons on the downlink path from the access point to the client device. The tool does not take into consideration the uplink signals transmitted by the client radios and received at the access point. Remember that the minimum received signal strength and SNR apply to both the client radio and the access point.

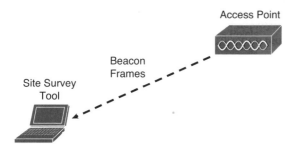

Figure 15-3 *Site Survey Tools Measure Only One Direction of the Communications Path*

Most access points have a significantly higher effective isotropic radiated power (EIRP), which is the transmit power plus antenna gain, than wireless clients. Figure 15-4 illustrates this point. Access points, for example, are typically set to their highest transmit power. This is done to seemingly maximize the signal propagation and coverage from each access point to minimize the number and costs of access points. Client radios, however, tend to have a much lower EIRP because of smaller, lower-gain antennas and the desire to conserver battery power. In addition, it's generally desirable to set the transmit power of the client devices to a relatively low transmit power to maximize battery life. In this situation, the downlink signal strength will be relatively high, and the uplink signals will be much weaker. This means that the effective range between the access point and the client device is governed by the uplink signal strength, not the downlink.

Therefore, the use of only access point beacons (that is, downlink signals) for determining coverage will lead to much better coverage than what will actually be available when the clients interact with the access point. The downlink communications will be fine, but weaker uplink signals will limit the effective range and likely disrupt communications when client devices move into areas where uplink signal strength is not good enough to support communications.

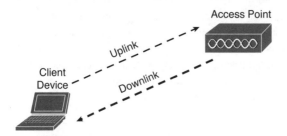

Figure 15-4   *The Uplink Signals Are Typically Weaker Than the Downlink Signals*

To avoid falling into this trap, perform the following steps:

Step 1.   Identify the client device that has the lowest EIRP. The goal is to find the weakest client because it could impact the maximum range between the client device and the access point. Do this by looking at the specifications (transmit power and antenna gain) for the device. Be certain to take into account the transmit power that you will eventually be setting in the user devices. For example, you may have two client devices, with Client Radio A set to transmit power of 32 mW (15 dBm) and having antenna gain of 3 dB and Client Radio B set to transmit power of 16 mW (12 dBm) and having antenna gain of 1.2 dB. Client Radio A has an EIRP of 18 dBm, and Client Radio B has an EIRP of 13.2 dBm. Therefore, Client Radio B would be the device with the lowest EIRP. Keep in mind that it might be possible to turn the transmit power up higher or use a higher-gain antenna, which will help matters.

Step 2.   Determine whether to base signal coverage on uplink or downlink signals. Compare the EIRP of the access point and the client device that has the lowest EIRP. See the access point data sheet for details on the access point's EIRP. Take into account the access point's transmit power setting and the antenna that will be used during the propagation testing and assessment of signal coverage. If the EIRP values of the access point and client device with the lowest EIRP are the same, you can base signal strength on the uplink or the downlink. If the EIRP of the access point is higher than the EIRP of the weakest client device, base signal coverage on the uplink. In the opposite case, base signal coverage on the downlink. In most cases, you will find that the access point EIRP is higher than the client device EIRP, which means that usually the signal coverage must be based on the uplink.

Step 3. Apply a calibration factor, if needed, to the test tool. This step is necessary only if you must base the signal coverage on the uplink—that is, if the EIRP of the client radio is less than the EIRP of the access point (which is most often the case). Calculate the calibration factor by subtracting the client device EIRP from the access point EIRP. If the client device EIRP is 15 dBm and the access point EIRP is 23 dBm, for example, the resulting calibration factor is 8 dBm (23 dBm – 15 dBm). Add the calibration factor to the minimum received signal strength and SNR that you determined for defining acceptable signal coverage. You need to use the calibrated values when interpreting signal coverage in test tools that base signal strength indications on received beacons. For example, if the calibration factor is 8 dB, and you are using 20 dB SNR as constituting signal coverage, the actual value you should use when interpreting coverage using SNR is 28 dB (20 dB + 8 dB). If the downlink provides the basis for signal coverage, you can use the test tools without applying a calibration factor.

Identifying Optimum Access Point Antenna Installation Locations

A significant part of the wireless site survey is identifying the optimum locations for installing access point antennas.

Propagation Testing

As the basis for identifying antenna locations, perform propagation testing at sample areas to gain a good understanding of how radio waves propagate through the facility. This testing includes setting up an 802.11n and 802.11ac test access point at various positions inside the facility, measuring access point beacon signals in the surrounding area, and assessing signal propagation results.

While this chapter focuses on performing a wireless site survey in relation to designing a network, an organization may want to perform an assessment of the capabilities of an existing WLAN. This is often necessary today more than in the past because many companies already have a WLAN in place and want to consider the needs and costs of upgrading it to support newer technologies and applications. In this case, you don't need to perform testing with a test access point. You can simply use a signal meter while walking through the applicable areas of the facility and recording signal coverage of the existing network.

Test Access Point Configuration

The test access point should include both 2.4-GHz (802.11n) and 5-GHz (802.11ac) radios, with transmit power set to the same levels used when determining minimum signal values for defining signal coverage. Configure the access point to broadcast a service set identifier (SSID) that is easy to recognize, such as "TestAP." This makes spotting applicable signal data in the test tools easier. The test access point merely needs to send 802.11 beacon frames; therefore, there is no need to connect the access point to the existing wired network or configure security mechanisms, request-to-send/clear-to-send (RTS/CTS) threshold, and so on.

Antenna Considerations

At each test location, it is best to elevate the test access point antenna to the approximate level where the antenna will likely be installed, such as near the ceiling. Do not worry about getting the test antenna above the ceiling tiles. The difference in signal propagation above and just below the tiles is generally not significant. To minimize losses due to polarization mismatches, be certain to align the access point antennas perpendicular to the ground.

For indoor testing, either 2-dBi or 3-dBi omnidirectional antennas are usually the best choices. Using such antennas results in an access point density that is well suited for most applications. After testing, though, you might determine that a higher-gain omnidirectional antenna, such as a 6-dBi antenna, might be best to reduce the number of access points (and associated costs) needed to cover the facility. This is possible because an increase in gain of an omnidirectional antenna increases the range in all directions for both uplink and downlink paths. Just be sure to include the difference in antenna gain as a calibration factor when interpreting the propagation test results. If increasing the antenna gain by 3 dB, for example, interpret a signal value of –75 dBm at a particular location as –72 dBm instead.

When testing outdoors, there may be advantages to using directional antennas to cover a specific area. In this case, perform the propagation testing using a directional antenna that has the gain and beamwidth necessary to adequately cover the area. This will usually take some planning. Observe the outdoor area that needs signal coverage and consider the antenna parameters. Figure 15-5 shows a parking lot that needs signal coverage. Based on the layout of the parking area and buildings, a directional antenna with a beamwidth of 120 degrees and mounted on the roof of the building will best cover the parking area. It is not possible to accurately predict the gain needed with directional antennas in this case, so you should perform the testing using directional antennas with different gains.

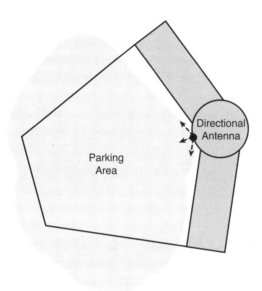

Figure 15-5 *Directional Antennas Are Generally Best for Covering Outdoor Areas*

Identifying Test Locations

Choose propagation test locations (possible access point installation locations) that maximize propagation through different parts of the facility while still supporting utilization requirements. For example, you could first position the test access point toward the center of each floor and measure signal propagation through as much of the construction and layout of the building as possible. This gives you an idea of how the signals will propagate through the facility. If each floor has similar construction and layout, you could test just one of the floors. The first level of a hospital, for example, may cover a large area and have a maze-like floor plan with a scattering of offices, clinics, and cafeterias. This will likely require you to perform propagation testing at several locations on the first level before feeling comfortable with how the radio waves are propagating. The higher floors of the hospital may include mostly in-patient rooms, and the layouts of the higher floors may be very similar to each other. Therefore, it would probably be sufficient to only test one of the higher floors.

After getting an idea of how the signals are propagating, use that data to determine where to install access points. Ideally, you should test each of the proposed installation locations by placing the test access point at the corresponding proposed installation location and using a signal meter to measure the signal coverage around that test access point. After you have tested a few of the access point installation locations, display the recorded signal information to ensure proper signal coverage overlap of the proposed access point locations. If needed, test additional access point locations to find the optimum installation locations.

For voice/data applications, avoid access point installation locations along the perimeter of the facility and stagger the access point locations in a way that prevents the access points from "seeing" each other (for example, along the same hallway). This avoids inter–access point interference and improves capacity. For the same reason, it's best to stagger the access point installation locations on adjacent floors.

If a WLAN needs to support location-based applications, you probably need to identify access point locations in the corners and along the perimeter of the area where location tracking is needed. For example, this could include the corners of the building and along the exterior walls. Cisco refers to this concept, shown in Figure 15-6, as defining the "convex hull" of the tracking area. In addition, other access points may be needed inside the convex hull for extending coverage for location tracking and other applications deeper inside the building.

> **Note** The design of a WLAN for location tracking applications will likely require access points installed near each other on adjacent floors since they need to be installed in the corners of the covered areas. This can't generally be avoided, and some resulting decrease in capacity may occur, depending on actual channel assignments and reuse. To minimize these issues, try staggering the access points along the perimeter of the covered areas on adjacent floors.

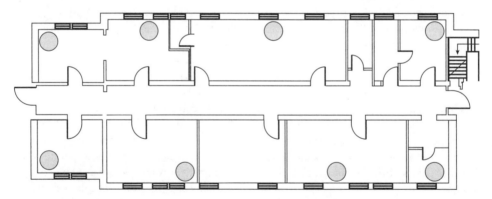

Figure 15-6   *The "Convex Hull" Includes Access Points That Encircle an Area Having Location Tracking Requirements*

For outdoor areas, place the test access point antenna as close as possible to where you plan to install it. For example, if you plan to mount the antenna on the roof of a building to cover a parking lot, perform the testing with the test access point antenna located on the building rooftop. For commercial buildings, this generally requires special permission and generally a facilities management escort. You also need to determine a method for temporarily mounting the antenna on the rooftop so that it is possible to aim the antenna at the area that needs signal coverage.

Measuring Test Signals

At each test access point location, use a signal meter to identify or record the received signal level and SNR throughout the range of the access point. Go into as many areas and rooms as possible to ensure accurate results. If you are testing a facility where you are not known, consider having a local person escort you into various offices and other rooms (especially ones that are normally locked).

Bear in mind that in some cases, you might not be able to enter all rooms (for example, in-patient rooms in hospitals). In such cases, you need to estimate signal levels in the untested rooms based on signal levels on different sides of the room. As shown in Figure 15-7, for example, the signal level in one room may be –65 dBm, and it may be –75 dBm two rooms down the hall and away from the access point. With these measured values, you can estimate the signal level in the untested room to be approximately –70 dBm.

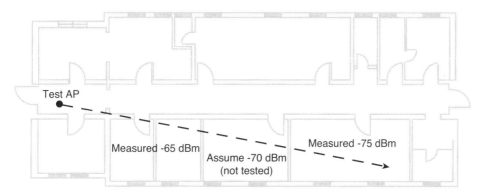

Figure 15-7   *It Is Possible to Approximate Signal Levels in Rooms That Cannot Be Tested*

Typically, the signal coverage on the floor above and below the floor with the access point is approximately 30 percent to 50 percent of the coverage on the floor with the access point/antenna. Figure 15-8 illustrates this. The access point Test AP, as shown in the diagram on Floor 2, provides signal coverage on Floor 1 and Floor 2. Do not take this as fact, though. The construction between some floors allows radio waves to propagate through to the next floor rather easily, but in other cases it does not. Be sure to perform tests on the floors above and below the access point to determine the actual behavior of radio waves in your facility. Keep in mind that the results for 2.4-GHz and 5-GHz bands will likely vary, so be sure to test both bands.

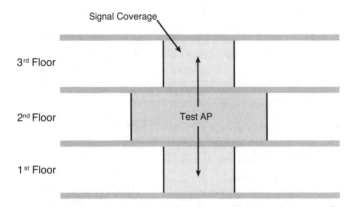

Figure 15-8   *Typical Interfloor Signal Propagation*

Note   Set the signal meter to measure only the RF channels that the test access point is set to. This prevents the meter from needing to scan dozens of channels, which causes delays when taking readings.

Assessing Propagation Test Results

After measuring the signals at each propagation test location, assess the results based on the minimum received signal strength and SNR for your applicable implementation. Do this for the 2.4-GHz and 5-GHz bands separately and do not forget to factor in any necessary calibration factor before analyzing the coverage. Many tools allow easy incorporation of the calibration factor to display the actual signal coverage. Ideally, use these tools to graphically portray areas where there is acceptable signal coverage. For example, Figure 15-9 shows a screenshot of AirMagnet Survey results for a 2.4-GHz test access point located in a building. Use of this tool included importing a floor plan of the building and walking into various rooms to record signal measurements. An access point (Test AP) was placed near the center of the building to maximize the area of propagation testing.

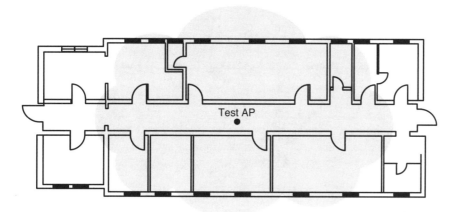

Figure 15-9 *Propagation Test Results*

Refer to guidelines provided by the applicable vendors when assessing access point coverage for location-based applications. From each specific location where tracking of a device is needed, vendors generally require at least three access points heard; the signal strength of one access point needs to be strong enough to support data or voice applications (for example, at least one access point heard at −67 dBm or better), and two additional access points need to be heard at −75 dBm or better (for triangulation purposes). In addition, the three access points must generally be in different quadrants relative to the specific location where a device needs to be tracked. In Figure 15-10, for example, Access Points A, B, and D provide sufficient signal strengths for tracking the location at the center of the four quadrants. You need to ensure that all these location design requirements are met throughout all areas where tracking is needed. This can become cumbersome as you perform the survey, but some test tools, such as AirMagnet Survey, make it much easier by displaying heat maps indicating coverage where these location design requirements are met.

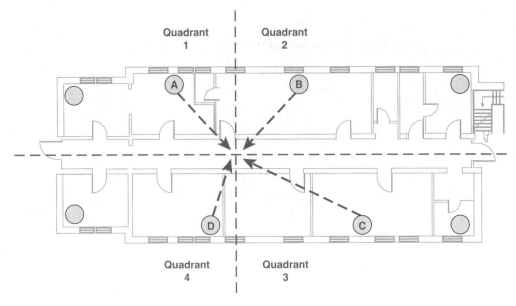

Signal strength relative to access points:

A = -71 dBm
B = -70 dBm
C = -80 dBm
D = -66 dBm

Figure 15-10   *Access Points in Different Quadrants for Supporting Tracking Requirements*

Note   See the section "Difficult-to-Cover Areas" in Chapter 12 for tips on covering elevators, stairwells, and parking areas.

Cell Overlap Considerations

In addition to propagation testing results, factor in the amount of necessary overlap among adjacent cells when identifying installation locations for access point antennas. For fully covered areas where roaming is critical, place access point antennas throughout the facility so that there is approximately 15 percent to 25 percent overlap among each of the adjoining cells. To satisfy roaming, 15 percent overlap is usually sufficient. For redundancy, 25 percent (and possibly more) is needed. Figure 15-11 shows applicable overlap.

In Figure 15-11, each cell represents acceptable signal coverage with an access point located at the center of the cell. The cells depicted in Figure 15-11 are for illustration purposes only. The actual signal coverage from an access point antenna will likely be fairly irregular, depending on the layout of the facility. In addition, the environmental conditions that impact radio wave propagation (such as interference, movement of people, and so on) will cause signal coverage to change in an unpredictable manner. Therefore, it is tough to provide an accurate amount of overlap, so you might want to target 25 percent just to be safe.

Note   A rule of thumb for access point density is one access point per 5,000 square feet for data only and one access point per 3,000 square feet for voice applications.

Figure 15-11   *Cell Overlap Impacts Access Point Antenna Installation*

Annotating Access Point Antenna Installation Locations

After performing propagation testing at enough locations in the building to understand how well the radio waves are propagating through the facility, you can approximate the range of an access point in various parts of the facility. Use this range as a "yardstick" for identifying the installation locations for access points needed to cover the entire facility. Be sure to take into account cell overlap, mounting considerations, and possibly needs for high utilization in specific parts of the facility. Figure 15-12 illustrates optimum installation locations for access points and antennas, based on the propagation testing results shown in Figure 15-11. Only two access points (AP 1 and AP 2) are needed to provide signal coverage and signal overlap throughout the entire floor of the building.

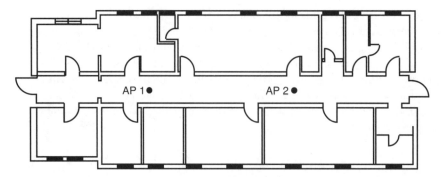

Figure 15-12   *Access Point and Antenna Installation Locations*

> **Note**   When identifying antenna installation locations, incorporate tips from Chapter 12 regarding covering multifloor facilities and difficult-to-cover areas, such as elevators and stairwells.

Writing an RF Site Survey Report

When you are satisfied that the locations of access points you have identified will provide adequate signal coverage, document your findings on the facility diagrams by noting the location of each access point and antenna. The installers will need this information.

A site survey report should include the following:

- **System requirements:** Include a review of all requirements that impact installation locations for access points and antennas. This is especially important if other documentation for the WLAN requirements is not adequate.

- **Test methodology:** Explain how you performed the testing by describing the test equipment, test access point configuration, and methods used for analyzing the spectrum and performing signal propagation testing. Be sure to explain the minimum received signal strength, minimum SNR, and calibration factors that you are using to represent acceptable signal coverage.

- **Inspection findings:** Describe the physical environment and existing network infrastructure, including the switches, available ports, and PoE capability for each floor of the facility. Include photos as needed to fully illustrate the details.

- **Test results:** Include screenshots of the output and results of spectrum analyzer and propagation testing. Explain any pertinent information, such as significant sources of radio signal interference.

■ **Recommended antenna locations:** Identify the locations of all access point antennas on layout diagrams of the facility so that the signal coverage requirements are met. Designate each location as supporting 2.4 GHz, 2.4 and 5 GHz, or 5 GHz only.

■ **Recommended infrastructure enhancements:** Explain additional switches and PoE necessary on each floor to fully support the WLAN.

Early Evaluation of Mounting Assets Beneficial for City-wide Deployments

When deploying city-wide wireless networks, municipalities need access to sufficient mounting assets, such as streetlamp poles, traffic light poles, and building rooftops. These are needed for installing mesh nodes and wireless backhaul equipment. The availability and location of the mounting assets have significant impacts on signal coverage and performance of the network.

An issue is that municipalities generally have rights to only a limited number of building rooftops, and some of the buildings may not be located in optimum areas from a radio propagation perspective. In addition, a municipality may not be able to use street light poles in specific areas, sometimes due to poor physical condition of the poles or resistance of the public based on poor aesthetics. For instance, light poles may be a decorative type, and residents of a neighborhood may balk at the idea of mounting mesh nodes or backhaul equipment on the poles. Therefore, system integrators must often explore mounting asset alternatives, which may require the installation of additional poles or towers or use unconventional radio technologies.

To avoid delays or ending up with an operational system that has insufficient signal coverage and performance because of limited mounting assets, municipalities should conduct a preinstallation site survey that thoroughly identifies the location, condition, and availability of every potential mounting asset. City maps identifying streetlamp and traffic light poles are a good place to start. Be certain to check the actual condition and availability of the poles, however. Also, perform radio signal analysis atop applicable building rooftops to understand whether existing radio-based systems may preclude the use of a particular rooftop.

Summary

Because of the unpredictable propagation of radio waves, it is important to conduct a wireless site survey before finalizing the design of a WLAN and installing access points. Start by reviewing the requirements of the WLAN. Elements such as target applications and client radios provide a basis for determining appropriate signal values that define acceptable signal coverage. The survey consists of inspecting the facility, assessing the existing network infrastructure, identifying potential radio signal interference, and identifying optimum installation locations for access point antennas. At the conclusion of the survey, write a report that fully documents the site survey.

Chapter 16

Installing and Configuring a Wireless LAN

This chapter will introduce you to:

- Wireless LAN Installation Considerations
- Planning the Installation
- Staging the Components
- Installing Ethernet Switches and Cabling
- Installing Access Points
- Testing the Installation
- Documenting the Installation

Once you have a solid design, you are ready to install the wireless LAN (WLAN), which includes access points, controllers, and possibly Ethernet switches and associated cabling. This chapter explains the steps necessary to install and configure these components.

Wireless LAN Installation Considerations

The installation of a wireless network requires the following steps:

Step 1. Plan the installation.

Step 2. Stage the components.

Step 3. Install the access points.

Step 4. Configure the access points.

Step 5. Test the installation.

Step 6. Document the installation.

The sections that follow cover each of these steps.

> **Note**   Be sure to complete a thorough wireless site survey before installing a WLAN. For more details on performing wireless site surveys, see Chapter 15, "Performing a Wireless Site Survey."

Planning the Installation

Spend some time planning the installation. Doing so will significantly reduce the number of problems that might arise. Without an effective plan, implementers will not know whom to contact when problems arise. They might not understand the tools needed to perform the installation, and they might be uncertain about the proper locations for devices.

Developing an Installation Plan

An installation plan explains how to install a wireless network and helps you focus on what needs to be installed. It also provides instructions for installers who might not have been involved with the design of the network and, therefore, do not have firsthand knowledge of the network's configuration.

The following are the major components of a network installation plan:

- Points of contact
- Safety tips
- Installation procedures
- Required facility changes
- Tools
- References to design documentation
- Schedule
- Resources
- Budget
- Risks

> **Note**   The project team should assign someone to be the installation manager; this person will develop the plan and be responsible for the installation.

Points of Contact

The plan should indicate someone as the central point of contact for each installation site if problems arise. This person could be the customer representative or someone who works in the facility where the installation will take place. Be sure this person can provide access to restricted areas and locked rooms. Also indicate who on the project team can answer questions regarding the installation procedures, network configuration, and frequency usage concerns.

Safety Tips

When network components are being installed, accidents are less likely to happen if you incorporate good safety practices and remind people about them. Plan for good safety by putting together a safety plan and requiring that everyone adhere to it. The following are some safety tips that you should consider:

- Insist that no installers work alone. Always use the buddy system. If a serious accident occurs, the other person can obtain help.

- Recommend that installers remove rings and necklaces while installing hardware components. A metal necklace can dangle into a live electrical circuit (or one that is not connected to a power source but is still energized by charged capacitors) and provide the basis for electrical shock. Rings also conduct electricity or can catch on something and keep you from removing your hand from a computer or component.

- Use proper ladders and safety harnesses if placing antennas on towers or rooftops. There is no reason to take high-elevation risks.

- Wear eye protection when using saws or drills.

- Identify any areas containing asbestos and take precautions as needed.

Installation Procedures

The plan should clearly describe the procedures for installing components. In general, you can use the procedures for installing and testing the network outlined in the next sections as a basis. Be certain to identify the installation locations for all access points and controllers. In addition, describe the communications rooms where controllers and other backend equipment must be installed and where the installation team can store equipment and supplies.

This is the overall process that the installation procedures should address:

- Install cabling and switches.

- Install and configure controllers and connect them to switches.

- Configure switches and VLANs to support the users.

- Configure RADIUS to accept Extensible Authentication Protocol (EAP) sessions from controllers.

- Configure Dynamic Host Configuration Protocol (DHCP) servers.

- Install and configure access points and connect them to switches. (Controllers will automatically discover and configure the access points.)

- Install and configure client radios in the client devices.

In addition, include procedures for verifying the installation and proper operation of the network.

> **Note**   Be sure to follow installation procedures supplied by vendors when installing network components.

Required Facility Changes

Be sure that the plan explains any major physical changes, such as drilling through walls and floors, that must be made to the facility to accommodate the installation of the wireless network. The facilities manager will likely need to review these physical change requests to determine feasibility and related costs. Substantial changes to the facility may be rejected if they could result in negative impacts to the facility. Therefore, it is generally best to keep facility changes to a minimum.

Tools

Be sure to identify the tools necessary to complete the job. If you have ever constructed a Barbie house, built a patio cover, or worked on a car engine, you certainly realize the need for having the right tools. Not having the proper tools results in time delays related to looking for the tools or rework due to using the wrong tools.

Installers might need the following tools:

- Wireless installation tools and utilities assist in planning the location of access points and testing wireless connections. They are generally available from the applicable wireless product vendors.

- Two-way radios provide communication among the installation team, especially when spread over a large geographic area.

- Specific test equipment verifies the network installation.

- Standard tools, such a flashlights, ladders, and crimping tools, should be readily available for the installation team.

- Safety cones are used to identify work areas.

References to Design Documentation

The installation will probably require use of design documentation to better understand the overall network configuration. Be sure to indicate the existence of the documentation and how to obtain it.

Schedule

Create a schedule that identifies when to perform each of the installation activities. This helps keep the installation process on schedule. Unfortunately, the best time to install network components is during downtime, such as evening hours and weekends. This minimizes disturbances. Hospitals and warehouses never close, but you should plan installation activities for when the organization is least active.

Resources

Make certain the plan identifies resources needed to perform the installation procedures. Generally, you will not have a staff of technicians experienced in installing wireless networks. If you plan to perform wireless installations as a service to other companies, then you may want to train existing staff to do the implementations. However, for a one-time installation, it is best to outsource the work to a company that specializes in network installations.

Budget

Create a budget to track expenses related to the installation. The project team should have already prepared a budget during the project planning stages. At this time, it may only be necessary to refine the budget to reflect the installation plan.

Risks

Identify any risks associated with the activities and explain how these risks can be minimized. You might be required, for example, to install 200 WLAN connections within a two-day time period. With only two installers, you run the risk of not completing the installation on time. Therefore, you need to look for additional help to stay on schedule. If someone needs to pre-approve your plan, it is best to identify risks and solutions before starting any work.

Coordinating the Installation

The installation of a network is much easier to accomplish if you first coordinate the installation activities.

Consider the following tips:

- **Communicate with network managers:** For example, the access points will tie back to switches via Ethernet; therefore, you need to communicate with the people responsible for supporting the existing Ethernet systems if they already exist.

- **Communicate with facilities managers:** The person designated as the facilities manager for each facility should have a chance to review the installation plan. In fact, he or she should have been active in developing the schedule to minimize any negative effects on the organization. Also, in larger facilities, you will likely come across locked doors leading to locations where you need to install access points or cabling. Therefore, coordinate access to these locked rooms before getting too far along. It is best to actually have a phone number of someone who can get you into rooms at the last minute if necessary. Also, work with the facilities manager to process any permits needed.

■ **Give the organization's employees a heads up:** If you have to install components of the network when the organization's staff is present, announce when, where, and for how long installers will be working in the area. Be sure it is clear to the employees when any existing system resources will not be available. People need time to rearrange their schedules if necessary to accommodate the installation. Have the organization send out a memo or an e-mail to announce the installation.

■ **Hold a preinstallation meeting:** The preinstallation meeting gathers together everyone involved in the installation to review procedures. Be sure everyone knows whom to contact if problems occur. This meeting is also the best time to remind people about good safety practices.

■ **Provide periodic installation status reports to the facility owner:** Identify progress made with installation of the WLAN, known risks, planned risk resolution, schedule impacts, and any other pertinent information.

When installing the network, ensure that all public areas remain clear or are properly marked during installation. If installation activities are disruptive to normal operations of the facility, you may need to perform the installation during off-hours. Be sure to coordinate specific off-hours installation times with the owner before proceeding with installation.

With an installation plan in hand and coordination behind you, you are in good shape to begin the installation.

Staging the Components

If you are implementing a wireless system at multiple sites, be certain to use a staging function to ensure the most effective pretesting and distribution of components to the intended operating locations. The staging process essentially puts together the system in a single non-user location to verify that it works as expected. It is best to do this testing before rolling it out to many sites because it significantly reduces the amount of rework necessary if a defect is found in the design or one or more of the components.

Staging involves the following functions:

■ Warehousing bulk components, such as boxes of radio cards and access points

■ Unpacking bulk components

■ Sorting and labeling components for each installation site

■ Installing and testing software on appliances

■ Configuring all controllers and access points to ensure that they have proper connectivity

■ Packing and shipping components destined for specific installation sites

The benefits of staging include reduced installation time at the users' sites, assurance that all necessary components are available at the installation site, and proper installation and testing of all subcomponents.

Installing Ethernet Switches and Cabling

Many facilities have existing Ethernet switches and cabling. This makes installation of a WLAN much simpler because all that is needed is to install and configure the access points, controllers, and client radios. However, in some cases, the installation may include switches and cabling. For example, the organization might have an existing Ethernet network but not have enough switch ports available to support the connection needs of the access points and controllers. Some facilities might require a dozen more access points for each floor, which can easily exceed the capacity of existing switches. Therefore, you certainly want to be prepared for installing Ethernet switches and cabling. The following are some relevant tips:

- For new buildings, run cabling above the ceiling with terminal outlets every 60 feet in a grid pattern. This way, it is possible to install cabling prior to positioning access points and allows flexibility in moving access points in the future. The incremental cost of this is not significant. Once you are installing cable, it is not much more expensive to place the additional terminal outlets. In addition, an access point can be placed within 30 feet of a terminal outlet.

- The installation may involve using cable trays beyond what is currently available within the facility, so plan on having them on hand during the installation.

- It is generally best to install controllers and switches in lockable equipment cabinets to prevent unauthorized reconfiguration of the network.

- Be sure to label all cables according to company specifications or methods that you define. The main idea is to identify each end of a cable by using some number scheme that lets you know which access point you are dealing with when connecting the wire to a patch panel and rewiring or troubleshooting the system in the future.

Some companies require that Ethernet cabling be installed within a metal conduit, which provides some additional fire safety. Therefore, you need to determine whether this conduit is required to properly install (and quote) the system. You certainly do not want to discover the need for a conduit during the final testing because it might mean you have to start from scratch.

Keep in mind that some organizations have preferred cable installation companies that regularly install network cabling in their facilities. In most cases, it is much more cost-effective to have these companies install the cabling. They know the facility very well and likely have staffing already assigned to the facility where you are installing the WLAN.

Note   Be sure to include protection against power surges, including lightning strikes, for all electrical and network connections.

Installing Access Points

The installation of access points usually involves more effort than installation of the other WLAN components. The difficulty of this part, however, depends on whether you implement a controller-based solution. Without a controller, you might need to configure each access point separately; with a controller, the configuration needs to be done only at the controller.

Place access point antennas as high as possible to clear obstacles and increase range between the access points and wireless stations. For example, position the access points above office partitions and away from metal objects, such as furniture, fans, and doors. Ceilings generally provide the best mounting locations for access points. In addition, install access points so that they are resistant to vandalism, accidental physical abuse, and extreme weather conditions (wind, precipitation, and so on).

Note   Plan on having 10 percent to 15 percent more access points on hand than planned in case there is a need to add more for coverage holes.

Mounting Practices

Most access points ship with mounting brackets. Use a bracket to mark the positions for mounting holes, install the bracket, and then attach the access point to the bracket. Be certain to install the mounting bracket and access point at the location indicated by the wireless site survey.

If mounting an access point on a vertical or horizontal flat surface, such as a wall or solid ceiling, install the bracket screws into studs to ensure that the access point will be securely fastened to the surface. If studs are not available, make use of wall anchors specially made to reinforce the surface for mounting hardware.

Note   Do not mount access points within 3 feet of metal obstructions, such as heating and air-conditioning shafts, and florescent lights.

Many facilities have suspended ceilings, and you can mount an access point either above or below the ceiling tiles. It is generally best to install access points above the ceiling tiles if possible, mainly because it keeps the access points out of view from people inside the building. This provides greater security because it is more difficult for hackers and vandals to find an access point, and it also looks better. In fact, some companies may require that access points be placed out of view.

Be certain, however, that the access points you are using are suitable for operation above ceiling tiles (in a building's environmental air space). Generally, an access point must have a metal enclosure and have adequate fire resistance and low smoke-producing characteristics for operation in a building's environmental air space (plenum rated). Section 300-22 of the National Electric Code (NEC) covers this requirement.

An access point generally comes with a bracket for mounting above the ceiling tiles. The Cisco access point mounting bracket, for example, integrates into the T-bar grid above the ceiling tiles. The T-bar box hanger and bracket mounting clip allow you to orient the access point antenna just above the top surface of the ceiling tile. There is no need to extend the antenna through the ceiling tile to be exposed to the room.

If you find that there is a need to mount access points below removable ceiling tiles, which could be the case if there is not enough room above the tiles, you can generally do so by using special mounting clips. An advantage of mounting below ceiling tiles is that it is much easier for an administrator to find and assess the status of the access point.

Some vendors provide a means for using a padlock to lock an access point to the mounting bracket to provide added physical security. Also, you can make use of special communications boxes for securing access points if you are concerned about theft or vandalism.

The following are warnings related to the installation of access points that you should consider:

- Do not install access points near unshielded blasting caps or in an explosive environment. Radio frequency (RF) signals from the access point (or radio clients) may cause explosives to ignite.

- Per the Federal Communications Commission (FCC) RF exposure limits, keep access point antennas at least 7.9 inches or more from the bodies of all persons.

Antenna Alignment

After connecting the antennas to the access points, ensure that they are vertical to the ground. For example, when mounting an access point near the ceiling, point the antenna down. This will maximize the signal propagation horizontal to the ground, which improves range. If the RF site survey was done with the antennas aligned vertically to the ground, and you align them horizontally during the installation, the signal coverage will likely be spotty. Users will not be able to communicate from some of the places within the facility, and roaming will likely not work properly.

Note   All outdoor-mounted access points should be designed to support ambient temperatures and wind applicable to the local environment.

Configuring Access Points

As part of staging and after physically installing the WLAN, you need to configure the access points based on the design of the system. This can be done via the controller (in a controller-based WLAN) or by interfacing directly to the access point (in an autonomous-based WLAN).

Configuration Setting Access

If implementing a controller-based architecture, the controller will automatically configure each access point based on global settings. In this case, all the configurations are done on the controller. To do this, log in to the management console on the controller. If you are implementing a WLAN with autonomous access points, you need to log in to the access point directly. In some cases, you must connect via a serial cable and use terminal emulation to initialize the controller or access point. For example, some access points, such as those made by Cisco, ship with no IP address configured, so you must configure the IP address before connecting to the access point via a WLAN radio. After setting some initial parameters, such as security set identifier (SSID), IP address, and so forth, you can access the configuration screens of the controller or access point from over the Ethernet or wireless network.

Firmware

The access points that you receive may have been manufactured a while ago, and there may be updated firmware available. Therefore, you should upgrade the access point firmware before configuring and using an access point. Be certain, however, to check vendor recommendations on which firmware release to use for voice applications. The recommended release might not be the most current version.

Note   Be sure to upgrade any existing controllers that support only legacy access points to an appropriate level for 802.11n or 802.11ac, if applicable.

Access Point Configuration Settings

The following sections summarize the primary configuration settings that you should be prepared to configure on access points.

802.11n/ac Enable

Be certain that the access points are configured to operate in 802.11n and 802.11ac mode as needed. This is not set by default in some vendor implementations. Figure 16-1 shows 802.11n mode globally enabled via a Cisco wireless controller for the 2.4-GHz radios in access points associated with the controller. An individual global 802.11n mode setting is available for 5-GHz radios in access points associated with the controller, too.

Figure 16-1 *Cisco Wireless Controller Configuration Screen for Enabling 802.11n Mode*

SSID

The SSID is the name given to the WLAN that client radios must have in order to associate with the network. It is generally best to use a common SSID for all access points to
improve the ability of client devices to roam. Figure 16-2 shows where the SSID setting is
configured in a Cisco wireless controller when creating a new WLAN. This SSID (which is
Test in the figure) is applied to all access points that are assigned to this new WLAN.

Figure 16-2 *Cisco Wireless Controller Configuration Screen for Setting the SSID*

The delivery traffic indication message (DTIM) interval is the number of beacons
that occur before 802.11 multicast/broadcast frames are sent by the access point. See
Chapter 6, "IEEE 802.11 Medium Access Control (MAC) Layer," for details about the
DTIM interval.

Beacon Interval

The beacon interval is the amount of time between transmission of beacons from
the access points. The default interval is 100 milliseconds, but it may be beneficial to
increase the beacon interval to allow power save modes to operate in a manner that is
more effective at conserving battery power. Keep in mind, however, that stretching out
the beacon rate can cause problems; for example, it may cause associated client device

roaming to be sluggish. Figure 16-3 shows the global 802.11n beacon interval setting (referred to as beacon period in the figure) via a Cisco wireless controller for the 802.11a (5-GHz) radios of the access points associated with the controller. In this example, the beacon interval is set to 100 milliseconds, which is the default setting. See Chapter 6 for more information about beacon intervals.

Figure 16-3   *Cisco Wireless Controller Configuration Screen for Setting the Beacon Interval/Period*

Radio Frequency Bands

If an access point is equipped with both 2.4-GHz and 5-GHz radios, you can choose either 2.4-GHz or 5-GHz operation (or both). In most cases, it is advantageous to operate using both bands. For more information about choosing RF bands, see Chapter 11, "Range, Performance, and Roaming Considerations," and Chapter 12, "Radio Frequency Considerations."

Transmit Power

The transmit power setting has significant impact on the range and performance of a WLAN. As transmit power increases, range and performance usually increase. It may be beneficial, however, to operate access points at relatively low transmit power to facilitate a microcell wireless architecture, which can dramatically improve the capacity of the WLAN. Figure 16-4 shows the global transmit power setting via a Cisco wireless controller for the 802.11a (5-GHz) radios of the access points associated with the controller. In this case, the power level is set to Fixed Level 1, which causes the access points to transmit at maximum transmit power. The selection of higher-level numbers (such as 2 or 3) causes the access points to transmit at lower transmit powers. Instead of operating at fixed power levels, you can choose the Cisco power level assignment method Automatic, and the controller automatically adjusts the transmit power levels of the access points as environmental conditions change. As with the other global settings, you can configure an individual global power-level assignment method for the 802.11b/g (2.4-GHz) radios, too. See Chapter 11 for more details on transmit power trade-offs.

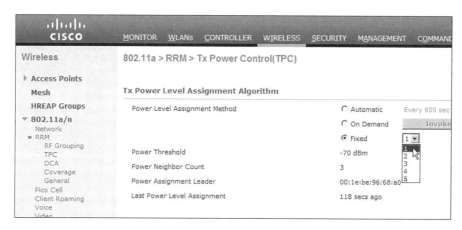

Figure 16-4   *Cisco Wireless Controller Configuration Screen for Setting Transmit Power*

Transmission Channel

Transmission channels should be set to specific non-overlapping channels to avoid inter–access point interference and avoid other interference sources, such as microwave ovens and neighboring WLANs. All access points allow you to configure a fixed (static) RF channel for each access point. As an alternative, you can choose to enable dynamic channel assignment, which Cisco implements. Figure 16-5 shows the global dynamic channel assignment configuration that automatically sets the RF channels of the 2.4-GHz access points associated with the controller to Channels 1, 6, or 11 as environmental conditions change. A similar configuration setting is available for the 5-GHz access points. For more information on strategies for setting transmission channels, see Chapter 11 and Chapter 12.

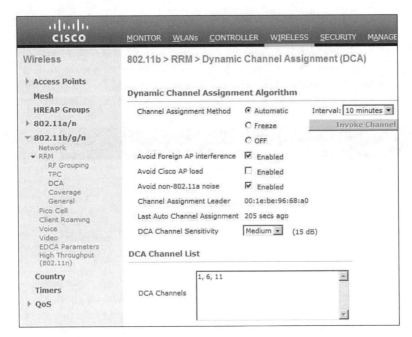

Figure 16-5 *Cisco Wireless Controller Configuration Screen for Setting Dynamic Channel Assignment*

Data Rates

Data rate settings can impact the range of a WLAN. By default, all data rates generally apply; however, you can set the access points to specific data rates if you prefer. For example, a data rate setting of 54 Mbps would require wireless client devices to be closer to the access point to maintain a reliable connection as compared to a data rate setting of 11 Mbps. See Chapter 11 for more details.

Antenna Diversity

Most access points have diversity antennas, but you must ensure that the diversity setting in an access point is configured correctly so that diversity is actually implemented. It is not set by default in all cases, so it is best to check and enable diversity to maximize range and performance. Figure 16-6 shows the global configuration screen on a Cisco wireless controller for setting the number of antennas (under Antenna Parameters) for 802.11b (2.4-GHz) access points associated with the controller. In this example, you can choose the number of transmit and receive antennas based on the level of diversity you want. For optimum operation with these applicable access points, the selection of three receive antennas and two transmit antennas (as configured in the figure) is optimum. A similar configuration setting is available for the 5-GHz access points.

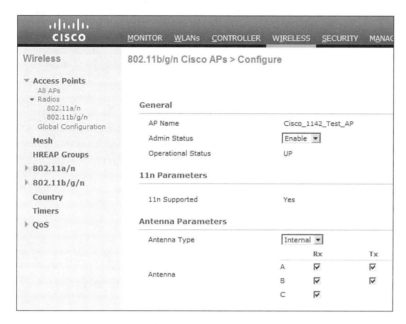

Figure 16-6 *Cisco Wireless Controller Configuration Screen for Configuring the Number of Applicable Transmit and Receive Antennas*

Channel Width

802.11n allows configuration of 20-MHz or 40-MHz channels, and 802.11ac extends that by offering 80-MHz and 160-MHz channel widths. For greatest performance, implement the widest channel width possible. If operating in the 2.4-GHz band, use only 20-MHz channel width. Figure 16-7 shows the global configuration screen on a Cisco wireless controller for setting the channel width for 802.11a (5-GHz) access points associated with the controller. Chapter 11 provides more details about the trade-offs of channel widths.

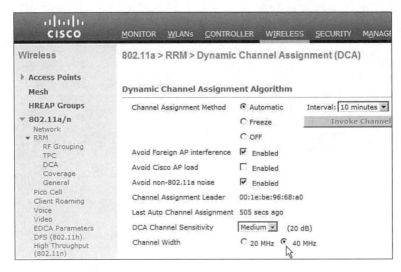

Figure 16-7   *Cisco Wireless Controller Configuration Screen for Configuring Channel Width*

Fragmentation Threshold

If RF interference is present, it may be beneficial to set the fragmentation threshold to a lower value. Keep in mind, however, that lower fragmentation thresholds generate greater overhead. Therefore, setting a lower threshold may reduce overall throughput instead of make it better. Refer to Figure 16-3 to see the global configuration screen on a Cisco wireless controller for setting the fragmentation threshold for 802.11a (5-GHz) access points associated with the controller. In this example, the threshold is set to 2,346 bytes, which effectively disables fragmentation. A lower setting would be necessary to enable fragmentation. A similar configuration setting is available for 2.4-GHz access points. For details on the operation of fragmentation, see Chapter 6. In addition, Chapter 11 describes how fragmentation can improve performance.

RTS/CTS Threshold

Request-to-send/clear-to-send (RTS/CTS) can improve throughput when hidden nodes are present. You can activate RTS/CTS (for different frame sizes) by setting the RTS/CTS threshold to a value lower than the default setting. As with fragmentation, however, the operation of RTS/CTS introduces additional overhead on the network, which can actually decrease performance when hidden nodes are not present. To better understand how RTS/CTS works, see Chapter 6. In addition, Chapter 11 explains how RTS/CTS improves performance.

Note   Be certain to review configuration guides supplied by the applicable vendor for specific instructions and recommended configuration settings for controllers and access points.

Testing the Installation

After installing a WLAN, you need to perform tests to verify that the network is operating sufficiently. You should do this before performing any acceptance testing and deeming the system operational. If you do not fully verify the installation, all requirements may not be fully met. This may lead to potential downtime and unplanned troubleshooting and repair of the network in the future.

You should perform these types of verification tests:

- **Signal coverage testing:** Verifies that it is possible to operate applications from all required areas

- **Performance testing:** Ensures that the WLAN provides the desired performance to users utilizing the applications

- **In-motion testing:** Determines whether client devices roam effectively from one access point to another

- **Security testing:** Ensures that the WLAN implements all required forms of security and is able to guard against unauthorized usage of the network and applicable resources

See Chapter 17, "Testing a Wireless LAN," for details on performing this testing.

Documenting the Installation

After you have tested the installation and taken care of any discrepancies, fully document the "as-installed" installation in sufficient detail to enable efficient and effective operational support of the WLAN. Support personnel will likely need to see this documentation periodically when troubleshooting and upgrading the system.

The installation documentation should include the following elements:

- **Identification of all installed equipment:** Include a list of all access points, controllers, switches, PoE devices, and so on, along with quantities and model numbers.

- **Installation locations of access points, controllers, and switches:** This should be done on building diagrams so that it is very clear where the equipment is installed. This is especially important for access points, especially if the access points and associated antennas are mounted above ceiling tiles and hidden from normal view within the facility.

- **Configuration settings of all equipment:** Describe all pertinent configuration settings, including rationale for choosing the settings.

Summary

Before getting started with a WLAN installation, do some careful planning. For example, describe the installation procedures, plan the schedule, and coordinate with the facilities manager. In addition, think about staging the component before the installation to ease installation at the actual facility. The installation will involve mounting access points at locations throughout the facility in addition to possibly controllers, Ethernet switches, and cabling. After installing the system and before deeming it operational, be certain to perform sufficient verification testing to ensure that the network satisfies all requirements. Finally, document pertinent aspects of the installation for support staff to reference as they maintain the network.

Chapter 17

Testing a Wireless LAN

This chapter will introduce you to:

- Wireless LAN Testing Considerations

- Signal Coverage Testing

- Performance Testing

- In-Motion Testing

- Security Vulnerability Testing

- Acceptance/Verification Testing

- Simulation Testing

- Prototype Testing

- Pilot Testing

- Test Documentation

Because of the use of radio waves, it is important to fully test a wireless LAN (WLAN) before users start using it. Be certain to perform testing after installing a WLAN to ensure that the WLAN system satisfies requirements. In some cases, during operations and maintenance, it might be necessary to perform testing when troubleshooting problems. This chapter covers the types of testing you should do.

Wireless LAN Testing Considerations

When planning the testing of a WLAN, consider the following forms of testing:

- **Signal coverage testing:** Signal coverage testing determines where client devices are able to satisfy coverage requirements. This testing may be part of a WLAN site survey or may be done after the network is installed to determine the as-installed signal coverage.

- **Performance testing:** Performance testing determines whether the WLAN can satisfy user needs for using specific applications over the WLAN.

- **In-motion testing:** In-motion testing determines whether users can continue to make use of applications while roaming throughout the coverage areas, especially when the roaming requires handoffs between access points.

- **Security vulnerability testing:** Security vulnerability testing ensures that the WLAN implements required security mechanisms and offers sufficient protection to unauthorized access and passive monitoring.

- **Acceptance/verification testing:** After installing a WLAN, it is important to run a series of acceptance/verification tests to ensure that the WLAN satisfies all requirements. This is especially important if the organization is having a contractor install the WLAN.

- **Simulation testing:** In some cases, such as when implementing a very large WLAN, it may be beneficial to simulate the behavior of the WLAN before actually installing it. This can provide helpful feedback for designing the system, especially if the WLAN will have critical performance requirements.

- **Prototype testing:** Prototype testing involves implementing an individual function of the WLAN that is not well understood before deploying the complete system. For example, an organization may not be very familiar with 802.1X authentication systems and may benefit by implementing the 802.1X authentication in a lab environment with a limited number of test client devices.

- **Pilot testing:** Before installing the WLAN across the entire organization, which may include numerous buildings and different applications, it is strongly advisable to install the system in a limited number of facilities (ideally one) and make that system work effectively first. After you work out all the problems, you can install the WLAN throughout the remainder of the organization without the need for extensive rework because the problems will likely have been solved during the pilot testing.

The remainder of this chapter explains the details of these forms of testing and applicable documentation.

Signal Coverage Testing

Signal coverage testing involves using a signal coverage tester (sometimes referred to as a signal meter) to measure WLAN signals throughout the coverage areas. The main objective is to ensure that signal levels are high enough to support the levels of performance that the users need when using applications over the WLAN.

Wireless Site Survey Coverage Testing

Signal coverage testing is often part of performing a wireless site survey and should be done before installing the WLAN. It is done by positioning a test access point at various locations throughout the required coverage area and using a signal meter to measure signal values in the vicinity of the test access point. The results of this propagation testing provide a basis for making decisions on where to install access points. For more details on performing coverage testing during wireless site surveys, see Chapter 15, "Performing a Wireless Site Survey."

Note When performing wireless site survey coverage testing, set the signal-measuring tool to record signal strength only on the channel that the test access point is set to. This eliminates the possibility of the tool missing access point beacons and improves accuracy.

As-Installed Coverage Testing

After installing a WLAN, it is important to perform as-installed signal coverage testing to ensure that the WLAN is providing signal coverage in all required coverage areas based on the final positioning of access points. As with coverage testing done during a wireless site survey, as-installed coverage testing involves using a signal meter to measure signal values throughout the required coverage areas. As-installed coverage testing, however, does not use a test access point. The actual installed access points that comprise the WLAN generate the signals that the signal meter measures. In addition, instead of testing only specific locations, you walk through the entire facility and measure the signal values. The goal with as-installed coverage testing is to ensure that the signal coverage requirements are fully met by the installed access points.

As with propagation testing done during a site survey, as-installed coverage testing requires you to determine minimum signal levels that constitute acceptable signal coverage. You can then utilize a signal meter to measure the signal values and generate coverage maps based on a minimum threshold. See Chapter 15 for more information about defining acceptable signal values for signal coverage.

It is generally advisable to generate signal coverage maps for the facility where a WLAN is installed. Many of the signal meters specialized for performing site surveys include this feature. You load in floor plans of the facility, and the signal meter indicates where there is acceptable coverage, based on the signal values that you have recorded during the testing.

Note When performing as-installed coverage testing, set the signal measuring tool to record signals on all relevant channels that the installed access points are set to. This ensures that all signals are recorded properly. See Chapter 14, "Test Tools," for details on signal meters.

Considering Beacon Rates

When using survey tools to measure signal strength for generating signal coverage maps, be certain to take into account the 802.11 beacon intervals set in the access points or mesh nodes. The default beacon interval is generally 100 milliseconds, and the default for most survey tools is to measure signal strength on each radio frequency (RF) channel for 250 milliseconds (sometimes called the scan time). With these settings, you are assured of the access points or mesh nodes transmitting a beacon while the survey tool is measuring the signals on a particular channel. In fact, at least two beacons will occur during that time, so the survey tool will not miss any of the beacons.

A possible problem may occur, however, if the beacon interval on the access points or mesh nodes is set to a longer value. For example, Tropos mesh nodes generally have default beacon intervals of 250 milliseconds. They do this to reduce overhead traffic (that is, beacons) on the network. In this case, if your survey tool is set to a scan time of 250 milliseconds or less, then there is a possibility that a beacon will not occur during the 250 milliseconds. In most cases, the scan time is adjustable. To ensure that the survey tool you are using is measuring all possible signal data, it is a good idea to be certain that the scan time of the survey tool is greater than the beacon interval.

City-wide Indoor Signal Coverage Testing Considerations

To create a municipal wireless network that enables full public access to the Internet, the network must offer signal coverage inside businesses and homes. At some point, you will need to verify that sufficient signal coverage exists in the desired percentage (for example, 70 percent) of inside locations. This type of testing is easier said than done.

A major problem is that the majority of indoor areas are not open to the public. As a result, a system integrator completing system testing or a municipality performing acceptance testing does not have ready access to indoor places. Understandably, businesses and homeowners are usually reluctant to let strangers inside their private establishments. Therefore, it might be possible to test only a very small number of indoor areas—those that are accessible to the public, such as restaurants, grocery stores, and so on.

A municipality may be able to boost the number of indoor test locations, however, by soliciting volunteers that allow test teams to enter their private businesses and homes. For example, a municipality may set up a system that automatically calls utility customers, explains the need to perform the testing, and asks the customers to participate in the testing (possibly by having the customers press a specific phone key). The municipality could then provide the volunteer list to the test team, which would greatly expand the number of indoor test locations. This also gets the community involved in the deployment in a positive way, which is always a good thing.

Performance Testing

A WLAN must have specific applications defined in the requirements, and to do so, it must be capable of passing a variety of tests.

Association Tests

Make sure that each of the client device types will associate with at least one or more access points that are part of the installed system. This is an initial test to see whether the client devices can establish a wireless connection, which primarily involves the 802.11 protocols and any vendor-specific enhancements. Confirm sufficient associations before moving on with other testing. This is important because sometimes client device radios are not fully compatible with the access points, even though they both comply with 802.11n or 802.11ac. If you do not ensure that the client devices have stable associations, other performance tests may indicate erratic and inaccurate results.

Note A problem with using client radio devices from different manufacturers on the same network is that vendor-enhanced features may not be usable. The functionality of the network may be reduced to the least common denominator—that is, the functions specified only by the 802.11 standard.

For example, with a wireless IP phone implementation, the phone should have an indicator that confirms that an association has been made. Power up the phone and check whether the phone indicates an association. If the phone does not associate with an access point, recheck the phone configuration, especially the service set identifier (SSID), authentication type, and security password. These parameters must match those configured on the access point in order for association to be successful. Also, ensure that you are operating the phone in an area where signal coverage exists. You can generally do this by observing the signal status on the phone.

When performing an association test, connect the client device to an access point and monitor the connection for at least 10 minutes. In some cases, the client device may initially associate with an access point without any issues but then disassociate after a few minutes. If such problems occur, research similar problems regarding the types of client radios and access points you are using and upgrade the firmware, if necessary, to fix the problem. Sometimes you must upgrade the firmware in the client device radios, access points, or both for the association process to work effectively.

Registration Tests

After confirming that the client devices associate effectively with access points, the next step is to ensure that each of the client device types registers successfully with the network and applicable applications. This involves protocols and processes that operate over the 802.11 protocols.

Authentication Tests

When a WLAN system implements 802.1X security mechanisms, ensure that the client devices are successfully authenticating with the network. You can do so by observing the access point authentication status table or RADIUS server administration.

If you are testing a wireless IP phone application, for example, you need to be sure that each phone properly authenticates with the system. Therefore, you need to verify that the phone is actually authenticating with the authentication server. To do this, you probably need to access the authentication logs on the server. If the phone is not authenticating, check that the username and password entered in the phone for the authentication system are the same as those configured in the authentication server.

Network Connection Tests

As a basis for communications between the client devices and the application, most wireless systems implement either TCP or UDP. In either case, ensure that the client device successfully connects to the network and has a valid IP address. This can generally be done by observing the association table found in the access point. It is also a good idea to ensure that the client device is capable of responding to a ping generated from the same subnet where the application resides. The ping result should indicate that the client device responds to the ping with acceptable delays and does not time out. If network connection tests indicate a problem, ensure that the client device has a valid IP address. You might also want to upgrade the firmware on the client device, access points, or both.

Application Connection Tests

Be certain to check whether each type of client device type properly connects to the actual application. With a wireless IP phone implementation, for example, ensure that the phone registers with the call manager software and receives the applicable phone number. If the phone does not register properly, which is usually identified by an indicator on the phone, recheck to ensure that the phone is actually configured in the call manager software. If the phone is configured in the call manager, recheck that the phone has the proper IP address, subnet mask, primary gateway, and DNS settings. Keep in mind that the phone may associate with an access point but not be able to obtain an IP address. The IP address should correspond with the address plan for the location where it is connecting to the network.

Application Tests

After you have verified that the client devices are successfully connecting to the system, confirm that each type of client device is able to interface with the WLAN with acceptable performance. For example, if you are testing a wireless IP phone system, you are now ready to see whether you can actually place calls. The goal is to determine whether the phone can make a connection with another phone and ensure that the voice quality is acceptable. This testing ensures that the wireless network and supporting wired infrastructure are supporting the phone calls adequately.

Start by placing a call on each phone from a stationary location. Place a call to preferably someone on a wired phone and talk for at least a minute while assessing voice quality. If you find that the quality is poor, check the signal coverage at that location. For instance, you should only observe from the phone's location a single access point on a particular non-overlapping channel (1, 6, or 11) with a signal level that is at least 15 dB higher than other access points set to the same non-overlapping channel. (Be sure to check recommendations from the specific vendor whose equipment you're implementing for signal level requirements.) The presence of more than one access point set to the same RF channel and having similar signal levels may cause significant interference that reduces voice quality. In addition to checking the wireless network, you might recheck the quality of service settings on the call manager software to be sure that they are correct.

Note   In mixed-mode implementations, ensure that 802.11n/802.11ac devices are indeed operating at 802.11n/802.11ac rates by checking client association tables.

Load Tests

As a final step when testing the performance of a WLAN, ensure that multiple users can use applications on the network. The goal here is to verify that the WLAN can continue to satisfy all requirements while users are using the system; you need to test with both the typical and a maximum number of users. The best way to test the load on the network is with actual users and client devices. In some cases, however, you may need to resort to simulation, as explained later in this chapter.

For example, with a wireless IP phone system, make use of multiple wireless IP phones throughout the facility. Ideally, distribute and use the phones in a manner similar to how they will actually be used when operational. Find volunteers or actual users to help you with these tests. You can give them each a phone, instruct them on how to use it, and have them initiate calls with others. To simplify testing, you can start by having the group of callers place calls from the same location and then have them move to separate locations within the facility while continuing voice conversations and monitoring voice quality. If requirements in parts of the facility specify a need for higher capacity, have an appropriate number of test users make use of the phones from that area. Again, strive to test the system as users will use it.

While performing the load tests, monitor the system by using network analyzers or system management tools, if available. Also, be sure to receive feedback from the users who are actually using the devices and identify any related issues. If problems arise, note the applicable time and location in the facility where the problem occurred. Doing so makes it easier when looking through the results of the monitoring tools to identify the underlying problems.

Note   Consider using load test tools, such as PureLoad, to simulate multiple user connections to the wireless network.

In-Motion Testing

Once stationary usage of the applications is working satisfactorily, run tests to verify that users moving throughout the coverage areas are able to continue operating the applications successfully as they roam. When testing, be certain to move about the coverage area at typical and maximum speeds at which users will operate the applications. This is necessary because roaming tends to break down at higher speeds. Also, run a wireless packet sniffer to record packet transmissions between the client device and the network. This will help you better understand the underlying issues if you run into problems. For example, you might see significant delays when the system is reestablishing the flow of packets when the client device radio hands off from one access point to another. By looking at the packet trace, you may also see that a client device is experiencing significant retransmissions with a particular access point before handing off to another access point with better signal quality, which would point to issues with the client radio's ability to roam.

For wireless IP applications, place a call and walk through the facility while talking to someone on a wired phone. As you walk, monitor the voice quality. If everything is working okay, you should hear consistent quality as you traverse the facility and the phone roams from one access point to another. If you detect poor sound quality at any point, check the signal strength indicator on the phone. A reduction of sound quality may occur when the signal strength is low. To make roaming phone call tests easier to perform, wear an earpiece while listening to the voice quality and monitoring the signal strength indicator on the phone at the same time.

When performing the roaming tests, ensure that the phone can "see" at least two access points (on non-overlapping channels and at acceptable levels) from anywhere within the covered area. This can often be done by observing the phone's wireless connection utility. If two or more access points cannot be seen on non-overlapping channels, a phone roaming from one access point to another may not be smooth enough to maintain good voice quality. To make voice quality consistent, you might need to reengineer the wireless network by moving access points or adding additional access point.

If the phone is connected to a particular access point and does not roam even if located directly under another access point, there may be more than one access point having relatively high signal strengths on overlapping RF channels. In this case, you may be able to fix the problem by adjusting the transmit power of one of the access points; on the other hand, you might need to reengineer the WLAN. Another reason that the phone may not be roaming in this scenario is that the nearby access point may not be operating, so check the status of the access point.

Another problem with roaming is that the phone may roam from one access point to the other too slowly. In this case, check the phone wireless utility to ensure that there is indeed another acceptable access point to roam to. The problem could be that there are no other access points that have strong enough signals for the phone to roam. If the phone appears to roam promptly to the next access point, there might still be excessive delay problems on the wired network infrastructure.

Sometimes a phone may roam okay with regard to the network but lose connection with the call manager. In this case, check to be certain that the phone is not traversing different IP subnets, which can cause a layer 3 connection loss and disconnection from the call manager. In addition, if using Cisco LEAP, make certain that some of the access points are not blocking TCP ports associated with LEAP.

Security Vulnerability Testing

It is important to regularly run a series of tests to verify the security of a wireless network. This is necessary to ensure that the network satisfies all security requirements. If possible, employ someone (an "ethical hacker") who has knowledge and experience regarding wireless security and hacking methods. In addition to verifying proper configuration of devices on the network, you should attempt to break into the system.

Security Settings Verification

You need to review the security configuration settings in client radios, controllers, and access points. This includes confirming that encryption and authentication functions are configured correctly in relation to design specifications. For example, if design specifications indicate use of Advanced Encryption Standard (AES) encryption, ensure that the access points are configured to require AES encryption. Do not assume that the WLAN has the proper configuration; be certain to look at the configuration of the actual equipment.

Once you are sure that the network's security settings are correct, determine whether authorized client devices can successfully connect to the network using the applicable security mechanisms, such as AES encryption and 802.1X authentication. In addition to ensuring that it is possible to connect, verify that the actual security mechanism is in use. You can do so by running a wireless packet sniffer to identify the applicable security mechanism that corresponds to the client device being tested.

Penetration Testing

Testing the ability of authorized client devices to connect to the network is only part of security testing. You also need to verify that unauthorized client devices cannot connect to the private side of the network or reach the protected network from the public side of the network.

Private-Side Testing

A good place to start with penetration testing is to attempt to connect unauthorized devices to the private side of the network, which should be configured with encryption and authentication mechanisms that allow only authorized client devices to successfully connect. Assume that you know the SSID of the private network because that can be easily found by monitoring 802.11 association requests from client device radios. Configure an unauthorized client device with this SSID and verify that you cannot connect to the network. Of course, if it is possible to connect to the private side of the network without applicable encryption passwords, there are major problems with the security of the network. In this case, review the security settings on the access point.

Public-Side Testing

Some networks, such as public hotspots, encourage open connections and do not have any security mechanisms. However, such a network may also include a private network as well. In such a case, run tests to verify that client devices connecting to the public side of the network cannot access any sensitive resources.

As part of analyzing the security vulnerabilities of a wireless network, run a TCP port scanner, such as SuperScan or Retina, to find open TCP or UDP ports that may offer security holes. SuperScan runs on a Windows laptop and scans all ports via the wireless network. Most of the time, SuperScan returns information (for example, IP address) about open port 80 (HTTP) interfaces on access points and printers, but it also finds other open ports that are made available by the installation of various applications.

Note   You can download SuperScan, a free port scanner, from www.mcafee.com/us/downloads/free-tools/superscan.aspx.

You can place the found IP address of a node, such as a printer, in your web browser and reach the configuration screen for the associated device or application. For example, because most users do not implement admin usernames and passwords on printers, hackers could configure some printers to send all printed data to a capture file on their laptop, which of course is not good. Be sure that there are no ports available that will make the network vulnerable to a hacker. If open ports are found, consider redesigning the security of the network.

When running penetration tests, use a port scanner with a test computer, which should be the same as the target client device, connected to the network at various locations, as follows:

■ **Scan the test computer from within the same subnet:** This test determines the extent to which a public wireless user can access user devices that are in the same subnet as another user. This scenario is common with public hotspots, where the hacker is connecting to the network from the same area as a targeted user (for example, from the same coffee shop). With the port scanner connected to the same subnet as the test computer, initiate a scan of all applicable TCP/UDP ports of the IP address of the test computer.

■ **Scan the test computer from a different subnet:** This test determines the extent to which a public wireless user can access user devices that are in a different subnet. This scenario is common with public hotspots, where the hacker is connecting to the network from a different area than a targeted user (for example, from different parts of an airport). With the port scanner connected to a different subnet than the test computer, initiate a scan of all applicable TCP/UDP ports of the IP address of the test computer.

- **Scan the test laptop located on a private subnet from a public subnet:** This test determines the extent to which a public wireless user located on a public subnet can access devices that are on a private subnet. This scenario is applicable where a hacker is trying to compromise the security of users connecting to the protected side of the network. With the port scanner connected to the public subnet and the test computer connected to the private network, initiate a scan of all applicable TCP/UDP ports of the IP address of the test computer.

In addition to scanning a test computer, perform a scan of all devices that connect to the network, such as access points, controllers, switches, and application servers. In addition to wireless components, be certain to include devices that are not part of the wireless network, such as printers. If scanning all ports, you probably need to limit the number of devices (by IP address) or the scanned ports, or the scan may run for days. Be sure to scan the more vulnerable ports, such as port 80. Before running the tests, talk to your local network security manager to decide which ports are most important to scan.

Acceptance/Verification Testing

When an organization hires a contractor to implement a WLAN, it is important for the organization to conduct acceptance/verification testing to ensure that all technical system requirements are met and that the overall system is functioning effectively. The organization needs to verify that the overall system has adequate signal coverage, performance, capacity, and security and that management systems are in place and operating properly. Therefore, acceptance/verification testing includes the testing explained previously in this chapter, but it is a formalized process. In fact, it is a good idea to make acceptance/verification testing part of the contract with a system integrator and possibly stipulate successful completion of acceptance/verification testing as a requirement for part of the payment for the system.

The following are benefits of acceptance testing:

- Determines whether the system is fully operational prior to being given operational status, which avoids potential issues with usage and support

- For potential legal purposes, provides expert technical evidence of system elements that do not meet contracted requirements

- Provides a form of insurance to service providers that the system will support intended applications prior to their investing in the deployment of applications

In addition to the testing covered earlier in this chapter, acceptance/verification testing should address the following elements:

- **Installation practices:** Tour the facility and ensure that access points are installed properly, antennas are aligned correctly, and cabling is neat and organized. For more information about installation best practices, see Chapter 16, "Installing and Configuring a Wireless LAN."

- **System documentation:** Review all documentation, such as system design specifications, as-installed signal coverage maps, cabling diagrams, and operational support plans. The various chapters throughout this book explain what this documentation should include.

- **Operations and maintenance:** Look over operations and maintenance procedures and make sure that all applicable staff have proper training. Test the reaction time of support staff by triggering a failure event, such as disabling one or more access points. This should be done without any notice to the support staff. Observe how long it takes support staff to fix the problem and verify that this falls within required times.

Simulation Testing

Simulation uses software models that artificially represent the network's hardware, software, traffic flows, and use. You can run simulations that replay or generate various types of traffic or protocol streams to validate results quickly; days of network activity go by in minutes when simulating traffic using such tools. Simulation tools can assist a designer in developing a simulation model. Most simulation tools represent the network using a combination of processing elements, transfer devices, and storage devices. Simulation tools are generally costly, with prices in the tens of thousands of dollars. You might be better off hiring a company that already owns a simulation tool.

Consider the following when using simulation to verify the technologies on a system:

- Results are only as accurate as the model; in many cases, you need to estimate traffic flows and utilization.

- After building the initial model, you can easily make changes and rerun tests.

- Simulation does not require access to network hardware and software.

- It does not require much geographic space—just the space for the hardware running the simulation software.

- Simulation software is fairly expensive, making simulation infeasible economically for most one-time designs.

- The people working with the simulation program will probably need training.

Consider using simulation for the following situations:

- When developing a type of WLAN product that does not yet exist

- When it is not possible to obtain applicable WLAN hardware and associated software for testing purposes

- When testing performance requirements based on predicted user activity (because it is often not practical to do this with physical prototyping)
- When it is cost-effective to maintain a baseline model of a product or system to test changes to the baseline

Prototype Testing

A physical prototype represents a part of the product or system you want to verify through construction and testing. It consists of the actual hardware and software you may eventually deploy. Prototyping generally takes place in a laboratory or testbed.

Consider the following when using physical prototyping:

- It yields accurate (real) results because you are using the actual hardware and software, assuming that you can include applicable user utilization loads.

- It is relatively inexpensive as part of a system installation because you can obtain components under evaluation from vendors.

- It takes time to reconfigure the prototype to reflect changes in requirements.

- It requires access to network components, which can be a problem if you do not have easy access to vendors.

- It requires space to lay out the hardware and perform the testing.

Consider using physical prototyping for the following situations:

- When initially testing the design of a new WLAN product before going into mass production

- When testing the system design of a WLAN solution before vendor selection, especially when the operating environment may have a high degree of signal impairment (such as multipath distortion and RF interference)

Typically, you do not need to physically prototype the entire system. You especially don't need to prototype the parts that other companies have implemented without encountering problems. Consider prototyping any solutions that have not been tested before, especially elements dealing with performance and range.

Pilot Testing

Pilot testing involves installing a real version of the WLAN system that users actually operate. This testing enables the evaluation of realistic use and long-term performance issues. The results of this testing also provide a blueprint for the installation of WLANs in other common facilities.

Consider the following when doing pilot testing:

- It yields the most accurate (real) results because you are using the actual hardware and software under realistic conditions.

- It involves the purchase of applicable hardware and software.

- It depends on relatively firm requirements to minimize costly changes to the installed system.

- It requires a live facility to install and use the system.

Consider using pilot testing for the following situations:

- When testing the design of a new product before going into mass production

- When testing the system design of a WLAN solution before installing the system

The implementation of a WLAN pilot test generally involves the installation of multiple access points to cover a significant portion of the overall intended coverage area. Before installing the pilot system, perform a wireless site survey to determine the number and location of access points (see Chapter 15). This data will provide a warning about issues that you might need to consider before installing WLANs at other facilities.

Test Documentation

At the conclusion of testing, produce a test report that addresses the following elements:

- **Background:** Explain what is being tested and why the testing is being done.

- **Test team:** Identify all people who were involved with the testing and their roles.

- **Requirements summary:** Briefly describe the WLAN requirements and reference the requirements document for more details.

- **Test methods and tools:** Describe how the testing was accomplished and the tools that were used to collect the data.

- **Test results and analysis:** Include all applicable test data. Many test tools put data in a format that you can include in your test report. If this is too cumbersome for inclusion directly in the test report, reference applicable test files. Also, explain the results, including any underlying issues that might be causing problems.

- **Recommendations:** Explain what changes should be made to the network to counteract issues found during testing.

Test documentation is a vital part of a WLAN. Managers and support staff can refer to test reports in the future to better understand why changes were made to the network and what might help avoid or fix future problems. Therefore, be certain to fully document any testing that you do.

Summary

Sooner or later, you will likely be involved with testing a WLAN. You need to test signal coverage when performing a wireless site survey and after installing the access points (as-installed coverage testing). Performance testing includes a series of tests, including association tests, registration tests, application tests, and load tests. Performance testing should be done from stationary locations and while users are in motion and roaming throughout the facility (if applicable). To verify security of the network, perform a series of security tests, including security settings verification and thorough penetration testing. For many deployments, especially when an organization has hired a contractor to install the system, you should complete more formal acceptance/verification testing. At the conclusion of any testing, always produce a test report that fully documents the testing, such as what was tested, why the testing was performed, and results and recommendations.

Chapter 18

Managing a Wireless LAN

This chapter will introduce you to:

- Operational Support Considerations
- Help Desk
- Network Monitoring
- Maintenance
- Engineering
- Configuration Management
- Trouble Ticket Coordination
- Preparing for the Transfer to Operational Mode

Operational support can contribute to nearly 50 percent of the total life cycle costs of a wireless LAN (WLAN) system. Therefore, be sure to fully plan related operational management support, which includes elements that are similar to those of wired networks. Wireless support, however, must take into account the uniqueness of radio wave propagation. In addition, the effective operation of a wireless application depends a great deal on the precision of the configuration of the WLAN. As a result, WLANs require unique management techniques and tools.

Operational Support Considerations

When managing a WLAN, consider the following elements:

- **Help desk:** Users with problems should be able to contact a centralized help desk staffed with people who can help with problems that are relatively quick to solve.

- **Network monitoring:** Plan on monitoring various aspects of the WLAN continuously to detect any unforeseen problems.

- **Maintenance:** It is important to define a maintenance function that can perform preventive maintenance and troubleshoot and fix problems as they occur.

- **Engineering:** For monitoring/testing new technologies and redesigning the network to accommodate higher utilization levels and new applications, be certain to define an engineering role for applicable staff.

- **Configuration management:** Many equipment settings and components significantly affect the operation of a WLAN. Therefore, carefully manage the configuration of the network.

- **Security management:** Continually monitor the security of the WLAN to ensure that network resources remain safe.

- **Trouble ticket coordination:** To ensure that all management functions work together effectively, institute an organized trouble ticket system.

- **Operational support transfer preparation:** Before "flipping the switch" and allowing users to access the network, be sure that all management elements are in place and ready.

The following sections describe each of these elements in more detail.

Help Desk

A help desk provides first-level support for users. It is the first stop for users who are having difficulties with the network. Therefore, when a problem arises, a user should know how to reach the help desk. The mission of the help desk is to solve relatively simple problems that users may be having and act as a conduit to the rest of the support operations. Help desk staff should mitigate problems by helping the users, not make changes to the network.

Note   Review help desk usage statistics to determine optimum staffing.

When planning the operational support for a WLAN, establish a help desk that can respond to the problems described in the following sections.

Connection Problems

Users commonly call the help desk when they have connection problems. People at the help desk should be able to solve simple connectivity issues, such as helping users configure their radio card and operating system to comply with the proper service set identifier (SSID), IP address, and Wi-Fi Protected Access (WPA) key.

Poor Signal Coverage

Poor signal coverage sometimes occurs because of improper site surveys or changes made to the facility. If a user complains about coverage, help desk staff could ask the user to temporarily operate from a different area, if possible. Meanwhile, they should introduce a repair ticket for the maintenance group to fix the problem. An access point may have a broken antenna or require rebooting because of a software bug.

Poor Performance

Occasionally, a user may mention that applications are running slowly. In this case, the help desk will probably need to pass the problem to engineering to find the source of the problem. Possibly, network monitoring may indicate a high occurrence of broadcast packets on the network that is introducing delays to users. Or there might be too many users active on the network. Major configuration changes or upgrades to new technology might be necessary.

System Status

The help desk should have up-to-date status on the well-being of the WLAN system. Users want to know more than just that the network is down for a particular reason; they want to know when the network will be fully operational again. The job of the help desk is to help users, so be sure it can provide status information. If a user calls in with a problem, be certain to let that user know when it has been fixed.

Additional Considerations

Most enterprises integrate the WLAN help desk functions into the existing corporate help desk. A company should, however, provide applicable training to the help desk staff to ensure that they are ready to support WLAN-specific issues. Radio wave propagation leads to impairments, such as radio signal interference, which is beyond the knowledge of most existing IT staff. Fully train the help desk team in network operation principles, particularly in user applications.

If the help desk cannot solve a problem by working directly with a user, procedures should be in place to escalate the problem to advanced support functions. Help desk staff should have a communications interface with maintenance and engineering to solve more complex problems that arise. In fact, the help desk often alerts maintenance when problems occur, primarily because users first contact the help desk when they have trouble using the network.

Note Establish a single phone number (with multiple-call handling) for the help desk and ensure that all users know the phone number.

Network Monitoring

Network monitoring continuously measures attributes of the WLAN. This is a key part of proactively managing the network in a way that enables smooth upsizing to support a growing number of users and may enable you to solve issues before they hamper performance and security.

When planning operational support for a WLAN, consider doing the types of monitoring described in the following sections.

Performance Monitoring

Continually measure the usage of access points and application servers to gather valuable information you need to properly scale the WLAN system as user traffic changes. Access point utilization acts as a gauge to indicate when additional access points and WAN bandwidth are necessary. In addition, network monitoring should keep an eye on sources of radio signal interference and raise flags when the interference is high enough to cause significant degradation in throughput.

The following performance metrics generally merit further attention and possible corrective action:

- The number of concurrent users per access point goes above 20 users.

- Access point utilization goes beyond 75 percent.

- Controller utilization goes beyond 50 percent.

- Retry rates of client radios and access points are consistently above 10 percent.

Access Point Monitoring

In extreme situations, an access point may become inoperative due to a broken antenna or firmware fault, and it must be maintained or rebooted before users can associate with the access point. Because most companies deploy WLANs that have radically overlapping access point cells, however, total loss of connectivity may not occur. Instead, users usually experience lower performance and possibly erratic connectivity in certain parts of the facility. In this case, users tend to not complain too strongly to the IT group about the problem, making it difficult to know whether an access point is down.

Network monitoring is certainly a remedy to this problem. Incorporate alerts that inform maintenance staff when an access point is not operating properly or not operating at all. An access point can be down for days, weeks, or months without anyone knowing it. Keep a close eye on this and take corrective actions when necessary (preferably before partial coverage affects users too badly).

Note Some access points can monitor coverage holes and send alerts to the wireless control system if received signal strength interference (RSSI) levels fall below a specific value. In addition, management software can send an alert to the administrator when an access point becomes non-operative.

Configuration Monitoring

When installing access points, you set several configuration parameters, such as SSID, radio frequency (RF) channel, and transmit power. It is important to monitor these configuration settings over time. Network managers should be aware of the configuration of all access points to facilitate effective updates to the network. Documentation of the access point configurations can be easily lost. Monitoring of the configurations enables accurate, centralized records of the setting values.

In addition, a hacker may attempt to reconfigure an access point to a default configuration that is unsecure and that comprises network security. Tools should continuously monitor all the access points in the network and alert IT staff if anything strange occurs. The IT staff can set the performance and security thresholds at any value they want and change them at any time. Some software packages also have automatic repair features that automatically return the access points to their proper settings if someone tampers with the settings or a maintenance person reboots the access point after a malfunction.

Security Policy Management

In general, the security element of operational support WLAN systems, or any system for that matter, involves managing the network to ensure that no issues persist that can hinder the network. Good security policy requires foolproof encryption and authentication, as well as solid WLAN system configuration policies that the company enforces.

When planning operational support for a WLAN, keep in mind the security policies described in the following sections.

Installation Control Policies

Enterprises should have policies in place that require anyone installing wireless access points and base stations to first have approval from a designated IT group. The company should strictly forbid the connection of unauthorized wireless access points to the corporate network. In fact, all access points should satisfy specific configuration policies. The reason for this is to keep someone from attaching an access point that does not have adequate security configurations to the corporate network, which would allow a hacker to easily access corporate resources.

Monitoring Policies

It is important to continually monitor for the presence of rogue access points to ensure that there are no open, unprotected entry points into the corporate information system. You can do this by placing monitoring pods throughout the facility to detect unauthorized access points, or you can (ideally) do monitoring over the Ethernet side of the network. If possible, a company should integrate the network monitoring function into tools in use for monitoring the existing Ethernet corporate network. Most access points offer Simple Network Management Protocol (SNMP), which provides an interface to existing wired network monitoring tools.

Periodic Testing Policies

Access points should be subject to periodic penetration tests and audits to ensure compliance with configuration policies. Without this testing, there is no way to tell whether the WLAN actually conforms to security requirements. A combination of effective network monitoring and configuration management can replace the need for some of this testing, but be sure to conduct periodic testing to ensure that you do not miss anything.

Maintenance

When deploying a WLAN, be certain to have a plan for fixing problems as they arise. Try to proactively find trouble spots and mend them before they affect users. By doing so, you can reduce downtime and thus certainly make users much happier. These types of efforts fall into what most companies call the maintenance function. Effective maintenance staffs include hands-on people who can troubleshoot problems and apply appropriate fixes.

The maintenance staff should be ready to repair the types of WLAN problems described in the following sections.

Inoperative Access Points

Firmware bugs sometimes cause access points to fail in a manner that keeps wireless client devices from associating with the access point. Often, a solution to getting things back to normal is to just reboot the access point. Doing so generally puts the access point back on the air. After rebooting an access point, determine whether updates to the firmware are available and report the problem to the vendor. Update the firmware if yours is currently out-of-date. In some cases, you might need to replace the access point.

Poor Performance

WLANs are difficult to design and install in a way that provides good performance at all times, especially when there are lots of users or high-performance applications, such as voice traffic phone calls. The shared medium access protocols of the 802.11 standard lead to widely varying throughput as conditions on the network change. Therefore, maintenance staff need to be ready to respond to user complaints about sluggish performance. Possible remedies include ensuring adequate coverage, implementing bandwidth-control mechanisms, and using a WLAN switch architecture.

Poor Signal Coverage

You should perform a wireless site survey to properly position the access points and determine whether any harmful interference sources are present that may disturb performance. Often, however, either a company does not perform a survey or alterations made within the facility change WLAN propagation and coverage. In either case, users may eventually complain about having poor coverage in certain parts of the building. Maintenance staff then need to evaluate the areas that have poor coverage and reorient the access points in a way that satisfies required coverage.

Broken Hardware

The two primary components of an access point that physically break are antennas and cable connectors. If a telephone technician who is rewiring phones accidentally clips off an antenna from an access point, poor coverage will result. The access point will still probably continue to operate, but the range will be reduced without the antenna. Breaking a data cable, on the other hand, completely disables the access point, especially when using Power over Ethernet (PoE) to supply electricity. Such mishaps will happen sooner or later, so have adequate numbers of spare antennas and cables on hand. Having a spare access point or two is also a good idea.

Staffing a maintenance crew that can fix problems associated with WLANs is one step toward having successful maintenance. Being proactive is much more important. To minimize WLAN downtime, consider the preventive maintenance suggestions outlined in the following sections.

Firmware Updates

Newly purchased access points and client cards generally do not have the latest software; after all, they may have been sitting in a warehouse for months or even years. Instead of waiting for the devices to fail, update the firmware when new releases become available. Doing so ensures operation with the latest features and freedom from defects to maximize performance and security of the network. Before moving to a new release of firmware, however, be sure to adequately review and test the new firmware. New releases have been known to cause more problems than the previous versions, especially when supporting client radios with older versions of firmware.

Note   If software updates change the user interface or there is some indication to the user that a change was made, be sure to give users a heads up that the changes are taking place.

Signal Coverage Verification

After a WLAN becomes operational, conditions may change within the environment and thus alter the range of the access points. The addition of a new wall inside an office, for example, will reduce RF coverage in that area of the facility. If you know of a change that might alter signal coverage, perform a wireless site survey of the affected areas. In addition, you should be proactive and retest the coverage of a WLAN at least every six months to ensure that signal coverage is optimum. In larger companies, changes can easily go unnoticed. In other areas where changes occur more often, such as warehouses, consider retesting coverage more often.

Access Point Inspections

It is important to periodically walk around and visually inspect the access points. The frequency of these inspections depends on the environment. With outdoor systems, consider checking antenna and cable connectors every few months. You might get by with inspecting indoor installations every six months or so.

Check for any existing or potential damage. For example, you may walk through a large medical center and find several access points dangling by their data cables over some beams. Perhaps a construction company came in to replace ceiling tiles and left the access points in these vulnerable positions for several days. Ideally, the access points should be neatly tucked away above the ceiling or securely mounted to beams or walls. It is also best to keep access points out of easy reach in order to avoid security problems.

Troubleshooting

When problems arise, maintenance staff will likely need to troubleshoot the WLAN. This involves using test equipment, such as a spectrum analyzer, signal coverage tester, or wireless protocol analyzer. In addition, the staff will need specific training and experience with WLANs to resolve most problems, such as connectivity issues, poor performance, and excessive roaming delays.

Note   For more information about troubleshooting methodology and tips on fixing typical WLAN problems, see Chapter 19, "Troubleshooting a Wireless LAN."

Sparing

In addition to the minimum hardware necessary, plan on having some spare hardware on site to replace components that may become defective. With any system, it makes sense to have spares for elements that offer a single point of failure. For WLANs, a failed access point will cause the most havoc, at least for the users it serves.

If you have a spare, you can replace an access point within an hour or less, but it may take 24 hours to replace one if you need to purchase a replacement. You need to make an assessment of the importance of availability and how long the network can be down, but it does not hurt to have at least one spare access point. So, when planning a WLAN, factor the costs of these extras into your budget.

Engineering

A company with a WLAN should establish an engineering function that assesses needs for changes and defines corresponding solutions. Engineering, of course, is a critical task when initially designing a WLAN system, but it is also important to have available on an ongoing basis. Engineering and maintenance work together in a way that lengthens the life of the system.

The staff for engineering tasks may consist of staff working directly for the company, most likely within the IT group. Especially after having a WLAN for a number of months or years, employees of the company can become experts in understanding the applicable technical aspects. In most cases, however, the engineering function will likely be an initial outsourcing venture.

Advanced Problem Resolution

Because of the nature of WLANs, difficult-to-solve problems will likely arise. Users may have periodic loss of connectivity that causes applications to malfunction, or interference may inflict significant loss of throughput. In these cases, engineers might be necessary to analyze the problems and recommend how to proceed with a solution. For example, users may complain that the batteries in wireless IP phones do not last very long. An engineer may diagnose the problem and find that the radios in the phones are continually scanning for access points because the access points are not installed in locations where signal strength is sufficient throughout the facility. This would lead the engineer to redetermine the proper placement of access points.

Coverage Expansion

Companies occasionally expand the reach of a WLAN to cover new areas. This generally requires engineering input to determine the effective placement and channel settings for access points. A hospital, for example, may begin with having only WLAN applications in the emergency department. After better understanding the advantages of wireless applications, the hospital may decide to expand the system to include other departments. Doing so requires designing the existing network to handle the greater amount of traffic and the addition of greater signal coverage.

Capacity Increases

In the early days of a WLAN, the number of users is normally much lower than the total available capacity. As time goes by, however, the company is likely to deploy additional applications that increase WLAN utilization. It is important to have network monitoring in place to watch throughput levels and engineer upgrades to the network, when needed, to handle ongoing needs to support a greater number of users.

Firmware Review

Within the maintenance function of operational support, technicians may find it necessary to upgrade the firmware of access points. Before making upgrades, however, engineering should first test and evaluate the new firmware in a test lab or with a limited number of users. By so doing, they can verify that the changes being made will not adversely affect the network.

Technology Upgrades

Engineers should continually monitor the evolution of WLAN technologies and products to ensure effective migration in a manner that meets growing network utilization. For example, the engineering function should proactively review the potential upgrade from 802.11b and 802.11g to 802.11n to 802.11ac. A change in technology should be made only after careful deliberation.

Design Review

The engineering function should also be involved in reviewing and verifying compliance of new designs with the common architectural design of the WLAN system. This avoids haphazard expansion of the network that might lead to negative operational conditions. A design review involves examining requirements and making certain that the requested changes fully satisfy requirements.

> **Note**   From time to time, reassess WLAN requirements to determine whether changes to the WLAN are needed.

Configuration Management

Configuration management involves controlling changes made to the WLAN after installation. Changes may involve installing or moving access points, altering access point configurations (such as RF channel), or updating firmware. In larger systems, configuration management may also be necessary to keep requirements for additions to the system from expanding endlessly without good reason.

Network managers must review any changes that might impact WLAN performance or security. This type of review ensures that relevant impacts are taken into account—impacts that involve additional costs and use of resources necessary to support the requests. In some cases, changes may merely involve supporting a larger number of users, which may or may not require modifications made to the network. Other instances could include a need for wider RF coverage and additional access points.

Change-Control Processes

Consider incorporating a change-control process to manage the configuration of the WLAN (see Figure 18-1). In larger enterprises, this may be a formal, company-mandated process, and the actions and decisions made by the various groups (for example, technical review panel [TRP] or configuration control board [CCB]) may be made by multiple people. For smaller deployments, however, one person (possibly you) may satisfy all parts of the change-control process. In the latter case, at least keep these change-control processes in mind when making changes to the WLANs.

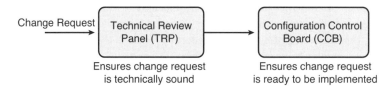

Figure 18-1 *Change-Control Process*

To make a change to the configuration items, the person wanting to make the change must submit a change request to a TRP, which will assess the technical nature of the change. This should be conducted by appropriate staff who have experience in the type of change being requested and includes an evaluation of whether the change complies with the company's technical standards. If the TRP believes the change is technically feasible, it forwards the request to a CCB for final approval; otherwise, the TRP should return the change to the requester for further refinement (or disposal). The CCB mainly evaluates whether the project team has prepared adequate levels of support for the implementation and that the change has been coordinated with the proper organizations. With approval of the change, a project team must then ensure the modification of support documentation.

A company should utilize a change request form as an input into the configuration management process. The purpose of this form is to summarize the requested change in a manner that makes it fairly simple to determine the level of review needed to accept or reject the proposed change. For instance, the addition of a new application would likely require review by security and engineering functions to determine whether mechanisms are in place to safeguard the application and provide adequate levels of performance.

A key aspect of configuration management is the development and management of a baseline architectural design and support plan. When someone proposes or requests the deployment of a WLAN or a change that prompts modification to an existing WLAN, the company should use this baseline as the basis for validating and verifying the design and assessing the impacts. This process includes determining the impact of the proposed change on the overall WLAN and peripheral systems.

The implementation of an effective configuration management process also includes the establishment and use of a configuration management database, which includes a list of all installed components, configuration settings, and applicable diagrams that document the current state of the WLAN. This database should include a list of all hardware and software (including configurations) that are part of the WLAN. As the company accepts changes to the WLAN configuration, it needs to update the database to reflect the new state of the system. Without this type of documentation, it is possible that only one or a handful of people will have knowledge of the WLAN composition; if that person or persons left the company, the knowledge would go with them.

Security Management

After deploying a WLAN, you should implement security assessments regularly to ensure that the WLAN complies with effective security policies. For most situations, this is necessary whether or not the network implements effective security mechanisms. Do not put too much trust in the design of a system. It is best to run tests to be certain that the network is hardened enough to guard against unauthorized persons attacking company resources.

In fact, companies should conduct regular, periodic security reviews to ensure that changes to the WLAN do not make the system vulnerable to hackers. A review once each year may suffice for low-risk networks, but a review each quarter or more often may be necessary if the network supports high-risk information, such as financial data, postal mail routing, and manufacturing control functions.

When performing a WLAN security assessment, consider completing the steps discussed in the following sections.

Reviewing Existing Security Policies

Become familiar with the company's WLAN security policies. You need a benchmark for determining whether a company is complying with its own policies. In addition, having this benchmark will help you make an assessment and corresponding recommendations for policy modifications. Determine whether the policy leaves any room for a hacker (for example, a disgruntled employee) to access or harm company resources.

For example, the policy should describe adequate encryption and authentication mechanisms. Also, the policy should mandate that all employees coordinate with the company's information systems organization before purchasing or installing access points. It is important that all access points have configuration settings that comply with the policies and provide the proper level of security. In addition, you need to ensure that methods are in place for disseminating security policies to employees in an effective manner.

Reviewing the System Architecture

Meet with information systems personnel and read through related documentation to gain an understanding of the system's architecture and configuration of access points. You need this to determine whether there are any design flaws that provide weaknesses that could allow a hacker inside the system.

For example, if static WEP is in use, a hacker could use tools such as AirSnort to break through the encryption process. In addition, the dependence on 802.11 authentication alone will only verify the radio network interface card (NIC) and not the user, which means an unauthorized person who has stolen someone's wireless-equipped laptop could access the corporate network.

Reviewing Management Tools and Procedures

Some security weaknesses are inherent in supporting a WLAN. Therefore, learn as much as possible about existing support tools and procedures to spot potential issues. Most companies, for example, configure access points over the wired Ethernet backbone. With this process, the passwords to open a connection with a particular access points are sent in cleartext (that is, unencrypted) over the wired network. As a result, a hacker with monitoring equipment hooked to the Ethernet network would be able to capture the passwords and reconfigure the access point.

Interviewing Users

Be sure to talk with a sample of employees to determine whether they are aware of the security policies, at least to a level of security that they can control. For example, do the users know that they must coordinate the purchase and installation of WLAN components with the appropriate organization? Even though the policy states this, do not count on everyone having knowledge of the policy. A new employee or someone who has not seen the policy may purchase an access point from a local office supply store and install it on the corporate network (without any security settings enabled) to provide wireless connectivity within his office. It is also a good idea to verify that people are using personal firewalls.

Verifying Configurations of Wireless Devices

A portion of the security policy should define appropriate access point configurations that will offer an appropriate level of security. As part of the assessment, view the configuration settings of the access points and determine which security mechanisms are actually in use and whether they comply with effective policies. For example, the policies may state that access points must disable the physical console port, but while testing, you might determine that most access points have the ports enabled. Of course, this would indicate noncompliance with the policies, and it would enable a hacker to possibly reset an access point to factory default settings, with no security enabled. In addition, look at the firmware version of each access point to see whether it is up-to-date.

Older firmware versions might not implement the more recent patches that fix encryption vulnerabilities.

Investigating Physical Installations of Access Points

As you walk through a facility, investigate the installation of access points by noting their physical accessibility, antenna type and orientation, and radio wave propagation into portions of the facility that do not have physical security controls. The access points should be mounted in a position that would make it difficult for someone to physically handle the access point without being noticed. Placing an access point on top of a bookshelf, for example, would make it easy for a hacker to swap the access point with an open one that does not have any security enabled. Or the hacker could attach a laptop to the console port to reset the access point. If the access points are all mounted above the ceiling tiles and out of plain view, however, someone would need to use a ladder and would probably be noticed by an employee or a security guard.

Identifying Rogue Access Points

A problem that is difficult to prevent and significantly undercuts the security of a WLAN is employees installing "personal" access points in their offices. Most of the time, these installations do not comply with security policies and result in open, non-secure entry ports to the corporate network. In fact, a hacker can use sniffing tools to figure out when such opportunities exist. Therefore, you should scan for these unauthorized access points as part of the assessment. Most companies are surprised at how many of them they find. Ideally, to effectively monitor rogue access points, you should use tools built in to the access points, controllers, and management software that automatically identify potential rogue access points and alert the appropriate staff to take action.

If your budget is not large enough to cover sensors to automatically discover rogues, periodically walk through the facility with tools such as AirMagnet Analyzer or NetStumbler to identify and find access points that are not part of the official WLAN. If you find a rogue access point operating inside your facility, investigate the security threat.

Performing Penetration Tests

Try accessing corporate resources from the wireless side of the network. If possible, employ someone (an "ethical hacker") who has knowledge and experience with wireless security and hacking methods. By doing so, you can ensure that the WLAN is locked down and secure.

Note   For details on performing penetration testing, see Chapter 17, "Testing a Wireless LAN."

Analyzing Security Gaps

The information you gather during the assessment provides a basis for understanding the security posture of a company. After collecting information in the previous steps, spend some time thinking about potential gaps in security, including issues with policy, network architecture, operational support, and other items that weaken security, such as presence of unauthorized access points and ability to penetrate the network. You need to think like a hacker and uncover any and all methods that make it easier for someone to penetrate and access (or control) company resources through the WLAN.

Recommending Improvements

As you spot weaknesses in the security of a WLAN, research and describe methods that will counter the issues. Start by recommending improvements to the policies that dictate what the company requires in terms of security for the WLAN. This provides a basis for defining technical and procedural solutions that will strengthen the security of the system to a level that protects the company's interests.

Trouble Ticket Coordination

To effectively operate a network, all management functions must work together in an organized manner using a trouble ticket system. To make this work well, assign responsibilities for resolving problems to the different departments within the organization. Figure 18-2 illustrates the typical coordination of trouble tickets.

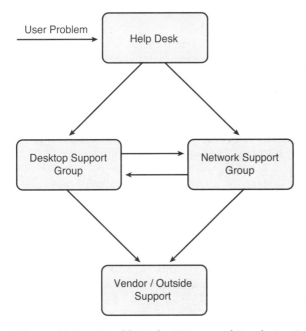

Figure 18-2 *Trouble Ticket Triage and Escalation Process*

Help Desk Group

The help desk should be the focal point for all new trouble tickets based on problems reported by users, and it should provide initial frontline support to users. The help desk should attempt to directly resolve client connectivity issues and other problems by using fault-isolation trees, which are flowcharts that instruct the help desk personnel how to resolve problems. Using a fault-isolation tree minimizes "knee-jerk" fixes, such as simply rebooting access points and reenabling client radio cards before the root cause of the problem has been found.

The help desk staff generally work remotely via telephone instead of responding directly to the user's location. If a problem cannot be resolved immediately, the help desk should escalate the problem to a desktop support group or network support group, depending on results of working through the fault-isolation tree. This generally makes the best use of resources.

To proactively manage a WLAN and minimize the number of trouble calls, the help desk staff should track trends regarding WLAN issues and periodically report findings to the network and desktop support groups for resolution. Sometimes resetting a client radio, for example, might fix the immediate user problem, but this information should be recorded to determine trends that may need more detailed analysis and resolution.

Note   For examples of fault-isolation trees for resolving WLAN problems, see Chapter 19.

Desktop Support Group

Most companies have a desktop support group that configures and supports desktop computers, such as PCs. In many cases, the desktop support group takes on the role of supporting users with mobile devices, too. If the help desk cannot resolve a problem that appears to be related to connectivity issues, the help desk should escalate the problem to the desktop support group, or whoever is responsible for supporting user client devices. Desktop support staff usually go directly to the user's location and attempt to fix the problem. If the desktop support group finds that the problem is network related, it can forward the trouble ticket to the network support group for resolution.

Network Support Group

The network support group is responsible for configuring and supporting the network infrastructure, and this likely involves the WLAN. If the desktop support group cannot fix a problem, the issue should be escalated to the network support group. Likewise, if the help desk cannot resolve the problem that appears to be network related, the help desk should escalate the issue directly to the network support group. The network support group should include network engineers who have the experience to resolve WLAN infrastructure problems. In some cases, however, it might be necessary to contact the vendor of the infrastructure components or other outside resources to help fix problems. In addition, if the network support group finds that the problem is network related, it can forward the trouble ticket to the desktop support group for resolution.

Preparing for the Transfer to Operational Mode

The transfer of the system from a project status to operational mode should be well defined. Otherwise, it is not clear who is supporting the network, and finger pointing is likely to occur if any problems arise. The main task in preparing for the transfer to operational mode is to develop a turnover agreement that will be put into effect after the installation and testing phases are complete. At the beginning of the project, the project charter gave the project manager responsibility for implementing the network. The turnover agreement transfers this responsibility to the supporting organizations handling system administration, network management, and so on.

As with all other phases of a project, documentation is important to convey the ideas from one phase to other project phases. In the case of operational support, a plan is necessary to effectively carry out the support. An operational support plan describes how the organization will support the operational network. This plan should indicate which network elements require support and which organizations are going to support them. More specifically, the operational support plan should describe how the organization will support the various operations and maintenance functions.

Summary

The operational support of a WLAN system is significant. If you do not effectively manage the configuration, monitor the network, periodically review security, and perform maintenance, help desk, and engineering functions, users will likely experience poor performance. Through configuration management, you need to keep track of elements such as RF channels, transmit power, and new applications to ensure that the system continues to provide good service. Network monitoring can spot issues with the network before they cause problems to users, and periodic security assessments shield a system from hackers and help protect company assets. The maintenance staff should be in place to troubleshoot and fix problems, such as access points that need to be rebooted, and engineers should be on hand to tackle more in-depth issues that may require redesign of the network. The combination of all these support elements will keep the system effectively supporting intended requirements.

Chapter 19

Troubleshooting a Wireless LAN

This chapter will introduce you to:

- Troubleshooting Methodology
- Connection Problems
- Performance Problems

After installing a wireless LAN (WLAN), you might find that it does not support applications as expected. Users may complain of erratic connections or slow performance, which hampers the use and benefits of the wireless applications. When this happens, you need to do some troubleshooting. This chapter will help point you in the right direction.

Troubleshooting Methodology

Troubleshooting involves the following steps:

Step 1. Identify the problem.

Step 2. Identify the underlying cause of the problem.

Step 3. Fix the problem.

Step 4. Document the fix.

The sections that follow explain the first three of these steps in further detail.

Identifying the Problem

The first step of troubleshooting is to gain a firm understanding of the actual problem. This includes knowing what the user is experiencing and when and where the problem is happening. For example, a user may complain that he is experiencing connectivity issues. In this scenario, ask the user to explain more about what he is experiencing. Is the connectivity erratic or nonexistent? In what parts of the facility does the connectivity problem occur? If you find out as much as possible about the situation, troubleshooting will be more successful.

You will likely learn about most problems directly from users because they are actually using the network. They will come to you, and you may not need to proactively look for problems. In addition, the help desk or other support staff may uncover a technical problem, such as a signal coverage hole, when troubleshooting connectivity difficulties that a user is experiencing. As a result, the solution to one problem may lead to the identification of another problem.

Identifying the Underlying Cause of the Problem

This is the most difficult step, where the "real" troubleshooting takes place. It might include using test equipment to measure signal strength or monitoring 802.11 protocol communications. This step requires an investigative attitude and constantly using the facts that point toward the culprit.

When troubleshooting, focus on finding the underlying cause. This process may lead from one problem to another, but eventually you should find what is causing the problem (or series of problems). For example, troubleshooting user connectivity issues may lead to signal coverage problems, which may lead to an inoperative access point with a broken antenna. In this example, the broken antenna is the underlying cause in terms of the system. You might also want to explore why the antenna is broken and possibly take corrective actions so that it does not happen again.

Fixing the Problem

Once you know what caused the problem, the final step is to fix the underlying cause of the problem. Doing so might be as easy as replacing a broken antenna or reconfiguring access point settings. Other fixes, such as minimizing radio frequency interference or installing more access points, may be more difficult or costly to achieve.

> **Note**   Make sure that your troubleshooting tools are 802.11n and 802.11ac compliant.

Connection Problems

A common problem is a client device being unable to reliably connect to the WLAN. When troubleshooting this issue, first investigate whether the user has an 802.11 connection, which indicates that the client radio is connected (associated) to the access point. You can do this by observing the user's connection status on her client device (for example, Windows wireless connection status window) or by logging in to the access point and looking at the client association table.

If an 802.11 connection exists, confirm that the client device has a valid IP address. If the IP address is not valid, the client device might not be reaching the Dynamic Host Configuration Protocol (DHCP) server, or the static IP address set in the client device might not be correct. In addition, there might be issues with 802.1X authentication, such as improper credentials or authorization.

If you find that the client radio has no 802.11 connection (association) to the access point, investigate the possible underlying causes described in the following sections.

Insufficient Signal Coverage

The most common reason for 802.11 connection problems is insufficient signal coverage. Either the user is too far away from an access point or the transmit power in the client devices is too low. In either case, the received signal strength at either the client radio or access point (or both) is below the receive sensitivity (or noise floor), which makes it impossible for the client radio to associate or stay associated to the access point.

To test whether insufficient signal coverage is causing connectivity problems, check the signal strength at the client radio and the access point. For the client radio, you might be able to read the signal strength from the client device. Some client radios have vendor-specific software utilities that display the received signal strength in dBm. You can often check the received signal strength at the access point by logging in to the access point and observing the client's connection status. These methods are fairly accurate because they include the specific antenna gains of the client radio and access point. If you cannot obtain the signal values directly from the client device or access point, use a signal meter or site survey tool to measure the signal strength at the same location as the client device and access point.

If the signal value at the client radio is below the receive sensitivity of the client radio (or the signal value at the access point is below the receive sensitivity of the access point), insufficient signal coverage is likely causing connection problems. Also, signal values at either the client radio or access point resulting in a signal-to-noise ratio (SNR) of 0 or less will certainly cause connectivity problems, and SNR of under 10 may cause the connection to be unreliable.

Also, you can monitor the flow of 802.11 frames between the client radio and the access point to see whether a successful exchange of association frames occurs. If you do not see the access point send an association frame response, the signal strength at the access point is likely too low for the access point to receive and process the initial association frame from the client radio. This is a common scenario because the transmit power of client devices is usually much lower than access point transmit power. The client device will have received the access point beacons successfully and attempted to connect with the access point, but the access point is unable to hear the client radio.

Note   To learn more about how to provide acceptable signal coverage, see Chapter 15, "Performing a Wireless Site Survey."

Radio Signal Interference

Sometimes, severe radio signal interference may cause 802.11 connectivity issues. This is especially true for client devices operating in areas that have relatively low signal coverage. In these areas, the impact of interfering signals is greatest because it causes the SNR to be relatively low.

The best way to check whether radio signal interference is causing connectivity problems is to use a spectrum analyzer and observe the presence of interfering signals. Radio signal interference generally varies throughout the day, so you should attempt to perform the testing when the user is actually experiencing the problem. Try to characterize the interference based on its duty cycle. A wireless paging system that emits a signal every 10 seconds only, for example, is not severe enough to cause connection problems. A microwave oven constantly throwing out –60 dBm signals across the frequency band within the signal path between the client radio and the access point, however, will likely cause connection problems.

> **Note**   For more information about radio signal interference, see Chapter 4, "Wireless LAN Implications."

Access Point Failure

Access points occasionally become inoperative. When this happens, signal coverage holes may crop up in the area of the affected access point. So, when troubleshooting 802.11 connectivity problems, verify that the access point is operating. Check that it has sufficient electrical power. Also, you might need to reboot the access point to recover from a software problem.

Even if an access point status indicator indicates that the access point is functioning properly, it might not be sending out any beacons. With an 802.11 protocol analyzer, check whether the access point within range of the client device is sending beacons. If you do not see any beacons, the access point is likely inoperative. Alternatively, you can use a signal coverage tester to verify whether the access point is transmitting. If no signals are coming from the access point, it is probably inoperative.

Incompatible Client Radio

To connect to an 802.11n access point, the client device must have an 802.11b, 802.11g, or 802.11n radio. (An 802.11ac access point requires the client to have an 802.11a or 802.11ac radio.) The problem is that some older client devices may not have compatible radios. Consequently, check whether the applicable client radio is compatible with 802.11n (or 802.11ac) networks. If the radio card is a "Pre-N" type (not Wi-Fi 802.11n draft 2.0 compliant), for instance, connectivity is likely not possible. With 802.11 frequency-hopping spread spectrum (FHSS) or non-802.11 client radios, connectivity is definitely not possible. To solve connectivity problems, replace the older incompatible client radios with ones that are fully compliant with 802.11n (or 802.11ac).

Faulty Firmware

Old firmware on either client radios or access points can cause 802.11 connectivity problems. For example, the firmware might not fully comply with the ratified version of the 802.11n or 802.11ac standard. Check the firmware versions and upgrade if needed.

Incorrect Client Radio Configuration

Several settings on a client radio can cause 802.11 connectivity problems. The following client radio configuration settings can impact connectivity:

- **Service set identifier (SSID):** The SSID in the client radio must match the SSID configured in the access point. If it doesn't, the client card cannot connect to the access point.

- **Network type:** If the network type setting in the client radio is set to ad hoc mode, the client radio will not connect to an access point. Be sure that the network type is set to infrastructure mode to enable connections to access points.

- **Radio frequency (RF) channel:** The RF channel setting on the client radio applies only to ad hoc networks and has no impact on connectivity to access points. If the client device is intending to connect to an ad hoc network, be certain that the RF channel is set to the RF channel that corresponds to the ad hoc network.

- **Security settings:** Most WLANs require the client device to be configured with the correct 802.11/Wi-Fi security password before the client radio can connect to the access point. Therefore, be certain that the user is inputting the correct password.

- **Transmit power:** A very low transmit power setting in the client radio may cause connectivity issues because the signal level at the access point might be too low (well below the receive sensitivity of the access point). If this is the case, try increasing the transmit power in the client radio.

Check these configuration settings on the client radio if the user device is having trouble connecting to the network and make appropriate corrections to fix the connectivity problems.

It is also possible that incorrect settings on the access point could be causing client radio connectivity issues. It is possible to configure most access points to allow only specific types of client radios to associate. For example, this setting could be configured to allow only 802.11n client radios to associate with the access points. If this were the case, 802.11b and 802.11g client radios would not be able to associate with the access point. Check these settings and ensure that they are configured to allow association with the specific type of client radio that is having problems connecting.

Note For more on the trade-offs of various client radio and access point settings, see Chapter 11, "Range, Performance, and Roaming Considerations."

Performance Problems

Sometimes users complain of sluggish performance, usually when accessing applications on the network. They might be experiencing significant delays when using applications, such as downloading files or browsing the Internet. This is not quite as bad as unreliable connectivity. The client radio may stay connected to the network, but the throughput is just too low.

Keep in mind that when troubleshooting performance issues, the problem may lie outside the realm of the wireless network. The Internet connection, for example, might be too slow, or a router may not be configured correctly and so may be causing significant delays. Therefore, it is a good idea to do some troubleshooting on the wired network before getting too far with troubleshooting the wireless network. This requires knowledge of wired networking, which is beyond the scope of this book; other publications focus on troubleshooting wired networks.

If you are fairly certain that the wired part of the network is not causing performance problems, you should troubleshoot the wireless network by examining the possible underlying causes described in the following sections.

Insufficient Signal Coverage

The most common reason for performance issues on a wireless network is insufficient signal coverage. Signal strength at the client radio or the access point may be above the receive sensitivity (and noise), but the signal might be only high enough to support the lower data rates. This causes overall throughput and corresponding performance, as experienced by the user, to be under par.

Test the signal strength at the client radio and access point. You can compare the signal strengths to radio specifications to determine whether signal strength may be causing the performance problem. If the signal strength is in the range where the radio will support only 2-Mbps data rates, signal strength coverage may be the problem. If the retry rate of 802.11 data frames associated with the client radio is also high (30 percent or higher) and the signal strength is relatively low, poor signal coverage is likely causing the performance problem. If the retry rate is low, signal coverage is likely not causing the problem.

Radio Signal Interference

Radio signal interference is much more liable to cause performance problems than 802.11 connectivity issues, even for client devices operating in areas where signal strength is relatively high. Radio signal interference causes bit errors to occur in 802.11 data frames, which triggers retransmissions. Repeating data transmissions contributes to lower throughput and performance, as experienced by the user. As with troubleshooting connectivity problems, you can use a spectrum analyzer to visualize the presence of radio signal interference, with emphasis on understanding its duty cycle. Interference with relatively high duty cycle (above 30 percent) will generally cause degradation in performance, depending on the signal level of the interference and the 802.11 signals.

Faulty Firmware

Sometimes firmware bugs or imperfections impact performance, causing an access point to lock up periodically. When troubleshooting performance problems, review firmware release notes for the client radio and the access point. It is common to find notes that explain changes made to the firmware to fix performance-related problems. For example, the methods used in software to encrypt 802.11 data frames might not be very efficient, resulting in poor performance, and the vendor may publish updated firmware that makes the encryption process more efficient. So be certain to upgrade firmware to the most current level.

Non-optimal Client Radio Configuration

Some settings on a client radio can cause 802.11 performance problems, including the following:

■ **Data rate:** If the data rate setting is configured too low, such as 2 Mbps, the client device may experience slow performance. In most cases, changing the data rate to a higher data rate (or "auto") will improve performance. Bear in mind, however, that higher fixed data rate settings will decrease range, and the data rate setting in the client radio usually affects only the data rate of the 802.11 data frames going from the client radio to the access point.

■ **Transmit power:** A relatively low transmit power setting on a client radio may cause performance issues because the corresponding signal level at the access point may be too low (only high enough to support low data rates). If this is the case, try increasing the transmit power in the client radio.

Check the preceding configuration settings on the client radio if performance issues exist and make appropriate corrections to fix the connectivity problems.

Non-optimal Access Point Configuration

It is possible that non-optimal configuration settings on an access point may be causing poor performance. Consider the following:

■ **Data rate:** As on a client radio, a low data rate setting on an access point may cause poor performance. The data rate setting in an access point usually affects only the data rate of the 802.11 data frames going from the access point to the client radio. Therefore, you should set both the client radio and access point data rates to sufficient values. In most cases, the "auto" setting provides effective performance.

■ **Transmit power:** Also as on a client radio, a low transmit power setting in an access point may cause performance issues because the corresponding signal level at the client radio may be too low (only high enough to support low data rates). If this is the case, try increasing the transmit power in the access point.

- **Transmission channel:** The transmission channel setting in an access point may coincide with radio signal interference in the area. This can result in low performance because the SNR will be relatively low, and retransmission may prevail. If you set the transmission channel to a channel where less interference is present, the performance will likely improve because of higher SNR and fewer retransmissions. Making this change might require moving to the 5-GHz band, where the RF spectrum is fairly quiet compared to the 2.4-GHz band.

- **Channel width:** If operating with 20-MHz RF channels, you can probably increase performance by switching to 40-MHz channels. This is practical only in—and currently only implemented in—the 5-GHz band.

- **Fragmentation:** If fragmentation is enabled, its corresponding threshold might be set too low, causing excessive overhead on the network. Check the retransmission rates of 802.11 data frames. If the retransmission rates are under 10 percent, try increasing the threshold or disabling fragmentation. Doing so might cause the throughput and corresponding performance to improve because of the reduced overhead. Be certain to check the retransmission rates, though. If they are higher, the performance may actually worsen. In this case, you might see a performance improvement by lowering the fragmentation threshold. Fragmentation is difficult to set for maximum performance. Also, because fragmentation thresholds are set manually, it is not usually practical to tune them as radio interference comes and goes. Because of this, for best overall performance, it is generally best to disable fragmentation.

- **Request-to-send/clear-to-send (RTS/CTS):** As with fragmentation, a low RTS/CTS threshold may generate significant overhead on the network (due to RTS and CTS frames). If the retransmission rates are under 10 percent, try increasing the threshold or disabling RTS/CTS and then recheck the performance to see whether this helps. Because the presence of hidden nodes will probably change periodically, it is not practical to optimize the RTS/CTS threshold settings for the sake of improving performance. Performance will probably be best in the long run if you disable RTS/CTS.

Note For more on the trade-offs of various client radio and access point settings, see Chapter 11.

Misaligned Antennas

For optimum performance, check whether the antennas on an access point are aligned as they were when they were tested during the wireless site survey. Generally, the correct antenna alignment for omnidirectional antennas is vertical to the ground. For an antenna mounted relatively high (for example, on top of a two- or three-story building), you might need to tilt the antenna down toward the ground to ensure that the radiation pattern covers the area on the ground closer to the antenna. Some directional antennas, such as sector antennas, have built-in down tilt. If antennas are not aligned properly, the resulting mismatch in polarization can cause the signal strength at the client radio and access point to be lower. This will impact performance because the lower signal levels will support only lower data rates.

High Utilization

When there are large numbers of active wireless users or the users are operating high-end applications, such as using Wi-Fi phones or downloading large files, the utilization of the network may be reaching the capacity of the access point. In this case, the retry rates will be relatively high (greater than 10 percent), even if signal levels are high and noise levels are low (that is, high SNR). The result is lower throughput per user due to the additional overhead necessary to retransmit data frames. Thus, high utilization can result in performance issues.

You can increase capacity and resolve this problem by placing access points closer together with lower transmit power to realize smaller radio cells. This "micro-cell" approach reduces the number of users per access point, which enables users to have more capacity. Another method for handling high utilization is to move some of the applications to a different frequency band. For example, you might consider having wireless IP phones interfacing with a 5-GHz network and data applications running over a 2.4-GHz network.

Note   For more about improving the performance of a WLAN, see Chapter 11.

Summary

Eventually, something will go wrong with your WLAN. When this happens, you need to be prepared to do some troubleshooting. Start by identifying the problem by learning when and where the problem is happening. The next step is to analyze the problem and try to identify why the problem is occurring. Many of the issues that users experience are connection problems; possible causes are insufficient signal coverage, radio signal interference, access point failure, incompatible client radio, faulty firmware, and incorrect client radio configuration. Performance problems may also crop up, including insufficient signal coverage, faulty firmware, non-optimal client radio or access point configuration, misaligned antennas, or high utilization.

Chapter 20

Preparing Operational Support Staff

This chapter will introduce you to:

- Support Staff Considerations
- Availability of Existing Staff
- Experience Requirements
- Education and Training Requirements
- Certifications
- Staffing Sources

When deploying a wireless LAN (WLAN), you need to consider the staff that needs to support the system and ensure that applicable preparations are done as needed. This includes finding qualified people to perform the services and possibly training your existing staff. This is crucial, especially for organizations that are not familiar with performing the various support functions.

Support Staff Considerations

The following are elements that you should consider when choosing candidates for supporting a WLAN:

- **Availability of existing staff:** Review existing staff and determine which qualified individuals may be available to support the WLAN.

- **Experience:** This is generally the most important attribute of a person's background regarding their ability to effectively support a WLAN. Question candidates about the related work that they have done in the past. Focus on the actual experience a person has with implementing and supporting WLANs.

- **Education and training:** This can include courses taken at vocational schools, vendors, and colleges. Obtain details about all relevant training that an individual has completed. Ideally, this training should include real-world and hands-on elements.

- **Certifications:** Check which certifications the person has but carefully consider what has led to the person receiving the certifications. A certification based on required attendance at courses that prepare the person to complete relevant tasks is much stronger than a certification that is based merely on knowing details about the technology or for which the person did not need to complete hands-on training.

Availability of Existing Staff

Review existing IT staff and identify individuals who are available or can be made available to support the WLAN. Ideally, these should be people who participated in implementing the WLAN. They will likely meet experience requirements because they were actively involved with the deployment of the WLAN. If existing staff cannot fulfill all WLAN support functions, then you need to hire additional staff.

Experience Requirements

The type of experience that a person needs depends on the support function he or she will be undertaking and the level at which the person will be providing these functions. The following are some tips on the various types of experience that staff should have:

- **Help desk staff:** These people, who will be answering support calls from users, should have a background in troubleshooting wireless connectivity problems and experience with the operation of client devices that operate on the network. This can be an entry-level position if there is someone who can provide these staff with adequate training and where there is good documentation, such as fault-isolation trees, that the staff can refer to when helping users resolve problems. Otherwise, the help desk staff should have one or more years of experience performing help desk functions for a WLAN.

- **Maintenance staff:** People who will be responsible for performing preventive maintenance and repairing the network should have experience installing and configuring the type of access points deployed in the network and background with installing cabling and antennas. In addition, they should have experience testing WLANs, such as performing wireless site surveys.

- **Network engineering staff:** Engineers may be needed from time to time to fix problems that help desk and maintenance staff cannot resolve or to redesign the network to accommodate changes in the usage of the network. These staff need extensive experience with analyzing signal coverage and roaming problems, analyzing radio signal interference, and configuring IP networks. In most cases, engineering staff should have several years of experience implementing and supporting WLANs.

Note For details on the operations and support functions that support staff needs to fulfill, refer to Chapter 18, "Managing a Wireless LAN," and Chapter 19, "Troubleshooting a Wireless LAN."

The amount of experience a person needs to fulfill a role depends a great deal on the size and complexity of the WLAN. For example, a person who needs to support a WLAN with only a few access points and that has only occasional user connectivity to the Internet can probably get by with very little or no experience. The support person in this case can likely get by with learning as problems occur.

However, a larger WLAN, especially one that supports wireless IP phone applications, needs people with extensive experience. A person being considered for this situation would need several years of experience implementing and supporting WLANs, assuming that he or she would be fulfilling a maintenance or engineering role. As mentioned earlier, someone working for the help desk may be able to be an entry-level person with very little or no experience with WLANs.

Note Passion for wireless networking is a worthy trait to look for in candidates you are considering for WLAN support staff positions. You want to work with and depend on people who are clearly excited about working with wireless networks and have experimented on their own with wireless networking technologies and equipment.

Education and Training Requirements

Support staff for a WLAN should have evidence of completing training related to the functions and tasks that they will be expected to perform. In addition, they should have general education in computer and networking technologies, such as computer operating systems, switched Ethernet networks, and IP addressing. They should also have training on the types of networking equipment that the organization has deployed.

Vendor-Neutral Training

Vendor-neutral training is important because it usually focuses on common industry best practices and does not include any biases that vendors may include in their training. Many companies offer this sort of training, but ensure that the training includes hands-on exercises and laboratory work. Be certain that all support staff have hands-on, vendor-neutral training as part of their background.

Vendor-Specific Training

The majority of WLAN vendors, such as Cisco, offer training focused on the actual equipment that staff need to support. It is critical that support staff receive vendor-specific training for all components that comprise the WLAN, such as access points, controllers, and switches.

College Education

In most cases, a college education is not required for support staff, but having a college degree in a related field, such as MIS, engineering, or computer science, may allow an individual to eventually advance into management or other positions. The exception to this is the engineering support role, where it is usually best to have at least one support person with an engineering, computer science, or MIS degree.

Certifications

The majority of certifications are vendor specific (for example, Cisco CCNP), and others are vendor neutral (for example, CWNP). Look for candidates who have a mix of certifications. Ideally, support staff should have certifications emphasizing WLANs and including hands-on training where the person had to actually perform tasks before receiving the certification. Certifications based on merely passing a multiple-choice exam primarily indicate what the person knows about a particular topic, not what they can actually do.

Most wireless vendors have certifications based on satisfactorily passing their training courses and exams. For example, the following are some of Cisco's certifications:

- **Cisco Advanced Wireless LAN Sales Specialist certificate:** Indicates an understanding of WLAN features and benefits and the ability to assess customer needs. This certification is intended for Cisco channel partners.

- **Cisco Certified Network Associate Wireless (CCNA Wireless) certificate:** Indicates associate-level knowledge and skills to configure, implement, and support Cisco WLANs.

- **Cisco Certified Network Professional Wireless (CCNP Wireless) certificate:** Indicates advanced knowledge and skills to configure, implement, and support Cisco WLANs.

- **Cisco Certified Internetwork Expert Wireless (CCIE Wireless) certificate:** Indicates broad theoretical knowledge of wireless networking and a solid, practical understanding of WLANs.

The Certified Wireless Network Professional (CWNP) program, which is vendor neutral, offers the following certifications:

- **Certified Wireless Technology Specialist (CWTS) certificate:** Indicates knowledge of the terminology and basic functionality of enterprise 802.11 wireless networks.

- **Certified Wireless Network Administrator (CWNA) certificate:** Indicates knowledge of WLAN fundamentals and provides a foundation certification for the CWNP program.

- **Certified Wireless Security Professional (CWSP) certificate:** Indicates knowledge about securing WLANs.

- **Certified Wireless Design Professional (CWDP) certificate:** Indicates knowledge about designing WLANs.

- **Certified Wireless Analysis Professional (CWAP) certificate:** Indicates knowledge about analyzing, troubleshooting, and optimizing WLANs.

- **Certified Wireless Network Expert (CWNE) certificate:** Demonstrates advanced skills in designing and supporting WLANs

Staffing Sources

When looking for candidates for WLAN support positions, consider the following sources:

- **Online sources:** There are many online job sites (for example, Dice.com and Monster.com) where you can post requirements for open positions and search for résumés of potential candidates. When posting announcements of open positions, be sure to state that specific requirements must be met, such as having certifications.

- **Colleges and vocational schools:** Schools often supply names of potential candidates who may be capable of fulfilling specific job requirements. Contact local colleges and vocational schools and ask for recommendations on any qualified students who have either completed or are nearing completion of their studies. The advantage of contacting schools is that you can often obtain qualified candidates because the school will have had experience working with the student and can comment on their abilities.

- **Employment recruiters:** When you are in a hurry to fill a position, an employee recruiter is a possible source for candidates. An issue, however, is that you will likely have to pay a sizable fee if you end up hiring someone referred to you by the recruiter. The advantage is that the recruiter takes care of filtering résumés and corresponding with candidates. The recruiter is also likely to pre-interview the candidates and eliminate those who do not fully meet your position requirements.

Of course, there is always the old-fashioned way of advertising for open positions in local newspapers. The effectiveness of this approach, however, is not as good as the methods described above.

Summary

When preparing staff to support a WLAN, the first step is to consider existing staff that might be qualified and available. Of course, this might require finding someone to fulfill duties that the individual gives up in order to focus on supporting the WLAN. If existing staff cannot satisfy all support functions, you need to hire or contract additional resources. When determining whether a person is qualified to fill a support role, consider the person's experience, education and training, and certifications. The type and sufficiency of experience depend on the function the person will need to satisfy. In addition, look for a mix of vendor-specific and vendor-neutral training. It is important that the person has experience and training relevant to the type of WLAN that you need to support.

Glossary

Numbers

4-way handshake   802.11 communication back and forth between an access point and client radio that results in determining the common key used to encrypt data.

802.3   A standard published by the Institute of Electrical and Electronics Engineers (IEEE) that defines the signal characteristics and operation of a wired LAN. It defines the use of CSMA, which is similar to 802.11 WLANs.

802.11   A standard published by the Institute of Electrical and Electronics Engineers (IEEE) that defines the radio characteristics and operation of a medium-range radio frequency LAN. Specifies the use of CSMA as the primary method for sharing access to a common air medium.

802.16   A standard published by the Institute of Electrical and Electronics Engineers (IEEE) that defines the radio characteristics and operation of wireless MANs.

A

access point   A type of base station that WLANs use to interface wireless users to a wired network and provide roaming throughout a facility.

active scanning   A roaming function for 802.11-based clients that sends probe request frames to search for other access points.

ad hoc mode   A configuration of a wireless network that allows communications directly from one user device to another, without the need to travel through a base station. Ad hoc mode applies to both wireless personal-area networks (PANs) and WLANs.

analog signal   A signal where the amplitude of the signal varies continuously as time progresses. A radio wave is an example of an analog signal.

antenna   A physical device that converts electrical signals to radio or light waves (and vice versa) for propagation through the air medium. Antennas may be omnidirectional, distributing radio waves in all directions, or directional, focusing radio waves more in one direction than others.

association   A process whereby an 802.11 station (computer device) becomes a part of a WLAN. After association, the user can use network services.

authentication   The process of proving the identity of a user or base station. The use of usernames and passwords is a common authentication method, but many other more sophisticated authentication mechanisms exist. For example, digital certificates can offer a means of authentication without user intervention.

B

base station   Hardware that interfaces wireless computing devices together and to a wired network. Access points and wireless routers are types of WLAN base stations.

Bluetooth   A specification published by the Bluetooth Special Interest Group that defines the radio characteristics and operation of a short-range, low-power radio frequency network. Many devices today support Bluetooth, and 802.15 has developed applicable standards.

bridge   A device that interconnects two networks at layer 2. A bridge forwards data packets to another network based on the MAC (Medium Access Control) address found in the packet header. Bridges play a key role in the deployment of wireless MANs.

C

carrier sense access   A process of sharing a common medium by first determining whether the medium is idle before transmitting data. This is part of the CSMA protocol.

carrier signal   The primary RF signal that "carries" data through the air medium.

Various modulation types vary the carrier signal frequency, phase, or amplitude to represent information.

CCMP (Counter Mode Cipher Block Chaining Message Authentication Code Protocol, Counter Mode CBC-MAC Protocol)   An 802.11 security protocol that utilizes AES encryption.

CDMA (code-division multiple access)   A process whereby each user modulates the signals with a different, non-interfering code.

CF (CompactFlash)   A very small NIC for PDAs, cameras, and other small computer devices. Bluetooth and 802.11 CF NICs are readily available.

client device   Hardware having a user interface that enables the use of wireless network applications. A wireless client is a type of client device. Also known as a computer device.

client radio   Hardware that implements the 802.11 standard and interfaces the client device to an access point (infrastructure mode) or another client radio (ad hoc mode).

CSMA (carrier sense multiple access)   A process that allows multiple 802.11 stations to share a common air medium. Stations attempt to transmit data only when no other station is transmitting. Otherwise, collisions will occur, and the station must retransmit the data.

D

DCF (distributed coordination function)   A part of the 802.11 standard that defines how stations will contend for access to the air medium. DCF makes use of CSMA to regulate traffic on the network.

DHCP (Dynamic Host Configuration Protocol)   A protocol that automatically assigns unique IP addresses within an assigned range to network devices. Most home and public WLANs implement DHCP, which makes it very easy for users to gain access to the network. DHCP automatically assigns a valid IP address to each user.

digital certificate   An electronic message that contains the credentials of a particular user. Digital certificates are used as a means for authenticating users or their computer devices.

digital signal   A signal that varies in amplitude steps as time advances. A digital signal represents data within a computer device. The digital signal must be converted to an analog form (via a process known as modulation) before the data can be sent through the air medium.

directional antenna   A type of antenna that focuses radio waves and range more in one direction than in others. Directional antennas are commonly found in wireless MANs and wireless WAN systems. The directivity of the antenna increases range in one direction and decreases range in other directions.

distribution system   A system (wired or wireless) that physically interconnects access points in a WLAN. A common distribution system for WLANs, for example, is Ethernet.

DSSS (direct-sequence spread spectrum)   A type of spread spectrum in which a spreading code increases the signal rate of the data stream to spread the signal over a wider portion of the frequency band. 802.11b WLANs make use of direct sequence.

E

encryption   The scrambling of data bits according to a key prior to sending the data over a network. WEP (Wired Equivalent Privacy) and WPA (Wi-Fi Protected Access) are examples of protocols that WLANs use to implement encryption.

Ethernet   An 802.3 wired LAN. Ethernet is a common type of network that companies use to interconnect PCs and servers. Ethernet provides the distribution system of most WLANs.

F

FDMA (frequency-division multiple access)   A process that divides a relatively wide frequency band into smaller sub-bands, where each user transmits voice and data over his or her assigned sub-band.

FHSS (frequency-hopping spread spectrum)   A type of spread spectrum in which the transceiver hops from one frequency to another, according to a known hopping pattern, to spread the signal over a wider portion of the frequency band. Older 802.11 WLANs use frequency hopping.

frequency   The number of times per second that a signal repeats itself. Often measured in Hertz (Hz), which is the number of cycles occurring each second. Frequencies of WLANs, for example, are within the 2.4-GHz and 5-GHz bands.

FSK (frequency shift-keying)   A modulation process that makes slight changes to the frequency of the carrier signal to represent information in a way that is suitable for propagation through the air.

G

gatekeeper A device that provides most of the call control actions, such as access control, bandwidth management, translation between telephone number and IP address, and call transfer for H.323 systems.

gateway A device that provides connections between voice terminals and the standard public switched telephone network (PSTN).

GPS (Global Positioning System) A system that enables people having a GPS client device to easily determine their geographic position. GPS offers the basis of an excellent navigation system and location-based services over wireless networks.

H

H.323 An umbrella specification defined by the International Telecommunications Union–Telecommunications Standard Sector that includes a group of protocols for sending voice and video over IP-based networks.

hacker A person who has the ability to steal information that resides on a network. Hackers often try breaking into corporate systems for fun and exploit the vulnerabilities of wireless networks. Not all hackers, however, are criminals.

hotspot The location of a public WLAN. Hotspots are found in areas where people congregate with computer devices, such as at airports, in hotels, at convention centers, and at coffee shops.

I

interference Unwanted signals that disrupt the operation of a wireless network. The presence of interference decreases the performance of a wireless network.

interoperability A condition whereby computer devices are able to successfully interface with a wireless network.

IP (Internet Protocol) A protocol that routes packets between computer devices attached to a network. IP places a header field in front of each packet that contains the source and destination IP address of the packet.

IP address A number that represents the address corresponding to a connection of a network device to the network. For example, every wireless NIC has an IP address. Each NIC must have an IP address associated with it if the user is to make use of TCP/IP applications, such as sending and receiving e-mail, browsing the web, or interfacing with a corporate application server.

IPsec (IP Security) A protocol that supports secure exchange of packets at the network layer of a network. IPsec is commonly implemented in VPNs and encrypts data packets across the entire network (often referred to as end-to-end encryption).

L

LAN (local-area network) A type of network that spans the area of a building or campus. A LAN uses wired cabling (Ethernet) or wireless connections (IEEE 802.11) to interface client devices to resources, such as application software and databases, on the network.

LEAP (Lightweight Extensible Authentication Protocol) A Cisco proprietary authentication mechanism for securing wireless networks.

location-based services The ability to track the location of users and deliver information to them that relates to position within a particular area.

M

MAC (Medium Access Control) layer   A part of a network architecture that manages and maintains communications on a shared medium. The MAC layer is the brains of a NIC or base station and enforces the rules that all devices must follow.

MAN (metropolitan-area network)   A type of network that spans a city or metropolitan area. A municipal network, which may use mesh network technology and point-to-point links, is a type of MAN.

medium   The space in which communications signals, such as radio waves, propagate. With wireless networks, the medium is air.

medium access   A process whereby multiple computer devices share a common medium. The most common medium access method for wireless networks is CSMA.

modulation   A process that creates a radio or light signal from the network data so that it is suitable for propagation through the air medium. Examples of modulation types are FSK, PSK, and QAM.

N

NAT (Network Address Translation)   A standard that maps official IP addresses to private addresses that may be in use on internal networks. For example, a broadband Internet service provider may offer only one official IP address to a home. NAT, along with DHCP, enables the homeowner to have multiple PCs and laptops sharing the single official IP address.

NIC (network interface card)   A hardware device that interfaces a computer device to a network. Also known as a radio card or a client card.

noise floor   The amplitude of unwanted electromagnetic energy in a particular area while a wireless network is not operating.

nonce   A random number generated by an 802.11 client radio and access point that provides a basis for calculating the key used to encrypt data.

O

OFDM (orthogonal frequency-division multiplexing)   A process that divides a modulated signal into multiple subcarriers prior to transmission through the air medium to improve performance. The 802.11a and 802.11g WLANs and some proprietary wireless MANs use OFDM.

optical fiber   A long piece of glass that has a very small diameter and is able to carry light signals from one end to the other. An optical fiber cable has a protective coating, making it difficult to visually distinguish from copper-based cables.

P

packet trace   A representation of the series of 802.11 frames that have been sent among client radios and access points.

PBX (private branch exchange)   The hardware and software necessary to process phone calls for a company over the standard PSTN.

PC Card   A credit card–sized device, also called a NIC, which provides extended memory, modems, connectivity to external devices, and, of course, wireless network capabilities to small computer devices, such as laptops and PDAs. Many PC Cards implement Bluetooth and 802.11 technologies.

PDA (personal digital assistant)   A small device that people can use to store contact information, schedules, and to-do lists. Some PDAs run software programs, such as e-mail clients and web browsers.

point-to-multipoint system   A system in which communication occurs directly from one user to several others.

point-to-point system   A system in which communication occurs directly from one user to another.

power save mode   An 802.11 function that allows wireless client radios to enter a sleep mode that draws less current and extends battery life.

PSK (phase shift-keying)   A modulation process that makes slight changes to the phase of the carrier signal to represent information in a way that is suitable for propagation through the air.

PSTN (public switched telephone network)   The standard circuit-switched telephone system that supports phone calls between most homes and businesses.

public wireless LAN   A type of WLAN, often referred to as a hotspot, that anyone having a properly configured computer device can access.

Q

QAM (quadrature amplitude modulation)   A modulation process that makes slight changes to the amplitude and phase of the carrier signal to represent information in a way that is suitable for propagation through the air.

R

radio NIC   A type of NIC that transmits and receives RF signals.

RADIUS (Remote Authentication Dial-In User Service)   An authentication and accounting system that many WISPs and high-usage enterprises use to handle access control and billing on wireless networks.

repeater   A device that receives and retransmits signals for the sole purpose of extending range.

RF (radio frequency) signal   A signal that is designed to propagate through the air medium.

rogue access point   An access point that is unauthorized and has configuration settings that may enable someone to gain access to network resources.

router   A type of base station that routes packets from one location to another, based on a destination IP address. A router implements special networking protocols, such as DHCP and NAT, that enable users to use TCP/IP applications.

RTP (Real-Time Transport Protocol)   A protocol that provides end-to-end functions suitable for applications transmitting real-time voice and video over IP-based networks.

S

SCCP (Skinny Client Control Protocol)   A lightweight alternative to the full-blown H.323 standard implemented in Cisco wireless and desktop IP phones.

SIP (Session Initiation Protocol)   A protocol developed by the Internet Engineering Task Force (IETF) that is based on Internet specifications, such as Hypertext Markup Language (HTML) and Simple Mail Transfer Protocol (SMTP), for sending voice and video over IP-based networks.

snooper   Someone who casually and sometimes inadvertently interfaces with a wireless network. A war driver, who drives around to find active WLANs, is a type of snooper.

SNR (signal-to-noise ratio)   A value, measured in decibels (dB), that is the signal power (in dBm) minus the noise power (in dBm).

spread spectrum   The spreading of the carrier signal over a wider part of the frequency spectrum. DSSS and FHSS are two types of spread spectrum.

SSID (service set identifier)   A name given to devices on a particular WLAN in which the SSID assigned to a wireless client must match the SSID configured in the access point.

T

TCP (Transmission Control Protocol)   A protocol that establishes and maintains connections between computer devices attached to a network. TCP operates at the transport layer and is used in conjunction with IP; the combination is commonly referred to as TCP/IP.

TDMA (time-division multiple access)   A process that allows only one user to transmit in any given time slot. Each user has use of the entire bandwidth during its assigned time slot.

terminal   Endpoints of a VoWLAN system, such as wireless IP phones.

terminal emulation   A mechanism for users to interface over a network to applications running on a centralized computer. VT-220, 3270, and 5250 are types of terminal emulation.

TKIP (Temporal Key Integrity Protocol)   A protocol that enables each wireless station to use a different encryption key that changes often. TKIP fixes the key distribution problem of WEP.

transceiver   A device, such as a client radio, that both transmits and receives information.

U

UDP (User Datagram Protocol)   A connectionless protocol that runs at the transport layer and is similar to TCP, except that UDP offers very few error recovery services.

V

VLAN (virtual LAN)   A logical collection of network devices that communicate with each other over the same physical network but where network devices on one VLAN cannot communicate with network devices on another VLAN (unless provisions are made to connect the different VLANs).

VoIP (Voice over IP)   A technology for sending voice signals over an IP-based network.

VoIP endpoints   Hardware devices, such as wireless IP phones, at both ends of a voice conversation conducted using VoIP technology.

VoWLAN (Voice over WLAN)   A WLAN that supports the transmission of voice information, generally through the use of VoIP.

VPN (virtual private network)   Special software on a client device that controls access to remote applications and secures the connection from end to end, using encryption.

W

WAN (wide-area network)   A type of network that spans a continent or country. Enterprises often use a WAN to interconnect their facilities located in different areas.

WEP (Wired Equivalent Privacy)   A part of the 802.11 standard that defines encryption between devices connected to a WLAN.

Wi-Fi   A brand name given to WLANs that comply with standards as defined and published by the Wi-Fi Alliance. Wi-Fi is based on the 802.11 standard.

wireless IP phone   A mobile phone specially designed to send and receive phone calls over an IP-based network, such as a WLAN.

wireless MAN   A network that satisfies wireless networking needs within the area of a city. Wireless MANs make use of 802.16 and proprietary standards.

wireless WAN   A network that satisfies wireless networking needs over a large geographic area, such as a country or the entire world. Satellites offer a means for extending radio signals over a wireless WAN.

WISP (wireless Internet service provider)   A company that offers wireless connection services to the Internet for homes and offices. WISPs often provide wireless access in public WLAN hotspots.

WLAN (wireless LAN)   A network that satisfies wireless networking needs within the area of a building or college campus. 802.11 and Wi-Fi are popular standards defining WLANs.

WPA (Wi-Fi Protected Access)   A security protocol defined by the Wi-Fi Alliance that enables computer devices to periodically obtain new encryption keys. WPA version 1 implements TKIP and WEP; WPA version 2 implements the full 802.11i standard, which includes AES.

Y

yagi antenna   A specialized directional antenna that uses multiple signal-reflecting elements attached to a boom.

Index

I

Q

R

cisco

ciscopress.com: Your Cisco Certification and Networking Learning Resource

Subscribe to the monthly Cisco Press newsletter to be the first to learn about new releases and special promotions.

Visit **ciscopress.com/newsletters.**

While you are visiting, check out the offerings available at your finger tips.

–Free Podcasts from experts:
  • OnNetworking
  • OnCertification
  • OnSecurity

Podcasts

View them at **ciscopress.com/podcasts.**

–Read the latest author **articles** and **sample chapters** at **ciscopress.com/articles.**

–Bookmark the Certification Reference Guide available through our partner site at **informit.com/certguide.**

Connect with Cisco Press authors and editors via Facebook and Twitter, visit **informit.com/socialconnect.**